HUMANIST ETHICS
DIALOGUE ON BASICS

HUMANIST ETHICS
DIALOGUE ON BASICS

EDITED BY MORRIS B. STORER

 *Prometheus Books*

Buffalo, New York 14215

Published by Prometheus Books
1203 Kensington Avenue, Buffalo, New York 14215

Copyright © 1980 by Morris B. Storer
All Rights Reserved

Library of Congress Card Number 80-7456
ISBN 0-87975-117-7 Cloth
ISBN 0-87975-118-5 Paper

Printed in the United States of America

Contents

Editor's Preface

Is humankind floundering toward a fate like that of the beached whales? We think of the threatening deterioration of our environment—sea and sky and shore, air and water and food. We think of the menace of East-West conflict—more than half of our industrial labor force addressed to munitions manufacture—nuclear and otherwise—and a heavier concentration on *their* part. We think of our generation's rape of the resources of the earth. We think of the swelling rate of violent crime, disorder and cynicism, drugs and abandonment in schools, decline of literacy under the impact of television, the runaway concentration of wealth and income, the despair of the exploited, corruption of leadership. It is hard to reject the sense of a mortally sick world.

Why, in the face of this, a symposium on humanist ethics? (1) Because the health and harmony of the human world, of its nations and its communities and its individual members, depend on their morality (or call it "justice"). (Plato even *defined* morality as "health and harmony.") (2) Because humanists have an especially heavy responsibility for these things today. And (3) because humanists are at odds about the meaning of morality. There is an imperative need for a fuller humanist consensus in this area. We have to *work* for it.

Humanism has to face special responsibility in this area because a large majority of the educators of America and of the western world are humanist in their outlook. The faculties of American colleges and universities are predominantly humanist, and a majority of the teachers who go out from their studies in the colleges to responsibilities in primary and secondary schools are basically humanist, no matter that many maintain a nominal attachment to church or synagogue for good personal or social or practical reasons. Critics of secular humanism are apt to hold responsible (for problems in the schools) not simply the humanist educator, but the educator's humanism. There is a need for humanists to be clear and responsive to all the realities in ethics.

What is humanism, and who is humanist? For our purposes I will identify as "humanist" all who, in the basic deliberations and action decisions of their lives, have set aside faith in revelation and dogmatic authority (if they ever *had* it), and have settled for human experience and reason as grounds for belief and action, putting human good—the good of self and others in their life on earth—as ultimate criterion of right and wrong, with due concern for other living creatures. It has been estimated that as many as thirty million Americans—around one out of every seven—are of this mind, but the number is probably much larger. And the world population of humanists defined in such limited terms, may be numbered at close to a billion, remembering that 95% of China's 700 million were reared to a mix of humanist Confucianism, naturalist Taoism, and atheistic Buddhism, and that the Soviet Union's 250 million population have been officially committed to a somewhat corrupted mode of Marxist humanism by fiat of a dictator State.

It is clear that world dialogue, if it is to make progress toward the international consensus which Konstantin Kolenda represents as next plausible step toward world reconciliation, will have to move in humanist terms, with primary respect for the realities of our common world and common human nature, and without reference to any supernatural enlightenment.

The various theistic world religions have had their successes and their failures in bringing people together on one or another common moral standpoint, on the basis of faith and authority. Hundreds of millions have united under the banners of Christianity and Judaism and Islam and Mahayana Buddhism and Hinduism and Shintoism. But Christianity and Islam have clashed in some of the bloodiest wars in history. And the peace is not yet secure between Judaism and Islam in the Middle East, or between Catholic and Protestant in Ireland, or between Muslim and Hindu in Pakistan and India and Bangladesh or between Shiite Mohammedan in Iran and whatever stands in the way. Julian Huxley was facing these hard realities in 1946 as he worked with the task force shaping the United Nations Organization. "A world organization," he wrote, "can not be based on one of the competing theologies of the world, but must, it seems, be based on some form of humanism..., a world humanism..., a scientific humanism..., an evolutionary humanism." "Huxley thought it possible," observed the *UNESCO Courier*, "to establish a moral system which was purely scientific in inspiration and which would be capable of uniting mankind."

In his emphasis on such a possibility and such a goal, Huxley pointed the direction for this book, but our purpose is more modest. It is apparent that humanists today are almost as widely dispersed in moral standpoint as the "community" of world religions. We will not be able to agree on a moral system overnight, but we are confident that we can make solid progress toward mutual understanding and consensus by interchanges of views, by continuing efforts to clarify the meanings of our terms for ourselves and for others, and by continuous review of the facts on which our judgments and those of others rest.

Humanists *are* largely united in emphasizing human fulfillment, a measured freedom, the dignity of the individual, a factor of situational relativity, and a broad spectrum of human rights as cornerstones of humanist ethics. But it is clear that, beyond these essentials, we differ widely. Is *personal* advantage the measure of right and wrong, or the advantage of *all affected*: Humanists differ. Is there *truth* in ethics? We differ. Are "right" and "wrong" expressions of heart or head? Do people have free wills? Do you measure morality by results or by principles? Do people have duties as well as rights? We have our differences on all these and more. And it appears that our contribution to peace on earth (and to life itself) by way of humanism will be proportionate to our success in transcending these differences and achieving a realistic consensus.

Much work has already been done toward these ends, of course. For instance, Paul Kurtz ten years ago brought the lights of humanism to bear on the issues of the time in editing a volume entitled *Moral Problems in Contemporary Society: Essays in Humanistic Ethics*, which I have had occasion to use and value, and in 1973 he took the initiative, as editor of *The Humanist* magazine, in drafting the landmark consensus statement, *Humanist Manifesto II*. The need for efforts in this direction have been widely felt, quite independent of humanist concerns, prompting the Rockefeller Foundation, recently, for instance, to convene a conference to "analyze the current absence of a value consensus in American life, and to examine the possible grounds for a new consensus." The deliberations of this conference were published in a working paper of the Foundation called *The Search for Value Consensus*.

In approach to our symposium, we started with the conviction that the problems of ethics are among the most difficult and demanding problems that humans have to face, and that we would need the help of the most careful and realistic thinkers, the lifetime students, the most articulate writers in the field, and we would need to include in our panel spokespersons for as many as possible of the important contending views. "We shall find it no easy task to mold a natural ethic strong enough to maintain moral restraint and social order without the support of supernatural sanctions, hopes and fears," writes Will Durant in the article which introduces this symposium.

Confronting such a challenge, we have been exceptionally favored in the affirmative response of twenty distinguished specialists, representing a broad spectrum of standpoints and a worldwide geographic distribution, including leading thinkers from India, Yugoslavia, Austria, Norway, Scotland, Canada, and Australia, as well as the United States.

With our letters of invitation we directed attention to five sets of questions central to our differences, as follows:

1. THE MEANING AND SOURCE OF MORALITY

What is the rock-bottom concern of morality? What relation to local customs and laws? Is one culture "better" than another? Heart vs. head, sentiment vs. sense-and-reason as source? Are there facts that together determine right and wrong? Is there "truth" in ethics?

2. HUMANKIND AND NATURE—FREE WILL AND RESPONSI-BILITY

The meaning of "rational animal"? Freedom of choice and responsibility for choice vs. universal determinism? What facts support the alternatives? Can we have both? Is there a middle ground?

3. MORALITY AS WORKABILITY VS. MORALITY AS JUSTICE

Is it right "if it works?" Toward whose ends? Do ends justify means? Greatest happiness of greatest number vs. justice vs. love? What facts argue for one or the other as hub of morality? Is there an unexceptional place for a morality of principles?

4. THE BASIS OF RIGHTS AND DUTIES

Any rights without duties? Or vice versa? What place for "obligation" in a humanist ethic? To what principles? What is the *meaning* of obligation? Are people obligated if they do not feel it? What factors underneath obligation? Human equality? How are people equal? What determining facts, if any?

5. PRINCIPLES OF SITUATIONAL MORALITY

When is deviation from principle justified? How then determine the right course? By thinking of consequences entirely? Or by searching for new principles appropriate to the particular situation? Is private interest sometimes an ultimate consideration? Situationism vs. opportunism? Any absolute factors in humanist ethics?

We invited our contributors to center their articles on whatever question or questions might seem most significant and of greatest interest at the time, but we encouraged them to include their views on a major cross-section of the questions posed. As the articles started coming in, our formula developed with a kind of inevitability. We determined early that we must not let pass the occasion and opportunity for real dialogue, and so laid a plan to invite responsive commentary to each article from two other contributors with different views. To top it off, we then invited authors of original articles to return with rejoinders to comments, if they were so moved.

The response of our panel to this exchange plan was inspiring, and the more appreciated because no such unfolding of the project was in view in the original letters of invitation. Words are inadequate to express the Editor's thanks to this great panel of contributors and to all who have invested so much of themselves in this undertaking. I acknowledge with special warmth the continuous counsel and support of Paul Kurtz, editor-in-chief of Prometheus Books, in designing and actualizing the symposium volume, and I remember with appreciation the contributions of Victor Gulotta, assistant editor of Prometheus, of Diane Sparks, copy editor, and of Margaret Wells and others associated with the office. But most of all I acknowledge with deep thanks the immensely important part played by my wife Gretchen at every stage of the journey, which extended far beyond the work of homemaking for the project. Her studied counsel on major decisions and her ever ready help on details of the project including especially my own writing, were invaluable resources without which there would have been no such book.

M.B.S.

Humanism in Historical Perspective

Will Durant

Humanists believe, with Alexander Pope, that "the proper study of mankind is man." We are content to be wholly a part of Nature—of the magnificent and impartial panorama that greets our senses and instruments. We accept the *supersensory*: we acknowledge that our senses perceive only a part of the objects and operations that surround us; but we believe that those supersensory realities are subject to the same approximate laws that govern our bodies and souls. I define the soul as the sum and operations of the powers of a living body.

Belief in the supernatural flourishes in the beginning, and again in the collapse, of a civilization, when life is insecure and apparently dependent upon hidden forces demanding worship and sacrifice. When social order is restored and a confident economy spreads security, a growing minority ignores the supernatural, and a minority of that minority seeks understanding through science, history, and philosophy. The age of Pericles in ancient Athens was almost an explosion of humanism, with Democritus, Anaxagoras, Euripides, Hippocrates, Thucydides, and Socrates, and with Pericles and Aspasia supervising all.

In Greece, this Golden Age of humanism neared its end when Alexander led Greek armies to the conquest of the Near East, Persia, and Egypt. The intermarriage of the victors with the defeated—a procedure recommended and exemplified by Alexander—and the slow merger of Hellenistic with Asiatic cultures opened a highway by which Oriental migrants, ideas, and religions passed westward into Europe. For example, St. Paul left Jerusalem to preach Christianity in Ephesus, Antioch, Phil-

6

ippi, Corinth, and Athens. The population of Attica had been depressed by defeat and impoverishment in the long Peloponnesian War, by its own submission to Philip and Alexander of Macedon, by the greedy concentration of wealth, and by the corruption of politics and private life; it turned angrily from its old and evidently helpless gods and finally accepted the gospel of Christ. The new religion gave a heaven-based morality and order to the Hellenistic world, but it ended the age of humanism in classic Greece.

A like evolution of spirit colored the history of Rome. For a century or so—from the Gracchi through Caesar and Augustus—the imported wealth of a conquered Mediterranean world allowed education to free some minds in the upper classes for a humanistic naturalism; thus, Lucretius, Catullus, Cicero, Caesar, Ovid, Horace, Tacitus, Seneca, and Marcus Aurelius were liberated souls, to whom the gods and goddesses of Rome had become poetic adornments and a moral aid to the commonality. But as Alexander's conquests had opened the road for Eastern manners and creeds to move from Asia into Greece, so the Roman conquest of Greece (149 B.C.) allowed Greek families, teachers, literature, and philosophy to spark a Roman Enlightenment; and soon thereafter, a wave of Greek and Oriental immigration brought a dozen new faiths to displace the old deities and the new humanism of Rome. By the time of Marcus Aurelius, Christianity had prevailed over its competitors; by the time of Constantine, its followers had won such distinction for their moral life and social order that the victorious emperor gave it his official support, and for the next thousand years it dominated the culture of Europe. There were many pleasant, as well as some unpleasant, aspects in that medieval millennium, but humanism hid its head.

It was resurrected by the monks who so fondly, or unwittingly, preserved ancient manuscripts, and by the scholars who, in the enthusiasm of the nascent Renaissance, discovered these relics of a pagan antiquity. In forgotten corners, Petrarch and Boccaccio, in about 1350, found the lost classics—"gentle prisoners," Petrarch called them, "held in captivity by barbarous jailers" or innocent devotees. In the famous monastery of Monte Cassino, Boccacio was shocked to find ancient manuscripts rotting in the dust, or mutilated to make new gospels. Poggio Bracciolini, secretary to Pope Innocent VII (1404 ff.) toured monasteries in Switzerland, Germany, and France, and unearthed eight orations by Cicero, the *De Rerum Natura* of Lucretius (a veritable epic of naturalism), twelve plays of Plautus, parts of Tacitus, and even more. We must add, in fairness, that leading ecclesiastics paid Poggio's traveling expenses and readily forgave his sins.

In the half-century before the Turks took Constantinople in 1453, a dozen Italian humanists traveled to Byzantine Greece and returned with texts of Herodotus, Thucydides, Euripides, Demosthenes, and Aristotle. Fearing the collapse of Greek rule in Constantinople, several Greek scholars left the Byzantine capital, and came to teach the Greek language and its literature in Italy. Cosimo de' Medici, in 1446, establihed the Platonic Academy in Florence and paid Marsilio Ficino to give half of his lifetime to the study and editing of Plato's works. The enthusiasm that the Italians had for the classic texts of Greece spread to those of Rome. A hundred scholars hunted Latin manuscripts, edited or translated them, and helped to restore the literature of pre-Christian Rome to its place in the humanistic heritage.

The effects of this literary resurrection were endless. It revealed to a Christian world a civilization that had never known Christ and how a bold minority had emerged that put aside supernatural beliefs and terrors and accepted Nature on its own terms of earthly good and evil and was willing to work with natural means to natural ends. Amid the theological disputes of the Reformation, Erasmus pursued his classical studies and trusted to the growth of reason. Montaigne took the torch and passed it on to millions of readers in a dozen lands. In England, Bacon "rang the bell that called the wits together." Spinoza survived a terrible excommunication and went on to write a noble philosophy identifying the laws of Nature with God. Taking up Bacon's challenge, the intellectual giants of the French Enlightenment issued the world-shaking *Encyclopedia*, summarizing the progress of science. A century later, Darwin and Spencer placed man in the natural succession of living forms. These were high moments in the history of the human mind, and in the history of humanism.

Our victories of course, are never complete, and may never be. As long as poverty, suffering, or grief exists, the unfortunate will seek supernatural aid. We should not begrudge them these consolations; and we should not attack such creeds unless they attack our own freedom of belief. Moreover, we shall find it no easy task to mold a natural ethic strong enough to maintain moral restraint and social order without the support of supernatural consolations, hopes, and fears. Nor should we let our critics suppose that we worship man; we know that our species has soiled itself with a thousand absurdities, enmities, crimes, and even with massacre and genocide. Our aim is to protect our freedom to work for the *improvement* of man—for men brave enough to stand with their feet on the earth rather than in the sky; and for the multiplication of such men and women into a more humane society, state, and international order. I pass on to you Walt Whitman's tender challenge:

My spirit to yours, dear brothers,
We walk unheld, free, the whole earth over,....till we make

our mark upon time and the diverse eras,
Till we saturate time and eras, that the men and women of
races, ages to come, may prove brethren and lovers as we
are.

Originally published in The Humanist. *Reprinted by permission.*

PANEL I

PAUL KURTZ
MIHAILO MARKOVIC
KAI NIELSEN

Does Humanism Have an Ethic of Responsibility?

Paul Kurtz

WHAT IS HUMANISTIC ETHICS?

Is there such a thing as "humanist ethics"? How does it differ from other forms of ethics? Can those who identify themselves as "humanist" reach a consensus? Does humanist ethics provide a basis for moral responsibility and obligation? I am wary of any *ism* (including human*ism*) that sets itself up as a doctrine or creed, seeks uniform agreement among its proponents, or attempts to legislate a moral code.

The term "humanism" has been invested with such a variety of meanings that it is difficult to find a singular definition with which everyone will agree. Nevertheless, I have argued elsewhere that humanists by and large are secularists. They are committed to free thought and to the view that ethical values are relative to human experience and needs. This means that ethics need not be derived from any theological or metaphysical propositions about the nature of ultimate reality, that it can be autonomous, and that ethical judgments to some extent may be grounded in reflective inquiry.

Perhaps the above assertions may be taken as overly general; yet they enable us to distinguish a whole class of ethical theories that call themselves humanist—both on the meta and normative levels—from those that are not. In particular, humanist ethics may be contrasted with those moral systems that are rooted in some belief in God and other theological or quasi-theological doctrines. Such humanist theories reject a metaphysics of the universe which depends upon a divine purpose or origin, has theories

11

of reincarnation or immortality, ties ethics to some doctrines of *karma* or judgment day of divine reward and punishment for what is done in this life, or seeks to derive a moral code and concepts of sin and responsibility from divine commandments. There are, however, ethical theories that are anti-theistic yet differ on fundamental meta and normative issues. Existential-ism, emotivism, pragmatism, and utilitarianism are all humanistic in one way or another, but disagree, for example, on the meta level concerning the role of reason in the moral life or the relationship of fact to value. Pragmatists and utilitarians believe in naturalistic ethics; existentialists and emotivists tend to be subjectivists in ethics, maintaining that values may be rooted in the last analysis in attitude, not simply belief.

Similarly, many so-called humanists may differ about any number of concrete normative recommendations. Some will be for or against capital punishment, euthanasia, abortion, the sexual revolution, the use of nuclear power. They may also differ fundamentally on the political and social implications of their moral judgments. Some may be liberal or radical, others moderate or conservative. Some may be for socialism, others for capitalism; some prolabor, others probusiness. Humanists from the earliest days to the present have emphasized an ethic of freedom, though they may differ about the meaning of freedom. Nonetheless, they have invariably argued for the liberation of individuals from repressive social institutions; they have defended the free mind and the right of individuals to live their life styles as they see fit so long as they do not harm others or interfere with their rights.

"Humanism" contains the term *human*, which has been charged with emotive, often vague, meaning. Thus humanist ethics means for some to be opposed to "dehumanizing" or "depersonalizing" institutions. "Human nature" is often taken as a given and has been considered an ideal to be fulfilled. The core idea here apparently is that *human* or *humanity* are "natural" and "good," and that artificial or environmental devices that limit or restrict them are "wicked." Some in the ecology and no-growth movements recently have called themselves "humanist" in this neo-romantic sense, opposing technology and science as "unnatural" imposi-tions on humanhood. This is in sharp contrast to historical humanism, where the use of scientific method was considered essential to the humanist outlook.

Some humanists have sought to play down an ethic of individual freedom (sometimes called libertarianism), identifying it with a conserva-tive political philosophy, especially where it also involves economic poli-cies; instead, they have emphasized equality and fraternity. Under this view ethics is concerned primarily with how individuals relate to others in the community; the devotion to a beloved cause is the center of one's moral concern (Marxist humanists have usually concentrated on this aspect of ethics). Some have identified humanism with "humanitarianism"— support for underprivileged minorities (racial, sexual, etc.), the dispossessed, retarded, and handicapped. Some critics believe that this is a form of "bleeding heart liberalism," for it distributes rewards to the poorest members of the community without sufficient appreciation for merit, talent, innovation, and productivity. Others identify humanism (as in *Humanist Manifesto II*) with a commitment to "humanity as a whole" as a basic moral obligation. There are both secular and religious humanists who may subscribe to any or all of the above normative principles, even though they may differ about first principles concerning the universe and man's place within it. How humanism translates into specific moral prescription in any one age is sometimes difficult to say, given different social, ideological, and political forces at work.

The truth is that humanism has attracted many diverse tendencies in the world under its banner, and it may be impossible to find agreement among all those who claim identity with the humanist philosophy. This difficulty is especially pronounced when there is rapid social change. There are always new problems to face, hence there is continued need to revise principles and values in the light of altered social conditions. There may be honest and fundamental disagreement among humanists (as indeed among Christians) about a whole range of questions: economic, political, social, and ethical. Perhaps I am overly pessimistic. But I believe that there is little guarantee of getting a consensus of thought or action, other than in the broadest terms. Perhaps we should not seek it, else humanism is in danger of being transformed into a new dogmatism. Better to keep open the doors to continued critical inquiry; at best, we can clarify the moral problems we face and learn from one another, humanists as well as nonhumanists. Humanism thus does not represent a fixed program or platform, but rather is a general outlook, a method of inquiry, an ethic of freedom, and it is committed to a limited number of basic values and principles.

FREEDOM VS. RESPONSIBILITY

Does humanist ethics have a theory of moral responsibility? Can it provide a ground for obligation? The critics of secular humanism maintain that it fails to do so. There is the familiar argument against "relativistic ethics." Without some belief in God, we are admonished, obligation collapses. This argument is as old as ethics itself. The theist believes that if religion is absent, ethical duty has no source. Many philosophers have been concerned with this challenge. Kant attempted to provide a foundation for ethics without deriving it from God—though he was confronted in the last analysis with moral antinomies.

The view that belief in God is a secure ground for ethical obligation is fallacious. Since there is insubstantial evidence and surely no proof that God exists, the problem of ethical obligation is only pushed one step back to a premise that is itself precarious. The theistic universe presents an ethical order full of inconsistencies: the problem of evil for one, the abandonment of genuine moral freedom for another. If one's ethical principles depended in the final analysis upon the existence of God and His moral commandments, then one's free moral conscience is compromised. Doing something because God commands it, not because it is right or good, is not itself morally worthy. In the *Old Testament*, God commanded Abraham to sacrifice his son Isaac and he was willing to obey God's command. This illustration of faith and obedience is hardly morally commendable. The fact that God then bade Abraham not to do so is insufficient reason for Abraham's desisting. It was wrong for Abraham to sacrifice Isaac and one does not need a theological system to say so. Ethical judgments should have autonomous grounding in moral experience, and we would expect people to be truthful, honest, sincere, generous, whether or not they believe in God. Moreover, individuals who believe in God derive contradictory moral commandments: Christians and Jews are for monogamy, Muslims for polygamy. Most Protestant sects are for freedom of choice in abortion, Roman Catholicism is opposed. Christians will turn the other cheek to an offender, Muslims will cut off his hands. Theological moral codes depend as much or more on doctrines of revelation, church dogma, and a priestly class than on simple belief in divine power. From belief in the Fatherhood of God any number of opposing moral prescriptions—full of stern admonitions of duty—have been drawn.

Now one can understand the concern of the theist that humanist ethics without religious guidelines and the institutionalization of a code may not provide sufficient support for moral responsibility. There have been modern secular movements that have brutalized man: Nazism and Stalinism as quasi-theological, ideological doctrines abandoned traditional norms and ended up by creating infamous Gulags and moral monsters. Surely the humanist cannot be burdened with or blamed for the totalitarian excesses of the twentieth century. Humanists generally have defended human rights and democracy, and they have been among the first to condemn such tyrannies. Theistic religious institutions, particularly where they have had a monolopy of religious power, are surely not immune to the suppression of freedom, as the Crusades, the Inquisition, the wars between Muslims and Hindus, Protestants and Catholics, Jews and Muslims, vividly demonstrate.

Nevertheless, the humanist is faced with a crucial ethical problem: Insofar as he has defended an ethic of freedom, can he develop a basis for moral responsibility? Regretfully, merely to liberate individuals from authoritarian social institutions, whether church or state, is no guarantee that they will be aware of their moral responsibility to others. The contrary is often the case. Any number of social institutions regulate conduct by some means of norms and rules, and sanctions are imposed for enforcing them. Moral conduct is often insured because of fear of the consequences of breaking the law or of transgressing moral conventions. Once these sanctions are ignored, we may end up with the Thrasymachian man—concerned with his own personal lust for pleasure, ambition, and power, and impervious to moral constraints. The broader question is not simply, can you have morality without religious sanctions, but without *any* political, legal, or economic restraints; without, that is, any of the rules of law and order that govern a civilized community.

Some utopian anarchists maintain that human nature is basically beneficent; it is restrictive societal laws that corrupt human beings, and not the contrary. Their solution is to emancipate individuals from them; this they believe will untap a natural propensity for altruism. Regretfully, there is no guarantee that this will occur. Human motivation is highly complex and human nature is capable of both good and evil. Love and hate, self-interest and generosity, sympathy and jealousy, cooperation and competition are so deeply ingrained that we cannot be assured that only the best will in the end prevail. Thus we have no guarantee that individual moral beneficence will reign once all institutional sanctions are removed. Moreover, even *if* the world were only full of people with good intentions, they might still differ in their interpretation or application of their moral convictions, and this can be a further source of conflict.

Let me say at this point that I do not believe that secular humanists, who are devoted to a philosophy of freedom or of social progress, need be any more altruistic or responsible than the nonhumanist or theist. Humanists can be as deceitful and nasty, full of pride and as moved by the lust for fame and power—or conversely as beneficent and other-regarding—as anyone else. No one group can claim a privileged possession of the moral virtues. There is no moral exclusivity for any one philosophical, religious, or ideological party. Life would be oversimplified if all the good guys were on one side and all the bad guys on the other. Thus there is no assurance that if one is identified as a "humanist" that he or she will be moral, especially in regard to the common human decencies. Indeed, some modern day humanists are prone to an exacerbated moral self-righteousness that may be more wicked than the wickedness they wish to extirpate. Traditional morality, often unthinking, carries with it the smug complacency of the double standard. Humanists are critical of the devout businessman (the modern day Cephalus) who prays on the Sabbath, yet uses sharp and exploitative business practices during the week, condones conventional morality as sacrosanct, and is insensitive to hypocrisies and injustices. Often pitted against him, however, is the moral reformer, who—though reform is necessary to the cause of human moral progress—may become an intolerant moral fanatic, willing to chop off the heads of those whom he judges to be unjust or disagrees with. Regretfully, some egalitarians are impervious to the complexities of problems and are willing to impose simplistic moralistic solutions to them.

In raising the basic question, "Can humanist ethics provide a framework for responsible action?," I am leaving aside still another challenge, which is often presented to the secular humanist, "Can humanism adequately answer the question, 'What is the meaning of life?'." I have addressed myself to this question elsewhere at length.[1] The theist mistakenly believes that life is not meaningful if God is dead, or if there is no divine purpose to the universe. To that I answer, life has no meaning *per se*, but is full of opportunities. The meanings we discover depend on what we are willing to put into life, the dreams and ideals we cherish, the plans and projects we initiate. A vital virtue for humanist ethics is the courage for a person to become what he or she wishes. Here one can say that the good life is possible for individuals without the need for an external support system. Such an ethic emphasizes independence and self-reliance, the development of one's potentialities, the cultivation of critical intelligence and creative self-actualization. For such autonomous persons, an exuberant and full life, overflowing with meanings, is readily available. This does not deny that our fullest happiness involves other persons and presupposes some harmonious relationships with them. But the problem of the ground of moral responsiblity is a separate question. A eudaemanistic theory may indeed be self-centered and the desire for one's own self-realization egoistic. A central question of ethics thus concerns our relationship to others: What are our responsibilities and duties to our fellow human beings?

MORAL EDUCATION

I am persuaded that a humanistic ethic of freedom by itself is not sufficient without fulfilling at least two further conditions: First, it presupposes the theory and practice of moral education, and second, insofar as reason can be applied to moral choice, it presupposes a set of *prima facie* ethical principles that should have some claim upon our action.

As I have said, moral freedom is a central humanist value: the freeing of individuals from excessive restraints so that they may actualize their potentialities and maximize free choice. However, such a normative value is hardly sufficient unless a moral growth takes place. It is not enough to release individuals from authoritarian institutions, for some individuals may degenerate into hedonistic fleshpots or amoral egoists; thus we need also to nourish the conditions for moral development, in which an appreciation for the needs of others can emerge; and this is dependent upon moral education.

This need seems to be particularly strong in affluent postmodern societies today where narcissism is epidemic: Many individuals are consumers first and foremost. The entire domain of their universe is immediate self-gratification. The quest for pleasure is located in buying and consuming, using and discarding things, the gluttonous waste of food and drink, the dictates of fashion and adornments, the amassing of trinkets and gadgets to play with and show off. Much of this consumption is not based upon rational use but upon capricious tastes that are conditioned and titillated by advertisers. The banal bipolar syndrome of narcissistic morality alternates entertainment and boredom. The never-ending quest of the passive consumer and spectator is to be amused, but ennui always lurks in the background. The heroes of the consumer morality are comedians, show business personalities, and sports figures, who exemplify the surface character of life: all show, no depth. If affluent societies have solved the problems of poverty and disease for large sectors of their societies—the bane of all societies heretofore—they now have the problem of enhancing the level of taste.

The need for moral education has been recognized by philosophers from Aristotle to John Stuart Mill and John Dewey. This has at least a twofold dimension: First, the elevation of standards of taste and appreciation, the cultivation of qualitative pleasures and creative enjoyments, intellectual, aesthetic and moral; second, the development of moral virtues and moral character.

There are different pedagogical views about how to develop moral character. The traditionalist opts for training in discipline. He uses Sunday sermons, rote learning, and the threat of punishment to engender good habits. Religious indoctrination has always attempted to instill respect, fear, and love for the moral code. More recently, educational psychologists have argued that moral education in children and young adults involves a process of growth and development. Although at the most elementary level, moral education depends on some training and example, eventually the goal is the cultivation of autonomous agents, free to choose, aware of moral principles, cognizant of their responsibilities to others, capable of some reflective judgment.

The cognitive element in moral education, though, is not sufficient by itself. Morality must enlist the whole person and must address itself to the emotive and aesthetic components of the moral life: to develop attitudes in which some genuine concern for the needs of others is rooted in rational comprehension at the same time that it is fused with sentiment and feeling. Aristotle recognized this in the *Nichomachean Ethics* when he observed that students would not appreciate his course in ethics and politics unless they had already developed some of the moral virtues through experience and living.[2]

The question of moral responsibility is as much a psychological question as it is a theoretical one: How does one develop an appreciation for others, the moral point of view, a sense of altruism and giving, honesty, truthfulness, sincerity and trust. Some individuals are autistic, self-centered, selfish, concentrating on their own private gratifications. Such individuals lead the lives of crippled moral dwarfs. How does one develop moral growth in them?

Some say by exposing such individuals to the free give-and-take of moral inquiry and by examining moral dilemmas. I agree, though regretfully at times the result may be moral skepticism and nihilism, rather than a developed moral sense. Whether moral sympathy is innate or acquired is difficult to say, given the complexities of human nature.

Psychologists have differed on this point: Some, such as A. H. Maslow, maintain that moral sympathy is intrinsic to human nature and that the inner self which needs to unfold is basically good.[3] Others, such as B. F. Skinner, believe that various forms of moral behavior can be conditioned by operant reinforcement.[4] I believe that both theories have an element of truth: the roots of morality are found in our dependence and reciprocity as social animals, but whether morality is actualized depends in part upon cultural conditions. Surely the schools alone cannot accomplish the task of nurturing moral character, even though they still remain a vital source, for all of the institutions of society have a formative role in developing character.

One issue concerns the question of the neutrality of the schools, particularly in pluralistic democratic societies, where opposing sets of values may compete. Should the teacher simply seek to clarify existing values that the student already possesses and has brought to the classroom, or should the teacher attempt to "indoctrinate" (a bad word for libertarians and democrats) new values? Some believe that the schools should remain neutral, merely placing value problems under cognitive scrutiny. This is the position of the values clarification movement.[5] Those such as Jean Piaget and Lawrence Kohlberg believe that there are stages of moral development.[6] Whatever one's approach, values clarification or moral development, some values are being assumed by the teacher: intelligence, democracy, and tolerance as a minimum, the quest for fair play or a universalistic criterion as a maximum.

Secular humanist educators have suffered heavy attack, particularly in the United States, at the hands of theists who maintain that in teaching moral education in the schools, a new religion of secular humanism is being indoctrinated and this is contrary to the constitutional prohibitions against the establishment of a religion.

I think that this latter charge is unfounded, for if it were generalized then the schools could not teach science (some indeed refuse to allow them to teach evolution without also teaching creationism), contemporary literature, classical philosophy or ethics, or many other fields without being accused of indoctrination in the "religion of secular humanism." What the critics wish to repeal is the modern world, and they wish a return to fundamental Biblicism.

Nonetheless, I believe that the schools need to engage in moral "instruction"—a better term than "indoctrination"—of some kind; they do it anyway. In one sense virtually all education is moral. In so far as education strives to expand the horizons of the person, even his intellectual understanding, there is some modification, however subtle, and reconstruction of values going on.

Even in a democracy, the schools can, and should, consciously do this by focusing on the most basic and commonly shared moral values as the fabric of the community and the basis of human relationships: truth, honesty, sincerity, trust, kindness, generosity, friendship, sharing, concern for others, et cetera. This can be accomplished without raising ultimate ontological questions of where these values are rooted—in theology or nature. Moral education thus attempts to develop within the child and the young person both an emotive and intellectual basis for character formation. That this should be done is the message of philosophical ethics from the Greeks to the modern world: the autonomy of the moral virtues independent of a religious or nonreligious framework.

Now a good deal of the opposition to moral education in the schools concerns the attempt to offer solutions to specific moral issues that are under dispute in society. Granted, the schools cannot live in isolation from the concrete moral problems that trouble society; but courses in sexual education, discussion of abortion, euthanasia, women's rights, homosexuality, racial integration and intermarriage, war and peace, are saddled with opposing viewpoints in society. Here it is enough for the schools to discuss such moral dilemmas, examining alternative positions, without imposing the viewpoints of the teachers or of the community. But this is distinct from *the need to root within the psychological makeup of each individual a set of moral dispositions and virtues.* If they are absent, then libertarian societies may be faced with an increase in the number of morally retarded individuals, free to do what they want, insensitive to the hurt they may cause others.

A tragic illustration of the problem faced by democratic societies that do not have programs of moral education is the wanton murders of Charles Frankel, his wife, and two neighbors in Bedford Hills, New York. The Frankels and their neighbors were brutally shot and their homes rifled by thieves. Charles Frankel, an eloquent defender of humanism and democratic freedom, had faith in human intelligence. He was sacrificed by the excesses of passion and violence unleashed by those in a free society who lacked the moral virtues.

Some sociobiologists believe that moral turpitude may be in part genetic and that some individuals, particularly hardened criminals, are incorrigible. How, for example, should the penal system deal with repeated offenders? By coddling or punishing them? Should the legal system be rehabilitative or retributive in its approach? The humanist does not wish to give up in his constant effort to reform the institutions of society so that the best that human beings are capable of will emerge. Konrad Lorenz and others, however, maintain that aggression is innate in the human species.[7] Human vices, such as selfishness, laziness, vindictiveness, hatred, sloth, pride, jealously are so widespread in human behavior that we are all capable of their temptations at times. Perhaps humanists have been overly optimistic about the full reaches of human nature. Perhaps "original sin"—in natural and biological terms—is present in some individuals, who are immune to our efforts at amelioration. What we need is a deeper empirical understanding of human nature, without reading in what our values demand.

The difficulty in postmodern society is that moral education no longer can be entrusted to the family or the schools, and it surely cannot be left to the churches in so far as they preach false doctrines of redemption and salvation. In the Western world moral values often are a product of an economic system that prizes consumer entertainment as the highest value, and the mass media, in which violence, pornography, born-again religion, and the paranormal are sold to gullible consumers. I am not here simply indicting capitalism nor am I approving governmental regulation of the free market in ideas. What I am pointing to rather is the critical need for some measure of moral education in the larger media of communication.

Those who live in democratic societies need to influence the content of the media in an effort to raise the standards of appreciation—if we are to have any hope, that is, of developing moral character. Totalitarian Marxist societies have hardly solved the problems either, for they have imposed in their systems of education and in the mass media encapsulated moral programs. They have abandoned an ethic of freedom in favor of indoctrination in egalitarianism. The result is that the individual is lost. He is dispossessed of his rights; he has only duties to the state, but few freedoms against it.

PRIMA FACIE ETHICAL PRINCIPLES

But this still leaves open the question for one committed intellectually to a humanist ethics, Can the question of moral responsibility be resolved? How does one reconcile self-actualization and personal freedom with the rights and needs of others? On the scale of human values, which have higher priority, *my* needs and interests or *yours*?

There is, in my judgment, no ultimate resolution of this problem, no deductive proof of the "moral point of view." It seems to me that some constructive skepticism is a necessary component of moral philosophy; although a reflective person will, in general, come to abide by the moral point of view, it is not universally binding. To some extent, one's own best interest—such as in cases of his health or survival—ought to have a person's first commitment; in others, one's responsibility to other human beings (his children, family, friends, colleagues, or countrymen) should have a stronger claim on his action. In still other cases, a person recognizes an obligation to consider humanity as a whole and future generations yet unborn (as in questions concerning worldwide pollution or nuclear holocaust). What our duties and obligations are always depends upon the situation at hand and the kinds of questions being raised. We must be prepared to examine and revise our options by means of deliberative inquiry.

Yet I do not think that we need be led to a completely relativistic position in which no general principles are relevant. On the contrary, I submit that a naturalistic and humanistic ethical theory can incorporate general ethical principles that have significance in a situation.

How do we decide what to choose? I do not think that utilitarianism gives us an accurate guide for all moral choices. Surely, we need to take into account the *consequences of our action* in evaluating various alternatives, a pragmatic rather than a strictly utilitarian criterion. The greatest happiness principle, though relevant in some contexts, is too general to be of much help. If a teleological ethics by itself is insufficient—even though it is essential for any balanced ethical theory—some naturalistic form of deontological ethics should be recognized. Problems of ethical choice for the humanist involve an individual's quest for happiness; he will undertake those things that activate him and contribute to the fullness of his life. But maturity of judgment soon enables one to recognize that his deepest well-being is tied up with others and that *caring* is an essential nutrient in human relationships. Still it is not simply a question of the prudential calculation of one's long range self-interest. There are general principles of behavior that a developed moral agent will come to accept and these will have some bearing upon his conscience and conduct.

These ethical principles are not derived from God or divinity, nor do they come simply from some moral law implanted within the womb of nature or human nature. Nor indeed are they absolute or final in the sense that they are inviolable. I prefer the term "general" rather than "universal," since they are only approximate guides for conduct and there may be exceptions to them.

W. D. Ross uses the term *prima facie* to denote the fact that some duties are conditionally obligatory, but whether it is our actual duty to fulfill them depends upon a full examination of our obligations within the situation. According to Ross, among the *prima facie* duties are those that rest upon a person's previous acts, those resting on the acts of others, the contracts and commitments entered into, and the claims made upon us. There are also middle range duties incumbent upon us: positive duties, such as keeping our promises or paying our debts, and negative ones such as not cheating others. But there are more general duties as well: such as nonmaleficence, not injuring others; justice, attempting to distribute goods as widely as possible; and beneficence, helping to relieve distress where we are able to do so.[8]

I prefer to use the term "principles" rather than "duties," because we can generalize various kinds of action, and recognize that these are general prescriptions, rules, and policies that we ought to observe. Most of these are part of the proverbial wisdom, such as, "Honesty is the best policy," or "Do unto others as ye would have them do unto you."

Now the question that can be raised is, What is the foundation of these *prima facie* general ethical principles? Many who have defended them have done so on intuitive grounds. They have said that either they cannot be proven and are true without proof, or that they are self-evident to the reflective conscience.

I deny their intuitive character. Such general principles are not mysterious or sacrosanct, but naturalistic and empirical phenomena. They have developed in social relationships over long periods of time—in part because of common human needs and necessities, and in part because they have come to be recognized as imperative in human relationships if we are to realize social harmony. They are tested by their observable effects in human conduct. A relationship between two persons cannot long endure if there is insincerity between them, and a human community cannot long endure in peace if there is widespread duplicity. General ethical principles, however, are not simply justifiable as instrumental; in time they come to have some intrinsic merit, and we come to feel strongly about them for their own sake: they are both means and ends. Those who consider them simply expedient may have no compunctions about breaking or compromising them at will and may be corrupted in the process.

There is an ironic legacy that dependence upon some forms of purely utilitarian or pragmatic moral systems have bequeathed us; that is, some individuals and groups have been willing on utilitarian grounds to justify the use of *any* means to achieve ends that they considered worthwhile. The conclusion that Machiavellians have drawn is that if they are to remain in power, they must be ready to employ unscrupulous means. Authoritarian defenders of the status quo have applied the full force of the state, violating human rights, in order to secure their ends; and despots have always employed heinous methods of torture and terror. The paradox of moral compromise—that one is prepared to use dastard means to achieve noble ends—has also undermined Marxism as an ethical philosophy. Marxists are critical of the injustices of capitalism; they wish to usher in a utopian system of ideal values. But some apparently feel that this justifies them to use terrorist means to defeat their opponents, even if it results in the slaughter of innocent bystanders. Totalitarian communist regimes have, on the same ground, crushed dissent and opposition of so-called enemies of the party or revolution.

Humanists are not immune to moral corruption either. I have learned from direct personal experience in humanist organizations that even so-called "humanists" will at times use mendacious means to achieve their goals, and that they are as prone to vanity, jealousy, vindictiveness, and other foibles as other human beings. I was dismayed to discover that some so-called "humanitarians" and "philanthropists" make contributions or are devoted to a cause not for the good they will achieve, but for personal power and acclaim. And even more distressed that others will stand by and allow the rape of the moral dignities to occur, on the mistaken assumption that sin is always committed by nonhumanists (bishops, divines, and other such personages), not by the emancipated. The result is often that the emancipated, bereft of all conventional standards, are left without any viable principles of ethical conduct at all. All the more reason why humanist ethics needs double rooting: (1) a teleological interest in realizing worthy ends, goods, values, *and* (2) a deontological concern for fulfilling obligations, responsibilities, duties; an ethic of principles, as well as an ethic of ideal ends.

Which of these roots ought to prevail in ethics? Which ought to have the deepest priority, the good or the right? I am unwilling to affix an *a priori* solution to this question. As I have said, it all depends upon the situation at hand. In problems of moral choice, we need to take into account empirical and pragmatic criteria: the facts of the case, the means at our disposal, the consequences of our actions. We also need to consider the *prima facie* ethical principles that are relevant. Our actual duties, obligations and responsibilities will depend upon the situation and the social milieu in which we live. These are always particular and concrete, growing out of our commitments and values, the contracts entered into, the claims made upon us. Only empirical inquiry can tell us what we ought to do in a given situation.

In moral problems there is often a conflict between values, not all of which we can attain. We may wish to travel widely, raise a family, and have a successful career all at the same time—which may be difficult or impossible (unless we become a travel agent or airplane pilot). In other cases, there may be a clash between a good to be achieved and a responsibility to be fulfilled, as in a conflict between what one may desire and what others expect of him—and one may have to give way to the other. Similarly, an act may be justifiable, even though in itself evil, because of the preponderant long-range good that will ensue, as when we reluctantly decide to go to war to defend ourselves or others against aggression. In still other situations, all of the alternatives may be bad, and we may be compelled to choose the lesser of two evils, as in the case of a person suffering from an incurable disease, who is faced with death, a prolonged and horrible one, or euthanasia, but death in any case. The point is, we need to *balance* the competing claims of our values and principles, considerations of the good and the right.

Humanist philosophers have recognized that our ultimate obligation, in the final analysis, is the use of rational thought to resolve, as best we can, such moral dilemmas. What we will decide to do, as I have said, presupposes some moral education, and a sensitivity to general ethical principles—an important concomitant of humanist ethics. Still, it is the autonomous person capable of reflective choice who is the best guide. We need to appreciate at the same time the limitations of absolute moral certitude and the possibilities of moral wisdom. Authoritarian and legalistic moralists will no doubt object to such a conclusion and will wish for something more. Humanist ethics can only provide something less than they desire, but this does not mean that ethical choice need be capricious or subjectivistic, nor that it is unamenable to some form of objective critical appraisal. Indeed, humanist ethics, although the least pretentious of ethical theories in what it promises, may yet be the most reliable; for it may be best able to allow both the good life to be realized and the moral decencies to prevail.

NOTES

1. See: *The Fullness of Life* (New York: Horizon Press, 1974), and *Exuberance* (Buffalo, NY: Prometheus Books, 1977).
2, *Nichomachean Ethics*, Bk. I, ch. 3.
3. Maslow, Abraham H., *Toward a Psychology of Being* (New York: 2nd Ed., Van Nostrand Co., 1968).
4. Skinner, B.F., *Walden Two* (New York: Macmillan, 1948).
5. Raths, Louis, et al., *Values and Teaching: Working with Values in the Classroom* (Indianapolis: Merrill, 1966). Simon, Louis, et al., *Values Clarification: A Handbook of Practical Strategies for Teachers and Students* (New York: Hart, 1972).
6. See: Piaget, Jean, *The Moral Judgment of the Child* (London: Routledge and Kegan Paul, 1932), and *The Childs Conception of the World* (New York: Harcourt, Brace, 1929). Kohlberg, Lawrence, "From Is to Ought," in *Cognitive Development and Epistemology*, ed. T. Mischel (New York: Academic Press, 1971), pp. 131-256, and "Stages of Moral Development as a Basis for Moral Education," in *Moral Education*, ed. by C.M. Beck, et al. (Toronto: University of Toronto Press, 1971), pp. 23-92, and "Stage and Sequence: The Cognitive Development Approach to Socialization," in *Handbook of Socialization Theory and Research*, ed. by D.A. Goslin Chicago: Rand McNally, 1969), pp. 347-480.
7. Lorenz, Konrad, *On Aggression* (New York: Bantam, 1970).
8. Ross, W.D., *The Right and the Good* (Oxford: Clarendon Press, 1930).

Comment by Morris Storer on Kurtz Article

Paul Kurtz has given us in his article two things of vital importance: (1) a landmark discussion of moral education, and (2) a highly significant study of the place of principles in an ethic of freedom.

The former points the way to a critically needed emphasis on ethics in public and private school education, in the home, and in mass media programs, to counter the influence of "an economic system which prizes consumer entertainment as the highest value" and of the mass media "where violence, pornography, born-again religion, and the paranormal are sold to gullible consumers." The need is "to nourish the conditions for moral development, in which an appreciation for the needs of others can emerge."

Item (2) above points the way to an ethic that builds on the reality of the human condition, an ethic of entirely "naturalistic and empirical principles," recognized as "imperative in human relationships if we are to realize social harmony:" sincerity, truth, honesty, justice, beneficence, keeping promises, paying debts—a golden rule morality: no cheating or injury or duplicity—an end of Machiavellian violence to morality—principles that people begin by valuing just instrumentally—as expedient—but come to feel strongly about for their own sake. But appropriately and predictably, Kurtz reaffirms the dependence of obligation on the particulars of the situation in hand.

One major significance of this combination of emphases—on moral education and on a humanist morality of principles—is the prospect that it opens up for cooperative relations in education to replace the tensions that have been rife between humanism and various religious institutions. The general principles that Paul Kurtz emphasizes are foremost among the main principles that church and synagogue are concerned to implant and elicit in their membership. Where there are differences, everything is to be gained by closer relations of communication. Where there *have been* differences of major emphasis in ethics (as concerns those principles), Kurtz's emphasis points the way to resolution of the most serious tensions, and to new possibilities of reasoned consultation. Humanists ought to, and can afford to, acknowledge every person's right to freedom of belief and faith in the ultimate areas, so long as the implications of those beliefs and of such faith do no violence to the principles which Paul Kurtz has here emphasized or which are elsewhere expressed in humanist consensus statements.

Reply by Paul Kurtz to Storer

Morris Storer has correctly identified the two main points of my essay: the need (1) to support a program of moral education and (2) to recognize the role of general moral principles in moral situations. I agree with Professor Storer's view that if humanistic ethics would clearly incorporate these aspects, it would most likely reduce the level of conflict with powerful religious institutions, which often consider humanism to be "wicked" and "immoral." It is important to recognize that humanist ethics shares with other ethical systems, including religious ones, a set of *common* ethical norms as the common heritage of human history and experience. We should not overlook, however, the genuine differences that still persist in other areas between humanistic and theistic ethics. If we are to use the same roads and highways, we need to respect the rules of the road and abide by the traffic system. But we may differ fundamentally about where we wish to arrive at the end of our journeys. Humanists have a different view of the meaning of life than theists. They place a different value on autonomy and independence; they believe that human beings can create the conditions for the good life without the need for God or clergy: we are responsible for our own destiny, no deity will save us, we must save ourselves. Humanists take secular values, such as creative happiness and joy, as the end of life, not the vain hope for immortality. There is, accordingly, a genuine—and perhaps irreconcilable—difference in most values that we cannot easily brook.

Nevertheless, we *do* share common moral principles which we recognize as necessary preconditions for living and working together. One basic rule is tolerance: the right of differing individuals and groups within a pluralistic world to coexist (this does not mean that they are immune from criticism). This vital democratic principle had been denied for a long time by many theological dogmatists. It is only after a long history of suppression that religious believers have come to share with humanists an appreciation for them.

Comment by Kai Nielsen on Kurtz Article

Paul Kurtz well conveys the sense of reasonableness that is embedded in humanistic accounts of ethics and the tragic dilemmas that often are part of the moral life. He also wisely would have us be wary of both absolutism in ethics and relativism and seeks to define a form of objectivism that undermines both absolutism and relativism. My problems about his account turn on Section Four of his essay. I think too much is made of the conflict between egoism and altruism, between self-interest and concern for others. The moral point of view, as Kurt Baier, among others, has powerfully argued in his *The Moral Point of View*, requires impartiality, not altruism. In moral reflection each is to count for one and none to count for more than one. The moral point of view does not require a denial of the self but willingness on the part of the moral agent to be impartial. He counts his own interests but he need not give them either more or less weight than the interests of anyone else. (This is not negated by the practical, if you will, tactical, point that often, since most people know best what their own interests are, we are all better off, if we, in standard circumstances, take care to protect our own interests. There are egoists—that is, amoralists—who do only that or give their interests pride of place over the interests of others, but a moral agent who tends prudently to his own interests does not do that). A recognition of this does not make the moral point of view something which is not universally binding, as Kurtz claims. For the moral agent, for someone committed through and through to doing what he, morally speaking, regards as the right thing to do, there can be no alternative but to accept the moral point of view as universally binding. Indeed, to say this, is to say something which very much appears to be true by definition. The problem about the universal bindingness of the moral point of view emerges around the question, "Why should I be moral?". An amoralist will not find the moral point of view binding at all. He will only use moral conceptions manipulatively to achieve his own ends. But that is not, again by definition, a possible option for a humanist. (That is true, even if we construe humanism, as Kurtz does, in a very broad sense, covering many tendencies of thought).

I also think that Kurtz is unclear about his backing for his general ethical principles. He denies that they are intuitive. But it is hard to know what to make of his claim that they are "naturalistic and empirical phenomena." Indeed it is at least plausible to believe that they have *arisen* because of common human needs and necessities, but their *origin* does not decide the question of what their present status is. Religious notions also arise out of needs, as Feuerbach and Freud show, but this does not make religious statements empirical statements. "Have regard for others," unlike "People tend to have regard for others," does not appear to be an empirical claim which is true or false in the same way the second quoted remark is. "People *must* have concern for others" seems to be no more an empirical statement of fact than "Have regard for others." How we would establish its truth is unclear. How, more generally, we would establish the truth or warrantability of fundamental or general ethical principles is left quite mysterious by Kurtz. It is this problem, among others, that I tried to deepen and confront in my own essay.

Finally, Kurtz is unfair to Marxists, at least Marxists who have views like those of Marx or Engels. They do not wish to "usher in a utopian system of ideal values." Indeed their critique of utopian socialism makes it quite plain why they think that is a mistake. Furthermore, Marx, Engels, and Lenin, as one can see from their criticisms of the Anarchists, were definitely against terrorism. With mass support terrorism is unnecessary, indeed just a senseless cruelty. Without that mass support it is worse than pointless, for it will only alienate what may be potential supporters of socialism.

Reply by Paul Kurtz to Nielsen

Kai Nielsen opens his essay be recognizing with me the tragic dilemmas that are often part of the moral life and the difficulties that may arise in adjudicating conflicts in obligations between an individual's interests and those of others.

Nielsen raises three objections, particularly to the last section of my paper. First, he thinks that I make too much of the conflict between egoism and altruism. The moral point of view, he says, involves impartiality, not altruism, and is universally binding. Would the problem be so easily resolved, for there is at times a conflict between egoism (or self-interest) on the one hand, and impartiality on the other. Also, many moral philosophers have held that an individual's primary obligation is to his own self-interest or that of his immediate relatives, friends, or countrymen, and not to the generalized other. Libertarians have argued that this indeed is our basic duty and that if each would tend to his own garden before tending to others, we would all be better off; this they maintain is the conclusion that an ethically impartial spectator would reach. Thus, there is some dispute precisely about what an *impartial* moral observer would find as his first responsibility: universal beneficence vs. concern for his own well-being or those within his immediate sphere of interest. Merely to say that the moral point of view is universally binding is a truism—true by definition—for what may be in dispute is *what* the moral point of view is.

Professor Nielsen also glosses over the fact that many or most individuals find it difficult or impossible to be completely impartial about matters that concern their vital interests, although they may gladly be impartial about that which concerns others. That is why whatever one's views of impartiality (or altruism) are, we still need to develop a system of moral education to cultivate such a concern, for it is not apparent or axiomatic that individuals will recognize the priority of impartiality.

Nielsen objects to my view that ethical principles are "naturalistic and empirical phenomena." By this I simply meant that they did not have some mysterious ontological status, nor could they be discovered intuitively. To say that they are "empirical" means that they are characteristics of human behavior or institutions that have developed over a long period of time. It does not mean that I deny their prescriptive or normative role, nor believe that they are descriptive assertions. He correctly points out that if ethical principles are empirical, so are religious beliefs and practices: they too are human, not "sacred," phenomena, growing out of human needs and interest. *Both* ethics and religion are empirical in origin and function. However, the question of how to evaluate ethical principles is another matter and here I would suggest several criteria: (1) the relevance of facts, (2) the analysis of means, (3) the consequences of various courses of action.

To these, I would consider the relation of any principles under analysis to (4) human needs, (5) existing values, and (6) other *prima facie* general principles. Ethical principles are practical, they are judged by what they accomplish in the observable world. Some of the criteria by which we judge them are accordingly empirical and pragmatic; but the principles themselves are prescriptive not descriptive in function.

Lastly, Nielsen maintains that I am unfair to Marxists, who, he claims, do not wish to create a utopian system of ideal values and are against terrorism. It is true that Marx was a critic of utopian socialists for being unable to achieve socialism by simply enunciating visionary views of the world. He thought that the only way to bring about socialism was by the use of practical action. In this sense he was a realist rather than a utopianist. But surely Marx—and many of his followers—have been motivated by utopian ideals, for they deplore the fact that justice does not exist in feudal and capitalist societies and they present an ideal picture of a classless society where it would. This is a utopian vision, however unclear Marx was about the exact contours of the society that would ensue after the destruction of capitalism.

To deny that Marxists have defended terrorism as a method of achieving communism and maintaining it against counterrevolution is puzzling. Surely, Lenin used it, as did Trotsky, Stalin, and many other disciples of Marxism. Granted that terrorism may be senseless and counterproductive, democratic socialists have long argued that democratic methods of persuasion must be the chief road to socialism. But Leninists have vigorously opposed this strategy. Indeed, a profound moral tragedy of our time is precisely that Marxist revolutions have been betrayed, that many Marxist revolutionaries who are out of power are willing to use terroristic means to achieve it, and, once in power, to suppress opposition to maintain themselves. It illustrates a chief problem for my paper, namely that a Marxist theory of ideal ends is insufficient without also recognizing the need for a theory of general ethical principles. A basic defect of Marxist theory, in my judgment, is that it has not developed an adequate theory of ethics, largely because of the centrality of the sociological interpretations of history. Ethical standards allegedly reflect the conditions of production and the class structure.

In any case, I do not believe that humanism should be tied to a specific ideology—Marxist, liberal, conservative, or others—but that ethical concerns transcend the limits of politics. This does not deny that we have political convictions and that many ethical issues have social and political solutions. But ethics, like other human interests—art, religion, or science—cannot be reduced to a single ideological-political stance. To attempt to do this would not only impoverish humanism, but make it narrow in focus and banal in meaning.

Comment by Mihailo Marković on Kurtz

While the paper of Professor Kurtz is focused on the possibility of building a humanist ethics of responsibility, he also deals with two other issues: (1) the meaning of humanism and humanist morality, (2) the need of moral education. I share his critique of irrationalism, obscurantism, and any form of totalitarian repression. Most of what he says on moral education does not seem controversial to me. Also some of his ethical principles certainly express a minimal basic core of any ethics.

My main difficulties with his paper are *first*, to reconcile several apparently incompatible things that he says about humanist morality, and, *second*, to understand what he really means by ethical principles and how he expects to justify them.

In his attempt to characterize humanism and humanist morality, Kurtz has at least two very different positions.

The view that prevails and which probably is the one with which he identifies himself is what he describes as "constructive skepticism." What characterizes this skeptical, minimalistic position is a strong commitment to scientific rationality, secularity, and individual freedom and a rather weak commitment to some kind of "caring" for others (while one pursues his egoistic goals) and to "helping to relieve distress" ("where we are able to do so"). From this point of view the author struggles against religious irrationalism and totalitarianism, but also against Marxist humanism. He seems to be aware that this emphasis on freedom of isolated, unequal individuals may have conservative political and economic implications. But he is ready to defend it philosophically by emphasizing that hate, self-interest, jealousy, and competition are as deeply ingrained in human nature as love, generosity, sympathy, and cooperation, and that, therefore, one should not blame social institutions and laws for so much misery in the human condition. Such a weak anthropological ground turns out to generate a remarkable tolerance toward those who oppress and exploit others. Professor Kurtz actually agrees that "humanists can be as deceitful and nasty, full of pride and moved by the lust for fame and power" as anyone else. It looks almost as if everyone is a humanist who chooses to label himself or herself that way—in the same way as everyone becomes a Christian by joining a church. The concept of humanism becomes quite uninformative and redundant if it does not cover anything more but secular individualism. On that ground one cannot build a very attractive ethics but at least this can be developed as a consistent (traditional liberalist) position.

However, Professor Kurtz in his paper tries to incorporate a number of more attractive moral ideas and these may be shown to be incompatible with the ethics of contemporary business and of bourgeois society in general. He says, for example, that humanist ethics "emphasizes independence and self-reliance, the development of one's potentialities, the cultivation of critical intelligence and creative self-actualization. For such autonomous persons an exuberant and full life overflowing with meanings is readily available. This does not deny that our fullest happiness involves other persons and presupposes some harmonious relationships with them."

This is now an essentially different ethical position. Freedom in the sense of "development of one's *potentialities*" is a very different thing from freedom in the sense of "economizing what one *wishes*" (which according to Professor Kurtz is a "vital virtue for humanist ethics"). One's potentiality to communicate meaningfully, to reason and act creatively is an *objective*, universally human, latent structure of dispositions which is present in an individual even after a very unbearable and crippling socialization process. On the other hand, the *subjective* wishes of a person who was crushed by the misery of the whole social environment may be so limited that "becoming what one *wishes*—the leader of a gang for example—could turn out to be precisely the opposite of *self-realization*. Here the author who moves most of the time on traditional liberalist ground of negative freedom (as absence of external impediments to do or become what one actually desires) suddenly assumes the standpoint of *positive* freedom, of self-realization of an autonomous person. And this is not merely a matter of terminology since he suddenly here speaks of "cultivation of *critical* intelligence" (rather than mere accumulation of positive specialized knowledge), of "creative self-actualization" (rather than any growth), of an "exuberant and full life overflowing with meanings" (rather than accumulation of wealth and power).

This kind of inconsistency, while logically unacceptable, need not be condemned if one consciously moves from a poorer, more limited position toward a richer more general one. Only one must also accept the implications and make necessary corrections elsewhere. Namely his kind of humanist ethics that is based on the idea of positive freedom (in the sense of self-realization) is not only extremely critical toward totalitarian, Stalinist society (and all Professor Kurtz's critical arrows go only in that direction) but also toward capitalist society (the oppressive dehumanizing features have hardly been mentioned in this paper.) The vast majority of human beings in both prevalent forms of contemporary society are utterly dependent, they waste their potential, develop a receptive rather than critical intelligence, produce but not create, and live anything but "exuberant, meaningful lives."

These profound and exciting humanist ethical ideals which express the noblest strivings of our historical epoch, once formulated by Kurtz, disappear from the list of his ethical principles. In that list we find elementary duties which constitute the very minimum of any morality (such as "keeping promises," "paying debts," "not cheating and injuring others") or very abstract categorical frameworks which wait to be filled by content ("justice") or vague obligations (such as "attempting to distribute goods as widely as possible"). (How resolutely should one attempt? What does "widely" mean here?)

It is not clear what is the theoretical status of those principles. At first they are construed as flexible, violable, approximate guides for conduct, as conditional obligations, the fulfillment of which is contingent upon an examination of the given situation. Furthermore, they are regarded as mere "empirical phenomena," "they have developed in social relationships over long periods of time as expression of human needs and necessities, and come to be recognized as imperative in human relationships." From here Professor Kurtz makes a jump and asserts that these are not merely duties but principles, "because we can generalize various kinds of action and recognize that these are general prescriptions, rules, and policies that we *ought* to observe." It remains quite unclear where this *ought* comes from. It is one thing to describe a *variety* of actual historical patterns of conduct and moral habits. It is a completely different thing to make a *choice* among them and to say that we *ought* to observe some of them. Why some and not others? If we adopt certain norms merely because they are observable over long periods of time as social facts then either we are ignorant of other incompatible but equally empirically observable moral habits, or we have to adopt a completely *relativist* approach. In the latter case we can no longer oppose to patriarchal or feudal morality which is equally a matter of empirical fact. On the other hand if their *ought* does not follow from *is*, why does it in our ethics? A naturalist, humanist ethics can only be founded on a philosophical theory of human being. Else it lacks any foundation, stops being a (normative) *ethical* theory and turns into a positive (sociological) description of various existing forms of morality.

Reply by Paul Kurtz to Marković

Mihailo Marković asks whether the position that I am defending is anything more than a form of "secular individualism." He claims to find this incompatible with other views that I express in my paper, especially my emphasis on creative actualization and moral development. It is clear that humanism has been identified with the classical liberal position. I share this libertarian viewpoint. It does not necessarily imply, however, a rampant egoism immune to moral development. This surely was not the case for John Stuart Mill, who was a libertarian humanist and who emphasized the need to develop the higher pleasures: moral, aesthetic and intellectual. Nor was it the case with John Dewey who sought to cultivate growth and democratic values in education. For the liberal humanist freedom in *both* senses, negative (freedom from) and positive (freedom to), are essential and not incompatible.

Accordingly, I would affirm the need of humanist ethics to develop an appreciation for the moral virtues of caring, helping others, having a regard for justice, nonmalfeasance, beneficence and other basic moral principles. (Incidentally, this is not a distinctively humanist position. Surely Christianity has emphasized the altruistic virtues.) I would also include in my catalogue of moral principles many others, such as fairness, equality, fraternity, etc. Professor Marković is entirely correct that I prize individual *freedom*—of creatively developed persons—in the last analysis as a central, but not the only, value. Marxists have all too often been willing to sacrifice individual freedom at the altar of Social Reconstruction. The kind of Marxist-humanism which Marković represents has not done this (thus far it has not met with much success); and it has attempted to keep alive an appreciation for human rights and freedom. In my view it is unfortunate that twentieth century humanism had been identified with certain repressive varieties of Marxism. Leninism, Stalinism and Maoism consider themselves to be "humanistic" in so far as they have a "humanitarian" concern for justice and progress, but they have abandoned freedom in the process. In retrospect, I consider Marxist communism to be the opium of the intellectuals and the poison of the masses, for it has led to hatred and intolerance. On balance, it is more destructive of humanist values than most of the systems that it seeks to replace. Humanists have surely not defended the status quo. They have been critics of the inequities of capitalist societies. They have sought to reform societies, to remove obstacles to individual growth, such as poverty and discrimination, to enhance individual development by helping to satisfy basic economic needs and providing for educational and cultural opportunity, and other ameliorative programs. It seems to me to be apparent, based upon the historical evidence thus far, that voluntary pluralistic societies that encourage individual initiative and innovation are more likely to achieve both freedom and a better life for the common man than are controlled totalitarian societies.

Intellectuals in general and humanists in particular have not recognized the moral contributions that democratic capitalism can make to human freedom and well-being. On the contrary, if you eradicate all economic freedom, and centralize control in a state bureaucracy or in a one party system, you end up by losing most other freedoms—political, intellectual and cultural. What is the point of dreaming about the theoretical democratic possibilities of an ideal Marxist-humanism when empirical reality vividly demonstrates the opposite.

I reiterate that I do not believe that humanism—as a secular ethic of freedom—should be tied to a specific ideology or even a specific economic, political or social system. If it was humane for humanists to have defended socialism at one period of history as a way to guarantee and enhance freedom, to do so now is questionable, especially in view of what has happened to human rights and freedoms in so-called Marxist societies. Accordingly, one can surely be a humanist today and defend humanistic capitalism. Perhaps other social systems will emerge in the future more appropriate to world conditions, and humanists along with others will need to revise their ideological commitments. The terms "conservative," "liberal," or "bourgeois" meanwhile have lost all identifiable meanings. In one sense, a *democratic* humanism is still the most *radical* of ethical postures in so far as it wishes to expand the dimensions of human freedom. Its chief enemies today are authoritarianism and totalitarianism, whether communistic or capitalistic, secularist or ecclesiastical.

Marković's last point concerns *obligation*. I can find no ultimate basis for ought. I can find no roots for moral principles in God or History, only in human needs, interests and ideals. Obligations can only be tested in the last analysis by their consequences in human experience. In this sense I remain a situationist and pluralist in ethics, though modified by my commitment to a set of *prima facie* ethical principles. I view such ethical principles as the common heritage of the human race, based upon funded experience. That is why I believe that it is vital that they be psychologically grounded in human motivation—in feeling as well as thought—by programs of moral education. While obligations are relative to human situations, they need not be subjective, but are amenable to reflective criticism and can be revised in the light of a process of inquiry. In this sense, the position that I hold is a form of objective relativism.

Historical Praxis as the Ground of Morality

Mihailo Marković

HUMANIST ALTERNATIVES

Once a humanist rejects the idea of the divine origin of morality he seems to have essentially the following four alternatives:

(1) A *static, ahistorical relativism* exemplified in any empiricist, pragmatist, or structuralist approach. From this point of view each particular society, each civilization, has a set of rules which regulate human relationships and maintain a necessary level of social cohesion. These sets are different and incommensurable paradigms of morality—like Bachelard's different types of rationalism or Kuhn's scientific paradigms or Levy Strauss's "codes" for the expression of specific social structures. This type of approach allows an objective study of each particular paradigm but rules out the possibility of speaking of a universal human morality. Moral systems cannot be compared, all concepts of morally "good," "right," "ought," or "true" become relative to a specified system and it does not make sense to evaluate one morality as "better" than the other.

(2) If this relativism does not satisfy us, because it tends to devoid general ideas of "human being and history" of any meaning, we may turn to an *absolutism* of a Kantian or phenomenological kind. There is a transcendental concept of man, and of his practical reason; an ahistorical autonomous good will, a universal moral law—the "categorical imperative"—provides the basis of all morality. Those who, like Schiller, reject the identification of the *a priori* with the formal and of the *a posteriori* with the substantial may project moral values into a particular realm of

validity (*Geltung*) outside of both spheres of material world and human consciousness.

(3) Those who, in an age of a fast historical progress, do not see much merit in such a static conception of both a formal ethics of duty and of an axiology of values "in themselves" may prefer the *historical absolutism* of Hegel. Any particular moral order within a family, a nation, a civilization, and morality in itself as a form of consciousness are only objective stages in the development of an absolute spirit. This approach opens the possibility of comparison and critique of various moral systems, of seeing their inner limitations, of evaluating one as merely a particular moment of the other. However the basic assumption of an *absolute* mind implies the absence of history, of possible creation of new forms of morality in the future. The system had to be closed if it claimed absolute truth: all real development took place in the past.

(4) The legitimate heir of Hegel's thought, Marx left behind an ambiguous body of ideas. Those which constitute nowadays the foundation of official Marxist ideologies offer a *historical but relativist* conception of morality. According to it there is a true development of morality in history. History—and not only the past but also the future—may be seen objectively, as a process of growth of social productive forces, and a succession of increasingly rich and free socioeconomic formations. But history may also be seen more subjectively as a history of class struggles. Each class has its own morality rooted in objective material life-conditions of that class. An overemphasis of the class character of man, a reluctance to see elements of universal humanity in each individual and class leads back to relativism. This is obvious not only in the Marxist orthodoxy of both the Second and Third Communist International, but also in the Marxist structuralism of an Althusser. Rather than seeing in the future what Hegel established in the past: a process of totalization of man in general, his progressive enrichment and emancipation, both orthodox and structuralist Marxists construe history as a series of modes of production which are separated by social ruptures—revolutions, and cultural ("epistemological") gaps.

While it could be argued that Marx himself is very much responsible for this relativist interpretation (consider Marx's Sixth Thesis of Feuerbach: "Man is *ensemble* of social relations."), he also made essential contribution to a humanist, truly historical conception of morality that goes beyond the wrong dilemma of absolutism versus relativism.

The view of man as a universal self-consciousness, developed in Hegel's *Phenomenology of Mind*, was transcended by a conception of man as a *practical* being, who creates his history, his material life conditions, social forms, and morality beyond any preconceived limit.

THE CONCEPTION OF MAN AS A BEING OF PRAXIS—A BASIS FOR ETHICS

If we don't wish to give ethics a theological foundation, and if we, furthermore, don't want to build it on the basis of an arbitrary, dogmatically postulated absolute standard, we must look for human history as a possible ground of morality. However if history is taken to be a mere collection of facts or a mere series of several disintegrated, incommensurable systems, we would simply relapse into a relativistic positivism—and that is what happened with official Marxism either in its earlier social-democratic or later Bolshevik version.

One has to ask if human history as a whole is a *meaningful* process or not. Before answering such a difficult and complex question one could ask a simpler, more general one: What constitutes the meaning of any life process? Jacques Monod's answer was: *teleonomy*, a unique primary object of preservation and multiplication of the species. One could ask here: What makes this basic project "valuable"? Why is preservation of species better than disappearance? Why is it *better* to multiply than to simply restore the already achieved quantitative level?

The only answer to such a question is: What is here described as "better" or "worse" is not merely a matter of subjective preference; it refers to a tendency which is a necessary part of the very definition of life. Surely not all individuals and species survive and multiply. But while they do— they are alive. In a similar way one should add that life involves a tendency to maintain and increase order and structural complexity: a process of change in the opposite direction of lesser order and complexity is "bad" for a living organism since it leads to destruction of life; it is therefore being described in negative value terms as a process of degradation.

The comparable question with respect to human history is: What is the primary project of historical development? Which are objective conditions necessary for survival and development of man, not as a mere living organism, but as a *distinctly human* being? A good deal of things which actually occurred in the course of history do not belong to such conditions: famines, floods, earthquakes, massacres, destruction. What made human history possible and indeed unique—in view of an explosive development during the last few thousand years—was a specifically human activity— *praxis*. Praxis is *purposeful* (preceded by a conscious objective), *self-determining* (choosing autonomously among alternative possibilities), *rational* consistently following certain general principles), *creative* (transcending given forms and introducing novelties into established patterns of behavior), *cumulative* (storing in symbolic forms ever greater amounts of information and conveying them to coming generations so that they can continue to build on the ground already conquered), *self-creative* (in the sense that young human individuals, after being exposed to an increasing wealth of information and new environmental challenges develop new faculties and new needs). Praxis is a new high-level form of the human species. It retains genetic invariance, self-regulation, teleonomy. But it goes far beyond them. The plastic genetic material will be shaped in countless different ways by social conditioning; self-regulation will become more and more conscious and autonomous, the conservative *telos* of species—preservation and multiplication will be replaced by an entirely new basic project: creation of a rich, manifold, increasingly complex and beautiful environment, self-creation of men with an increasing wealth of needs. Many human activities are clearly not instances of praxis, nor are they characteristic of human history. Repetitive work of a slave, serf, or modern worker resembles more the building of a beaver's dam than creative work.

As in the discussion about basic inherent teleonomy of life, it is possible to ask the question: What is the *good* of all this creation and self-creation? Is it not better to go back to simple organic life in as natural an environment as possible, with a minimum of needs? And as in the earlier case, the answer is: A different *telos* is possible but it would not be the *telos* of human history. The emergence of man is this gigantic step from the simple, organic, repetitive, narrow, *natural* world to the complex, civilized, continuously developing vastly expanded *historical* world, from a poverty of needs and abilities to an increasing wealth of goals and life manifestations.

A judgment of this kind is still *factual.* What has been argued so far is that, as a *matter of fact*, the specific characteristic of man and human history is *praxis.* A basic *normative* standpoint is taken when one commits himself to supporting, stopping, or reversing that trend of growing creativity in history. This is the point of a crucial bifurcation in ethics.

To commit oneself to increasing creativity in history, to *praxis* as the basic axiological principle, means to assert that it *ought* to be universally accessible, that it ought to become a norm of everybody's life. This again means to encourage discovery of the essential limitation of given social forms, institutions, and patterns of action; it means to try and explore new hidden possibilities of a different, richer, more complex, self-fullfilling life, to express them in the form of ideals, to examine strategies of bringing them about. This type of ethical orientation is clearly *critical and emancipatory.*

A *conformist, status-quo preserving* approach involves a tendency to reserve praxis for the elite and to condemn the vast majority of human beings to inferior, not characteristically human forms of activity, offering *receptivity* as a surrogate for creativity, and condemning emancipatory ideals as utopian. It resists further liberation processes but at least tends to retain the level of freedom already achieved.

A *retrogressive* normative attitude to history involves a commitment to the reversal of the historical trend, to the restoration of already dismantled master-slave social relations. *Servility* is offered as a substitute for creativity; the glory of conquest and domination on the one hand, the honor of serving and patiently, loyally enduring on the other.

These three basic attitudes to history are mutually incompatible. The dialogue between those who advocate them makes sense only in order to establish whether they have been taken consistently and whether they can be lived in practical life. If this is the case, discrepancy in value judgments cannot be overcome.

Assuming that we accept the *universalization and continuation of praxis* in history as our fundamental normative standpoint, the question is: What else does it involve, how could it be further analyzed? What is meant by saying that man *is* and *ought* to be a being of praxis?

(1) In contrast to traditional materialism and empiricism, man is not merely a reflection of external natural and social forces, a product of education; he is not only a superstructure of a given economic structure, but also a *subject* who, within the constraints of a given situation, creates himself and reshapes his environment, changes the conditions under which certain laws hold, and educates the educators. On the other hand, in contrast to Hegel, man is not conceived as a self-consciousness only, but as a subject-object who is constrained not only by the quality of existing spiritual culture but also by the level of material production and the nature of social institutions. However, precisely because he has both subjective and objective dimension, both spiritual and material power, he is able not only to understand his limitations but also to overcome them practically.

(2) Man is certainly an *actual*, empirical being. An ethical theory becomes irrelevant when it merely imposes on him norms which are completely divorced from that empirical reality and have no ground in it. Certainly, using sophisticated means of manipulation and brute force, certain obligations and duties can be forced upon a community, but a true morality cannot be produced in such a way. It has to be autonomous, and only an actual (individual or collective) subject can lay down its own moral laws. On the other hand, moral norms, by the very nature of being *norms*, are never a mere reflection of actual existence. Morality, like every act of *praxis*, begins with an awareness of a limitation in actual empirical existence, in the way we habitually, routinely act. Norms may be already present in our customary behavior, but these are either *legal* norms imposed by force, by the threat of social overt coercion, or *customs*

unconsciously accepted in the process of socialization and blindly followed like any conditioned reflex. Morality involves a conscious, free choice among alternatives and that choice transcends the immediate selfish needs of our actual existence—it expresses long-range needs and dispositions of our potential being.

Human potential is not a part of directly observed empirical existence but it belongs to *reality* of a person or community, and is empirically testable. Far from being a vague metaphysical concept, the notion of a potential capacity or of a disposition can be operationalized by stating explicitly the conditions under which it would be manifested (provided that those conditions can be produced in specified ways, and the reality of dispositions tested).

(3) Both in actuality and potentiality man is in the first place a unique person with quite specific capacities, powers, and gifts. Man is also a particular communal being: only in a community he becomes a human, brings to life his abilities, appropriates accumulated knowledge, skills, and culture created by many preceding generations, develops a number of social needs: to belong, to share, to be recognized and esteemed. The levels of particularity are many: an individual belongs to a family, to a professional group, class, nation, race, generation, civilization.

That is where all relativists stop: as a particular being man invariably has a particular morality; there can be no universal standard of evaluation. Philosophers who developed such universal criteria had either to eliminate history—like Kant in his transcendental ethics, or like Hegel to construe history as the process of actualization of a potential universal spirit—both lead to absolutism. The problem becomes solvable only when the absolute spirit is replaced by the idea of a universal human species—being. As we saw, that universal is not only spiritual but also practical, it does not exist *in abstracto* but only as the basic potential of concrete living individuals. The *descriptive* concept of this universal human nature is constituted by a set of conflicting general dispositions; some supporting development, creation, and social harmony, some causing conflicts and destruction. From the standpoint of historical praxis the former are evaluated as "good" and enter into a *normative* concept of human nature. This concept is not fixed since history is, in contrast to Hegel, an open-ended process. This point of view is not absolutist as Hegel's: man continues to develop and in the future ever new forms of morality may be expected to evolve. And yet one need not relapse into relativism. Development in history is continuous; a translation and incorporation of former practical products and experiences into the latter remains possible and there are transepochal invariants. Therefore there are good reasons to argue that, in spite of all discontinuities between particular epochs and civilizations, there is one universal human knowledge, there is one material and spiritual culture that grows, one human species-being that evolves through the life of all various individuals and particular communal beings.

At a given moment of history there may be one theory that expresses this accumulated knowledge, that already achieved wealth of human being better than other preceding or coexisting theories. In the future this theory will also need revision, but at the present its author could have sufficiently good reasons to hold that his views are more true than those of his opponents. He may be wrong, but that must be shown by superior arguments. In the same sense an ethics may be regarded as a superior expression of a historically already achieved possibility of the good life, of social harmony and solidarity, in other words: of moral praxis. While refusing to claim its absolute validity, such an ethics may indeed demonstrate that it transcends the limitations of all preceding ethical theories and thus incorporates them as its special cases.

IDEAL COMMUNITY PRAXIS

Once we have established what constitutes the specific nature of human being and his history our next step will be to project an ideal community in which praxis would be a universal principle, that is, in which each individual would have equal opportunities to act in a purposeful, self-determining, rational, creative way.

Here we have a different theoretical context than the one in the preceding section. There we considered actual history but abstracted from it only those intervals and communities where decisive acts of creativity took place—whether in the sphere of material production, or building institutions, or in the realm of culture. It was made clear that most of historical space and time was filled by dull, repetitive work, unproductive conflict, or mindless leisure. However, those moments of free creation are distinctive of man and human history.

Now we turn to another context: what kind of social situation, what kind of human relationships are implied by maximalization of conditions for praxis of each individual. We have to bear in mind three basic considerations:

First, belonging to a community is, on the one hand, a necessary condition for any self-development and realization of one's potential; on the other hand, it poses certain *limitations* for the praxis of each individual. In order to protect the rights of each individual there must be some democratically established *rules* of communal life. It is true that it is in the very nature of praxis that one acts not only in order to bring to life his capacities and affirm oneself but also to satisfy the needs of others. And yet there is a minimum of basic needs that society must recognize and protect independently of individual initiatives. These rules are neither legal (because they are not supported by state violence) nor moral (since they are external and no matter how much the expression of a general will, they may be to some extent heteronomous with respect to an individual will).

In order to meet basic needs of the whole community a certain amount of *work* is necessary. Surely at a very high level of productivity the amount of socially necessary work will be substantially reduced. It will also be so enriched and humanized that it will *tend* to coincide with praxis. And yet there is a clear conceptual difference between *work* and *praxis*. The former inevitably involves a degree of external order and hierarchical organization which is alien to praxis.

Another limitation is *scarcity* of those goods which may be necessary for creative activity. Top quality material products, cultural performances, space, time, and healthy environment will be scarce in any conceivable community. Too much self-affirmation limits others; on the other hand, too much self-restraint limits and cripples oneself.

Second, the very idea of universality of praxis (and since Kant it is hardly controversial that only those norms are ethical which can be universalized) implies that in some important respect all members of the community must be *equal*. The concept of equality needed is neither equality of personal property and income nor mere equality of opportunity. If individuals with a different genetic endowment were equally treated (offered equal amount of parents' and teachers' time, expected to do equal kinds and amounts of work), initial inequalities would only be fixed or even increased.

This is why in an ideal community of praxis social measures for achieving true equality must be undertaken right after birth and not much later, in the sphere of formal education and work. Supplementing whatever parents may themselves offer, society must provide optimal conditions, for discovery and realization of most creative dispositions of each child. In contrast to a society based on uniformity of thought and life-style, in which one becomes identical with others by destroying his self-identity, here all equally create their self-identity while staying different from each other.

Only when it comes to limitations to praxis these are distributed in a way that is alien to praxis, that is, treating all adult members as identical. Rules of communal life hold equally for all and when it comes to decide on them by vote, each person must have neither more nor less than one vote. Socially necessary work is obligatory for all, although allowing the choice of work that best suits one's capacities, interests, and skills. Unwanted, unattractive roles may have to be shared by all, in turn. Analogously, concerning scarce goods, the starting point for trade off or any comparable arrangement must be equal right of each member of the community.

Third, within the framework of those indispensable social constraints, an ideal community offers at any stage of life maximally favorable conditions for praxis of each individual.

This presupposes accessibility of an ongoing education, the purpose of which is less to convey technical knowledge and skills for socially necessary work, and more to bring forth potential talent, to generate a wealth of needs and a concern with the well-being of others.

Reduction of socially obligatory work allows increasing emphasis on unstructured, innovative, spontaneous activities.

Abolition of any monopoly of economic or political power opens room for universal participation in social decision-making.

BASIC MORAL VALUES FROM THE STANDPOINT OF AN IDEAL COMMUNITY OF PRAXIS

The vision of such an ideal community of praxis, which tends to fully realize all that is distinctly human in history, constitutes the ethical ground in our present alienated society.

In this ethics the idea of *summum bonum*, the highest good, is more distant from actual reality than in other nonreligious ethical systems. Most of these systems coincide with an already existing morality and are compatible with given social arrangements, no matter how unjust. For example, *utilitarianism* from Aristippus to Epicurus and from there to Bentham, Mill, Sidgwick, and Moore did not really challenge the established society, whatever it was. Seeking pleasure and calculating how to achieve it is an invariant in customary human behavior and even when it is a maximum amount of it, or highest quality of it and for a maximum number of individuals, it remains a morality within a given social framework. The same holds for ethics of duty, whether one of Kant or of Ross and Pritchard. The sense of duty is formal and it could direct different people in divergent ways. The apologist of an oppressive system may be prepared to will that the maxims of his actions should become universal law.

Dewey's pragmatic ethics, with its emphasis on continued growth, in the sense of an increasing variety of needs and harmony in their satisfaction, clashes with traditional static morality but expresses quite well the ideological needs of any modern industrial society.

Examples of ethical theories that involve rebellious elements but in a harmless individualistic form are Stoic and existentialist ethics. They offer moral solutions to individuals in unbearable external conditions. One expresses the ideal of spiritual independence, and serenity that can be achieved by reduction of desires and withdrawal from the world's competition and conflict. The other commits one to absolute freedom, disregard of all bonds and imposed constraints, involving even the risk of death. These two retain their validity for individuals in exceptional situations but are essentially escapist.

Humanist ethics based on the notion of praxis projects an idea of *eudaemonia*, of good life, which requires radical social transformation. That each human individual should be able to live as a being of praxis involves a very revolutionary moral demand of economic, political and cultural liberation, of maximum possible creativity, of social solidarity. Most of what various ethical theories praised as basic virtues and ultimate ends finds its place and a new meaning within this context. Plato's virtues—wisdom, courage, temperance, and justice—are no longer related to a contemplative reason but to a rational activity of shaping the world according to human capacities and needs. As Butler noticed in theory and John Stuart Mill in his own life, very little pleasure can be achieved when it becomes an end in itself; it is only a byproduct that attends attainment of ends other than pleasure. Stoic peace of soul and spiritual independence is of limited value when it goes with a poor life emptied of almost any content; it becomes an entirely different value at a much higher level of material and cultural development and of social emancipation. Then it will be attained by renouncing dominating power and accumulation of material wealth, by aspiring to a free, productive life in a healthy harmonious social environment. In this context freedom is much more than mere freedom of thought or a desperate act of choice of an uprooted, isolated existence; it is a way of life that recognizes needs and interests of other individuals and society as a whole, that within such inevitable constraints creates ever new possibilities, chooses autonomously among them and brings the chosen project practically to being.

The idea of a natural moral law, in the sense given it by Hugo Grotius, as a set of rules based on the universal nature of man, plays an important role in each humanist ethics; however, it requires a dynamic reinterpretation. Since human nature evolves in history and is exemplified in a different unique way in each individual, moral goodness is not an abstract static concept. Dynamic concepts of traditional ethics such as self-realization and self-perfection are therefore indispensable, although they get a new meaning. The self is not an isolated selfish individual but essentially a communal being, therefore "self-realization" means bringing to life those potential capacities which do not only affirm its individual interests but also promote social good. Self-perfection means development of rational, creative capacities rather than spiritual ascent to God, as in medieval ethics. However there is one great idea in Christian tradition which is superior to the abstract and uniform treatment of man by many susequent rationalist and humanist ethicians. This is the idea that moral goodness is in doing one's best with one's specific natural endowments and in given circumstances. This principle of individuation or of personalism has rarely been respected in traditional ethics which in a rather formal way emphasized general principles, rules, and duties. Even Hegel, who in his critique of Kant's formalism required a concern about the content of ethical judgments, thought that content came from the customs, norms, and laws of the particular society in which the agent lived. This obviously leads to moral conformism—that is why Hegel saw the highest expression of morality in the state.

Here we have a dilemma between an extreme *subjectivist* conception of morality resting on self-interest and self-preservation of the individual agent, and an opposite *objectivist* view of morality as subordinated to God, or to the state (which itself is an objective form of Absolute Spirit), or to an abstraction of social good. In order to resolve that dilemma we must assume that man is both a unique person and a social being, that he feels genuinely concerned about certain general needs, without ever surrendering his personal autonomy and integrity. As a result of socialization an individual internalizes the values of this community; unless he grows together, communicates, and interacts with other members, one never develops any moral consciousness. However, as a being of praxis man has a unique capacity of critical self-consciousness. Therefore, he can come to believe that there are certain general limitations in the prevailing morality and that he should not always conform to its norms. He may be wrong and become a social outcast. But he may also be right and contribute by his deviant moral behavior to the emergence of a new superior morality.

New morality lives for some time only in the praxis of the most developed individuals or in the form of ethical theory. It prevails and begins to be lived by large masses of people in the times of profound social crisis when the whole social fabric and the official ideology of the ruling elites collapses and the need for social restructuring is felt irresistibly.

New morality rejects some traditional norms or weakens them in the sense that they lose their former high place in the hierarchy of values. Humanist ethics that emphasizes *being* rather than *having* will no longer give a high priority to the protection of property or of other characteristically bourgeois institutions. It will no longer be considered right to kill in the defense of property, to compel one to pay debts, even when these are unjust and when it involves leaving his children hungry, to keep promises even when they have been forced by manipulation and repression, to stay married without love, to get wealthy without work, to discriminate against certain people because they belong to a different class, sex, race, or church. Traditionally socialist elements in this new morality are demands that each member of the community ought to contribute his share of socially needed work, and that all social goods should be distributed according to the amount and quality of this contribution but also according to the specific nature of individual needs. Such norms exclude any kind of exploitation and privilege on the one hand, and any distribution according to inherited social status or property, on the other. Socialist ethics has also always with good reasons insisted on a principle of solidarity, mutual support, and aid to the weak, poor, old, ill. However there is a void in traditional socialist ethics which must be filled: neglect of moral issues concerning personal self-determination, integrity, and inner harmony. Since society cannot be really emancipated without emancipation of the individual, socialist morality must allow the possibility that an individual or a particular community may be morally right against any existing organization, institution, or society as a whole. Praxis transcends any established order, whenever this order becomes too narrow for creative novelties. Therefore, moral self-determination is more than a mere freedom of will: it involves the moral right of the individual to go beyond social constraints and create new possiblities, also it involves not only an autonomous act of choice but also action according to choice.

From such an ethical standpoint personal integrity is placed very highly at the scale of moral values—in contrast to duplicity of bourgeois morality which divorces thought, will, and action. An obvious example may be found in ethics of Hobbes who adopts Christian moral rules but considers it a folly to act according to those rules, since all people are selfish, therefore not likely to keep them. The possibility of such morality depends, then, on the state authority and the law which must guarantee keeping the rules. Once Hobbes's assumption of the antisocial nature of man is abandoned, there is no need to split oneself into a beast during the weekdays and a saint on Sundays, and to support a coercive state machinery in order to force people into observing an indispensable minimum of morality. An individual must take the risk and live his moral philosophy— only then will he satisfy his genuine need for harmony between his beliefs, verbal utterances, and overt acts.

Obviously one could resolve inner conflicts and restore integrity in different ways within a continuum between egoism and altruism. The optimal solution is such a self-affirmation which also involves a concern for the well being of other persons. This principle analytically follows from the very concept of praxis; it excludes both the giving away of one's life, and abuse and disregard of others. It does not impose love for everybody but recognizes a basic respect and sympathy for another human being and awareness of his needs.

SOME META-ETHICAL ISSUES

Moore distinguished between two basic problems in ethics: What states of affairs are good? What actions are right? He tended to identify "right" with "ought" and having a "duty." Ross made an important point when he noticed that there may be special claims on a person (keeping promises, supporting parents) such that special duties will arise that outweigh the general duty of producing the greatest possible good.

When we reconsider those concepts from the philosophical standpoint of praxis we may notice in the first place that the concept of the morally good is no more undefinable as in Moore. Praxis is the highest intrinsic good. Consequently all those states of affairs are good which maximally bring to life human potentialities for free creative, rational activity in a given historical situation.

Concepts of "good," "right," and "ought" (duty) overlap. In most cases what one "ought" to do is "good," and when we evaluate such action we shall call it "right." However, in calling it "right" we emphasize conformity with the rules of the accepted moral "code," and since the rules in principle can never cover all phenomena and never do full justice to development, there may be cases where the right action according to moral rules is not the best one, if good at all. For example, in the Yugoslav partisan struggle it was considered right to assign women somewhat less dangerous and physically difficult tasks, but in cases of some strong, gifted women it diminished their chance of reaching more responsible roles, which eventually had undesirable social consequences.

On the other hand, there are situations where one "ought" to act according to his subjective moral conviction although an objective analysis would show that the act turned out to be neither "good" nor "right." This is not only the case of special obligations Ross speaks about, but also all those cases where one is deeply convinced that certain moral principles do not apply, where he has an immediate moral insight that it would be wrong to apply them. This discrepancy between "ought" and "good" may be reduced when "ought" is interpreted in an objective way—as what everyone "ought" to do in *a type* of situation. Since the preservation of personal integrity is also one of objective duties and social goods, it may override other considerations and make an otherwise wrong action the right one. However the basic source of discrepancy is one between subjective and objective evaluation; what an agent believes he ought to do need not coincide with what is really good. This discrepancy cannot be always removed, although in ethics based on the idea of *praxis* the distinction between the subjective and the objective is not so sharp as in other philosophical trends.

It is true, morality is an *objective* social phenomenon, a set of rules governing behavior, which can be expressed in symbolic form and studied scientifically. But this is not the objectivity of a divine order, nor of an Absolute spirit. The rules are products of human historical praxis. They are applied to a specific situation as it is known *to us* and not *in itself*. From what we believe about the situation, not from the situation as it is, it will depend what our moral duty is. We cannot know all the consequences of an action although they are accessible to empirical study. Even less can we be sure about all the motives and intentions of the agent. And practical reasoning by which we derive specific moral judgments from ethical premises is fallible—as we know ever since Aristotle.

And yet moral evaluation is not an entirely *subjective* matter—just an ejaculation of emotions, or an authentic individual choice totally unrelated to reason and any moral principle. An individual invariably makes a moral judgment as a member of community in which he was socialized. Therefore he can give reasons for his judgment and he will use objective logical rules for deriving it from certain general moral norms. Even when it comes to examining motives—the most subjective factors of an action—one may approach a reliable estimate of motivation by communicating with the agent, checking his reports against other reliable data from his life history and his conduct, comparing them with reports of other agents in comparable situations.

Thus subjectivity and objectivity of ethical judgments constitute a continuum without extreme poles and without a hard and fast line between two categories.

There is an analogous blurring of the distinctions between the *analytical* and *synthetic* and the *a priori* and *a posteriori*. The concepts retain their validity but they can be made very sharp only at the price of unacceptable simplification.

All moral judgments are *synthetic* in the sense that they inform us about certain characteristics of real human actions. Even basic ethical principles do not only state explicitly the meaning of ethical terms but describe the distinctly human properties of historical praxis. And yet once those properties have been selected and a *normative* concept of praxis constituted, certain rules follow analytically.

In a sense all such rules are *a priori*: they logically precede ethical analysis and evaluation. But this is neither the sense of *a priori* in Kant nor in modern analytical philosophy. Moral rules are not independent of any experience, a set of timeless, necessary postulates that determine the will, or a set of arbitrarily laid down premises of a language designed for moral discourse. In a *historical* conception of morality there cannot be any norm or principle which did not emerge out of practical experience, by formulating those habits and customs which over a long period of time succeeded in preserving social cohesion, in harmonizing human relations, and in liberating human energies for great creative efforts. In that sense, moral rules may be considered *a posteriori*. And yet at each historical moment the very possibility of moral thought and experience is determined by the existence of those rules and principles; *in that sense*, they are *a priori*.

Now if one rejects *a priorism* which tends to make ethical judgments absolute and *a posteriorism* which usually leads to relativism, the problem arises whether it is possible to resolve conflicts among ethical judgments which belong to different ethical systems. Is there anything comparable to truth in empirical theories?

The answer is: There is.

But, first of all, one has to clearly distinguish a value conflict from disagreement in relevant facts, incompatibility of theoretical framework used to describe the situation, and incongruity among alternative languages. Before there is consensus about relevant empirical evidence, use of theoretical paradigms (or at least the way of translating from one to the other), and the implicit logic of the given language, any debate on conflicting ethical issues is a waste of time.

Two strategies are at our disposal for the actual resolution of ethical conflicts. One consists in exploring the foundations of conflicting judgments, the other in testing them against direct moral experience.

The method of *theoretical examination* consists in asking the opponent to justify his judgment and in challenging the reasons given until one of the three things happen: (1) A logical mistake in practical reasoning may be discovered, which means that one of the judgments is wrong from the very standpoint of the system to which it belongs. (2) Both judgments have been correctly derived from their premises but the premises express totally incompatible attitudes to history. Continuation of a rational dialogue is not possible between those who try to reverse history and revoke an already attained level of emancipation, and those who support further historical development and a continuing human emancipation. The conflict stays unresolved in this case. (3) The dialogue between those opponents who share, at least incompletely, some basic common needs, same cultural heritage, same interest against third parties, may lead either to the establishment that one theory is more general and contains the other as its special case, or to the discovery of a synthesis of the two, of new, more general value principles which incorporate rational kernels of both conflicting values.

The method of *testing* ethical judgments is analogous to testing factual theories. In both cases all kinds of consequences will be derived and checked against experience, ordinary empirical experience in one case, value-experience in the other. (Dewey was right in taking an experience of harmonious satisfaction to be the test of right conduct. An experience of disgust and horror usually accompanies an evil action). In the absence of practical testing, acting roles that follow from the ethical judgments at issue may be simulated. Even in a purely verbal discourse, imagining and describing various situations in which one would have to act according to his judgment helps to spell out and more fully understand the meaning of that judgment. The conflict would be resolved if at least one of the opponents, having to practically apply his abstract judgment in unexpected and unusual circumstances, is not ready to accept its implications and decides to give it up.

The basic assumption on which a belief in the possibility of rational resolution of ethical judgments rests has been very well formulated by Ross. He admitted great variety of moral rules and evaluations in various civilizations but believed that these were *media axiomata* rather than ultimate rules. If circumstances are different and knowledge of relevant facts in various ways limited, ethical evaluations will have to be different even if fundamental needs and interests are the same.

And indeed a vast majority of people would agree that—*other conditions being equal*—life is preferable to death, creativity to destructivity, freedom to slavery, communal solidarity to brute egoism, material well-being to poverty, development to stagnation, independence to being dominated, dignity to humiliation, autonomy to heteronomy, justice to abuse, peace to war. Disagreements arise about *hierarchy* of such universal values and especially because *other conditions* are really not equal. Life need not be preferable to death when the price for it is loss of dignity, peace need not be preferable to war when it leads to loss of freedom.

Humanist ethics of this kind does full justice to historical variety without any support of relativism. And it secures a satisfactory degree of objectivity while rejecting any form of dogmatism and absolutism.

Comment by Paul Kurtz on Marković Article

There is much that I find sensible and can agree with in Mihailo Marković's rich and provocative essay. I find many of his comments responsible and humane. It is his basic ethical postulate and what he intends us to do with it in building the "good society" that concerns me. I am dubious of any attempt to locate in history an ultimate ground for ethics, and hence I find his concept of "historical praxis" somewhat troubling, for there are many tendencies and directions in history and different social and value systems. Accordingly, to attempt to read a progressive development or a higher standard of value into history is open to any number of skeptical questions. I fear that the reasoning is circular. History is used by Marković as a mask for his values—many of them I share and are humanistic and democratic— but is he not selecting those features that he finds preferable from his moral vantage point? Why cannot a Christian do the same, by reading some Divine plan into history and interpreting events as they relate to the Second Coming of Christ. A Muslim will no doubt view history as the fulfillment (or lack of it) of Mohammed's word, always using that as a criterion for evaluating social systems. A liberal democrat might consider from his vantage point the so-called existing socialist societies in the world as totalitarian and *retrogressive*. A devotee of the space age might argue that the whole of human history and the destiny of man is focused on our effort to escape from the solar system and populate the universe beyond. Marković seems to be committing one form of the naturalistic fallacy by defining as intrinsically "good" one aspect of human history ("praxis") and then reading that into the process as a ground for his preferences. All moral judgments, he says, are "synthetic," and basic ethical principles (in part) "describe the distinctively human properties of historical praxis." But we may ask, why should we accept this definition of Marković's as binding?

I believe that Marković and the praxis school of Marxist Humanism that he represents have made important modifications of Marxist theory, but have they gone far enough? Or is the ontological Dialectic (which is no more than a guide for analysis) still lurking? For I do not know what it means to say that history as a whole is a "meaningful process." This seems to me to be substituting one theology for another.

Marković focuses on a set of ethical values that he relates to praxis. By "praxis," Marković means "creativity." He wishes to expand this concept and to make it universally accessible as a norm of everyone's life. His standard apparently is the continuation and universalization of praxis in history. "In spite of all discontinuities," he argues, "...there is one material and spiritual culture that grows, one human species." He goes on to say that "at a given moment of history there may be one theory that expresses this accumulated knowledge..." But again this may be viewed as an expression of Marković's own value bias.

Not that I do not agree with him about the value of "creative praxis," or the need to be concerned with humanity and the species as a whole.

Simply, 1 do not believe that it can be enshrined in the womb of history or "historical praxis." Human history can go either way, as the recent Gulags of Stalin and Hitler tragically testify. Various forms of repression have existed in the world at different epochs: feudal, monarchial, capitalist, and communist societies. The recent totalitarian horrors are in many ways more reprehensible than anything that appeared earlier. Clearly there are progressive developments in human history: the elimination of illiteracy, the increase of knowledge and education, the overcoming of poverty and disease, the improvement of the standard of living for the average person, the advance of modern technology and science, the development of freedom, the opening up of many societies to mobility and reform. But I am apprehensive of any mono-historical theories and submit that a pluralistic view of history, in which new and often unexpected changes and trends occur and in which there are many values and norms that emerge, is more accurate.

I am especially worried about Marković's theory when he goes on to develop the concept of "an ideal community in which praxis would be a universal principle." By this he means "each individual would have equal opportunities to act in a purposeful, self-determining, rational, creative way." A liberal democrat might not disagree with this latter principle, but the key question concerns first, the role of freedom and its precise meaning, and second, the kind of "radical social transformation" that it would necessitate. As to freedom, one cannot help but fear that it may be subjected to "equality" and "solidarity." "Self-realization" and "self-perfection" says Marković, though indispensable, "get a new meaning." The self is not an isolated selfish individual but essentially a "communal being." Marković talks about a "new morality" that will transform society. What guarantee do we have that new elites will not develop and new repressive systems instituted that will *compel* individuals to be creative, as defined by someone else? Marković is opposed to bureaucratic elites, but what is the assurance that they will not again emerge? Why should any one group, offering what it believes to be a superior theory, attempt to transform the basis of existing society, religion, science, or ethics in order to bring into being a new one consonant with its vision? Why should any group be allowed to guide or control the destinies and fortunes of the entire human species? I am surely not against social change, even radical change, but the risk of dealing with the totality of human existence in the name of a utopian ideal raises the question: what right does any one group claim to serve as the guardian of all? I have no objection to democratic persuasion, but if the majority never agrees, then what? I have no objection to postulating imaginative images of the future, drawn from the study of history, but I demur when there is an effort made to impose them on everyone else. I am not suggesting that Marković would seek to do this, but I am apprehensive of those who in the name of history have.

In the later part of his paper, Marković discusses theoretical questions and he asks how we go about testing ethical judgments: against experience, he says, and by practical means. I agree with this statement fully. I wonder why then we must seek to anchor our judgments and/or give them the sanction of history. Why not deal with them in their own terms without seeking to justify them by the myth of history? Why not recognize that "praxis" is a normative value that if spelled out in concrete terms has meaning and can be illustrated and/or justified without resort to a mystique? Why not have a free society in which those who wish praxis *for themselves* can have it, but in which those who do not wish it are allowed to go their own ways fulfilling any destiny that they may wish, however disparate it may be from the current utopian ideal defended by the intellectuals?

Reply by Mihailo Marković to Kurtz

I understand Paul Kurtz's worries and share his concern about any repressive power that would try and *impose* one system of ethics on the entire human species. He seems to believe that *either* one has to merely assert the fact that there is a plurality of moral values *or else* one tends to impose a utopian ideal on others. I agree with him that one has to recognize the existence of different moral systems but this recognition is a mere *sociological* judgment. And even if one recognizes the *right* of all those different value systems to exist, one is still on the ground of law and not yet of morality. Since Kant, it is clear that the minimal requirement that a norm has to meet in order to be qualified as *ethical* is its claim to universality. There is indeed a plurality of moral views and each of them is moral if and only if its norms can be formulated as universal rules. Kurtz is surely aware of that when his own moral principles are in question: he surely does not believe that freedom is good for some people and not good for others. It is a moral principle precisely because it is good for all human beings.

Kurtz does not see, apparently, the distinction between *claiming universal validity* of our own moral norms and *imposing* them by force on others. As to the latter, it is not only equally unacceptable to me as to Kurtz, I even consider it a duty to struggle against that form of repression, and this duty is *moral* since I believe that everybody ought to engage in this kind of struggle. But, on the other hand, there cannot be any tolerant ethical dialogue unless opponents have genuine convictions. There cannot be ethical *pluralism* without those conflicting claims to universal validity. A situation in which each group would consider its values as bad for others should be described as lack of morality rather than moral pluralism. The latter is the case when various groups or individuals have genuine moral convictions with implicit claims to universal validity—but these convictions are different or even incompatible.

That is where the need for a *foundation* of ethical values arises. One has to answer the question: What is the ground on which his implicit claim to universal validity rests?

Kurtz says that he is "dubious of any attempt to locate in history an ultimate ground for ethics." Where else? Where else does he believe he can locate his own ground? There are two other possibilities. One is God—that one I shall rather not discuss. The other is cosmic order. Much of ancient ethics was based on a belief in an ideal world order which is to become a prototype for an ideal conduct of human life. Certainly one was able to find in the cosmos as much ethically relevant order as one put it there. It would be somewhat odd if a present day humanist would study galaxies and black holes in order to establish ground for his ethics. Consequently, where else to look for ground of ethics but in human history?

Of course, all kinds of things can be found in history or projected into it. Paul Kurtz misses the whole point if he really believes that anyone can justify anything by referring to a mere multitude of events and tendencies of history. The crucial question is: *What made possible the survival and development of man as a distinctly human being?* That an impressive development *did* take place is an indubitable *fact*. This is not something that I invented and projected into history. This is not an eschatological *goal* comparable to the second coming of Christ, fulfillment of Mohammed's word, or making a trip to some neighborly star. Not only is the development of knowledge, of power to control natural forces, of a wealth of forms of social life, of political institutions, or arts, of the means of communication an indubitable fact, it is a fact most *specific* for human history. This manifold development of communicative power, of reason, of creativity is precisely what distinguishes men from animals, plants, and all other objects in the world.

So far we are entirely on factual ground, discussing general features of the past history. What has been asserted and is open to debate is a matter of fact, not of values. The *normative* dimension in this whole procedure of grounding ethics, the step from *is* to *ought*, appears only when we ask the question: Whether this creative development ought to continue—therefore, *ought* to be supported—or ought to be stopped or reversed. Kurtz again misses the point expressing his disbelief that creative praxis can be "enshrined in the womb of history." Surely, history can go in different ways. But history is history of human individuals—no need, Paul, for capital H: I am not Hegel, nor even Lukacz. Whether it will go toward new fascist empires, Gulag and Vietnams, or in some better direction, it will depend on the activity, ideas, commitments, and sense of responsibility of us who live and more or less, in one way or other, determine the course of historical events.

Paul Kurtz finds reasons to worry about my ethical commitment to an ideal community in which "each individual would have equal opportunity to act in a purposeful, self-determining, rational, creative way." What worries me is that a humanist and liberal democrat should worry so much about equality and solidarity. We are certainly not equal persons and for that reason should not be treated equally. Different persons must be treated differently in order to reach most important equality of condition for full development. What makes freedom an ethical concept (in contrast to the "freedom" to oppress and exploit and bore others) is precisely that it involves equal freedom of all to get a decent education, to be able to grow, work according to ability, satisfy basic needs, fulfill one's creative potential. Kurtz is afraid that all these things will be *imposed* on people, that people will be *compelled* to be creative. The irony of this argument is that he does not seem to be afraid, or alarmed, or disgusted by the fact that societies in which we live now are dominated by elites which at the one scale *prevent* people to be creative. But while no guarantee can be offered to Kurtz that new elites will not develop—there are too many variables in any historical process, and morality is only one of them—I may emphasize that from my ethical standpoint no form of repression is admissible. Ethics based on principles of self-determination and creativity implies norms which condemn any self-appointed elite of power and any striving for domination.

At the end of his comment Paul Kurtz raises the question: Why is it necessary to anchor ethical judgments and give them the sanction of History if we can test them and deal with them in their own terms? This is a general issue of justification of any theory—whether factual or normative. If immediate experience suffices to justify a theory, then, judging from what we all observe Ptolemy was always right after Copernicus. Anyway, once we got Kepler's laws why did Newton seek to anchor these in terms of a "mystical" gravitational force?

It is a basic characteristic of rationality to seek to establish connections between all elements of knowledge and to show how they necessarily follow from a minimal possible number of premises. An ethical theory that would merely postulate a number of ethical norms and leave them side by side without linking them and showing how they follow from a minimum of ethical principles (which are, on their part linked with the rest of knowledge)—would be a rather primitive theory.

I have tried to show how all ethical values may be grounded on one basic value assumption: *Praxis is good.* It cannot be *derived* from any factual judgment (which would constitute the *naturalistic fallacy*) but it is linked with a basic factual assumption—"Praxis is enente of history," or more clearly: "Praxis is the specific necessary *condition* of all historical development."

Morality and the Human Situation

Kai Nielsen

THE MEANING AND SOURCE OF MORALITY

Skepticism about morality is very pervasive in our society. It is itself a key element of modernism. Sometimes it is little better than a conventional posture, something that is simply accepted unreflectively by educated people as just being a part of the *Weltgeist* and an attitude of mind any knowledgeable tough-minded person would have. With others it is the result of probing and often agonizing reflection. The sources of this skepticism are varied but one very central source is what I shall call the *no-truth thesis* in ethics.[1] By this I mean the belief that over questions of fundamental values, including moral values, no question of truth or falsity can sensibly arise. That the benefits and burdens in the world are not equally distributed, is a plain matter of fact the truth of which is perfectly evident. We also have some sense of what it would be like for that claim to be false. We know, when we study some hunting and gathering societies which are approximately egalitarian, what makes that claim concerning their approximate equality true and we also have some idea of what it would be like for this to be true of the whole world. We do not, of course, expect it to be true, but we have some idea of what it would be like for it to be true. For the moral claim that each person irrespective of merit or desert has a right to an equality of concern and respect, it is far less clear what, if anything, could show that to be true or for that matter false. Many of us feel deeply committed to some such principle even when we have no idea at all what would or could show it to be true or—if it makes any sense to talk in this way about such a principle—probably true. There can be a deep and perfectly unwavering commitment to it by people who do not believe that it or any other fundamental moral principle could be true or false. For factual claims, finally rooted in empirical observation, we understand how to determine whether they are true or false or probably true or false, but with fundamental moral claims we can have no such basis of confidence. Yet, without the possibility of ascertaining the truth or falsity of our fundamental moral commitments, it appears at least to be the case that they must rest on arbitrary decisions of principle rooted in our emotions or perhaps our biology, culture, or even class. This is one persistent and nagging source of skepticism. I shall return in a moment to considerations about how this no-truth thesis might possibly be met.

This skepticism rooted in worries about truth in ethics is exacerbated by concern about the relativity of morals. Even a rather superficial study of social anthropology will reinforce something we learn from our reading of Herodotus, namely that moral beliefs, sometimes even very deeply embedded moral beliefs, differ widely from culture to culture and, sometimes even within a culture, cut across class. This would not be so serious a worry if we had a confident sense of truth in ethics. After all, that different tribes have different cosmologies does not make physics totter. It is when it is coupled with the no-truth thesis that cultural relativity is troublesome. With it there is reasonable worry that perhaps even our most deeply embedded and stubbornly clung to moral beliefs may be little more than the ingrained mores of our time and place. We may feel strongly about the way of life of the Ik or Dobuans, but without a coherent conception of truth in ethics we are hardly in a position to claim that one way of life is better than another. We can hardly claim, with any great confidence, that these ways of life are immoral or perhaps even irrational. What our morality is, we fear, is most fundamentally a matter of how we have been conditioned. Our moral responses are very much a matter of the heart, but what these moral emotions are is deeply affected by the culture and sometimes even by the class from which we come.

Such considerations threaten the rationality and objectivity of morals. It would be foolish to believe that there are any short or easy answers to the above challenges to the objectivity of morals. Indeed there may be no answers at all and something like what I have said above may be the truth about morals and if that is so, we had better learn to face it nonevasively.[2] However, before we acquiesce in that, given what is at stake, we would be wise to see if, without flights into the evasions of a religious ethic, we can discover any resources within a purely secular morality to meet such a challenge.

With respect to the no-truth thesis, it is first well to remember that it is over the fundamental claims of morality where it has its most obvious force. That we should have concern to protect the rights of Blacks whose rights are being denied in South Africa or that we should fight poverty and degrading working conditions at home can easily be shown to be true once we accept a fundamental moral principle such as the claim that each person irrespective of merit or desert has a right to an equality of concern and respect. We know something about the conditions under which such equality is possible and we know something about what undermines self-respect. Poverty, no work, certain kinds of working conditions, and racial assault do just that, so if we accept such a fundamental moral principle we can easily establish the truth of lower-level moral principles. And, as the pragmatists were fond of stressing, it is those principles, rather than the fundamental ones, which repeatedly come into play in moral argument.[3] Moreover, once this distinction is kept in mind, it is no longer so clear that science and ethics are, after all, so different in this respect. We should not forget that it is not altogether clear how we would establish the truth or falsity of the fundamental principles of science either.

Be that as it may, there is still the haunting suspicion that if we press real moral disputes sufficiently, we will quite naturally get to a moral terrain where conflicting fundamental moral principles will be brought into play. Our 'moral truths' will all be dependent on them and they will conflict and we will have no idea of how their truth or falsity is to be established. Even when we agree on the facts we will find such disputes intractable, since, for such deeply embedded moral beliefs, the no-truth thesis applies.

Perhaps the plausibility of the no-truth thesis rests on a bad model of truth. Perhaps what fuels it is a correspondence model; for example, the statement "The cat is on the mat" is true if and only if the cat is on the mat. But there is plainly truth in mathematics and the correspondence model does not work there. Perhaps that model is also entirely inappropriate in ethics and another more realistic model should replace it.

We could say that a moral claim or principle is true if it is required by the moral point of view.[4] This, of course, raises a host of questions of which probably the most obvious is, How do we determine what is the moral point of view—and indeed, is there something appropriately called the moral point of view which reason requires us to accept? Perhaps there are just different, largely culturally determined moral points of view extant in various cultures and perhaps there is no such point of view that a through and through reasonable and well-informed person must just accept to continue to be accurately so described.

Suppose, in trying to ascertain if there really is such an objective moral point of view which could determine truth in ethics, we ask why a society, any society, the Ik included, requires a moral code, any moral code at all. I think the answer is that in a world in which there are conflicting desires and interests and in a world where all people, including the dominating classes, are to one or another degree vulnerable, we need a device wider than the law for adjudicating those conflicting desires and interests which would be acceptable to all the parties involved were they to stand in positions of equality. Morality, no doubt, has many functions but this is a function it will have in all societies. In class societies such as our own where the ruling ideas are largely in the hands of the ruling class, and reflect their interests, this function will have a large overlay of moral ideology. That is to say, the dominating class will have a certain conception of what will constitute a fair adjudication of conflicts of interests. Moreover, with their control of the mass media and education, they will sell the dominated classes a certain conception of what is possible and what is an equitable adjudication of conflicts of interests. They will create a moral ideology which, if the legitimization function of the state is working well, will bamboozle them into believing that they must keep the social contract. But this is the compliment that vice pays to virtue. Such moral ideology is parasitic on a nonideological conception of morality and the moral point of view. An indispensable function of morality is to adjudicate between conflicting interests in an equitable way. The sense of 'equitable' would be given by what rational human beings would agree mutually to accept when they understood the causes of their various desires and the consequences of getting what they want. To achieve fairness in adjudication they would have to agree to the equal consideration of the interests of everyone. As both Kant and Sidgwick in effect show us, the very idea of a morality conceptually requires a commitment to fairness. There are indeed 'class moralities' but they can only rest on intellectual confusions and false consciousness. There can indeed be classist amoralists who self-consciously promote the interests of their own class and dominate the weaker classes by moral ideology and, where that does not work, by force. But this is not a moral point of view, but an amoral one parading as a morality.[5]

To take the moral point of view requires the equitable or fair adjudicating of interests. This comes, I believe, to adjudicating conflicting desires and interests so that everyone can have as much as possible of what he or she wants that is compatible with others being treated in the same manner when their wants and desires to be so treated are what they would be if people having the desires were fully informed, had carefully reflected on this information, and had taken it to heart. In many respects it would be better to cash in the fair adjudication of conflicting desires and interests simply in terms of interests and needs. Perhaps some day, when we have a more adequate account of needs and their proper scheduling, we should do just that. The worry about wants and preferences is that in class societies they are subject to ideological deformation. This impediment can only be removed practically through political action. But the theoretical conditions I placed on the relevant appeal to desires indicate in skeletal form the kind of desires that would not be ideologically manipulated desires. Perhaps such desires would also match with what human beings genuinely need or with what is in their interests.

With such a spelling out of the moral point of view, we could then determine what in the way of rules and principles the moral point of view requires and the ones they require would be our central moral truths. The *prima facie* obligations to tell the truth, to keep our promises, to be benevolent, and care for our children would plainly be such truths. Even the fundamental principle of equal concern and respect I stated at the outset would be a reasonable candidate for a true moral claim. With this conception and with a knowledge of how societies actually function and of the conditions of particular societies, we would have a yardstick, if not an Archimedean point, for assessing societies and ways of life and we would have grounds for not believing that morality was simply a matter of the differing mores of diverse societies.

HUMANKIND AND NATURE: FREE WILL AND RESPONSIBILITY

None of the above can be obtained if human beings are not capable of responding as rational beings. If Dostoevsky's underground man is humankind in microcosm, no rational humanistic morality is possible. But, while Freud has taught us to recognize that our capacity for irrationality is far greater than untutored common sense would suspect, it is still not the case that we are all through-and-through irrationalists incapable of reflective self-direction. Rationality like neurosis is something which admits of degrees. However, we can characterize what it is, ideally, to be a thoroughly rational person or, as I would prefer to say, a reasonable human being. Of course, none of us satisfy these conditions fully—a fully reasonable person is an *ideal* type—but we can approximate these conditions in varying degrees, and in optional social conditions (conditions such as could be had if a socialist humanism found a stable exemplification) far more of us could achieve far more of that reasonability than we presently do. Abstractly conceived a fully rational human being is a human being who takes the most efficient means to achieve those ends he most wants, who is capable of postponement of want satisfaction when it will contribute more fully to the ensemble of his wants, who will in the appropriate circumstances reflectively and critically inspect his desires and aims, and who, aware of the extent of a socially-imposed consciousness, sees through the ideologies and myths of his society and is aware of, and in control of, the distorting effects of his own distinctive psychological history. He will be a person capable of impartiality and fairness and will not in some fanatical or clever silly way be tied to his own hobby horses. He will be, for his time and place, an informed human being capable of acting in accordance with an accurate grasp of that information. With reasonable success, he will strive to achieve consistency and coherence in his beliefs and he will not, where he is in a cultural situation capable of combating them in the normal course of education, be held captive by irrational cosmologies such as those of Judaism and Christianity.[6] (This does not mean that a reasonable person cannot be a Christian, but it does mean a fully reasonable person in a society such as ours who has had the benefit of a sober and full education—plenty of anthropology, philosophy, and natural science—cannot be a Christian.)

Determinism is a difficult, if not impossible, thesis to prove and it indeed may not be true or even perhaps coherent. But it does appear at least to be both coherent and true or, at the very least, it appears to be something we find very difficult not to assume. My point is that in thinking in a fundamental way about morality it is not essential to prove its truth or probable truth, for as Hobbes and Hume argued, even if it is true, there is still a perfectly straightforward sense in which human beings can be both free and morally responsible moral agents. Freedom and responsibility, like reasonability, admit of degrees. It is often the case that a human being has the ability and the opportunity to do certain things. A human being is free when he has the ability and the opportunity to do such things and in those circumstances does what he wants. The hallmark of a free human being is a human being who is capable of self-direction and who actually exists in such social conditions that his behavior is self-directed rather than being compelled or constrained, either externally or more subtly by psychological forces, so that he or she lacks the ability or the opportunity to do what she or he wants to do. The opposite of human freedom is not determinism but compulsion or coercion. Even in a completely determined world there are some people in some circumstances who are able to do what they want to do when they want to do it. These people in those respects are free. To the extent that one lacks the ability or opportunity to do what one wants to do, one is unfree. This is invariably a matter of degree but the degree is all important. There are indeed certain Brave New World situations in which we could do what we want and still not be free, that is, self-directed individuals. But when the person is rational and is able to do what she wants to do, then she is free. Freedom and responsibility are crucially cashed in both in terms of being rational and being able to do what one wants to do. But both of those things are quite possible even in a fully determined world.[7]

To talk of taking the moral point of view plainly presupposes that people can be free and responsible agents. But this agency is perfectly possible and indeed is, with a not inconsiderable number of people, in varying degrees actual. In a truly human society it would be even a far more extensive social reality. Determinism does not defeat morality and there is no good reason to believe that we are such irrationalists as to make morality a Holmesless Watson.

MORALITY AS WORKABILITY VS. MORALITY AS JUSTICE

Surely the mere fact that some social arrangement works does not make it right. If Hitler could have succeeded in capturing all the world and destroying all Jews, his social system would still be quite accurately describable as bestial. That it worked would not make it one jot less bestial. And if South Africa holds out—or becomes a model for the world—and shows its social system to be more efficient and to create more capital accumulation than any alternative system, it still would remain a moral monstrosity. Efficiency and workability is more important in a political morality than is generally recognized. But it is not the whole of such a morality and Pareto optimality can be outweighed by other considerations.

From our characterization of the moral point of view, it is a conceptual requirement that, morally speaking, the interests of everyone be considered alike. This means that restrictions are put on a utilitarian determination of desirable ends. We must not only seek the maximizing of happiness or whatever else is taken to be intrinsically good, we must also seek a maximization constrained by a certain pattern of distribution. There are questions of individual justice which are a matter of entitlement, but social justice is largely concerned with patterns of distribution of the benefits and burdens of a society. Once a certain threshold of scarcity is passed—a threshold long since passed in the Western Democracies—what is the right thing to do is not determined simply by what will produce the greatest aggregate of instrinsic good. Situations could arise where the moral point of view would require opting for a slightly lesser total of intrinsic good more equitably distributed.

The equitable distribution I would defend is egalitarian. It seems to me that the principles of social justice which should govern the design of an affluent society are the following:

1. Each person is to have an equal right to the most extensive total system of equal basic liberties and opportunities (including equal opportunities for meaningful work, for self-determination and political participation) compatible with a similar treatment of all. (This principle gives expression to

a commitment to attain and/or sustain equal moral autonomy and equal self-respect.)

2. After provisions are made for common social (community) values, for capital overhead to preserve the society's productive capacity, and allowances are made for differing unmanipulated needs and preferences, the income and wealth (the common stock of means) is to be so divided that each person will have a right to an equal share. The necessary burdens requisite to enchance well-being are also to be equally shared, subject, of course, to limitations by differing abilities and differing situations (natural environment, not class position).

My first principle is like Rawls's in being an equal liberty principle. The stress here is on the importance for everyone of moral autonomy and an equality of self-respect. The crucial thing about that first principle is its insistence that in a through-and-through just society we must all, if we are not children, mentally defective, or senile, be in a position to control the design of our own lives and that we must in our collective decisions have a right to an equal say. Where conditions of relative abundance obtain (conditions similar to those in Japan, most of North America, and much of Europe) equal self-respect and moral autonomy require something like my second principle to be attainable. Without something like my second principle, disparities in power and authority, acceptable under a less egalitarian system, indeed even under a system as egalitarian as Rawls's, will undermine the self-respect of people on the lower rungs of that less egalitarian society. Once we have achieved relative abundance, a greater equality of self-respect and a more secure moral autonomy become preferable from a moral point of view to more goodies. (Skeptical query: Is this so for any through-and-through rational person or only for such a person if he also has a distinctive sense of justice?) Where one is in dire poverty one may not attach so much importance to such values but as one gains a certain threshold of economic security—attains conditions of moderate scarcity or relative abundance—effective control over one's life tends to gain in importance. If people act in accordance with my second principle, there will be a reduction of inequalities in primary goods—goods which are the source of distinctions that will give one person power or control over another. What is morally important to recognize is that status distinctions should be viewed with suspicion. A world of master and servant, boss and bossed, is not a world in which the principles of justice have received their most adequate exemplification. Justice requires that everyone should be treated equally as moral persons and, in spite of what will often be rather different conduct, everyone should be viewed as having equal moral worth. Justice in society as a whole ought to be understood as requiring that each person be treated with equal respect irrespective of desert and that each person be entitled to self-respect irrespective of desert.

THE BASIS OF RIGHTS AND DUTIES

The egalitarian principles of justice I articulated in the previous section determine the conception of rights I would defend. Given such a conception of justice, there must be certain human rights that any person simply possesses and unforfeitably possesses just in virtue of being a human being. People are, as a matter of fact, in important ways unequal. We are not all equally caring where others are concerned or for that matter even for ourselves, we vary not inconsiderably in our moral sensitivity, in our industry, in our perseverence, in our intelligence, in our courage, in our capacity for love, and in the development of our sense of justice. It is to be hoped and indeed expected that in a social environment which is changed in certain distinctive ways these differences, though not all differences, between human beings would be considerably lessened. But be that as it may, no doubt differences would remain. With the principles of justice I have articulated, there would be a fundamental respect in which those differences would be overlooked. Justice is not determined by desert. The morality I would defend commits me to a principle of equal respect for all human beings. Human beings, great and small, good and bad, deserving and undeserving, have a right to our equal concern for their well-being and self-respect. This, I take it, is what it means to say that persons must be equally respected. This does not mean that human beings are never to receive rewards or praise or have our respect for their various accomplishments and it does not mean that certain people cannot be rightly punished or deprived of certain liberties to keep them from harming others and even, under certain extreme circumstances, from harming themselves. What it does mean is that any human being, even someone who is vicious and untrustworthy, cannot be so treated that his vital interests are simply ignored, simply set aside as counting for nothing. We do well to protect ourselves against him but in our deliberations about what to do, his vital interests, as ours, count and count equally.

The rights we have flow from what we consider to be our vital interests. What exactly they are will be a matter of dispute and one way of marking the differences between conservatives, liberals, and socialists is to see how wide a scope they give to what they take to be the vital interests and thus the human rights of all human beings: the things a human being will have a *prima facie* right to simply in virtue of being human. These include such human rights as security of person, freedom from arbitrary arrest, the right to the means of life (food, shelter, clothing, health care), the right to work, to marry, to immigrate, to freedom of speech, assembly, and political self-determination. There will, of course, be a dispute about what exactly goes on the list and about the extent and nature of the heterogeneity of types of rights on the list, but all of the above, I would argue, must go on the list, for they are necessary to protect two very fundamental goods essential for sustaining the moral point of view, namely human autonomy and the good of self-respect. Where these rights are not in force, such fundamental human goods cannot be sustained or at least maximally sustained.

These human rights cannot be forfeited but since these rights, as all rights, are *prima facie* rights, they can be overridden. They cannot, however, be rightly overridden when overriding them would only provide, everything considered, some small utilitarian gain.[8] Thus, if we can show that in society C for a given time (say a decade) a marginal overall benefit would obtain by overriding the right to freedom of association and choice of domicile of a small minority M, this would not justify a denial of such rights. But during a catastrophic war where there was, in reality and not just in an inflamed popular imagination, a clear and present danger which would bring catastrophic harm to the society and perhaps suffering and death for a very large percentage of that society, then in such a circumstance one would, if there is no other way of preventing it, be justified in overriding such rights to prevent a catastrophe. It is not that the rights are forfeited for they can't be, but they are overridden, and rightly, to prevent some still greater evil.[9] But they cannot be justifiably overridden, as utilitarians suppose, simply by showing that some greater maximizing of overall utilities would obtain by overriding them.

People can have rights without corresponding duties or obligations. Infants, the enfeebled, and perhaps even some animals have rights without having duties and obligations and in any case the correlation does not apply universally, but many rights do carry with them duties and obligations. If you have the right to freedom of speech or assembly, I have a duty not to try to prevent you from doing these things, and it is the obligation of the state authorities to provide a social situation in which these rights can be exercised.

PRINCIPLES IN SITUATIONAL MORALITY

If my argument has been near to the mark, morality is not totally situational. And it is not (what is not quite the same thing) simply a matter of the mores of one's tribe or of what one just happens to like or happens to approve of. There can be true or false moral claims, an intersubjective validity to moral claims, and a rationale to a morality rooted in an underlying function of morality which in turn determines what it is to take the moral point of view. People have objective interests and genuine needs.[10] But not everyone's needs can always be satisfied and not all interests are compatible. It is a pervasive function of morality to adjudicate these conflicts in a fair way, but neither what constitutes a "fair way" nor what are the interests and needs of human beings can be determined purely situationally. There are needs and interests, such as the need for companionship, some privacy, security, and some meaningful work which are quite universal. They have, of course, a cultural overlay. Neither privacy nor meaningful work will have quite the same meaning for a Samoan as it will for a Swede. Thus, there must be a certain specific situational determination, but there are common features too and general parameters set by interests and needs which are quite pan human. Again fidelity between husband and wife will not be the same for a Samoan as for a Sicilian, and for a Swede it will still be something somewhat different again and within a given culture this will change over time. Still there are bonds of trust, getting different cultural phrasings and applying differently in different environments and different social structures, which will have a very similar rationale. This similar rationale is what gives sense to the very concept of fidelity. Because such key concepts in our lives have such underlying rationales, the actions of quite different peoples are intelligible to one another. The truth about situationalism is that there are many moral conceptions such as certain marriage relationships or certain property rights which only make sense in a determinate social setting. In short, the environment, both physical and social, sets limits to the appropriateness of moral actions. The treatment of the aged by aboriginal Tasmanians makes moral sense. But it would be vile in contemporary Tennessee. The cattle raiding of the Turkana, Nuer, and Dinka makes sense and perhaps is, everything considered, justifiable. Cattle rustling in Texas and Alberta is another thing again. But this kind of situationalism is neither relativism nor opportunism. The differences are best explained in terms of different applications of noncontextual general moral principles. We have culture—specific moral practices which make perfectly good sense in terms of general moral principles just as different conventions about what side of the road to drive on make sense in terms of an overall conception of safe driving. And just as there can be a coherent dispute about in which states or provinces driving regulations are the most adequate, so there can be an assessment, often mistaken and sometimes ethnocentric, but not necessarily either, of the moral practices and the overall moral code of different cultures in terms of what the moral code requires and a reasonable assessment of the facts in the case.

Perhaps in some sense morality is an expression of the whims of mortal will, but if so, it is a rational will, and it includes the possibility, and indeed the virtual certainty, that many such wills will be mistaken and that their very mistakes can be corrected from within the unfettering confines of a rational conception of the moral point of view. It is not the case that morality is simply a matter of the heart, though it is that too, and it is not a matter of "you pays your money and you takes your choice" in which decision and simple desire is king. What is good is determined by what answers to human interests, what satisfies human needs, and what furthers human self-realization. But morality is not simply what is in a person's interest, the interest of a ruling class, what is desired by an agent or approved of in his tribe. Kant and Sidgwick were far too rationalistic in thinking that morality is a "dictate of reason" but all the same it is none of the above-mentioned things and it is not an irrational response in an absurd world not of our own making.

NOTES

1. See my "On Deriving on Ought From an Is," *The Review of Metaphysics*, Vol. XXXII, No. 3 (March, 1979).
2. There can, of course, be truths *about* morals even if there are no moral truths. He who would raise fat geese need not himself be fat.
3. John Dewey, *The Quest For Certainty* (New York: G. P. Putnam's Sons, 1929). But perhaps even more fully Dewey's views on ethics, relevant to the above claim, come out in the excellent collection of his work in John Dewey, *Intelligence in the Modern World* (New York: The Modern Library, 1939), pp. 761-793. However, the best statement of this pragmatist view—a statement fully cognizant of the critical reactions to it—is to be found in Sidney Hook, *The Quest for Being* (New York: St. Martin's Press, 1961), pp. 49-70.
4. Kurt Baier, *The Moral Point of View* (Ithaca, New York: Cornell University Press, 1958) and Kai Nielsen, "On Moral Truth" in Nicholas Rescher (ed.) *Studies in Moral Philosophy* (Oxford, England: Basil Blackwell's Ltd., 1968). This account has been powerfully criticized by James R. Flynn, "The Realm of the Moral," *American Philosophical Quarterly*, Vol. 13, No. 4 (October, 1976). I try, in the present essay, to state my account in such a way so as not to be vulnerable to those criticisms.
5. See my "Rawls and Classist Amoralism," *Mind,* (January, 1977) and my "Morality and Classist Amoralism," *Philosophical Studies* (The National University of Ireland, 1979).
6. What I have said about rationality is cryptically expressed here. I have developed it in my "Principles of Rationality," *Philosophical Papers,* Vol. III, No. 2 (October, 1974), "The Embeddedness of Conceptual Relativism," *Dialogos,* Vol. XI, No. 29-30 (November, 1977) and my "Rationality, Needs and Politics," *Cultural Hermeneutics,* Vol. 4 (1977).
7. The topic of freedom, determinism and moral responsibility is an incredibly complicated one. I have, in what is perhaps an overly simple way, tried to hack through some of those complexities. For a fuller treatment see my *Reason and Practice* (New York: Harper and Row, 1971), Part One. Sidney Hook cuts through that tangle in an even brusker way in his *Quest For Being*, pp. 26-48. But it seems to me that what he says there is essentially sound.

8. This is powerfully argued by Ronald Dworkin in his *Taking Rights Seriously*, (Cambridge, Massachusetts: Harvard University Press, 1977).

9. Joel Feinberg, "The Nature and Value of Rights," in *Rights*, David Lyons (ed.) (Belmont, California: Wadsworth Publishing Company, Inc., 1978), pp. 78-91.

10. For some important discussions of needs see Ross Fitzgerald (ed.), *Human Needs and Politics* (Oxford, England: Pergamon Press, 1977) and William Leiss, *The Limits of Satisfaction*, (Toronto, Ontario: The University of Toronto Press, 1976).

Comment by Joseph Fletcher on Nielsen Article

I want to say no to Kai Nielsen's "moral point of view." He advocates it as a way to transcend class differences and conflicts, as well as cultural diversities, and rival social interests or claims. He cites Rawls; but we should remember that in order to establish such an ultimate *standpunkt*, Rawls had to abandon his utilitarian approach to ethics in favor of a contract doctrine, working out (at painful length) a Kantian metaphysic for the "original position" of human equality. Religious ethics, which Nielsen would like to reject in favor of humanist autonomy, enjoys, in fact, the longest record among objective or transcendental "moral points of view"—views in which there is indeed an "original position" of equality—provided, however, by the *mens creatrix* of the divine will and expressed in the biblical doctrine of man-made *imago dei*.

Nielsen, I would contend, cannot have it both ways. Either human equality is an original or given datum, or it is not. I cannot but think it is not.

I would be far more comfortable with the Marxists at this point than with Nielsen, much as I admire and agree with his overall contribution to recent philosophical ethics. The Marxists are sturdier. They make no attempt to claim any greater or "higher" justice for their proletarian claims—none, that is, except the greater justice that goes with the fact of much greater numbers of proletarians in the world. And it is *this* consideration which is sufficient, surely, to justify their aspirations as against the reigning interests of the privileged minority. (There may be, and indeed are, weighty political and economic reasons to oppose socialism, but—and here again I say "surely"—there is no *value* ground upon which to fault it.)

Perhaps Nielsen takes this tentative step down a blind alley because of an error in what he says about both Kant and Sidgwick making equal commitments to fairness. (They would make strange bedfellows but, of course, are not bedfellows at all, really.) Both ethicists may have been committed to fairness with equal force, but their reasons were radically different. Kant argued that fairness was grounded in reality and objectively valid, while Sidgwick *chose* fairness as a fundamental moral commitment—chose it positively or positivistically, but not, as in Kant's case, with metaphysical arguments to give it "truth" status.

Let me go one step further, just to make sure that the question is unmistakable and quite clear. Naturalistic ethics asserts, essentially, that good (value) complies with reality and evil (disvalue) falsifies reality. Thus right and wrong become questions of truth and nontruth. Since Nielsen has (elsewhere) tried to bridge the gap between "is" and "ought" it is not surprising to find him linking humanistic ethics with naturalistic ethics. But it won't work.

His argument takes the form of "objective" ethics, that is, the idea that good and evil, along with right and wrong, have their existence "out there" in a given moral order, so that the ethical problem is to *discover* what is right rather than to determine it. This giveness fits the religious ethic, based as it is on the objective, transcendental "will of God" or "divine imperative," but it does not fit a humanist ethic in which human beings must, as moral agents, themselves choose and freely posit or assert the ideals and values and standards of mankind, along with the reasoning to make their moral decisions coherent with the moral agent's values.

For those who like labels and categories, we may say that humanist ethics is *fundamentally* teleological or goal-centered, rather than deontological or duty-centered, just as religious ethics is fundamentally commandment ethics, based on a metaphysical (divine) "objective" moral order.

In short, Nielsen's engaging paper on "Morality and the Human Situation" compels me to go back to my own paper and, for safety's sake, clarify what I've said about the "combination" of both verification and justification. Verification has to do with whatever facts might happen to be involved in moral acts, precisely and only because they are matters of fact (truth). But justification is a matter of values or ideals which are embraced only subjectively; they are not objectively verifiable—they are, in Nielsen's phrase, no-truths.

Reply by Kai Nielsen to Fletcher

I am grateful to Joseph Fletcher for his generous remarks about my work, but I am also constrained to say that he rather fundamentally misunderstands what I say. I do not claim—nor does Rawls, for that matter—that values or norms have a distinctive ontological status. I do not defend ethical naturalism. One of the reasons why I reject the correspondence model of truth for ethical utterances is that I do not believe that values are "out there" to be discovered as part of some moral order. I reject both Sidgwick's self-evident ethical axioms and an ethical naturalism that would represent values as a distinctive kind of empirical fact. Moreover, I do not think that we can derive fundamental moral norms from matters of fact.[1] However, what I did argue is that, even if moral utterances have the status of universalizable decisions of principle, it still can be the case that morality has a point and an underlying social function. It is by noting what kind of activity morality is—why we humans, anywhere and anywhen, have a morality at all—that we can determine what moral claims are warranted and what truth and falsity come to in ethics. The claim to objective validity that Fletcher believes leads me into having it both ways is in reality a claim to an *intersubjective validity* and must finally rest on a *reflective consensus*. I am not claiming anything more, but I am also not claiming anything less.

Fletcher also misses my close affinity to Marx. Because, though not solely because, class divisions are so deep and because of the fact that the dominant capitalist class so effectively controls the consciousness industry, we are presently in a situation where such a reflective consensus cannot be attained. I have argued elsewhere, that the kind of moral point of view I defended in "Morality and the Human Situation" could only become a reality in a genuinely socialist society.[2] Equality is not an "original datum" but an ideal that some people have come to hold—indeed an increasing number of people have come to hold—after, historically speaking, long periods of moral reflection. This ideal will only be achieved or even tolerably approximated through class struggle and with a profoundly altered consciousness, in radically changed socioeconomic conditions. For this to happen the society will have to be both one of relative abundance and a society in which the working class has attained class consciousness. That one or another or both these conditions have not yet been met in the industrial world does not mean they cannot be.

NOTES

1. My "Why There is a Problem about Ethics," *Danish Yearbook of Philosophy*, Vol. 15 (1978) and my "On Deriving an Ought from an Is," *The Review of Metaphysics*, Vol. XXXII, No. 3 (March, 1978).

2. My "Class and Justice," in John Arthur and William H. Shaw (eds.), *Justice and Economic Distribution*.

Comment by James Simpson on Nielsen Article

Professor Nielsen's essay is intriguing with some well developed messages which cry out for additional reflection on a variety of topics. I will limit my observations to just two points, one of which is an extension of his thought on the no-truth thesis, while the other is an apparent logical inconsistency in his two principles of social justice.

The no-truth thesis in ethics is described by Professor Nielsen as a "belief that over questions of fundamental values, including moral values, no question of truth or falsity can sensibly arise." Although he prefers to focus on pros and cons of various viewpoints rather than strongly committing himself to acceptance or rejection of the thesis, a convincing argument is advanced concerning the need for a set of moral prescriptions. I would like to follow up on that thought.

Philosophers, much like physicists or chemists, have sought universal truths since the dawn of civilization. Researchers from all fields naturally seek *the one* inviolate law or principle about the field they are investigating. Philosophers, and perhaps many anthropologists, naturally feel uneasy about an ethics based on cultural relativism, for it automatically negates the possibility of *one* inviolate truth or code of moral precepts— exactly what the scientific community has dictated as a goal. Certainly, those holding a Christian position are placed in a quandary over the possibility that alternative moral codes are both acceptable and desirable. But, those holding a humanist position need not be concerned about numerous moral codes, *providing,* as Kai Nielsen points out, the codes are well defined so they can supplement as well as complement the legal process. In effect, the yardstick of a moral code is workability and recognition that attitudes about right and wrong change through time as civilizations evolve and mature. Mores about divorce, abortion, and women's rights are good examples. The most important foundation block of humanist philosophy is concern with life here on earth, and not in an abstract afterlife subject to the whim of some God. Thus, it would appear that to a humanist the moral code adopted would depend on the vision about the ideal society. Once we are able to articulate what we want, a moral order can be designed which best meets the ideal. I strongly suspect that the ideal would vary considerably between individuals but, if there were a full knowledge of the relevant constraints, agreement would be possible. This situational ethics, it seems to me, is a logical approach for a humanist ethics.

My second comment about Professor Nielsen's paper is an apparent logical inconsistency between the two principles of social justice. My concern is also tied to my previous comments. His first principle states that each person is to have, among other rights, equal opportunities for meaningful work and self-determination compatible with a similar treatment of all. Part of the second principle is the desirability of an income and wealth division (the common stock of means) so that each person will have a right to an equal share. Now, if by this Professor Nielsen means the common stock should be redivided at the beginning of life's race (or perhaps more correctly at the end), then his principles are compatible. But, if he is asserting that there must be a continuous redivision to ensure complete, or nearly complete uniformity in wealth and income levels, then there is a large inconsistency, for he has passed from an argument for equality of opportunity to one of equality—and there is a vast difference between the two concepts.

It may appear, to a thinker permanently settled in an ivory tower of romantic idealism, that people generally want equality, but I am prepared to argue that this is not true; rather, the more general desire is for equality of opportunity. Provide this, plus a practical recognition that I.Q.'s differ, interests are dissimiliar and abilities vary, and we are on the road to a harmonious society where individual wants and desires are recognized and sought for, but within a context of realistic achievement. Only recently, for example, has there been an acknowledgement that it is not necessary for a large proportion of society to be college graduates. If we move away from a conception that certain factors, such as a college degree, are necessary prerequisites for "the good life" and status within that life, then we are on the road to a better society.

PANEL II

KURT BAIER
HERBERT W. SCHNEIDER
KONSTANTIN KOLENDA
JAMES R. SIMPSON

Freedom, Obligation, and Responsibility

Kurt Baier

I.

Modern humanism, though not a sharply defined philosophical position, can be regarded as a descendant of Renaissance humanism. Both emphasize man's capacity to improve his condition in this earthly life through his own efforts within a framework of suitable political organizations. Both oppose established and uncritically accepted authority, including that of the church, and both accept the ideals of human dignity, autonomy, and freedom. Thus, Pico della Mirandola, in the first part of his oration entitled "On the Dignity of Man," puts the following words into God's mouth:

> I have given you, Adam, neither a predetermined place nor a particular aspect nor any special prerogatives in order that you may take and possess these through your own decision and choice. The limitations on the nature of other creatures are contained within my prescribed laws. You shall determine your own nature without constraint from any barrier, by means of the freedom to whose power I have entrusted you. I have placed you at the center of the world so that from that point you might see better what is in the world. I have made you neither heavenly nor earthly, neither mortal nor immortal so that, like a free and sovereign artificer, you might mold and fashion yourself into that form you yourself shall have chosen.—[Quoted by Nicola Abbagnano in *The Encyclopedia of Philosophy*, ed., Paul Edwards, Macmillan, 1967.]

Renaissance humanists, accordingly, also opposed the static institutions of the feudal world whose heads pose as the vicegerents of a parallel fixed cosmic order charged with determining what goods men may aspire to and how they may attain them.

Modern humanists have tended to adopt analogous positions. They have advocated the greatest possible freedom in politics and religion. They have embraced democratic as opposed to aristocratic, hierarchical or elitist political systems, and they have opposed all myths about the nature of man and the universe. Instead, they rely solely on hypotheses which are not merely compatible with, but best explain, all the carefully observed facts. While they have therefore been committed advocates of free scientific inquiry, as true humanists they have also rejected those forms of scientism which threaten their central commitment to man's freedom of will and to the autonomous shaping of his own destiny.

In a humanist ethics, there is, therefore, considerable stress on the power of reason to determine the soundness or unsoundness of moral precepts, a rejection of conscience as the authoritative voice of God and of all claims that would assign to particular individuals, in virtue of their political or religious positions, authoritative views on what is morally right or wrong. Also, there is insistence on everyone's freedom to adopt a way of life in accordance with his own conception of the good or optimal life, as long as that is compatible with the same freedom for others. Within this general secular framework, we must, however, be prepared to find among humanists significant disagreements on questions of how these and similar general precepts are to be reconciled with one another. How, for instance, is such freedom, especially in the field of economic endeavor, to be reconciled with the claims of equality, even if only equality of opportunity, which is a presupposition of everyone having the same degree of freedom to lead the life he regards as most worthwhile? Again, how is this principle of freedom to be brought into agreement with the equally plausible principle that since we have only one life to live, we should each of us be equally likely to advance (and not just have the same *opportunity* for *advancing* through his *own efforts*) an equal distance towards what each of us regards as the optimal life for him. If there is to be this same likelihood of an equally satisfying life, the society would have to intervene in social developments rather more incisively than it would on the equal opportunity doctrine. Finally, we should expect to encounter much disagreement on the question of how the demand for individual freedom is to be brought into agreement with the demand for social justice. We shall expect to find some humanists more concerned to ensure that those who have made a greater contribution are not shortchanged by society in its attempt to make things easier for the worse off, whether they are so through their own fault or through other people's fault or simply through misfortune, and others more concerned to ensure that no one is pushed, by the working out of the socially recognized social rules of desert, into a position significantly worse off than the social average.

I want in this short paper to examine the question of the relative stringency of the claims of freedom against those of responsibility for, and obligation towards, others. What I shall have to say will be more in the nature of an exploration of such claims and a pinpointing of the considerations that should lead us to a settlement of such conflicts rather than to an actual settling of them. For the latter task would require a great deal more than a short paper. I could not complete this task even if I confined myself to one small topic in this vast area, say, what, if anything, a mother owes to her child including perhaps her fetus, or what a person in a position to help owes someone who is in serious danger of important harm. Since the purpose of this anthology is to explore deep and central issues rather than actually settle issues which can be settled in a short paper, I hope my choice of topic will not be thought misguided. I am the more persuaded of the need for such an exploration as I am dissatisfied with many of the recent more specific inquiries in various areas of applied ethics, such as medical ethics, economic justice, legal ethics, and the social responsibility of business, which in their haste to arrive at solutions ignore the theoretical foundations their arguments must assume and so, to my mind, must fail to carry conviction.

II.

Well, then, let us begin at the beginning. I believe that obligations and responsibilities are special cases of what is, in a certain sense, the most basic and so the (practically) most important category relating to human conduct. There are various terms, 'the obligatory', 'the morally required', 'the wrong', and 'the morally impermissible', all of which can be used to place conduct in that fundamental category. The variety of terms is useful because in moral contexts we normally define 'conduct' in terms of the impact it makes on others and then, depending on whether the impact is morally wanted or unwanted, construe the not doing of what is morally wanted as *omitting* or *neglecting* to do it, and the not doing of the morally unwanted as *refraining* from doing it. We cannot, therefore, define 'the obligatory' and the other related terms except by including reference to whether it is a doing or a not doing. What it is obligatory (or required) to do, it is impermissible (or wrong) not to do; and conversely, what it is impermissible to do, it is obligatory not to do. What it is not impermissible, it is, of course, permissible (not) to do. Lastly, what it is both permissible to do and not to do may be morally indifferent since neither doing nor not doing it is either obligatory or wrong. It is not necessarily so, since, as we shall see, there are other, less basic moral categories such conduct may fall into.

The category just sketched is, I believe, a subclass of the broadest and so, in another sense, the (theoretically) most important moral category, the morally wanted and its opposites. The morally wanted covers a range of things culminating in the morally ideal. This ideal is an ideal limit of things, conduct, virtue, character, which are wanted of us from what we call the moral point of view. The moral point of view and its product, the morally ideal, must be distinguished from other points of view—which produce similar ideals, such as, expediency, prudence, and utility—from which, often, different things are wanted of us. These different points of view, by enabling us to work out what would be wanted of anyone adopting them, provide us with various kinds of derivative reasons for doing the things wanted of us. They are derivative reasons to the extent that we have reason for adopting any of these points of view. Of course, many philosophers think that we have adequate reason always to adopt the moral point of view and that the reasons derivative from that point of view are always those with the greatest weight. Those willing to satisfy what is wanted of them from the moral point of view are said to be persons of good will, that is, persons willing to give due weight to other people's interests and concerns. This point of view is therefore closely associated but by no means identical with altruism, which consists in the setting aside of one's own interests and concerns for the sake of the interests and concerns of others. We normally regard selfishness or egoism as immoral because it is the ruthless promotion of one's own interests and concerns, that is, their pursuit to the point where, because it does not give due weight to the concerns of others, it is morally unwanted.

This fits in well with the moral enterprise as I and many others see it. For on such a view, that enterprise concerns only conduct, dispositions, and attitudes which are, in a wide sense, other-referring, that is, affect others favorably or unfavorably, whether they do so directly, as when one stabs, kicks, insults, or lies to others, or do so indirectly, as when one acts on maxims or principles whose general adoption, however natural that may be, would have adverse consequences for all concerned, such as pouring toxic substances into the river, picking rare wild flowers, or never giving to any charity.

The moral point of view is, like the others I have mentioned, a completely general one: anyone and everyone can adopt it. It has, however, two asymmetries built into it, which have not been generally noted, and which distinguishes this point of view from these others with which it has often been identified or confused. The morally ideal and the demands to which it gives rise are met by giving due weight to the interests and concerns of *others*. When one adopts the moral point of view, one thus thinks of each individual as *a self* confronting *others*. The second asymmetry consists in that between the self as an agent and the self as a patient. The moral demands can be thought of in either of two ways: (1) as what is wanted of an agent, what he is asked to do or to refrain from doing *for the sake of another,* the patient, as when the agent is asked to give up a seat for an old lady or to refrain from smoking for the sake of sensitive passengers; or (2) they can be thought of as what is wanted of a patient, that is, what he should put up with *for the sake of another*, as the result of what the other does for his own sake, as when he is asked to put up with the other's smoking so that the other can concentrate, or as a result of what the patient himself is morally wanted to do for the other's sake, as when he is asked to jump into the water to save a drowning man, at the risk of catching cold and totally ruining his best suit.

The first asymmetry is noticed but one-sidedly emphasized by two moral theories known, respectively, as "ethical egoism" and "ethical altruism." Ethical egoism recognizes that every individual sometimes has to face the conflicting interests of others, but demands of every self that he entirely ignore them, unless doing so is detrimental to him indirectly or in the long run. Ethical altruism holds the exact opposite in that it demands of every individual that he completely ignore his own concerns and interests for the sake of the other or others whom he comes to confront.

Utilitarians do not recognize the first asymmetry. Mill has some glimmering of the asymmetry, for he recognizes that "everybody has an equal (claim or) right to happiness"[1] but he mistakenly thinks that this amounts to the same as the principle that "one person's happiness, supposed equal in degree..., is counted for exactly as much as another's."[2] Like other utilitarians, Mill, therefore, is committed to simply summing the utilities of all concerned with a view to maximizing the sum, instead of balancing the conflicting utilities of different individuals against one another in an equitable fashion.

Kant overlooks the second asymmetry. He treats the relation of an agent to himself as if it were the same as that of an agent to another. In his view, all rational patients are to be regarded in the same way, whether they are the patients of their own actions or of those of others. Admittedly, Kant notes an asymmetry between self and others in the case of two duties, to make happy and to make perfect: the former is a duty only concerning others, the latter only concerning oneself. But he explains these asymmetries, not on the basis of the quite general asymmetry between a person's relation to himself and to others, but on the basis of the peculiarities of these two specific duties: that one *cannot make others* more perfect and so cannot have a duty to make them so, and that one is *inevitably psychologically set on* seeking one's own happiness anyway, and so cannot have a duty to seek it. But in the absence of such peculiarities, the duties one has concerning oneself and concerning others are based on the same symmetrical principle, that "you must treat humanity, whether in your own person or in that of another, always as an end and never as a means only."[3]

What distinguishes morally ideal conduct from that which is expedient, prudential, or utility-maximizing is that it is wanted on account of its promotion of the concerns and interests of others and despite its nonpromotion of the concerns and interests of the agent. The expedient ignores and overrides even the legitimate concerns of others. When one is in a hurry, the most expedient thing may be to push the cripple out of one's way. The prudential weighs only the risks to the agent himself. It is not necessarily imprudent not to warn the tenants of one's cottage in the Lake District that it often rains and that the roof leaks. What makes conduct *morally* ideal is that it takes into consideration the good of another. What makes it morally *ideal* is that it gives that good the weight which, morally speaking, is optimal. Before I can be more specific about this, a few preliminary remarks are necessary.

There are two rather different senses of 'the morally ideal'. In one sense, that conduct is morally ideal which is such that it *would be* for the good of everyone alike, *if it were* generally practiced. In this sense, such conduct is morally demanded of one quite irrespective of whether this fact about such conduct is generally realized, let alone whether such conduct is generally practiced. That conduct is, in this first sense, morally ideal can make only a very weak and indirect moral demand on one. The demand is only that anyone who knows this fact about conduct of a certain sort do what he can to bring about conditions in which such conduct can be practiced by anyone and everyone with the minimal risk of detriment to him. Hobbes recognized such weak and indirect demands to do what is morally ideal. He called such demands the Laws of Nature and said of them:

> The laws of nature oblige in conscience always, but in effect then only when there is security. The laws of nature oblige *in foro interno*; that is to say, they bind to a desire they should take place: but *in foro externo*; this is, to the putting them in act, not always. For he that should be modest, and tractable, and perform all he promises, in such time, and place, where no man else should do so, should but make himself a prey to others...[4]

The curious phrase "bind to a desire they should take place" is best interpreted as meaning that what the laws demand of one is an effort to bring about a state of affairs in which one has the assurance that all or most will observe these directives.

In the second sense, conduct is morally ideal if both it is morally ideal in the first sense and, furthermore, its moral ideality is generally known and there is adequate assurance that others by and large will act in this way.

That conduct is morally ideal in this second sense makes a much stronger demand. For in the absence of such assurance, one can always reply to people reproaching one for not acting in the way which is morally ideal in the first sense: "But why should *I alone* be the sucker who gives up things for the benefit of others?" When there is assurance that others, too, will engage in morally ideal conduct, this reply is not available. One is then open to the reproach that others have made the sacrifices necessary if the good of *everyone alike* is to be promoted and have done so only because of their justifiable expectation that one will do likewise when one's own turn comes to make a similar sacrifice. One's refusal to do likewise turns these rule followers into suckers. It is not only that these others have reason to resent that, but that one has sufficient reason oneself to want to ensure the continuation of a state of affairs in which there is assurance that people by and large will do what is morally ideal.

Plainly, it is not easy to determine in an objective way what conduct is morally ideal. Hence even among people of good will, that is, among people perfectly willing to do what is morally ideal, there may be sincere disagreement. But if people are to have the assurance that others will by and large do what is morally ideal, it is desirable that such conduct should be publicly recognized and taught to the next generation. For that will apprise people of good will what exactly will be generally *regarded as* morally ideal. The problem, of course, is that if there is likely to be disagreement on this score even among people of good will, it is also likely that some will disagree with at least some of what is regarded as morally ideal, and indeed sometimes rightly so. Nevertheless, assurance of conformity may be more beneficial to all concerned than correct specification of what is morally ideal. The undesirable effects of such incorrect conventional specification (our conventional moral code) can be somewhat mitigated by allowing it to be subjected to public rational scrutiny. The impact of such criticism should help to improve and bring the public conception of what is morally ideal closer to what really is so.

It is also likely that, other things equal, it will be desirable to attach appropriate social sanctions to conduct thus conventionally recognized as morally ideal, though of course the cost of such sanctions must always also be borne in mind in the calculation of their desirability. The main beneficial effect of such sanctions should be that they will incline those who are not persons of good will to behave as if they were, and will thus reassure those of good will that their conformity and sacrifices are not in vain.

Our next question is whether we can objectively determine such classes of morally ideal conduct and if so, how we can go about specifying these classes. Bearing in mind that the morally ideal is the ideal behavior of persons whose interests and concerns have come into conflict with one another, what we must find are the various typical relations between individuals and how in these relations the give and take between them might be defined so that the outcome is in the interest of everyone, that is, all the involved role-players, *alike*. The major dichotomy between these relationships is that between those cases in which people face one another simply as human beings, and those cases in which they do so as institutional role-players. In the first type of case, individuals are thought of as independent goal-seekers, whether their goals are the same and compatible, like passengers on the same plane; or the same and incompatible, like standby passengers not all of whom can get on; or different and compatible, like passengers using the same airport facilities to get to different destinations; or different and incompatible, like passengers trying to share a taxi when their destinations are in opposite directions. In the second type of case, individuals face one another as players of roles they have voluntarily assumed or to which they have been assigned. In this sort of case, morally ideal conduct depends not solely on the relation between the interacting role-players, but on the function of the institution as a whole and its interrelation with the other institutions which together make up the social order.

The difference between the two types of cases is not that in the first there are no conventionally recognized moral rules governing the relation between individuals, while in the second there are such rules. For there are, of course, conventionally recognized rules for both types of cases. The difference is, rather, that in the first type, the morally ideal is determined solely by the relationship between those affected by the interaction, whereas in the second type, the determination of the morally ideal relationship between the role-players depends not on their relationship alone, but on their relationship with other role-players in the same institution and with those of other institutions as well. Where people compete for scarce and indivisible goods under conditions of equality, the principle of "first-come, first-served" is universally applicable and fair. But whether the division of domestic labor between husband and wife is fair cannot be determined by looking solely at the allocation of benefits and burdens in the house. It is necessary also to take into account the similar allocations outside the domestic sphere: the allocation of worthwhile activities, power, and rewards, as well as the allocation of burdens, such as military service, planning for the joint future, and so on, as well as the interconnection between the division of labor in the family and in other institutions; how, for instance, the division of labor in child rearing affects the right to career selection and the opportunity for achievement and advancement, and so on. In this paper, I confine myself to the noninstitutional type of case which is comparatively simple. The second type of case leads inevitably into the complexities of social ethics and social philosophy, which are beyond the scope of this essay.

Concerning the noninstitutional type of case, the two major questions are these: (1) What may one do *to* another and, conversely, what should the other put up with? (2) What should one do *for* another and, conversely, what may the other expect of one? The overall principle is that, to spell out the morally *ideal* conduct, guidelines, or principles or rules for answering these questions *must be for the good of everyone alike.* For then and then only does everyone have the best possible reason (which *everyone* can have) to follow these guidelines.

To get clearer about this, it will help us to see whether there are limits to what is morally ideal or whether there are none, just as there would seem to be no limits to one's altruism. Consider a simple example to bring out the differences between the morally ideal on the one hand, and the expedient, the prudent, and the utility-maximizing on the other. One morning, in crisp clear fall weather, a party of four hikers, one very experienced, one moderately experienced, and two inexperienced, are on their way to a peak with a magnificent view. Only the very experienced hiker has climbed the peak before. They are about halfway up when they hear cries for help from someone who has met with an accident and now lies injured in a precarious position on a rock some 150 feet below the trail. The most expedient thing for them to do would be to ignore his cries and move on, lest giving him assistance prevent them from getting to the peak at all or at any rate before the midday haze clouds the view. Any course of action involving assistance to the injured hiker would not merely be less expedient but also less prudent than simply ignoring him, for it would ruin their planned hike and expose them to some risk (even if small) of slipping and falling. At the same time, even merely acknowledging his cries for help might later expose them to unpleasant criticism and perhaps legal action, if they then did not make efforts to rescue him or at least go back to the village for professional help. If they quietly move on without taking notice, they can always later deny that they heard his cries for help.

However, the expedient and the prudent thing would not in this case also be the utility-maximizing. The optimal course, from the utilitarian point of view, would probably be for the most experienced to climb down towards the injured hiker, taking food and first-aid equipment with him, while one of the inexperienced climbers hurries back to the village to alert a rescue team, and the remaining two continue their climb to the peak.

Even this need not, however, be the morally ideal course of action. Morally speaking, more should in this case be done for the injured man than is required by utility maximization. Perhaps the three remaining hikers, led by the highly experienced one, should try to move the victim from his hazardous and uncomfortable perch on the rock and move him up the trail where he can rest in safety and relative comfort until the rescue team arrives. This course of action might well produce *less* overall utility than the previous one (if, as is plausible, the gain for the injured man does not make up for the loss for the two who give up their climb) yet be closer to the morally ideal.

Lastly, the morally ideal is not necessarily the most altruistic. Suppose the injured man tells his rescuers that his glasses and wallet had slipped out of his pocket and were now lying somewhere among the rocks and trees below. A refusal of the two most experienced hikers to embark upon the strenuous and dangerous operation of finding his valuables would then be less altruistic than their embarking on it. But would it be further from the morally ideal? Could one say that it would be better for everyone alike if people did this sort of thing in these sorts of circumstances rather than refuse to risk their necks to do so? If things appear too finely balanced in this case, then simply suppose that the party consists of ten hikers all of whom insist, from altruistic motives, on giving up their hike to the top in order to stay with the injured man, although five or six of them could, at very little cost in psychological benefit to anyone, continue their walk to the top. Surely, at some point the magnitude of the sacrifice gets out of proportion to the gain and thereby alone is not the *sort* of conduct whose general practice is for the good of everyone alike.

III.

Having clarified the basic moral category of the morally ideal, we can now return to our main quarry, the major distinction *within* that category, which it will be remembered, was to throw light on our main question, how freedom is related to responsibility and obligation, what people should be free to do, and at what point obligations to others should limit their freedom.

The morally ideal, we saw, is an ideal limit. Looked at from the point of view of an "agent," one who is about to choose from alternatives before him, it is *the maximum* which, morally speaking, he is wanted to contribute toward the well-being of another. Looked at from the point of view of the "patient" or "recipient," one who is affected by the other's action, it is *the minimum* which, morally speaking, he is wanted to put up with for the sake of the concerns or interests of others. Every noninstitutional moral situation involves both such an agent and patient, and every person (or self) plays now one, now the other of these roles. What is morally wanted of an agent is sometimes that he do something, and sometimes that he refrain from doing something, for the sake of the patient. Similarly, what is wanted of a patient is sometimes that he simply endure something the agent is doing *to* him, sometimes that he put up with an adverse side effect on himself of something he is wanted to do or refrain from doing, *for* another. In this last case, he is a patient of his own action, and so also an agent, though the aspect just now considered concerns only his role as patient.

The important point to note is that, if the morally ideal is this limit, then what is morally wanted of agent and patient can be wanted more or less strongly. It is wanted the less strongly the closer the wanted behavior approaches to the ideal limit. What is furthest away is the morally *required*, what is closer to the limit is the morally *demanded*, and what comes closest to the limit is the merely *welcome*. What lies beyond either of these points, is not morally wanted. If an agent does less than the minimum or if a patient is made to put up with more than the maximum required then the conduct in question is morally *un*wanted. If an agent does more than the maximum morally wanted or if a patient is allowed to get away with less than the minimum he is expected to endure, then this is neither morally wanted nor unwanted. It is simply not the case that it is wanted, rather than that its nonhappening *is* wanted.

The conduct minimally and so most strongly wanted *for* a patient is *his due*, what is due to him; the minimally wanted *of* an agent is what is *due from him*. If something is due from Jones to Smith, then it is wrong for Jones not to do or provide it for Smith, it is Jones's moral duty or obligation to provide it for him. The fact that someone failed to do what is minimally wanted (required) of him, that he failed to provide what is due from him, and that he thus has done wrong, justifies the community in imposing the strongest sanction, namely, coercion. I think Mill was essentially right when he said:

> It is a part of the notion of duty in everyone of its forms that a person may rightfully be compelled to fulfill it. Duty is a thing which may be *exacted* from a person as one exacts a debt....Reasons of prudence, or the interest of other people, may militate against actually exacting it, but the person himself, it is clearly understood, would not be entitled to complain.[5]

But Mill was mistaken when he said, "We do not call anything wrong unless we mean to imply that a person ought to be punished in some way or other for doing it—if not by law, by the opinion of his own fellow creatures; if not by opinion, by the reproaches of his conscience. This seems the real turning point of the distinction between morality and simple expediency."[6] Mill here identifies what is morally wanted of someone with what is morally required, that is, what is wanted so strongly that failure to satisfy it justifies coercion, justifies exacting it from him. He failed to see that what distinguishes morality from expediency is not that the morally wanted may be exacted, whereas the expedient may not. Indeed, it is clear from his own remarks that he did not consistently hold this view. For though we may perhaps speak of public opinion and the reproaches of conscience as administering punishment, we can hardly think of them as coercion or as exacting what is morally wanted. Mill himself sees this clearly when he distinguishes between "the moral" to which the person may be compelled and "the merely desirable (expedient)" or "laudable (worthy)" to which he may be "only persuaded or exhorted."[7] But surely public opinion and conscience belong in the latter, not the former category. Mill holds two mistaken doctrines when he claims that the realm of the moral is marked off from the other two realms of the utility-promoting, namely, "expediency and worthiness,"[8] in that coercion is justified by failure to comply with moral canons but not by noncompliance with the others. The first mistaken doctrine is to think that the moral is a subclass of the utility-promoting or maximizing, the second that every failure to do what is morally wanted justifies exacting it from one.

Consider his second doctrine in light of the distinction we ordinarily draw between (1) what is morally required, our duty, what it would be wrong not to do; and (2) what, though still morally wanted, is yet beyond the call of duty. To avoid confusion, we must bear in mind the difference, mentioned above, between the cases in which someone has relevant institutional duties and those in which he has not. The lifeguard, whose institutional (i.e., professional) and so also moral duty it is to come to the aid of swimmers in trouble, has done no more than his (professional and moral) duty when he rescues one. It would be wrong for him to refuse to come to a swimmer's aid when he needs it. It would be a failure to do his (professional) duty and so wrong even if the rescue involved considerable effort and danger. Although this fact will constitute a mitigating factor when considering the gravity of his wrong, it cannot call in question the fact that it was a breach of (professional and so moral) duty. Conversely, if he does brave the elements to rescue the swimmer, he still has not done *more* than his duty, though he did it heroically. Perhaps it would be misleading to say that he had done *only* his duty, for that might wrongly suggest that praise and gratitude would be out of place. In fact, what is out of place is merely the belief that the person rescued now "owes him," that is, owes him a comparable service.

For contrast, consider now the case of someone, not a lifeguard, but a good swimmer who is sunbaking alone on an unguarded beach. He sees a person in trouble, but does nothing to help her. We think that in such a case, the minimum morally wanted of such a man is that he try to rescue the person in trouble. Failing to do so is failing in his moral (not professional) duty and so is doing wrong. If that is correct, then such a good-Samaritan act is not, for such a man, an act beyond the call of moral duty. A rule requiring such good-Samaritan behavior of such people would be for the good of everyone alike, and so we should consider such an act, and it therefore is, a moral duty. We certainly think that if such a man fails to do this, he is rightly condemned and will rightly reproach himself later. Some people even argue that such good-Samaritan behavior should be legally required and failure to do so treated as a breach of legal duty.

But if the man is not a good swimmer, if the drowning person is a long way out and the sea is very rough, then attempting the rescue would be beyond the call of moral duty—for the man has no professional duty concerning the swimmer. His moral duty in such a case is not determined by his professional status but by the proper balancing of the relevant conflicting interests. The fact that it would be heroic for him to attempt the rescue suffices to show that it is beyond the call of (moral) duty. If he does not make the attempt, he is not to be condemned, let alone punished, by others or himself. If he does make the attempt, his act is supererogatory, heroic, deserving of gratitude, and giving rise to an obligation, on the part of the rescued, to perform a comparable service for the rescuer when he is in some comparable plight.

Summing up, we can say that the basic, though not the broadest moral category is that of the morally required. In noninstitutional cases, it is the minimum one person must do for another and the maximum he may do to him, that is, the maximum beyond which he must not go in what he does to another. This lower limit, this minimal moral demand is determined by a judgment which balances the interests of an agent and his patient(s) in such a way that the universal adoption of the principle governing the behavior of people related in the way this agent and his patient(s) are related would be for the good of everyone (affected) alike. Anything more than that, which an agent does, or a patient submits to, for the sake of another, is beyond the call of duty, though it may still be morally wanted.

There are at least two subclasses of what is beyond the call of duty, the subclass of the morally *demanded* and that of the merely *welcome*. I believe though I cannot argue for it here, that what is often called "the supererogatory" belongs in the last class, while what are often spoken of as imperfect duties belong in the class of the morally demanded.

IV.

What can we learn from all this about the relative moral weight of the claims of social responsibility and obligation, on the one hand, and the claims of freedom on the other? One important lesson we can learn, I think, is how that question is sometimes misinterpreted and so wrongly answered. Let me explain why.

Although duties, obligations, and responsibilities cannot be sharply distinguished from one another, typically these terms are used for somewhat different sorts of moral tasks. Duties typically are relatively simple and recurring tasks attached to one's status or position. Obligations typically are temporary moral relations between individuals which can be discharged and so terminated by a completion of the task which is their content. Responsibilities are rather more complex tasks, involving some degree of initiative, planning, and resourcefulness. If I am simply required to take my neighbor's greyhounds for a walk each morning, then that task is most naturally described as my duty. But if I am required to look after these dogs while my neighbor is on vacation, this is more naturally described as my responsibility. The task involved in a duty typically is an action, in a responsibility, a state of affairs. Either of them could also be called an obligation. In calling them that, the emphasis would be on their being something I *must* do whether it fits into my plans or not.

What is common to all three is that they last for a period, that during that period certain tasks are morally required of the person who has them, and that in each case if the task if not performed, that person becomes responsible, in the sense of 'answerable', that is, subject to the appropriate sanction unless he can satisfactorily *answer* the question why he did not perform the task, that is, provide an exculpatory explanation (excuse) for his failure.

Any one of the three can be acquired in one of the three ways. They can be assumed, that is, deliberately taken on by a specific act of assumption, such as a vow, commitment, promise, agreement, or contract; they can be incurred by something else one does, whether intentionally, like stealing something from someone, or unintentionally, like getting someone pregnant, or running into a fence and damaging it; or they can be imposed, that is, made someone's duty, obligation, or responsibility, by the imponent's behavior, as when a manager *assigns* to his secretary a duty (to make tea), or a responsibility (to look after office supplies), or imposes an obligation on her, either by putting her under an obligation by doing something for her, such as giving her time off to study, or by doing something, for example, putting three handwritten manuscripts on her desk which brings into existence a concrete obligation capable of being discharged or neglected by her, namely, to type these manuscripts forthwith, because she already had the *general* obligation, undertaken when she signed her employment contract, to type whatever manuscripts her superior will give her to type.

Lastly, we should note a systematic difference in the use of these three terms: a conventional, an institutional, and a moral use. The former refers to the conventionally accepted ways in which we come to have these three slightly different types of task, without thereby entailing that their performance is morally required of us, while the second entails that that performance is morally required of us without entailing anything about precisely how we have come to have them. The distinction is sometimes signalled by a difference in the way the terms are used. The moral use is indicated by the singular and the qualifying adjective 'moral', as in "It is Jones's moral duty (obligation, responsibility) to get the money to pay Smith back." The conventional use can be indicated by the plural and the absence of the qualifying adjective, 'moral', as in "Ordering periodicals for the library was one of Jones's many departmental duties (obligations, responsibilities)." Under the influence of the ethical doctrines of G. E. Moore and of the Logical Positivists, who believed they saw a logical gap between 'is' and 'ought', which made it impossible to argue from the former to the latter, some philosophers and social scientists have come to believe that statements involving the institutional use are straightforward empirical claims, albeit claims which involve institutional facts, that is, facts about the rules which govern the relevant institutions; thus, if one knows the university bylaws, one can tell whether it is true that ordering periodicals is one of Jones's departmental duties. And they also believed, therefore, that statements involving the moral use of these terms are logically separate from and independent of the institutional use and could not be derived from it. In actual fact, the relation is more complex. In the standard institutional use, these terms suggest that when someone has an institutional duty, he also has a moral duty. A conventional duty *purports* to be a moral one. But, of course, this purport may be false and can in principle always be rebutted, though the burden of proof is then on the objector. But because a conventional duty purports also to be a moral one, the critical activities allowed by an advanced social order will tend to bring about such modifications of conventional duties as will bring it about that conventional duties really are moral duties. Thus a wife's conventional duties have undergone this sort of modification, under the moral pummeling of the feminist movement.

Given these facts about duties, responsibilities, and obligations, what bearing do they have on the apparent conflict between our complete freedom and our duties, obligations, and responsibilities? Putting it in the most general form, the freedom of anything consists in the absence of external obstacles or impediments in the way of exercising its abilities. Hence it makes no sense to speak of the complete or greater or lesser freedom of a thing unless that thing can be said to have certain *abilities* and to lack others. For in the absence of that difference, we cannot distinguish between internal and external obstacles and impediments. But then we also cannot distinguish between what interferes with the thing's abilities or powers and what diminishes its freedom. An unbreakable thermos flask *cannot* break, though perhaps if suitably bounced on the floor, it can rebound in interesting ways. (I once saw this done to good effect by a salesman at a fair.) Its unbreakability, its being incapable of breaking though quite capable of rebounding, does not amount to its *having the ability* to rebound but *lacking the ability* to break. There is, therefore, no sense in distinguishing between external and internal obstacles to exercising its abilities. By contrast, we can say of a car that it has the ability to climb a hill but not another much steeper one. Concrete barriers at the country's frontier half way up constitute an external obstacle to the exercise of the car's ability and so an interference with its freedom. An empty gas tank constitutes an internal obstacle and so a reduction of its ability, not its freedom. If the brakes are on but it can still get up the hill, then we may think of this either as a reduction of its ability or an interference with its freedom. We shall think the one or the other depending on whether we think of the brakes as an internal or an external obstacle to its locomotion.

There are similar unclarities in the case of human freedom. We need not concern ourselves with what might be called psychological freedom, including the freedom of the will, which involves the absence of obstacles external to the will but internal to the person, such as compulsions, obsessions, phobias, and the like, whose presence makes it impossible or hard for a person to decide to do what he judges he has the best reasons to do. Our concern here is solely with *wholly external freedom*, that is, the absence of those external obstacles and impediments put in the way of the exercise of one's abilities by other people. Some of these, like airline strikes or police arrests, actually *prevent* one from doing, others, like threats, or legal sanctions make it *more hazardous and costly* for one to do things one has the ability to do.

The kind of external freedom we are interested in here is *freedom in a given country*, that is, the absence in that country of those external obstacles and impediments which prevent or impede people from doing what they have the ability to do. We could say of a given person that at a given time he is completely free or has complete freedom in that country, if there are at that time no obstacles or impediments in the way of his exercising any of the abilities he has at that time and he had never encountered any obstacles or impediments in the way of acquiring new abilities and retaining old ones.

How can a person's freedom be diminished or increased? The most obvious way in which it can be diminished is his being prevented by the actions of others from doing, and so made *unable* to do, what he nevertheless still has *the ability* to do, as when guerrillas erect a roadblock or one's own government or that of Albania withholds an entry permit so that one cannot go mountaineering there.

A second way of diminishing someone's freedom is by destroying his ability to do something, as when a border guard shoots and maims me when I want to enter illegally. But it should be noted that he prevents me from mountaineering, not indeed by eliminating my freedom, but my ability, to do so. He does not eliminate my freedom to climb the mountains, because I was not free to do so before he shot me, and because he can limit my freedom only in respect of the things I have the ability to do. Nevertheless, although he does not reduce my freedom to do things, his action is still an interference with or reduction of my freedom, for I am completely free only to the extent that there are no external obstacles in the way of exercising my abilities or acquiring new ones and retaining old ones.

A third way of interfering with someone's freedom consists in threatening him with some evil if he does something he has the ability to do. In such a case, he still can do that thing, but can no longer do it freely. He is not prevented from doing it, but he is no longer completely free to do it: a burden or impediment has been put on his doing it. If he chooses to do it, it is not a free choice. If the burden is very heavy, say, a gun at his head, he can be said to have been compelled not to do it.

It is important to see how a society's use of social sanctions is like and unlike this last type of interference with people's freedom. When a society, through its customs or laws, attaches social sanctions to various classes of conduct for various classes of people, it similarly *interferes with these individuals'* freedom. But such interference, though necessarily making them less free in some respects, is not necessarily a reduction of *freedom in that society*, and so not necessarily a *reduction* of their freedom. For normally we think of the freedom in a given society as increased only when everyone's freedom in it is increased. Suppose in a certain country, the law against killing with guns is abolished. We should not necessarily regard this as an increase of freedom in that country because the abolition of that law also necessarily involves a decrease of the freedom of the victims. It is not even necessarily an increase in the freedom of the gunmen for they may become one another's victims. Our ideal of complete freedom in a country thus has the ideal of equality built into it. We would not think that a society necessarily had complete freedom if it was, so to speak, Pareto-optimal, that is, if it were impossible to increase anyone's freedom in that society without reducing someone else's. We think an increase of freedom in a country involves an equal increase of freedom for all. In a society with a slave class, the level of freedom *in* that society is that of the slaves, not that of the owners. Abolition of slavery raises the level of freedom in that society even if it reduces that of the owners.

And now a last point about freedom in a country. Mill, and the other libertarians who have followed him are simply wrong in thinking that the laws of a country, because they interfere with the freedom of its members in some respect, *reduce* that freedom though they may do so legitimately if it is to prevent harm to others. As we have seen, the social order, and above all the law, *purports* to be just, that is, to settle equitably the conflict of interests of those whose interrelations it regulates. If it does so—and truly democratic institutions make it possible to improve the existing legal order from the moral point of view—then to that extent the restrictions are truly for the good of everyone alike, but that must include ensuring the maximal amount of freedom for anyone compatible with a like amount for everyone else. In such an order, everyone is free to do what he has the ability to do unless such freedom reduces a comparable freedom of others to do what they have the ability to do. In such an order, no one is free to do what he ought not to be free to do, and no one has an obligation to do what he ought to be free not to do. Hence moral and legitimate legal obligations do not interfere with anyone's freedom. There is thus no conflict between complete freedom in a country on the one hand, and obligation and social responsibility, on the other.

Is there, then, no genuine disagreement between libertarians and their opponents? Well, there probably are many such disagreements, though I suspect few of them are based on high-level principles. Still, there is one such disagreement that I should mention. I think libertarians would tend to balance the conflicting interests in a different way from utilitarians and contractarians. I think libertarians have, on the whole, favored the role of the agent over that of the patient. They have praised initiative, enterprise, activity, novelty, experimentation, change, and have not been much concerned with the impact this has had on the patients, the bystanders, the occupants of the old roles, the third parties, those who were the victims of progress. In wrongly representing as interferences with freedom laws which to protect patients prohibit such favored enterprises, they have sometimes advocated trampling on the freedom of such victims.

NOTES

1. J. S. Mill, *Utilitarianism.* Ed., Samuel Gorovitz, Ch. V, p. 56; text and note 7.
2. Op. cit., p. 55.
3. I. Kant, *The Foundations of the Metaphysics of Morals.* Library of Liberal Arts, p. 47.
4. Hobbes, *Leviathan.* Ch. XV.
5. J. S. Mill, *Utilitarianism,* p. 47.
6. Op. cit., pp. 46-47.
7. Op. cit., p. 47.
8. Ibid.

Comment by Herbert Schneider on Baier Article

1. This essay revives the classic concept of "moral freedom" in its positive form of the pursuit of what is wanted or needed in social relations. It is effective criticism of the negative demands of the "libertarians." This virtue is more than mere "self-realization" as the Victorians interpreted it; it is the free cultivation of the reasonably desirable. The criticism of J. S. Mill in this context is excellent.

2. The attempt to make a sharp distinction between the moral point of view or the moral ideal, and the prudent, expedient, and useful, seems to break down in view of the subsequent detailed use of these "utilitarian virtues" in explaining the complexities of the "moral ideal." It would seem that the relation between the moral point of view and the more practical virtues and needs is worthy of more "public rational scrutiny."

3. The attempt to present moral problems simply as they arise among "human beings as they face one another" and not as "role players" meeting each other as members of institutions with conventional rules, is no doubt humanistic in a sense, but it excludes many of the chief problems of "social ethics" and institutional relations which are inescapable, and which in fact are discussed reasonably in this essay.

4. It seems to me that the "agent-patient relation" is somewhat exaggerated.

5. The essay deals with a variety of complex moral problems, in both their theoretical and practical aspects. It thus makes an excellent basis for fruitful discussion.

Comment by Konstantin Kolenda on Baier Article

Professor Baier is right in pointing out that making deals or striking bargains is to be distinguished from reaching a moral consensus, and he is correct in claiming that it is important to examine principles that underly such deals or bargains. His misgivings are especially pertinent in the light of the unfortunate connotation of terms like "deal" or "bargain." One tends to think of them as expressing the motivation at best of expediency or prudence or at worst of exclusive self-regard on the part of those engaged in dealing or bargaining. Such a conclusion, however, would be too harsh and cannot be drawn in every case. It is always an open question whether those who face the task of adjusting their disagreements proceed with a degree of good will or mutual disinterestedness. Parties to a dispute are usually concerned about the spirit in which the other side enters into negotiations and are on the lookout for evidence, verbal and otherwise, whether the offers made are in good faith and not mere pretense. This means that both parties assume the presence of commitment to moral principles on the part of their opponents, and they are both morally and prudentially advised to withdraw from negotiations, should it become clear that they are in the presence of deceptions or sham.

We learn about the principles and moral commitments of the negotiating partners from the way they state their priorities. Consider Baier's follow-up questions on our relations with Mexico. Something important is communicated to us if we are told by Mexicans that they would rather burn their natural gas than sell it to us at the Canadian price. Similarly, Mexicans would learn something revealing about us and our moral principles if they were told that "we would rather let Mexicans starve in Mexico than allow them to take away jobs of Americans." Outsiders watching the dispute would have reasons to declare both sides morally insensitive, to put it mildly. In the world desperately short of fuel a deliberate flouting of the principles of energy conservation is not morally indifferent. Similarly, for a country that champions human rights, the indifference to people starving, anywhere in the world, is a sign of callousness. That in fact there are those who would rather burn gas than have it serve human needs, or would protect well-paying American jobs at the cost of starvation in the world, has nothing to do with the moral validity of principles that forbid the wasting of vital natural resources and condemn the acceptance of hunger.

The search for consensus must be permeated by a mutual desire to embody in the resolution of a given conflict appropriate moral principles, principles by which the parties can stand both *in foro interno* and *in foro externo*. The reason for this is that consensus, if it is genuine, not a fake or pretense, is subjected to public rational scrutiny. Consider another example of weighty current interest. A recurrent question about the Strategic

Arms Limitation Treaty (SALT II) is whether the parties can trust each other. Each pursues a self-interested objective: avoidance of a clear-cut destructive capability of the other. But presumably there is also one overriding moral principle on which both agree, namely, the desirability of mutual survival. The anxious world can only hope that the commitment to this principle is indeed serious and central, and what is needed most of all to calm our troubled world is the accumulation of palpable evidence that this principle really dominates the motivation of the negotiating parties. One may even say that the persons in whose hands the fate of the treaty lies *owe* it to mankind (as Professor Storer would like to put it), *morally* owe it to all of us, that this absolutely minimal degree of consensus on this issue of overwhelming importance be pursued with determination and dedication. What is needed, on both sides, is not pious lip service to the desirability of limiting nuclear proliferation, but a demonstration, in deed after deed, in a series of publicly proclaimed decisions, that there *is* a moral commitment to this one crucial moral objective: to save mankind from self-destruction.

At least in this one instance we have the right to expect a morally ideal conduct, in Baier's second sense. We must hope that the moral ideality of preventing a nuclear holocaust "is generally known and there is adequate assurance that others by and large will act in this way." But an achievement of this kind of assured consensus could mobilize efforts to move toward further moral consensus. When Baier reminds us that "it is not easy to determine in an objective way what conduct is morally ideal," he has in mind an all-inclusive moral code that seeks to escape incorrect conventional specifications. He is right in warning us that on the question as to what is to be generally regarded as morally ideal there is likely to be a disagreement even among people of good will. But he also seems to recognize that the general desire to achieve consensus has an important role to play when he adds: "Nevertheless, assurance of conformity may be more beneficial to all concerned than correct specification of what is morally ideal." The assurance in question cannot rest just on scientific or psychological facts; it must also involve an assumption of a commitment to a moral principle. The humanist cause rests on this assumption.

Comment by Archie Bahm on Baier Article

Kurt Baier long ago worked out a conservative humanistic system for discussing ethical problems with his students. His *The Moral Point of View: A Rational Basis for Ethics* appeared in 1958 and as an abridged paperback in 1965. He has adopted many definitions, convenient for his purposes, which seem unduly restrictive to me.

He has chosen, as have many others, to limit ethics to "the moral," interpreted as social and never as merely individual. "Moral reasoning comes into the picture only when the goals of different individuals come into conflict with one another." (*The Moral Point of View*, 1965, p. 110.) His "moral point of view" always is "other-referring" and involves a willingness "to give due weight to other people's interests and concerns ." He examines self-interest, even enlightened self-interest, and concludes that "morality and self-interest cannot be the same points of view." (Ibid., p. 93.) Exploring egoism and altruism, conceived in their extreme forms, he concludes that "Those who adopt consistent egoism cannot make moral judgments." (Ibid., p. 95.) Conduct is moral only when it makes impact on others. Moral terms, such as "obligatory," "morally required," or "wrong," thus all apply to actions of doing or not doing (either neglecting or refraining).

He has chosen, as have many others, to limit morality to conduct, thus deemphasizing choice and intention. He devotes a chapter to "What is the best thing to do?" but none to best intentions. He devotes two chapters to "Rules of Reason" (individual and social) and a main one to "Moral Reasons," but none to principles for choosing among apparent alternatives. Moral rules, he says, "are meant for everybody." He deals with the problem of exceptions to rules by saying first that "It is never right to make exception to a moral rule in anyone's favor" (*Ibid.*, p. 100) and then that one may make exceptions to legislated rules when morally justified, because "being morally justified" is itself determined by a moral rule (to which there are no exceptions). "Absolute morality is that set of convictions, whether held by anyone or not, which is quite true irrespective of any particular social conditions in which they might be embodied," (Ibid., 115). Each particular "true morality" contains all such convictions and much more.

Baier's limitations create consequent difficulties: (1) "It is not easy to determine in an objective way what conduct is morally ideal?" (2) Once determined, then how can one be assured that all others will comply, so that rule followers will not "be suckers"? (3) How explain "the apparent conflict between our complete freedom and our duties, obligation, and responsibilities?" He defines the conflict away by limiting freedom to "the absence of external obstacles... to exercising abilities," by limiting concern "solely with wholly external freedom," and by ignoring "freedom of will."

My reactions to Baier's multiply restricted conception of ethics is that, in spite of its humanistic intent, he is greatly handicapped in dealing with the full range of ethical problems. I miss a theory of intrinsic values as basis for his "reasons," an account of a person's duties to himself, a genuine motive for persons to accept duties to others, a more convincing rationale for willingly conforming to moral rules, a much fuller explanation of the nature and kinds of freedom, some understanding of the contributions of other sciences (social, biological and physical) to moral life, a distinction between actual and conditional oughts, and awareness that moral rules should normally be intended as including "other things being equal." He has not given "expediency, prudence, and utility," even with his own selected meanings of these terms, their full due.

Editor Storer, hoping for greater consensus among humanistic ethicists, looks for clues for mediating, or at least moderating, explicit differences. Each humanist has specialized somewhat in his interests, in the problems appearing most important, in his debt to historical thinkers, in his conceptions of problems, in a language he uses, in the habits he has adopted, and in the critics he is most anxious to rebut. What is needed now is not so much mediation as understanding. First, when each humanist understands what particular presuppositions are being made by another humanist, he is more likely to agree with the conclusions drawn in accordance with those presuppositions. Second, when each humanist understands that there is more than what is encompassed within his particular viewpoint, he should be willing to expand his perspective, in principle at least. Humanistic ethics includes many varieties of specialized perspectives and emphases. Exploring these varieties as parts does not by itself reveal a comprehensive whole. But bringing these parts together for comparison and challenging each to come to terms with the others improves our prospects for giving further attention to that whole.

Humanist Ethics

Herbert W. Schneider

THE MEANING AND SOURCE OF MORALITY

The wants and tastes of other animals are inherited and governed by their native sensitivities, capacities, and instincts. A human being's infant structure is peculiarly indefinite and lacking in instincts; its native impulses and abilities are a small percentage of what it soon becomes, when an observer can detect the beginnings of personality in its behavior. The baby soon becomes a person. Persons are socially created; they are characters. The human person is an interest group, and most of the interests are socially created. In the kinds of social environment that are normal in developed cultures, childish interests soon are transformed into social relations of many kinds, and before long the person is a bundle of vested interests institutionalized.

In maturity a person is compelled to examine his interests as they affect each other, and as they relate to the interests of others. Personal character becomes reasonable when it's interests become sociable, compatible with each other and with social systems of institutionalized interests. To have only a single, professional interest is monomania. To have more interests than one can manage is schizophrenia. An intelligent person then is obliged to select and arrange his interests so that they contribute to his physical and moral health, instead of frustrating each other or conflicting with the interests of fellow citizens. An intelligent citizen must govern his interests as a good legislature governs interest groups.

HUMANKIND AND NATURE—FREE WILL AND RESPONSIBILITY

Morality must be conceived in terms of moral standards generated in particular cultures. The standards imply an art, unless they are nothing but custom and so-called "mores." Formal standards or principles are evidence that morality has become one of the folk-arts of a culture. Morality must then function in the context of other arts and organized interests. But as cultures become more developed and civilized they become more interrelated and respond to each other's standards and criticisms. The "mores" and customs become subjected to the criticisms of other moralities. Thus the intercultural relations make folk-customs more conscious of themselves as local arts, and gradually more general and reasonable moral systems and standards emerge. A humanist ethics and humanism in general aim at standards for mankind rather than for local moralities. But this ideal of a morality for all mankind as a whole is still largely theoretical, for mankind is not a whole.

It is therefore necessary as well as reasonable to take the variety of moral systems seriously, and to make moral art a medium for better cultural relations, and for the separation of moral standards from particular religions. This calls for toleration as well as criticism. But toleration of diverse moral systems need not lower moral standards in any culture. On the contrary, intercultural contacts should promote more humane standards.

MORALITY AS WORKABILITY VS. MORALITY AS JUSTICE

In any art a performance may be either right or wrong, correct or careless. The specific meaning for right and wrong depends on the particular art and artist under examination. Morality is the basic art of living well together. Moral right and wrong must therefore be conceived in terms of moral standards generated in a particular society. And the particular moral judgment or action must function in the context of other arts and interests.

Doing things "just-right" is a delicate matter in any art, and being just or doing right morally is no exception. It implies being "true" to the standard which must be up-to-date, relevant to the actual problems. Since these problems are usually full of new circumstances, the standards must be kept relevant to changing times. A general norm, of course, cannot solve a particular problem, but it must be clearly applicable as a guide. A decision of right or wrong, in order to be intelligent, must have some plausible alternative solutions to guide the deliberation. Moral judgments and conduct are seldom clear and obvious; they must be done deliberately and be subject to justification and verification for correctness in these practical decisions involves both values and facts. The standard or rule for guiding the judgment is intended to clarify the problem by relating it to the facts and values that must be faced. To be useful in this way the norms and principles must be relevant to the actual circumstances which have created the problem. Absolute or abstract rules do not make good guides; nor are the emotions and motivations that are involved inherently or universally moral, so that they could be used as guides. "He means well, but" is a severe criticism.

In short, morality is an experimental art, needing both helpful standards and intelligent information and decision.

THE BASIS OF RIGHTS AND DUTIES

Morality has three dimensions: doing what *must* be done, or meeting needs; doing what is desirable, or pursuing goals; and doing what is a duty, or being responsible. Obligations, interests, and responsibilities are the elements of morality.

Liberty and rights are civil privileges and must be deserved. Only responsible persons deserve liberty and rights, for those who are responsible are responsive to what others expect or demand. Rights and duties are usually coupled, for granting a right to one is a duty for the other.

One of the most important obligations is to be equitable, that is, to treat others as equals.

It is in all three of these dimensions that justice and righteousness are involved. This is the moral art.

PRINCIPLES IN SITUATIONAL MORALITY

Standards, norms, or general rules are indispensable in any art. They are essential elements of morality. For it is a dangerous policy to trust social relations and conduct to the intelligence of individuals operating on their own resources and judgments. In so critical an art guidance is needed. But if standards become useless as guides to intelligent deliberation, either because they are antiquated or too abstract, problems are made more difficult by misguidance.

Taking each situation in isolation is opportunism or shortsightedness.

Since moral decisions are experimental, they are made less intelligent, more of a gamble, if they must be made without alternative hypotheses as guides at hand to guide reflection and avoid hasty, unwarranted decisions. But irrelevant principles merely add to the confusion.

POSTLUDE

Of course, not all problems are moral problems. There are other arts with their own standards and problems. They may take us far beyond morality. No humanist would wish to moralize all the arts in the good life.

Beyond morals is happiness itself, and play and joy and music.

A genuinely humanist ethics must not ignore the humanities, even if they transcend morality.

Comment by Konstantin Kolenda on Schneider Article

Professor Schneider's compact and concise statement of humanist ethics rightly encourages us to view morality as involving an element of art. Doing things "just-right" requires a sensitive and delicate balancing of relevant standards, rights, duties, interests, and responsibilities. It also calls on some occasions for the willingness to see one's local mores in the light of alternatives preferred in other cultures. One cannot disagree with this account. But Schneider moves beyond these objectives and proposes that we should contribute toward an evolution of comprehensive standards for all mankind, warning us, however, that "this ideal of a morality for all mankind as a whole is still largely theoretical, for mankind is not a whole."

The question I want to raise is whether it is morally desirable to be moved by this theoretical ideal. There are reasons to think that it is not. The notion of a comprehensive, all-inclusive set of moral standards for all mankind is both illusory and impracticable. It is illusory because we never invoke it, and it is impracticable because if we were to invoke it, its abstractness would fail to address the particular issue at hand. In saying this, I do not question the universal validity of a moral standard which is offered as a reason for an action or a policy. Nor do I deny the moral attractiveness of the idea of the whole mankind living in peace and harmony. My point is rather that moral disagreements are always *particular* in nature and that our proposals to deal with them must *single out* some specific standards in the light of which the disagreement could be adjudicated. A genuine moral disagreement, when each side has a valid claim, is not a conflict between a partial morality and a global morality, the former representing a point of view which falls short of morality applicable to the whole mankind. Rather, we have *two* visions of possible candidates for a global morality, and the question to be examined is whether there are reasons to prefer one to the other.

To be sure, the conflicts I have in mind are not those in which it is evident that one side to the dispute either does not have a legitimate moral claim or is downright immoral. In such cases we need not appeal to a *de facto* universal agreement to offer valid criticisms. There are practices that can be justifiably condemned even if mankind is not yet a whole in the moral sense. Such practices, no matter how regrettable and recalcitrant to the efforts to eradicate them, are not problems for moral deliberation. We *know* that murder, arson, and deception are wrong and do not fit into a civilized scheme. What we do not know is how to harmonize legitimate preferences, interests, and styles of life when they interfere with one another. It takes what Professor Schneider calls "the moral art" to reconcile and to harmonize them. This can be done not by presupposing and invoking an independent ideal for all mankind but by creating a particular instance of greater harmony where previously a partial discord prevailed.

Comment by Kurt Baier on Schneider Article

The papers by Professors Kolenda and Schneider make a central point with which I sympathize—that moral orders are coextensive with socio-political orders. The moralities of those who live in the United States or in France or in Japan have many important general principles in common, and conversely, the things each of these group moralities have in common also tend to distinguish them from, and to bring them into disagreement, opposition and conflict with, the others. Both papers draw from this the conclusion, which also seems plausible to me, that the humanist ideal of a morality for mankind as a whole is for the time being no more than an aspiration if not an illusion. Yet both authors appear to regard this aspiration as somehow attainable if it is worked for in certain ways. There remain, however, large questions in my mind about how this worldwide morality is to be achieved.

Professor Schneider appears to individuate moralities in the same ways as he individuates cultures. For every culture there is a distinct morality with a set of standards which imply an "art." This means presumably that each morality contains general canons capable of being used by the members of a culture in the solution of the practical problems they encounter. The existence of these canons implies that someone's "performance" (in solving moral problems) "may be either right or wrong, correct or careless." He also emphasizes, correctly in my opinion, that "not all problems are moral problems"; not even all practical problems, I want to add. A great deal of weight, therefore, rests on his definition of "morality" as *the basic art of living well*. But it is not clear to me how this definition can be used to distinguish morality from prudence or from Bishop Butler's self-love or from practical rationality, nor how it can be used to solve the central problem raised by Schneider and Kolenda: how to achieve a worldwide common morality when different cultures have dreamt up different and incompatible visions of how to live well.

Globalism vs. Consensual Pluralism

Konstantin Kolenda

One task of moral philosophy is to provide a theoretical framework in terms of which moral problems can be understood. Although any theory presupposes as its background some practical problems, the usual procedure is to start with the theory and then to supply concrete examples of how it may be supported and applied. In this paper the order will be reversed. I shall start with an account of a problem and will turn to theoretical considerations only after presenting it in some detail. It will be my contention that the very nature of the problem highlights one central issue of moral philosophy: how can we work toward a moral consensus? I shall claim that the desirability of a consensus is itself a moral value and thus cannot be approached in terms of pure theory. If one *begins* with an attempt to formulate abstract conditions for consensus, one is likely to overlook its special normative position. That position can best be brought to light by examining some actual conditions. For that reason, the paper is divided into two parts. The first outlines a problem, and the second attempts to show how a certain conception of moral consensus may help to solve it.

I.

1. Our century is witnessing something unprecedented in the history of mankind, namely, global integration. Never before were all corners of the world mutually accessible. By accessibility I mean many things. First of all, knowledge. By now every corner of the world is explored, in the sense that we know its central facts: geographical and cultural. Of course, the process of acquiring information was prolonged and gradual: it took many generations of explorers, countless expeditions, and repeated contacts. Secondly, the accessibility is physical. Due to modern means of swift and reliable transportation, we can move ourselves, our products, and our artifacts thousands of miles in just a few hours. Thirdly, almost instant communication is made possible through telephone, radio, or satellite-transmitted television. If an event is deemed of interest, it can reach billions of people from anywhere on earth. In addition, the word- or picture-based information proliferates by being transposable onto pages of newspapers and magazines in all kinds of languages. Never before in human history have all the inhabitants been so accessible to one another both physically and informationally.

2. It is natural for knowledge to precede action. If all mankind has become a possible universe of discourse, that is, if we can encompass in thought all the places inhabited by human beings, then the idea unifying them in a global organization will not be far behind. The idea of world conquest is not exactly new. As history students we have heard of Alexander the Great, Genghis Khan, and the Roman Empire. These conquests followed the discovery of people and places that aroused the would-be conquerors' curiosity and interest. To extend the boundaries of one's power is always enticing for the enterprising spirit. But the would-be world unifiers of the past had neither the physical nor the informational resources to give their ambitions a truly global scale. Only in our century did the idea of conquering the *whole* earth begin to be entertained with not unrealistic prospects of success. The marching German soldiers during World War II were encouraged to sing: "Today belongs to us Germany—tomorrow the whole world," and their visions seemed for a time realizable. True, even Hitler had to lower his ambitions and concede the rule of the Asian part of the globe to his Japanese Axis partners. But between them they would unify the world under only two banners: the swastika and the rising sun.

The idea of unifying the world, however, need not be linked to armed conquest. Indeed, the revulsion against the horrors of war may provide an impetus for the desire to organize the world into one political unit, thus preventing any national group from embarking on bloody conquests. The proponents of world government from the direction of parliamentary democracies envisage a situation in which a gradual modernization, an intense commerce, a steadily increasing exchange of goods, ideas, and people would naturally encourage the dropping of artificial barriers between nation states and economic blocks. From the direction of Marxism, a most powerful ideological movement of our time, the blueprint looks different. Within the Communist movement historically there was a difference of opinion whether it should proceed on a global scale or whether it could succeed in separate countries. Whatever the outcome of that debate, it is clear that Communists have as their goal the establishment of a global, political, and economic system which would not be threatened from without, that is, from societies that adhere to some rival ideology—political, economic, or religious. A perusal of the so-called "New Communist Manifesto" issued under Khrushchev in 1961 leaves no doubt that the objective of the Communist movement is the world modeled on the system now existing in the Soviet Union.

3.   The proponents of the idea of one world are encountering many difficulties. One difficulty, from the point of view of parliamentary democracies, is precisely this division into East and West, the Communist and the non-Communist world. Those who hoped that the United Nations would become a consultative forum from which an impetus towards a political unification of the world may gradually emerge were soon frustrated by the cold war of inter-ideological rivalries. Pursuing their ideological objectives, the Communist countries have closed off their societies and their economies from the rest of the world, except for some carefully controlled contacts and limited trade agreements. The emergence of China as a third world power complicated the picture, and the game of expansion and containment preoccupied successive generations of statesmen with particular brush-fires and imminent threats, be it in Berlin, in Cuba, in Czechoslovakia, in Vietnam, or in Angola. If one regards the attempts to transform western Europe into one state as a model for the unification of separate political bodies into one world government, the record of this attempt is not encouraging. Winston Churchill's hope to forge a United States of Europe has not materialized so far, although there have been some significant gains—the European Common Market and the European Parliament in Strasbourg, the latter, however, being little more than an idea-exploring body. Undoubtedly, the political division of Europe into Western and Eastern has complicated this particular project.

4.   There are other obstacles to the idea of world unification. One problem, perhaps the deepest and most fundamental, arises from the moral abstractness of the goal itself. The idea of political world unification is abstract in the sense that it attempts to *leap over* some crucial conditions. Recent decades have shown, both in the non-Communist and Communist spheres of influence, that the one-world idea cannot be artificially grafted onto existing conditions. It may be instructive to examine this phenomenon as it came to surface in the Communist world; given the rather homogeneous articulation of the Marxist creed, it may be surprising to see the increasingly serious rifts among Communist societies.

First we have an early example of Yugoslavia, the first Communist state to insist on deviating from the Stalinist model. Yugoslavia still remains on a political collision course with the Soviet Union due to its desire to build socialism of its own brand. Czechoslovakia went even farther, and under Alexander Dubcek's leadership was prepared to build a so-called "Socialism with a human face," only to be crushed by Soviet tanks. More cautiously, Rumania still tries to reserve some important decisions for itself. In the Eastern hemisphere, China, while implementing socialism in its own cultural setting, denounced the Soviet road to Communism and began to chart its own course. In Western Europe, still free of political control of the state, the Communist parties indulge in what the Soviets call "revisionist" activities and promulgate so-called Eurocommunism in which the totalitarian control of the state is abjured and democratic freedoms are acknowledged. In each case the countries dissenting from the model of the Soviet Union assert their right to be guided by their own perception of what is most appropriate for their conditions and resist the demands for uniformity emanating from Moscow. While on the whole accepting the general Marxist framework, they may be said to advocate various forms of Communist pluralism.

5. Lacking a backing of an organized ideological and political movement, the sentiment toward a world order based on parliamentary democracy expresses itself in a rather diffuse way. Apart from the more definite and deliberate steps taken toward establishing a United States of Europe, the aspiration toward a world government rests on no more than the hope that increased modernization of all parts of the world would generate forces that work toward establishing a world government. The crucial question is whether modernization, industrialization, improvement in the standards of living and of levels of education would encourage the sentiment toward political world unity.

Judging from the events of recent decades, the answer to this question must be no. The optimistic mentality of democratic Western intellectuals was in part inherited from the colonial past when the idea of the "white man's burden" was almost taken for granted. Confident that the industrial revolutions, themselves resting on the expectation that the application of science and technology would yield rational methods of maximizing production and economic welfare, Western thinkers were taking it as axiomatic that modernization is bound to be welcomed as a benevolent answer to all economic, social, and political problems. In fact, the word "modernization" has acquired an almost magic halo. Modernization was equated with progress, enlightenment, democracy, and justice, all wrapped into one.

To the surprise of the proponents of the Gospel of Modernization, things failed to turn out according to expectations. One of the reasons was simply historical. During the colonial period modern methods were imposed by force on so-called underdeveloped peoples. When the populations acquired a degree of political independence and started to translate this independence into concrete projects, they often tended to associate modernization with oppression. The most telling example of this sentiment is found in the writings of Frantz Fanon who urged the Africans to turn away from all European models on the grounds that they were destructive and corrupt.[1]

A telling example of how a Western power may be disappointed and disillusioned in its expectation that its ways of managing things and organizing society are the only possible way is found in the American experience in Vietnam. Somehow the South Vietnamese failed to embrace enthusiastically the norms of parliamentary democracy and of technocratic management, despite the massive infusion of advisers and of technological hardware. Perhaps the experience failed because the attempt to win over the Vietnamese people to the American way of doing things had to be conducted under the most unfortunate circumstances of a relentless guerrilla war waged by the Viet Cong. Nevertheless, as belated discoveries and analyses have shown, much of the failure was due to the American inability to understand the native traditional forms of life and the different values which entered complexly into the manner in which the Vietnamese conceived their problems and goals. If the information about Vietnam's history contained in Frances Fitzgerald's book *Fire in the Lake* had been available to the American statesmen, one may suspect that they would have made very different decisions. According to Fitzgerald, the American idea to build "a strong, free nation" was absurd. "How should the south build a strong anti-Communist government when most southerners continued to obey the old authorities of the family, the village, and the sect. Communist, anti-Communist, the next war would begin in a language that few of them understood."[2]

6.   From all corners of the world we get signals that in its drive towards self-determination each country and each region insists on making use of its own traditional experience as embedded in social structures, economic patterns, art forms, and religious beliefs. In some cases, as for example in Africa, these local values and loyalties seem to work even against the idea of Pan-African unity, and produce a whole spectrum of experimentation with economic, political, and social structures. Most recently, we have also

come to appreciate the resurging vitality of Islam as providing norms for social, economic, and political life. The idea of an Islamic state, put into practice in Pakistan, Libya, and now coming into being in Iran, may not be a total surprise to some political scientists but it certainly seems not to have been anticipated by most statesmen. A growing force on the international scene, Islam seems to complicate our expectations about the resulting balance of power in the Middle East and in the whole of Asia.

What is going on in Iran is indicative of at least some serious misgivings about modernization in other countries as well. Even countries that have adopted industrialization and modernization as a deliberate policy, such as India, are not finding its acceptance easy and unproblematic. Mahatma Gandhi had feared that massive industrialization would disrupt cultural patterns of rural India, and some of his followers today advocate an alternative plan of emphasizing cottage industry in villages. Proponents of a Hindu state oppose the secular basis of government, and, to complicate matters, South Indians propose regional independence based on cultural and linguistic differences.

7. All of these examples indicate that the idea of a homogeneous world order is too abstract to do justice to particularistic interests of nations and geographic regions. The differences among these particular interests cannot be eliminated by creating what Julian Huxley had called "a common pool of ideas." Huxley believed that "the more united man's tradition becomes, the more rapid will be the possibility of progress; several separate or competing or even mutually hostile pools of tradition cannot possibly be so efficient as a single pool common to all mankind."[3] We need to look around for a more realistic way of harmonizing the diverse interests of the world's populations. Unless we do so, the expectation of understanding, unity, and peace are bound to founder on the discrepancy between the ideal and the reality. An ideal that fails to take into account the concrete situation in which it is to be realized is not good enough *as an ideal.* We must attempt to construct a better one.

II.

1. Before outlining the main features of consensual pluralism as an alternative normative objective, we must make some theoretical distinctions. A social community is also a moral community when it shares a moral code. This code may be rich and complex or it may be limited, even minimal. As a rule of thumb one may say that the more behavior-guiding principles a group shares, the more it functions as a moral community. How does one test whether a moral principle is valid for a given group? By observing whether it is followed, acknowledged, in action and word, cited in justification or blame. Thus, we can say that the reality of morality is people-dependent.

A habitual enactment of a moral principle is a necessary condition for its reality, for its actual existence in society. Even though we may still want to say that a totally ignored moral principle is in some sense valid or justifiable, the fact of its complete absence from the practices of a group entitles us to say that this group does not regard it as true. On the other hand, if the principle were to be revived, brought back as a constraining or regulating consideration, it would *acquire* reality, or as William James said of all truth, it would be *made* true. Its reintroduction would be its verification.

Whatever we regard the origin of morality to be, it is up to persons either to uphold or to ignore the injunctions specified in a moral rule or principle. The central place of this phenomenon in moral life was recognized by Kant when he associated morality with a conflict in the will. In a sense, a moral principle is always, perpetually on the line. Whether it will or will not prevail is up to a particular agent who finds himself in the situation which the principle covers. When changes take place in a moral code of a given society these changes are due to people's discontinuing their commitments to some parts of the code and possibly introducing new components.

Consensus in ethical matters exists when a sufficient number of members of a group agree in consciously following the injunctions of a code. Consensus is not just an intellectual consent, but also an identity of attitudes. Persons "feel-with" (con-sent) one another with respect to some form of behavior described by the code. There is a carry-over from understanding a principle to a disposition to act in the light of it. There need not be any specific sort of feeling to go with this disposition; it may become a matter of habit, a matter-of-course performance. Nevertheless, it is not inappropriate in such a situation to speak of the presence of feeling, as in the phrase "we feel this way about it." To refer to feeling in such a context is to give to understand that the agent subscribing to the principle finds it important to uphold it, that he cares about it to the extent that its violation he would find regrettable or blameworthy. As Gilbert Ryle characterized morality, to have been taught the difference between right and wrong "is to have been brought to appreciate the difference, and this appreciation is not just a competence to label correctly or just a capacity to do things efficiently. It includes an inculcated caring, a habit of taking certain things seriously."4

2.   Changes in moral beliefs and shifts in moral codes do not occur on a single, one-dimensional level of consciousness. In Professor Morris Stor-

er's happy phrase, the truth of an ethical statement is not a "single thing" but is "an equation summing up a history."[5] In a recent work, Stuart Hampshire argues that rationality in ethics is not to be assimilated to some specialized type of rationality. Having primarily utilitarians in mind, Hampshire inveighs against something more general, namely, the "rational computational morality," and argues that in such computational approaches we have a wrong model of practical reasoning. In his positive view, indebted to Aristotle and Spinoza, he depicts morality as an internalization of a complex code involving prohibitions, injunctions, and ideals that have become immediate, spontaneous, and to a great extent governed by intuition. Morality is a vast system, in many respects analogous to language. Although it is true that moral reasoning must be sharable and reconstructible, it is not exactly like legal reasoning, to which it is also partly akin, for "the extreme case of the translator's skill in choice of words illustrates that element in practical thinking on serious moral issues which 'a computational morality' either ignores or means to banish."[6]

A search for consensus on particular issues, if it is to be successful, must take into account the feature of morality to which Hampshire calls attention. It is of interest that the utilitarian position which he criticizes may be stated in a way that acknowledges his insights. In his most recent book, *A Theory of the Good and the Right*, Richard Brandt suggests that in a situation when a person rejects an important moral code or a part of it, one should resort to what he calls "cognitive psychotherapy." This consists in trying to show that if a person were to examine rationally his actual desires and interests he would see that the code he now rejects is in fact optimally designed to secure them. The question that may lead to a resolution of a disagreement and thus to a consensus is a question which, according to Brandt, lies at the center of the justification of moral codes. "What kind of social moral code, if any, would you most tend to support for a society in which you expected to live, if you were *fully rational?*"[7] Since by being fully rational Brandt means being optimally informed about all the ramifications of the code, we may use this question to examine the ramifications of the particular consensus being aimed at by the disagreeing parties. The appeal of Brandt's approach is that it does not seek an arbitrary imposition of a solution but rather recommends a careful review of the entire framework of all existing values and motivating principles, bringing into the light the particular roles played by each.

3. With this preliminary discussion behind us, let us examine the way in which consensus may function as a moral principle. Consensus may be understood in two ways. One may take it in a descriptive sense, meaning that wherever there is a moral code, there is agreement, consensus. In this case it is open to us to judge a given code as morally defective, the *de facto* consensus as morally regrettable. But we can also have a situation in which the absence of agreement on a code or a part of it has morally undesirable consequences. In that situation the achievement of a consensus would lead to the removal of these bad consequences. Here consensus, being a goal to be obtained, functions as a moral principle.

That principle need not be always applicable. To see this we should introduce a distinction between moral diversity and moral disagreement. The importance of this distinction was clearly recognized in A. E. Murphy's undeservedly neglected *Theory of Practical Reason*: "Moral diversity *becomes* moral disagreement only when the diversity itself is made a moral issue. And in nine cases out of ten, the part of plain good sense is *not* to make a moral issue of it."[8] Members of one group, say, manifest a high degree of kindness and considerateness toward one another, while members of another group are content to abide by a rather hands-offish principle of live and let live—they adhere to some form of sober Hobbesian contractarianism. Expectations in each group correspond to the nature of it's own code. In the first one kindnesses are expected and taken for granted, in the other they are not; the second group is more comfortable with extreme self-reliance, and its members are reluctant to enlist the help of others. But suppose the two groups begin to interact, either individually or collectively. If they stick to their customary ways of acting, their mutual expectations will not be met and frustrations will ensue. One need not assume that the one code is better than the other, but it seems clear that a consensus to adopt one *or* the other is better than the lack of consensus. Whatever losses or gains accrue from shifting from the charitable code toward the Hobbesian or from the Hobbesian toward a charitable, both groups would be better off morally if they achieved *a* consensus than they would be if they persisted in approaching each other in contrasting ways native to their respective codes. Here is a situation in which we can say that the moral disagreement makes a consensus morally desirable.

4. There are times when the achievement of such a consensus is especially important and desirable. Whenever diverse groups come into active contact, the issue of consensus becomes relevant. On the basis of the description offered in the first part of this paper, I wish to claim that ours is such a time. Contacts that were never envisaged before now take place, and they take place on a global scale. As we have seen, the contacts are not just physical or superficial. Rather, they are massively cross-cultural and involve beliefs, dispositions, practices, and principles from the multiple arena of cultural phenomena—economic, religious, social, ethnic, aesthetic. The task of minimizing conflicts and maximizing harmony calls for a policy I wish to call consensual pluralism. What does it consist in?

In contrast to the vague, abstract code of world unity, consensual pluralism is piecemeal and concrete. It addresses itself to harm-creating disagreements whenever and wherever they are spotted. It does not ignore them or sweep them under the rug or under the umbrella of eventual global solutions. Since, as indicated before, not every diversity is a moral issue, it is a mistake to make an issue of it. But there are plenty of live issues around, and some of them are momentous. One such issue, for example, is the seemingly uncontrollable proliferation of atomic armaments. It is to be hoped that that urgent issue receives adequate attention from those directly responsible for it, namely, the producers and deployers of nuclear arms.

There are other issues, not as momentous but of considerable urgency for those affected by them. One must start with them, in one's very own back yard. For the populations of the American Southwest, for example, the immigration issue between Mexico and the United States is of direct interest. Whatever is done by either country affects millions of lives on each side of the border. As yet no consensus exists as to how it can be resolved. But unquestionably there is a *need* for a consensus; a mutually acceptable solution must be faced if trouble is to be avoided and good neighborliness is to prevail. How can a consensus be reached? Only if both sides try to be fully rational in Brandt's sense and lay on the table all the relevant rights, obligations, and potential benefits and losses, and seek solutions in open deliberation. Both sides should try to discover what compromises are required, at what price, and for the sake of what objectives. The guiding principle, to which reference must be made again and again, is the *desirability* of a consensus on this matter. Rigidity and stubbornness may well lead to losing sight of the relevance of this principle and when that happens the conflicting practices may escalate into open hostility. In a search for a *modus vivendi*, resort to hard bargaining should not be surprising. Each party can be expected to try to exploit its special advantages. Mexico's recent discoveries of oil, badly needed by the United States, can understandably become a topic of discussion in the search for mutual accommodation. Parties to a dispute would be foolish not to defend their best interests and not to make use of their leverage. But blackmail and ruthless pressure are bound to backfire, because they directly work against the key moral principle at stake: the desirability of voluntarily embraced consensus.

This kind of open, straightforward, honest pursuit of objectives that broaden the area of consensus can gradually improve relationships between nations. It is, of course, a painstaking, piecemeal work that does not solve all the problems at once. But if resolutely pursued, it can build mutual trust and good will, both these values being but a function of attained and sustained agreements.

The objective of building consensus starts from the assumption that claims reasonably put forward by parties seeking consensus have a moral basis. As we are increasingly becoming aware, such claims are not limited to strictly economic goals; they are often intertwined with cultural, ethnic, and religious values. Wherever we turn in the world we discover the pressure and the power of pride. People cherish their independence, collectively and individually, and they are likely to stiffen their backs when they see their pride trampled upon. To be sure, the appeal to pride can be exploited by clever demagogues, but this does not mean that it does not figure constructively in people's desire for dignity and self-respect.

5.   The idea that we replace the abstract ideal of a broad, undefined, and unspecified notion of global harmony by an ideal of gradual resolution of concrete disagreements has many things in its favor. If taken seriously, and practiced in good faith, it is likely to have cumulative effect, each success encouraging further attempts to eliminate areas of conflict and disharmony. Consensus added to consensus will gradually help to build a comprehensive moral code for the entire planet, eliminating distrust and enlarging harmony. It may encompass border disputes, fishing rights, trading policies, the use of the sky and the oceans, the optimal distribution of energy, the mutually beneficial sharing of material resources of every sort.

The conception of forging a pluralistic consensus will also take the wind out of the sails of those who claim that the situation of our world is hopeless until and unless all existing institutions and social and cultural arrangements are thoroughly leveled by a world revolution that will impose a new order based on a universal utopian scheme concocted by some ambitious brain. No one brain is capable of taking into account the multiple needs and interests that come to expression in the total resources of mankind. Only by respecting these resources and helping them to achieve a broad range of accommodation with all relevant and justified interests can we produce a humanly decent world.

Furthermore, the ideal of consensual pluralism puts in the hot seat those who are presently in charge of managing competing and conflicting interests. It puts them on notice that it would be a moral failing on their part not to work toward consensus from the best of their abilities. Passing the buck, blaming others, is a tempting way out for most of us; we are wont to point to some allegedly uncontrollable conditions that tie our hands. Thus one government agency blames another, in the meantime sitting smugly on its hands. If it is true that morality is people-dependent, then the growth of moral understanding and accommodation can occur only if some persons take initiative. This applies in particular to those in charge, those elected to lead, and especially those in places of power and responsibility.

6.   Economic inequality in the world is certainly one of the areas that generate moral disagreements. These disagreements deservedly occupy the forefront of our attention, since economic well-being is a necessary condition for any form of good life. But it may be a mistake to be preoccupied exclusively with the question of economic justice. Central as these questions are, they are usually combined with other questions, namely, those that turn on the *ways* in which exploitation or injustice occur. To arrive at a consensus of what would be just in any particular case, we must begin with a description of the entire transaction that usually results in some persons' interests being neglected or ignored. A company that exploits a poor country's natural resources can often excuse its practices by pointing out that its activities were arrived at by a mutual consent of all parties. But if the activity is examined in the light of overall results and if these results are iniquitous, the exploiters cannot, morally cannot, declare indifference to these harmful results by a recourse to mere legality of their activities. By broadening the issue to include the question whether one can conscionably consent to exploitation of the poor only because there is nothing legally wrong with the transaction, one creates the conditions for a fuller appraisal of what blocks the possibility of arriving at the desirable consensus.

Thus the concerns of economic justice will be better served if they are put into a broader context of a concern for more inclusive justice. The desired consensus is more likely to be reached when one examines *all* the conditions that would result in an equitable relationship between the contending parties. It may be a favorite procedure of those bent on exploitation to limit themselves to questions of strict legality, but if one prevents them from seeking this easy, morally irresponsible way out, the crucial components that block mutual accommodation and understanding will be given the weight they deserve. Furthermore, it is quite likely that when disputes are transferred to a level where all relevant factors that determine the situation are brought into the light of open discussion, humane considerations will be difficult to keep out. Economic justice is more likely to ensue if one emphasizes the all-inclusive framework in which moral consensus is sought.

7.   The invitation to shift from abstract globalism to concrete consensus-building is connected with a certain conception of humanity. It takes into account a feature that is responsible for whatever achievements we can claim to our credit as a species. I mean inventiveness. Humanity is a race of problem-solvers. But in solving problems people naturally enlist the modes

and forms of acting and behaving with which they are familiar—from their tradition, their culture. To insist that there is only one way of solving a problem, be it economic, political, or social, is either narrow-mindedness or arrogance. The expanding global horizons force us to develop a certain degree of humility before other countries, other regions, other religions. Even the notion of the primitive begins to lose its pejorative connotations. Negatively, this phenomenon manifests itself in the reluctance of so-called undeveloped countries to accept automatically the values developed in industrialized countries. Positively, it can be found in the growing admiration not only for so-called primitive art, but also for entire forms of life that differ from the mainstream of European civilization. Even the word "civilization" may need a redefinition.

In pursuing pluralistic consensus, we can be also beneficiaries of many brands of human culture brought about by accidents of human history. The conquest of local populations of Latin America by invading Europeans was not a lovely sight. But this violent mixing of races, nations, and cultures has nevertheless produced unique and positive variants. Latin American countries, in virtue of their historical backgrounds and present circumstances, present rich blends of attitudes, values, and practices that are precious to them and admirable to their visitors. There is such a thing as a Latin American spirit and it has many national forms: Mexican, Brazilian, Argentinian, Chilean. It would be in everyone's interest if each such concatenation of human abilities and talents were encouraged to express itself freely and creatively in all areas of human life: social, political, economic, and aesthetic. All humanity can benefit from seeing such a multiple display of human spirit coming to full expression on all continents, in all corners of the globe.

NOTES

1. "Europe now lives at such a mad, reckless pace that she has shaken off all guidance and all reason, and she is running headlong into the abyss; we would do well to avoid it with all possible speed.... Let us decide not to imitate Europe; let us combine our muscles and our brains in a new direction. Let us try to create the whole man, whom Europe has been incapable of bringing to triumphant birth." Frantz Fanon, *The Wretched of the Earth* (New York, 1968), pp. 312-313.

2. Frances Fitzgerald, *Fire in the Lake* (Boston, 1972), p. 71.

3. Julian Huxley, "A New World Vision," *The Humanist*, March/April 1979, p. 37.

4. Gilbert Ryle, "On Forgetting the Difference Between Right and Wrong," *Collected Papers II* (New York, 1971), pp. 387-388.

5. Morris B. Storer, "Foundation Stones of Humanist Ethics," *The Humanist*, March/April 1979, p. 43.

6. Stuart Hampshire, *Public and Private Morality* (Cambridge University Press, 1978), p. 33.

7. Richard Brandt, *A Theory of the Good and the Right* (Oxford University Press, 1979), p. 185.
8. Arthur E. Murphy, *The Theory of Practical Reason* (LaSalle, Ill., 1964), p. 339.

Comment by Kurt Baier on Kolenda Article

Kolenda talks in some detail of how he envisages the piecemeal buildup of a common worldwide morality, what he calls "consensual pluralism" by negotiations between different cultures, such as that of the United States on the one hand, and Mexico, various Latin-American, and Islamic states on the other. He draws an important distinction between mere moral diversity and moral disagreement when the diversity itself is made a moral issue. He stresses the importance of the *desirability* of the consensus. But how are we to take this? That a worldwide morality covers (or can cover) only those issues on which both sides want a consensus *more* than they want to adhere to the claims with which they begin their negotiations? To take the case of Mexico on which he concentrates: suppose Mexicans would rather burn their natural gas than sell it to us at the Canadian price and that we would rather not get their gas than buy at a higher than the Canadian price? Or that we would rather let Mexicans starve in Mexico than allow them to take away the jobs of Americans and that Mexicans would rather try to enter the States illegally than reorganize their economy and their population policy? Or suppose, alternatively, that we regard a consensus (a deal) as more important than holding on to our claims (principles, interests)? Is the bargain we then arrive at really a moral one? "In a search for a *modus vivendi*, resort to hard bargaining should not be surprising. Each party can be expected to try to exploit its special advantages." Would not a bargain, struck after such negotiations, reflect the relative bargaining advantages of the partners rather than genuine moral principles? Surely, some stipulations have to be introduced about the psychological endowment of the bargainers or their conditions of knowledge or ignorance, something like Rawl's "mutual disinterestedness" and "the veil of ignorance," if the agreement reached is to have a claim to being a moral one. The problem becomes plain when we attempt to generalize from such individual two-sided bargains and the principles underlying them, to the uniform moral principles of all of humanity which are supposed to underly all such bargains. Presumably, any one sociopolitical order has to strike such bargains with its many neighbors and clients, but they will be quite different bargains, not only in terms of detail, but also in terms of principle, depending on the relative strengths of the bargaining partners, their relative interests and leverage. I, for one, cannot see how this method could produce a uniform world morality.

Comment by James Simpson on Kolenda Article

Professor Kolenda's essay is of special interest for it probes directly into the heart of humanist ethics by asking, Why have a consensus? More important, he correctly determines that students of ethics can improve their perspective on issues surrounding the consensus question by focusing on a "consensual pluralism" rather than "globalism." Whereas the latter term could be defined as an attempt to unify the globe in political, economical, and ethical terms, the author defines consensual pluralism as the task of minimizing conflicts and maximizing harmony. In his essay he observes "in contrast to the vague, abstract code of world unity, consensual pluralism is piecemeal and concrete. It addresses itself to harm-creating disagreements whenever and wherever they are spotted."

Let us now relate the concepts of globalism versus consensual pluralism to Humanist Manifesto II. In fact, I am surprised that Professor Kolenda has not referred to this important document given that six of the seventeen articles relate to the world community. Article Twelve of the Manifesto states, among other points, "Thus we look to the development of a system of world law and a world order based upon transnational federal government. This would appreciate cultural pluralism and diversity. It would not exclude pride in national origins and accomplishments nor the handling of regional problems on a regional basis."

Professor Kolenda would appear to take exception to this article, and I tend to agree with him. There are several good reasons. As he points out, "perhaps the deepest and most fundamental (problem) arises from the moral abstractness of the goal itself." He then presents several rather convincing arguments about *why* we should be cautious about political world unity. Perhaps most convincing is his concern that *a* world government could easily fall into inappropriate hands.

I would like to extend Professor Kolenda's views by consideration of some moral dimensions inherent in one world government. It is reassuring that humanists drafting the Manifesto felt that a world federal government would "appreciate cultural pluralism and diversity," but it is difficult to really believe that such an institution could reliably have such a focus as part of its vision about world organization. After all, a principal reason for proposing a world government is *because* there is considerable cultural pluralism (and we can include political and economic attitudes as part of this pluralism). Another concern I have relates to size. The arguments which I advanced in my essay against bigness of businesses and national governments, hold for *a* federal world government.

Where does this leave us? Well, I come right back to Professor Kolenda's plea for a consensual pluralism in which gradual resolution has a cumulative effect in building a comprehensive moral code for the entire planet, eliminating distrust and enlarging harmony. Although I strongly support Manifesto II as a base document for humanists, as well as the United nations as an organization, it is apparent, as we search for consensus on humanist ethics, that wholesale promotion of *a* world government deserves additional scrutiny.

Comment by Marvin Kohl on Kolenda Article

Professor Kolenda's paper raises two major questions: First, is it true that adopting a consensus in cases of serious moral disagreement is always better than declining or failing to do so? And second, to what extent is consensual global pluralism a realistic and effective way of harmonizing the diverse interests of the world's populations?

That consensus is a moral value is a proposition which can scarcely be doubted. That agreement is always better than the lack of it is, however, a proposition which has been both fanatically maintained and denied. But if we follow Kolenda's suggestion that consensual pluralism addresses itself only to "harm-creating disagreements" and not to intrinsically undesirable states of affairs, then the first question is not a difficult one. As a teleologist one may say that consensus is preferable to disagreement if and only if that state of affairs, or perhaps the rule under which it falls, produces or will probably produce a greater balance of good over evil. One may, for example, face a situation where negotiations are taking place between an open and a closed society. In the open society members have natural rights which are protected by law and the general moral sentiment. In the closed society individuals have no rights except those which the state gives them and members of non-Aryan groups are exterminated. The issue for the open society is whether to adopt the latter's code or to go to war. Now some may wish to argue that in some situations war is a mistake and that appeasement is the best alternative. But no teleologist can consistently maintain that—no matter what the consequences—agreement is always preferable.

The second question is more difficult because it raises some very large preliminary issues, which I can only touch upon briefly. (1) Even as a rule of thumb it does not seem to be true that "the more behavior-guiding principles a group shares, the more it functions as a moral community." Morality depends on the nature of the respective rules and not their quantity. (2) If full rationality necessarily involves being disinterested or impartial, then it is especially problematic in the political arena because the role of a politician is largely and almost always defined as that of representing one party more than the other. Like many philosophical approaches to politics, Kolenda seems to be appealing to disinterested rationality in a world where rationality is, in fact, almost never disinterested. (3) Kolenda points out that many populations reject the norms of parliamentary democracy. But if this is true, as I think it is, then it is difficult to understand why consensualism and pluralism, two underpinnings of political democracy, should prove to be ideologically more palatable for those populations. (4) And perhaps most important, although he describes several obstacles to world unification, Kolenda fails to mention two of the most serious: nationalism or the herd instinct which tends to overpower rationality and the love of power which is often eagerly accepted as its substitute.

Where nationalism and love of power are rampant, and this appears to be the normal course of international politics, it is difficult to see how the proposed method can be significantly effective. If we add to this scenario an ideological rejection of altruism, consensualism, and an almost horrified rejection of the idea of pluralism because it allows for departures from the "true faith"—as recently illustrated by developments in Iran—then the picture becomes grim. Indeed, one may be tempted to say that where the method is most needed, it is least effective. And even if we temper this criticism and say that the success of public policy does not turn on its ability to handle the hardest cases, we have to add that neither does it just depend on its ability to handle the easiest.

Reply by Konstantin Kolenda to Kohl

Professor Kohl's observation that there is a distinction between "harm-creating disagreements" and "intrinsically undesirable states of affairs" is certainly correct. Nevertheless, when someone claims that a state of affairs is undesirable, he voices a disagreement with those who allow this state of affairs to continue, thus setting in motion a process of potential reform or change, in which the pros and cons of the situation can be aired and a mutually satisfying consensus may be reached.

Kohl is also right in noting that rationality is "almost never disinterested." Neither is morality, we could add. The question turns on whether in addition to the particular material objective of the moral principle one wishes to see prevail, one is *also* interested in finding a mutually acceptable set of reasons for embracing or rejecting the material objective or the moral principle. A person who is not interested in *that* much at least, cannot be a party to a rational dispute, with all the undesirable consequences of such a breakdown to follow. Such breakdowns usually characterize herd instinct, love of power, or some forms of exclusivist and intolerant nationalism or political ideology.

When we run up against such displays of rigid adherence to "true faith," undesirable states of affairs cannot even become a *topic* of disagreement, because at least one of the parties regards the matter as settled—in its favor, of course. The consequence of such a posture, however, is a disturbing lack of consensus, disturbing because it may find expression in outright hostility. And if the presence of hostility is assumed to be morally undesirable—because it exposes both parties to the danger of physical confrontation—then the lack of consensus should become a matter of concern not only to the opposing parties but also to bystanders, who might be adversely affected by the outbreak of hostilities. This is why the peace-making efforts, whether by President Carter in the Middle East, or by the United Nations in any corner of the world, are so important for our future.

Toward a Humanist Consensus on Ethics of International Development

James R. Simpson

Analytic effort is of necessity preceded by a preanalytic cognitive act that supplies the raw material for the analytic effort... This preanalytic cognitive act will be called vision (Joseph Schumpeter, *History of Economic Analysis*).

The forty years which elapsed between Humanist Manifestos I and II have been characterized by a widening of perspectives, and demands by a diversity of groups in all parts of the world for equal rights and economic opportunities. Humanist Manifesto II effectively captures this internationalism by devoting virtually all of the introduction and conclusion to the need for an "affirmative and hopeful vision." In this article a vision of development is set forth in relation to ethical questions such as freedom of choice, responsibility for choice versus universal determinism, the question of whether ends justify means, and the ultimate basis for private interest. The greatest attention will be given to the basis of rights and duties, and the place of obligation in a humanistic ethic.

INTRODUCTION

Humanist Manifesto II contains seventeen articles, six of which are related to the world community. These include condemnation of dividing humankind on nationalistic grounds, an attack on violence and force as a method of solving international disputes, the need for cooperative planning, a plea for expanded communication and transportation across frontiers (especially *ideological borders*), and a recognition that neo-

Romantic efforts to indiscriminately condemn all technology and science should be resisted. Perhaps the most important article is number fifteen which states:

> The problems of economic growth and development can no longer be resolved by one nation alone; they are worldwide in scope. It is the moral obligation of the developed nations to provide—through an international authority that safeguards human rights—massive technical, agricultural, medical, and economic assistance, including birth control techniques, to the developing portions of the globe. World poverty must cease. Hence extreme disproportions in wealth, income, and economic growth should be reduced on a worldwide basis.

This is a very significant and powerful statement, both in affirmation of a policy and vision, and in terms of a moral philosophical imperative. I would venture to say that the question of safeguarding human rights is intimately tied to the choice of economic systems, and that disputes over the "goodness" or "badness" of the various systems will be a major philosophical question among humanists for the next decade. As social protest against inequities expands, there will be even greater interest in "socialist" and "Marxist" varieties of humanism by those who consider themselves naturalistic humanists.

This article's objective is to set forth some ethical propositions which can serve as points of departure for discussions on economic growth and international development. Space limitations require that many of the points be confined to assertions or propositions, but every effort is made to develop logical consistency.

TOWARD A DEFINITION OF "BEING DEVELOPED"

The entire argument in this chapter is based on the premise that the focal point of all human activity is *people*. Now, by people I don't mean masses of people or groups, but rather *individuals*. It is a fundamental proposition that humanism is a people-oriented philosophy (as opposed to a theistic orientation). What I am asking for is acceptance of the notion that our focus be on *individuals*, and that we face the reality that each person's wants and desires are different. This is not a plea for acceptance of a philosophy of extreme individualism. Rather we are arguing that the end of economic and social activity is fulfilling the wants and desires of *people*, and *not* the development of a powerful nation-state, large business entities, or other ego related activities projected in the *name* of people.

If we are in agreement that a humanistic focus is on *persons*, then I propose that "being developed" be defined as a multifarious phenomenon that is relative to each person and nation. There is no set level at which a country or region can be said to be "developed," although some indicators such as GNP per capita are useful measures. A country, region, community, or individual can be considered developed when there is an environment of freedom, "sufficient" income, and adequate opportunities to achieve aspirations, security, and esteem.

It is fully recognized that this rather nebulous definition will leave many readers cold as they expect a neat classification. The point brought out by the definition is that development *is* a personal experience and that even though there are differences in incomes, the term "developed" is based on factors other than income such as the promotion of equality and harmonious living.

The definition of "being developed" is directly related to a vision of what life is all about, quality of life, the highest good, and factors which yield the "best" life. In other words, economic growth, increased incomes, greater freedom *from* want, and freedom *to* meet personal goals and desires are just tools to obtain the greatest amount of satisfaction from life. Clearly, one person's satisfaction is subject to numerous constraints or barriers, such as limitations on resources and obligation to assist other persons to obtain as much of the good life as possible. The important point is that the first step in attempting to reach a consensus among humanists about moral issues is in setting forth an ideal of what we want and where we are headed. Without a vision we are floundering at sea, much like a ship caught in a storm where the captain has forgotten about where the ship is headed and is simply meeting crisis situations.

Goals are frequently misconstrued as visions. This is quite unfortunate as goals should be dictated by the vision or ideal one has of society. Goals are for *specific* efforts, are quantifiable, and contain targets as measures of end results or steps during the effort. Policies are set to meet specific goals and also to wed goals to visions. Nearly all of article fifteen quoted above is a goal, which is reducing, on a worldwide basis, extreme disproportions in wealth, income, and economic growth. The problem is meeting that goal within the context of other goals and a vision concerning the makeup of a developed person or society. There are many goals in social and economic life. Their acceptability, and the tradeoffs between them, depends on the vision of the type of society we want. That in turn depends on how we view equity. More important, and now we are back to my argument, is that a vision of the type of society we desire depends on how we view individuals—their wants, desires, freedoms, and responsibilities.

It may still appear that the definition of "being developed" is so broad that it precludes use from a functional policy standpoint. Closer examination reveals that a whole political ideology with attendant programs and thrusts is based on a conception of whether the development goal is one of equality of opportunity (essentially what is being argued for in the definition) or equality (which means an effort to make a society as homogenous as possible, at least in economic and material ways). In brief, the definition is crucial to elucidating personal or nation-state philosophies (visions) about the direction programs should take.

A HUMANISTIC ETHICS OF INTERNATIONAL DEVELOPMENT

Questions of international assistance for economic development are directly tied to the imperative that "world poverty must cease." Even the most casual observers with a humanistic focus will recognize that, from both a practical and ethical viewpoint, poor people and lesser developed nations (LDC's) around the globe cannot permanently live on donations or aid, but must continually strive for self-sufficiency. Few people argue with the concept of foreign assistance, although long discussions can be created about the amount and type of assistance, methods of delivering it, and the ethical bases for providing assistance. Also, while it is fairly clear that the poorest of the poor should be helped, there is considerable disagreement about what the average level of income in a country must be before assistance is cut off. Although these are interesting questions, let us focus directly on the LDC's themselves and their obligations as a partner in the process of development. It will be useful to keep the definition of "being developed" in mind during this section. We will concentrate on three aspects set forth in article fifteen of the Manifesto; the role of assistance, human rights, and equality.

Many, if not most, people in the donor countries believe that LDC's should carry out certain changes as their counterpart contribution for receiving development aid. One of the first changes which comes to mind is population control. Another is modifying values, customs, and beliefs such as prohibitions against eating certain types of food, like beef in India. To drive the question home, consider the case of United States food aid and relief shipments from other affluent countries. The United States allows for sale of surplus grains at low prices with excellent credit to the extent that shipments are nearly gifts under Title I of Public Law 480. In the case of one Asian country there has been virtually no attempt to reduce population growth from its three percent annual rate nor has there been any serious attempt to reduce smuggling of rice to neighboring countries even though the nation in question could meet current basic minimum requirements if regimented distribution were instituted and the smuggling stopped. Furthermore, the government finds it cheaper to subsidize foodgrains than to increase wages.

The decision about suspending aid as the result of a country having a dictator or resorting to alleged violations of human rights is one of the most thorny questions in development ethics. There is a realization that governments change, while the people remain. Also, development is a long term proposition. In this light is it "right" to cut off a very effective aid program directly benefiting say, 200,000 people, just because an autocratic government is in power? As any change agent with much field experience will testify, cutting off successful ongoing programs is a very sad and disheartening experience. The larger aim, which is that of *helping all peoples* of a developing nation, must be kept in sight.

Human rights, in the fairly narrow sense in which they are dealt with by the Inter-American Commission on Human Rights (IACHR), are claims by individual persons for freedom from tyrannical control or domination by governments. But, governments must operate within a certain scope vis-à-vis their citizens. For example, governments must justify arrests and imprisonment and they cannot torture prisoners. These rights, which are primarily negative defenses against governmental oppression, are complemented with positive assertions of economic and social rights which revolve around a more equitable distribution of benefits. Apart from IACHR, which is a regional group, the other major organization is the United Nations Commission on Human Rights (UNCHR) which has given most of its attention to problems in Africa. The UNCHR follows the European Convention on Human Rights which is in force. The IACHR, in contrast, has no court, depending on publicity as the major sanction.

While the various commissions on human rights focus on individual problems, governments have multiple purposes. In all likelihood human rights has a low priority in comparison to survival, national security, and regime stability. In this regard, it is clear that cutting off aid as a tool for obtaining observance of human rights demonstrates that aid is a political tool, rather than being given in a humanitarian sense. To improve upon this, it would seem desirable to separate aid policy into two parts, long term and short term. By keeping an eye on long term objectives it would quickly be apparent that it is not logical to cut off aid for human rights violations, as this is simply demonstrating disapproval and exerting a sanction for humanist values in a given regime. It would also help to delimit the difference in government-to-government policy as opposed to government-to-people policy.

Another vexing question relating to LDC's and a definition of "being developed" is determining whether a country is better off aiming for income equality or equality of opportunity. If the first alternative is chosen, there are two broad possibilities: redistribute the world's wealth to the extent that everyone starts out on an equal basis and then allow each person to develop as he or she can or; second, continue to force everyone to remain at the same level after the redistribution. Promoting equality of opportunity is different from distributing income, for this concept specifically recognizes that income differences are a natural phenomenon in a heterogeneous society and that forcing income equality implies creating a homogeneous society reminiscent of that found in Huxley's *Brave New World*. It also means complete control by government and behavioral control as depicted in B. F. Skinner's *Walden Two*. Some people think that the acceptance of inequality of income smacks of self-defeatism. But does our position really imply that society has no alternative but to accept a second-rate solution? Not if inequality of income is combined with equality of opportunity which is tempered with limits of power and wealth accumulation.

It seems to me that the solution to the matter is equality of opportunity at the beginning of life's race with rules that allow for fair competition during the events. It also means having sufficient events such that everyone has a chance to excel in his/her own way. The optimal amount of equality in terms of efficiency is the point where the added benefits from more equality are just equal to the additional costs of greater inefficiency. In fact, this difficult-to-apply rule can be extended to ethics as a whole by continuously comparing the trade-off between a major benefit (such as freedom) against the costs (like greater competition). If one accepts the idea that there should be equality of opportunity rather than equality of income, significant advances are made in setting policies concerning income distribution.

The objective of a "better life," can be construed as improving people's satisfaction or happiness so that, at any point, they can look back on their lives and recognize mistakes, but cheerfully admit that at least they had had the *opportunity* to try something that interested them. By recognizing that current and future issues in international development have become as much ethical as economic or technological enigmas, we are at least pointed in the direction of helping people obtain a better life which implies living in a society that is as free *as possible* from the vicissitudes of hunger, squalor in living conditions, and undue hardships. A modern society is one where the opportunity for equality exists. It is one in which humankind uses technology but is not enslaved by it, where the emphasis in political and economic decision-making is on the contribution of a decision to human dignity, purpose, freedom, and enjoyment of life. This is the desperately needed alternative to dogmas and abstractions which fight to shunt our car of progress on a sideline of growth for the sake of growth.

Article fifteen clearly sets forth an imperative by the industrialized nations to assist the LDC's. But, it can be criticized for not going far enough in recognizing the obligation of LDC's and people within those countries. There *are* human rights violations and uncontrolled population growth in many countries. But those drawbacks cannot be overcome without a dialogue. This is why the United Nations is so important. I also feel uneasy about article fifteen's lack of a positive vision. It is true that hunger and squalor should be overcome, but sustenance is only a necessary condition—it is a long way from being a sufficient condition for being developed.

The key for a better life is recognition that people cannot be forced into certain molds. The development process is slow and there must be an understanding that the people of LDC's will not instantaneously move from a position of relative poverty to a medium income bracket even if the means are made available to them. Development is a measured, never ending process in which it is difficult to ascertain progress. It is a two-way street in which the onus of responsibility for a developed *world* falls equally on both the developed nations and those in the process of development. Both the LDC's as a whole, and the citizen in particular, have duties as well as rights. Reaching the good life on an international scale will require cooperation and a positive philosophical attitude. What we wonder is whether all nations and all people will attempt to meet the commitment. This is the practical ethical question.

TOWARD A CONSENSUS ABOUT ETHICS
AND INTERNATIONAL DEVELOPMENT

The definition of "being developed" and the foregoing discussion about LDC's and quality of life serve as guides in setting forth observations about some important ethical issues at the international level confronting humanists. The critical proposition is that each person has different wants and desires, from which it logically follows that the community or society is a mechanism for the good of people, rather than people living for the good of the community. This does not mean that people should not hold dear the principle of helping others and sharing. What it does mean is that, apart from a moral obligation to assist others, people should be encouraged to enjoy life as *they* see fit. In other words, the good of society is maximized by individuals fulfilling their aspirations to the fullest extent possible. The key is fostering a philosophy in which people assist others because they *want to*, not because they are forced to. This is the rock-bottom concern of morality.

An ethics at the international level must emphasize freedom of choice coupled with responsibility to be meaningful. From this it follows that development, whether it be economic or in the broader sense, as used in this essay, cannot be force or pushed. A substantially higher Gross National Product (GNP) is not an end which justifies any means, as higher per capita incomes are themselves only a means to the more important factor which is "being developed." I also hold that only through a system of private property rights, regulated to prevent abuses of the system, can people ultimately meet their wants and desires. People *ought* to want economic freedom but with a philosophy oriented toward limiting the size of businesses to prevent the accumulation of undue monopolistic power. There must be a "certain" amount of government intervention to insure economic stability, protect property rights, prevent coercion, and thwart undesirable market practices. There should be a belief and faith in the ultimate potential equality of all persons and their desire for, and capacity to, accept democracy as well as a concern for liberty and harmony of all. To these principles so strongly espoused by John Locke, is added a belief that, while self-interest is really the driving force behind innovation, the real threat to freedom is excessive individualism. The problem is one of effective and proper control of personal motivation to stimulate both useful creativity and a sense of moral obligation and duty. I feel that the free market economic system embodies the required ethical bases provided proper controls are instituted.

The foregoing thoughts lead up to what can be called a humanistic ethics of international development where the role of developmental humanism can be construed as promoting the "good life" to everyone. Developmental humanism is viewed as being culturally relative. There is no imperative to bring about a classless society; in fact it is recognized that economic heterogeneity just like cultural heterogeneity, leads to fulfillment of personal needs and desires. The key is preventing one person from infringing on the rights of another. With these thoughts, plus the earlier definition of "being developed," I would like to set forth twenty humanistic principles which could form the basis for an international humanistic ethics. The list is not all-inclusive and some principles are undoubtedly open to discussion. But, at least setting them down is a start in striving for a consensus amoung humanists. The principles are:

1) Humankind's purpose in life is living a life which improves both one's condition as well as that of fellow beings. This imperative is best carried out by holding the position that society is for the good of people rather than people being for the good of society.

2) The objectives of development are provision of subsistence, enhancement, and luxury goods and services as needed for individuals and nations to achieve what they consider to be an appropriate level of want satisfaction.

3) The highest goals are this-worldly happiness or satisfaction, and economic, cultural, and ethical freedom and progress of all mankind irrespective of nation, race, or religion.

4) Human beings, while conditioned by the past, possess genuine freedom of creative choice for developmental action and are the masters of their own destinies. This freedom of choice, within objective limits, is compatible with the rights of others.

5) The "good life" or "quality of life" is relative to each individual's preferences, desires, and needs.

6) The individual attains the good life by harmoniously combining personal satisfactions and continuous self-development with significant work and other activities that contribute to the welfare of the community.

7) All human values are grounded in this-earthly experiences and relationships.

8) The state is a service to people rather than people being instruments of the state.

9) Social protest should be encouraged; but every effort should be made to have it nonviolent—not only in form but in actuality.

10) There should be every effort to establish democracy throughout the world. Regardless of the political system adopted, there should be full freedom of expression and civil liberties, throughout all areas of economic, political, and cultural life.

11) Personal liberty is an end that must be combined with social responsibility in order that liberty will not be sacrificed for the improvement of material conditions.

12) Development efforts should be aimed at reaching a high standard of living based on a flourishing economic order, both national and international, but individuals should not be forced to live in life-styles or in economic systems which they dislike.

13) Development should be stimulated, not pushed.

14) A free enterprise system in which excessive competition, power, and "bigness" are avoided is deemed the highest economic order, since it maximizes freedom in the widest sense of the word.

15) There should be the greatest possible development of all the arts whether they be classical, contemporary, or indigenous, and an increasing awareness of beauty, including the appreciation of nature's loveliness and splendor, so that aesthetic experience may become a pervasive reality in people's lives.

16) There should be a complete social implementation of reason and scientific method combined with an unending questioning of basic assumptions and convictions, including those posited in this list.

17) Science must be used not destructively, but for the improvement of humankind.

18) Ends do not justify means. Furthermore, means and ends are viewed as being a continuum, that is, interrelated and continuously changing through time.

19) Developmental humanists respect each person's right to follow the religion of his/her choice. However, it is felt that both means and ends of development must be this-worldly oriented and completely nonreligious in order to maintain an objective stance, and also because it is unrealistic to believe that the world's religions can reach agreement about the goals and ethics involved.

20) The Humanist Manifesto II is accepted in its entirety as a guideline for an international ethics of development.

CONCLUSION

Behind the bravura of recent conferences held by the LDC's (such as the "Group of 77" nonallied developing nations) is a sense of failure, indecision and frustration about their future. Where are they going? What do they want? What is "progress"? How should they react to the increasing emphasis on "anticonsumerism"? Their leaders wonder about the LDC's relation with the developed countries. Do the latter have a "right" to utilize the relatively inexpensive manpower of the LDC's, extend their multinational corporations like tentacles over the globe and buy up substantial portions of LDC raw materials for their own use?

There are many moral questions which can be examined within the framework of international relations and the apparently rational conclusion that LDC's, just like industrialized countries, have obligations as their part in the development process. Many questions can be posited in evaluating the moral tradeoffs inherent in a discussion of two party obligations beyond those touched on in this essay. What are the limits on rights of one person or country to influence another country's norms or values? Should special efforts be made to achieve income redistribution and, if so, at what rate? Should international borders be dissolved? Should there be greater emphasis on labor intensive techniques versus introduction of greater mechanization? Should worldwide austerity be incorporated in a development philosophy? Space does not permit consideration of these formidable, practical, urgent problems. I have attempted, however, to set forth an integrated set of ethical propositions and views which can be used as a framework for those people interested in formulating a personal philosophy about ethics of international development. The point is that humanists should evaluate the above questions, as well as those goals set forth in article fifteen of Humanist Manifesto II, such as the belief "world poverty must cease," within a total philosophical framework of a vision about the term "being developed."

A definition of "being developed" has been set forth in light of accepted principles of naturalistic humanism. It is concluded that a vision or ideal of the ultimate essence of life is a vital first step in determining an ethics of international development. The conclusion is that, while humanism has exalted people and a "this-worldly" philosophy, the real essence is the individual, as wants, desires and needs differ radically between people not only across cultures but within them. A focus on *persons* leads to a conclusion that the touchstone for evaluating policies, ends, means, goals, political and economic systems is the extent to which they exalt the individual. This is not meant as an endorsement of extreme individualism, egoism, or related philosophies such as hedonism. Rather, it is an argument that the ethical question about the highest good should be reexamined as a recognition that everyone's tastes, wants, and desires differ.

I have posited that the rock-bottom concern of morality is the need to foster a philosophy in which people assist others because they want to, not because they are forced into it. Along with this approach is the view that one culture is not "better" than another, but rather that a multitude of cultural and subcultural settings are desirable as likes and dislikes vary between individuals. From there it also follows that great emphasis should be placed on freedom of choice as this is the essence of humans as rational animals. Ends do not justify means, in general, as the ends are always changing. Furthermore, we are a long way from a method of determining individual desires and aggregating them to society-wide utility functions. Until such a planning procedure is worked out, and adequately tested to avoid the production of biased answers, we may conclude that the greatest good or happiness for the greatest number is found through individual decision making with adequate information and alternatives to choose from.

There are no rights without duties just as there are no duties without rights. Certainly the discussion in this essay about article fifteen amplifies that point. But, while people are obligated not to infringe upon the rights of others, and are morally obliged to assist in seeking the harmony of humankind as a whole, they should not be obliged to be a tool for economic growth of a system in which they do not have full democratic rights to choose their own destinies.

The last article of Humanist Manifesto II calls for full international cooperation across ideological borders. I strongly support this expression aimed at fostering world peace, but I am skeptical of finding a common ground between socialist and nonsocialist humanists on ethical matters even though they share several basic characteristics such as rejection of any supernatural conception of the universe, humanitarian concerns, and an affirmation that ethical values have no meaning independent of human experience. The problem is that although so-called Marxist or Socialist Humanists express a concern for people, they do not focus on *individual persons* and individual rights. Rather, the discussions revolve around groups, such as an alienated society and the proletariat. Marxists expound at great length about the depravity of the bourgeoisie, but fail to come to grips with the practicalities of *how* there can be extensive state control without violating fundamental humanist propositions. They fail to consider that personal freedom to make decisions is the antithesis of an emphasis on widespread government control and planning. There is no inherent contradiction between being a social reformer and holding a free market philosophy; there is natural dichotomy between promotion of freedom and strong state control.

REFERENCES

Space limitations have prevented full development of many arguments in this essay. Further treatment of them, both pro and con, is found in the following references.

Caves, Richard, *American Industry: Structure, Conduct, Performance,* (Englewood Cliffs, N.J.: Prentice-Hall, 1964).

Daly, Herman, (ed.), *Toward A Steady State Economy,* (San Francisco: W. H. Freeman & Company, 1973).

Derfler, Leslie, *Socialism Since Marx: A Century of the European Left,* (New York: St. Martin's Press, 1973).

Dewey, John, *Freedom and Culture,* (New York: Capricorn Books, 1963). Reprint of the original 1939 book.

Ebenstein, William, *Todays Isms,* (Englewood Cliffs, N.J.: Prentice-Hall, Inc., 1967).

Fromm, Eric, *Socialist Humanism,* (New York: Doubleday & Company, Inc., Anchor Books).

Henry, John M., (ed.), *Free Enterprise...An Imperative,* (West Branch, Iowa: The Herbert Hoover Presidential Library Assoc., Inc., 1975).

Kamenka, Eugene, *Marxism and Ethics,* (New York: MacMillan & Co., 1969).

Knight, Frank, *Freedom and Reform,* (1942 reprint ed., Port Washington, New York: Kennikat Press, 1969).

Kurtz, Paul, "Humanism and the Freedom of the Individual," *The Humanist,* January-February, 1969, pp. 14-19.

Kurtz, Paul, (ed.), *Moral Problems in Contemporary Society,* (Englewood Cliffs, N.J.: Prentice-Hall, Inc., 1969).

Markovic, Mihailo, "The Basic Characteristics of Marxist Humanism," *The Humanist,* January-February, 1969, pp. 19-23.

Okun, Arthur M., *Equality and Efficiency: The Big Tradeoff,* (Washington: The Brookings Institution, 1975).

134   James R. Simpson

Schumacher, E. F., *Small is Beautiful: Economics As If People Mattered*, (New York: Harper & Row, 1973).
Schumpeter, Joseph, *History of Economic Analysis*, (New York: Oxford University Press, 1954), pp. 41-47.
Sher, Gerson S., (ed.), *Marxist Humanism and Praxis*, (Buffalo, New York: Prometheus Books, 1978).

Comment by Konstantin Kolenda on Simpson Article

Professor Simpson defends controlled economic liberalism on the grounds that it is more compatible with humanist ethics than are other economic systems—socialism, communism, or Marxism. These systems, in his view, "lead to depersonalization of the individual and primary emphasis on organization," and in many instances incorporate a radical antiindividualism. Salutary as the emphasis on the primary importance of people as individual persons is, it tends to underestimate the needs of persons to participate effectively in social, economic, and political processes.

If it is the case, as Simpson warns, that a free enterprise system can suffer from "excessive competition, power and 'bigness,' " (his principle 14), then people ought to be in a position, through appropriate institutional frameworks and not merely as isolated individuals, to impose necessary restraints and sanctions that would remove these distortions. We are told, however, that these "controls" are not to be entrusted to the government: "legislative action must stimulate or encourage human creativity rather than push people into it." Simpson would like to limit the role of the state "to the provision of choice-making information, providing freedom from coercion and assisting people to reach individual goals. ... In other words, government is viewed as having a facilitating function."

To my mind, humanistic ethics should be concerned not only with the defense of individual rights but should also encourage ways of effectively controlling economic developments which result in obvious injustice. The pursuit of justice through appropriate democratically arrived at laws is one of the activities to which individuals in a free society are entitled. What I find missing in Simpson's essay is an account of mechanisms and procedures by means of which "strong controls preventing excessive competition" (and other abuses) could be exercised. Without the recognition of a need to watch over the ways in which economic activity could get ethically "out of control," the insistence on individual rights becomes to a great extent as abstract as are the theoretical dogmas of Marxist humanism, against which Professor Simpson marshals convincing arguments.

Reply By James Simpson to Kolenda

Professor Kolenda highlights some useful points regarding my essay. I have three comments which should meet his concerns. The first refers to his statement "salutary as the emphasis on the primary importance of people as individual persons is, it (controlled economic liberalism) tends to underestimate the needs of persons to participate effectively in social, economic, and political processes."

Now, it is quite apparent from this comment that Professor Kolenda, like (unfortunately) the majority of people throughout the world, has just plain overlooked the real essence of the free enterprise system. This is the voting which people do everytime they make a decision to purchase or reject a good or service. The polemics of advertising are well-known, but the point is that *only* in a properly controlled free enterprise system are people offered the wide variety of goods and services to meet their personalized wants, needs, and desires. When production is controlled by the State or by monopolistic business, consumers effectively lose part of their vote. The amount retained depends on the benevolence of those in control. At the risk of appearing redundant, let me reiterate that I am advocating free enterprise, and not unfettered capitalism.

My second comment refers to an apparent misreading of my essay by Professor Kolenda when he states that I have "underestimated the need of persons to participate effectively in the political process." This is erroneous, as the need for humanists to embrace democracy is brought out several times.

My third comment refers to Professor Kolenda's concern about my not discussing the mechanisms and procedures to avoid excessive competition and other potential abuses of a free market economy. This aspect was not considered because of space limitations and the objective of pointing out the need for a vision about society. But, since the subject is raised, I would like to encourage the reader at least to skim through a textbook on American industrial organization. Just an abbreviated journey through the history and essence of such legislation as the Clayton Act, the Robinson-Patman Act, and the Wheeler-Lea Act of 1934 will provide an exciting eye-opener. The reader will discover that the law—the foundation of control in our free enterprise economy—clearly spells out the nature of abuses except for one major area, and that is provision of an exact definition of what constitutes excessive *size* of business. This aspect was deliberately left to interpretation as the legislators involved with the act recognized that forms of business *should* change through time.

Let me close by quoting a few lines from the Sherman Act of 1890, a piece of legislation which grew from an unusual period of American economic history following the Civil War when "monopoly versus competition," as a general question of economic policy, first came to the fore at the national level. The most important aspect for our consideration, is the first half of Section 2, which states "every person who shall monopolize, or attempt to monopolize, or combine to conspire with any other person or persons, to monopolize any part of the trade or commerce among the several states, or with foreign nations, shall be deemed guilty of a misdemeanor." In my own mind the rules are set, at least in the United States, for effective control of the economic system. What is left to judges and philosophy—and philosophy is everybody's business—is a vision of what constitutes excessive control and power.

PANEL III

MAX HOCUTT
V. M. TARKUNDE
MARVIN KOHL
ALASTAIR HANNAY

Toward an Ethic of
Mutual Accommodation

Max Hocutt

THE MEANING AND SOURCE OF MORALITY

The fundamental question of ethics is, Who makes the rules? God or men?
The theistic answer is that God makes them. The humanistic answer is that
men make them. This distinction between theism and humanism is the
fundamental division in moral theory.

A few moralists contend that nobody makes the rules, which just
exist, written in the nature of things or in the consciences of men, where
they may be read by all those who know how to read nature or consciences;
nobody inscribed them there, but they are inscribed there nevertheless.
However, as Jean Paul Sartre has noted, this position is untenable. Worse,
it is unintelligible—an attempt to believe in a God-given morality without
believing in God. Atheists must take their atheism seriously. As Dostoevsky pointed out, if there is no God, anything goes. If there is no God,
there is also no table of divine commandments, no transcendent morality
which men are required to obey. Furthermore, if there were a morality
written up in the sky somewhere but no God to enforce it, I see no good
reason why anybody should pay it any heed, no reason why we should obey
it. Human beings may, and do, make up their own rules. All existing
moralities and all existing laws are human artifacts, products of human
society, social conventions. Morality is not discovered; it is made.

Does that mean that one set of rules is as good as another? Of course
not. Automobiles are made, not God given, or found in nature, but it does
not follow that one automobile is as good as another, and that is not true.
Medicines are made, not God given, and not often found in nature, but

that does not mean that all medicines are equally valuable, and they are not. Sometimes we make inferior automobiles and harmful medicines, and sometimes we make very bad rules. As some people drive the wrong cars for their purposes and take the wrong medicines for their ills, so some societies have the wrong moral and legal practices. Indeed, inferior moral and legal practices are at least as common as inferior medicines and automobiles.

As evaluated by what standard? If there is no morality laid up in heaven, by what yardstick will we measure earthly moralities? The answer, of course, is that we should use the same yardstick we use to evaluate any other human artifact: satisfaction of our needs. Penicillin is a good medicine because it cures our ills; Toyotas are good cars because they provide economical transportation; honesty is good morality because it facilitates human cooperation for the sake of common ends. The value of a moral practice, as of any other human creation, is its utility. Does it achieve the purposes we desire it to achieve? Then it is insofar a good practice. Does it defeat any of our desires? Then it is insofar a bad practice. In short, men make the rules to achieve certain ends, and, if men are rational, they will judge their rules by the ends they achieve. They will not ask, Is this rule in accordance with transcendent morality? They will ask, Is this rule doing what we want it to do?

As judged by such a standard, some moral codes are better than others. Some ways of doing things are much better at satisfying the needs of their practitioners, and some ways of doing things defeat the purposes of their practitioners. The measure of the difference is happiness. Where there is pain and misery and discontent, something is wrong; where there is pleasure and contentment and happiness, something is right. Where people are hungry and sick and alienated from their lives, something is amiss; where people are well-fed and healthy and happy in their work, something is being done well.

Hence, even though there is no such thing as an absolute, divinely instituted morality, there is nevertheless a distinction between truth and falsity in ethics. Saying "Honesty is a good policy" is saying something either true or false. Like other judgments, moral judgments have truth values. Furthermore, since moral judgments can be false as well as true, we can make mistakes. We can think to be good, practices that are in fact bad. We can feel very strongly that something is right when in fact, it is utterly wrong. We can have deep moral convictions that are wholly misguided. Indeed, we often do.

To put the point another way, denying that there is an absolute right and wrong laid up in heaven does not require us to subscribe to the confused doctrine usually mislabeled "ethical relativism"; it does not require us to believe that right and wrong are mere "matters of opinion."

On the contrary, the latter doctrine, which should be called "ethical subjectivism," is as objectionable as theological absolutism. Thinking something true doesn't make it true, either in ethics or in anything else. Thinking the earth to be flat doesn't make the earth flat, and thinking a practice right doesn't make it right.

To be sure, X's thinking the earth flat, makes true
> *The earth is flat to X,*

because that sentence is elliptical for
> *The earth is flat according to X,*

and merely means
> *X believes the earth is flat.*

Similarly, X's thinking flagellation of the flesh to be good makes true
> *Flagellation of the flesh is good to X,*

for that is merely a short way of saying
> *Flagellation of the flesh is good according to X,*

and just means
> *X thinks that flagellation of the flesh is good.*

When we come to Principles of Situational Morality, we shall see that right and wrong are "relative" in the sense that a practice right for one society in one situation might be wrong for another society or under different circumstances, but relativity to objective conditions is one thing and relativity to subjective opinions is another. Penicillin is not good absolutely. It is good for some diseases, not good for others, not because some people think it good and others disagree, but because it will cure some diseases and not others. We must not confuse
> *A is right to X,*

with
> *A is right for X.*

The first is elliptical for
> *A is right according to X,*

which just means
> *A thinks X is right.*

The second means something very different. It means
> *A will do X good.*

But what will do a person (or society) good is not always what he (it) thinks will do him (it) good. So what is good *to* X is not always good *for* X. For example, flagellation of the flesh, though good to those who believe in it, is not good for them.

FREE WILL AND RESPONSIBILITY

The notions of a Free Will and responsibility (i.e., culpability, liability to punishment) are not humanistic notions. The first is tied to a theistic metaphysics, and the second is tied to an inhumane retributivism. Enlightened humanists therefore have no use for either notion. What we have a use for is not the concept of "having a Free Will," but the concept of acting "of your own free will"; not the concept of being responsible (i.e., culpable) for your misdeeds, but the concept of acting responsibly (i.e., with due considerations for the consequences of your behavior). Let me explain these two distinctions.

The concept of a Free Will was invented by Plato, who thought of one's will as that part of one's soul which remains independent of the body only by exercising its capacity to side with Reason against Desire. Freedom of the will thus consisted, for Plato, in being uninfluenced by one's desires, in transcending the natural order of things. The hypothesis that we have wills free in this sense seemed to Plato necessary to explain the fact that some people have the self-discipline to do what is right and reasonable even when they might desire the contrary. For example, knowing that it is not good to get drunk, some people can refuse another cup of wine.

Although Plato's concept of a Free Will has had enormous influence, it is wrong in two important respects. First, people have no capacity to transcend the physical world. Second, liberty cannot be equated with such a capacity. Let me say something about the second point before I return to the first.

As we normally use words, a person is said to do something of his own free will if he does what he wishes to do. It is only when he is being compelled to do something against his wishes that he is said to act against his will. In short, liberty is doing what you want to do; slavery is being compelled to do what somebody else wants you to do. Plato's usage is the exact reverse of this. According to Plato, you are free only when doing what you don't wish to do, only when acting contrary to your desires; when you are doing what you wish to do, you are a slave to your desires. In short, Plato calls slavery "freedom" and freedom "slavery."

Plato's double-talk has caused serious confusion. It led Epictetus, the slave, to conclude that, because he was indifferent to his slavery, he was really free; that, by ceasing to wish for his freedom, he had secured it. In our own time, the same idea has led Jean Paul Sartre to write a novel, *The Age of Reason*, in which he illustrates his concept of Free Will by having the novel's neurotic heroine stick a knife in her arm, not because she wants to, but because she does not want to. Had she wished to do so, her action would have been the product of her desire, not an act of her Free Will. Simone de Beauvoir exposed both Sartre's and Epictetus's error when she asked wryly "Must we grant this curious paradox: that from the moment we recognize ourselves as free, we are forbidden to wish for anything?" Contrary to a wide-spread impression, voluntarists, believers in a Free

Will, are not libertarians, advocates of liberty. On the contrary, they are enemies of liberty. They merely conceal this fact by calling liberty "slavery" and vice versa.

So much for liberty. Let us now look at transcendence. Belief in it has no evidential basis whatsoever. To say that we have a capacity to transcend all physical influences on our behavior is as much as to say that we sometimes act without being caused to do so. As Roderick Chisholm has noted, it is to say that our Wills are prime movers: they move our bodies but they are themselves unmoved. What is wrong with saying that? Just this: to claim that something has happened without cause is to make a claim for which there can be no evidence. We cannot know that something is uncaused; we can only fail to know what its cause is. Therefore, all arguments for an autonomous will are arguments from ignorance. For example, the popular argument from introspection (we seem to ourselves to have Free Wills; so we do) reduces to the claim that, since we are unaware of what causes our behavior, therefore nothing causes it. Plato's argument (that one's transcendence of desire is proved by one's refusing a desired glass of wine) is also an argument from ignorance, which overlooks the influence of one's greater desire to remain sober.

If the concept of a Free Will is so confused, why have so many people been bamboozled by it? Why has it had such an enormous influence? Part of the cause was Plato's unfortunate proclivity for metaphors. They make good poetry, bad philosophy. Mainly, however, people believe in Free Will, not because it is required by the evidence, but because it is required by their theological and moral prejudices. Let me now say something in explanation of these two points.

The trouble began when Plato personified the unobserved causes of observed behavior. Seeing one man push back the extra cup of wine, another accept it, Plato postulated that, inside each visible man, there are three invisible men, Reason, Will, and Desire. Desire is dictating the Will of the man who takes the wine; Reason is governing the choices of the man who refuses it. As a metaphor, this is brilliant, but because Plato took his metaphor literally, he made both of the mistakes mentioned above. To represent one person as responding to the imperious commands of another person is to represent him as acting under compulsion. Hence Plato's metaphor led him to embrace the paradox that those doing what they wish (i.e., doing the bidding of Desire) are acting against their wills. (A double standard was maintained for those doing the bidding of Reason, Reason being a more admirable tyrant than Desire.) Having personified the causes of behavior, Plato read

X's behavior was caused by Y
Therefore, X did not act voluntarily

as meaning

X's behavior was compelled by Y
Therefore, X did not act voluntarily,

and failed to notice that, unlike the second inference, which is valid, the first is a *non sequitur*. In other words, Plato's animism led him to confuse causation with compulsion and to argue, wrongly, that the only free actions are uncaused actions; that causation is incompatible with liberty. Plato thus got himself into a terrible muddle. Causation constitutes compulsion only when one is caused to do something by the threats of another person. Your desires are not another person. Therefore, they cannot, in any literal sense of the word, compel you to do anything. Hence, desires are not threats to liberty; only dictators are threats to liberty. Plato's mistake was to construe desires as dictators.

Other people have shared in this confusion partly because primitive animistic habits of mind are difficult to overcome and partly because our social institutions have been made to depend on it. Plato invented the concept of a Free Will, but St. Augustine perpetrated it, not because of its merits as psychology, but because it enabled the saint to reconcile God's goodness with human suffering. Reasoning that God commanded us to keep our souls uncorrupted and that he gave us Free Wills with the capacity to do so, Augustine was able to conclude that our suffering is the price we pay for disobeying the divine command.

In modern times, the same argument has been used by Kant to justify, not divine, but secular punishment. As Kant saw, if we thought that misdemeanors were due to antecedent causes, we would take measures to correct, not the miscreant, but his environment. However, since Kant was utterly committed to punishing those who misbehave, he concluded that we must suppose their actions to be the actions of autonomous wills. Never mind that there is no evidential basis for this assumption. Morality requires it. In short, we believe in Free Will, not because the evidence supports it, but because our religious faith and our social practices do.

What we fail to recognize is that thus basing your metaphysics on your morality is irrational. It is rational to base your practices on the facts as you know them, but irrational to base your beliefs as to the facts on what you wish to do. "I have a healthy bank account; so I can spend freely" is sound reasoning, but "I am spending freely; so I must have a healthy bank account" is wishful thinking. If the institution of punishment presupposes a false metaphysic, then we must give up the metaphysic, not argue that, since the institution entails it, the metaphysic must be true.

The impulse to revenge is irrational, something to be discouraged, not something to be shored up by bad rationalizations. Why? There are many reasons, but the best was stated by Martin Luther King, Jr.: The law of an eye for an eye and a tooth for a tooth leaves everybody blind and toothless.

There is evidence that punishment does more harm than good, that we make people behave worse by punishing them for their misdeeds. If this is true, seeking retaliation is as foolish as spitting in the wind. (I am not talking about seeking recompense. Although retributivists usually confuse the two things, they are distinct. Revenge is not recompense and compensation is not revenge.)

A more rational policy would be to seek the causes of misbehavior, in order to learn thereby how to effect its cure, but this outlook does not presuppose Free Will. On the contrary, as Moritz Schlick pointed out, this policy is based on determinism. We can seek to improve behavior by changing its causes only if it has causes.

MORALITY: WORKABILITY OR JUSTICE?

Does the end justify the means? Of course. If not what does? In order to adopt a means, what more reason does one need than knowledge that it will help one to achieve one's ends?

To be sure, the fact that my means will achieve my ends may not justify them to you, and justifications are relative. If I am trying to justify my means to you, merely pointing out that my means will achieve my ends won't do the job. To justify my means to you, I must show you that they are consistent with your ends. Indeed, the problem of justice is constituted by the need of one person to justify his actions to others, whose ends would be better served by different actions. The problem of justice arises in the conflict between ends.

How should that problem be solved? I know no answer which could satisfy everybody. Having different, perhaps even incompatible, interests, we all wish to see the problem solved in the way that is best calculated to maximize the achievement of our own ends. Therefore, if I told you how the problem ought to be solved, if I laid down my ideas of "justice," I would be doing no more than trying to get you to accept a set of principles that would maximize my interests. Instead of putting out that kind of dishonest propaganda, I prefer to engage in open and forthright negotiations: let me have things partly my way, and I won't stand in the way of your having them partly your way. The alternative is to fight, and I'm a coward.

In spite of the self-evidence of what I have just said, many people persist in believing that there are principles of justice laid up in heaven somewhere. Well, if there are any such principles, I don't know what they are, and if I did, I don't see why I, or anyone else, should accept them. What could justify your attempt to impose them on me and others?

For example, suppose that you think justice is equality, more or less. Many people do, but why should anybody who is superior to others buy egalitarianism? Rawls says, in effect, "Because he would do so if he did not know that he were superior to others." But why should this counterfactual influence anybody's behavior? Rational choices are based on facts, not on counterfactual suppositions.

Kant said that one ought to do one's duty, and regard others as equal to oneself, whether doing so is in one's interests or not. But how can one have an obligation to do what is not in one's interests, and why should one treat clear inferiors as if they were equal to oneself? Kant had no good answers to these questions, and I know of none.

What is worse, I see a great injustice in this teaching of duty and justice. It can be used, and has been used, to encourage some people to reduce their efforts in their own behalf on the baseless supposition that others are doing so. Those who believe this are apt to find themselves exploited even more than previously.

The moral problem is a practical one of figuring out how best to get along with one's fellow human beings, whose needs and interests partly coincide with one's own, but also partly conflict with one's own. I know of no high-minded solution to that practical problem. To repeat, so far as I can see, we must either negotiate or compete.

THE BASIS OF RIGHTS AND DUTIES

In response to a claim that you ought to do such and so, it is always appropriate to ask, Why? (When you may not ask this question, the answer is all too obvious.) This fact indicates, I think, that you ought to do something only if you have a good reason to do it. So far as I can see, however, the only good reason for doing something is that it is in one's interests. If this is right, you ought to do something only if doing it is in your interests. Furthermore, since saying that you have an obligation (or a duty) to do something, implies that you ought to do it, you have an obligation (or duty) to do something only if doing it is in your interests. One has no obligation to do what is not in one's interests.

I am not preaching selfishness, just rationality. A rational person does what is in his interests, but we must distinguish what is in one's interests from what is in one's selfish interests. A rational person may care for his fellow human beings, or even, like St. Francis, for all of God's creatures. Indeed, a rational person may care more for something else than he does for himself. For example, a man may love his daughter, or his friends, or his country, even more than he loves himself. In that case, their welfare is his interest, and he has a good reason to do what benefits them, even if it won't benefit him.

The point remains that, whatever a person cares for, whether himself or something else, must constitute the basis of all moral argument. Those who are rational choose effective means to their ends, but if our end is to influence someone's behavior, we are more likely to be successful if we appeal to his interests. Ethical argumentation is an exercise in practical psychology. So, it would be perfectly silly to say to someone not himself irrational, "I know that doing X is in your interests and that doing Y is contrary to them, but you have a duty to do Y nevertheless." If that means anything besides "I wish you would do X," it can only mean "I know that doing X seems to you to be in your interests, and that doing Y seems to you to be contrary to them, but you are mistaken about that. Given a larger view of things, you would see that doing Y is in your interests." For example, it makes sense to say, "Reneging on your promise might pay off now, and keeping your promise will cost you something, but you must also consider the costs to your reputation of reneging, and more importantly, you must consider the damage you will do the institution of promise-keeping, on which you, like everybody else, depend."

Because each of us naturally wants things to be done in his own interests, and because we all know that the interests of others conflict with our own, we resist accepting the principle just announced. We say, "People ought to do their duty whether it is in their interests or not," but, since each person devoutly believes that things ought to be just as he wishes them to be, this only means "I wish that people would do what is in my interests, whether their doing so is in their interests or not." That, however, ought not to prevent any of us from recognizing that influencing others requires us to appeal to their interests, not ours. If I want a raise, I must show my boss that giving it to me will increase his profits. In order to reduce cheating on insurance claims, we must convince prospective claimants that the costs of cheating outweigh its benefits. When somebody's doing X is in his interests but contrary to ours, the best hope for getting him to refrain from doing X is so to rearrange things as to make not doing X to be in his interests. If, as things stand, insurance cheaters can profit from their crimes, then we must crack down on insurance fraud. If our bosses won't pay us what we are worth, we must deprive them of our labor. The ultimate appeal in practical moral argumentation is the *argumentum ad baculuum.* Offer a carrot, but carry a stick.

What applies to duties also applies to rights, which are just their reciprocals: if X has a duty to treat Y in way W, that is because Y has a right to be treated in way W by X, and vice versa. Therefore, X has a right to be treated in way W by Y where, and only where, so treating X can be shown to be in Y's interests. As the lawyers say, there is a right where there is a remedy. For example, I have a legal right to a piece of land, which you have a duty to respect, if and only if I have the means of protecting my claim to it. I establish my right when I get the agents of the law to arrest you for trespassing. If I cannot thus protect the "right" I claim, then claiming it is whistling in the wind.

Are there no moral rights unprotected by the law? Yes, but only so long as they are protected by our moral codes and institutions. We have moral rights to truth in packaging even when we have no legal rights, but only to the extent to which we are willing and able to use informal sanctions against merchants or manufacturers who misrepresent their products. As our legal rights are protected by our legal institutions, so our moral rights are protected by our moral institutions.

Are there no natural rights, no rights protected neither by legal conventions nor by moral conventions, no rights that we have by virtue of our human nature and independently of any set of social conventions? Yes again, but only insofar as we make such rights the price of our adherence to the social conventions. As Locke understood, to claim something as a natural right is to declare that being granted it is a necessary condition of one's being willing to adhere to the social contract. To claim something as a natural right is to claim that one has no good reason to obey the rules (legal or moral) unless that right is granted. Hence, our natural rights are those we ourselves protect by threatening civil disobedience, insurrection, sabotage, or revolution.

If this is correct, might makes right. Speaking of "rights" where there is no protection for those "rights" is senseless. Since there is no God, if the state won't protect your "rights," or other people won't protect them for you, then you must protect them yourself. Should you also be unable or unwilling to protect them, you are better off recognizing that they don't exist. Demanding what you can't have is not merely foolish but dangerous. People usually don't take kindly to threats.

This account has several important morals. One is that we must not be surprised if the leaders of other nations dislike preachments about natural rights: such talk sounds to them like incitements to civil disorder. Another is that we must not demand something as a natural right unless we are deadly serious, lest our demands meet with indifference, or worse, provoke attempts at suppression. Furthermore, we must not demand something as a right without giving due consideration to whether granting our demand is consistent with the abilities and interests of those on whom we make the demand. We can expect others to be responsible (i.e., to respond constructively to our needs) only if we ourselves are responsible (i.e., respond constructively to their needs).

PRINCIPLES OF SITUATIONAL MORALITY

When discussing the meaning and source of morality, I said that intelligent behavior is adjusted to the situation, that what is right here and now might be wrong there and then, that what is right for me might be wrong for you, and so on. This, I said, is so, not because opinions differ, but because conditions do. Means effective under one set of conditions might not be effective under another set. So a course of action recommended in this set of circumstances might be utterly misguided in that one. This principle seems to me to hold in moral matters as well as in prudential ones. Indeed, I admit no distinction between the two; that is, I deny that any imprudent action is morally binding, and I deny that one is obliged to refrain from what is prudent.

Let me repeat here that I am not advocating a dog-eat-dog morality. I am not advocating that you do whatever you think you can get away with if you think there is something in it for you. On the contrary, I think we are all obliged (to use a good Anglo-Saxon expression that seems to me to have a far more exact meaning than its gassier counterpart 'obligated'· much less the still further inflated 'morally obligated') to give considera- tion to the needs and interests of others—not because doing so is right according to some transcendent standard of morality laid down by some almighty deity, but because doing so cannot be avoided if we wish to pursue our own ends effectively in a world that contains other people. As John Donne remarked, no man is an island unto himself. We need each other, and, therefore, we must help each other. Those who offend each other are liable to find themselves objects of offense. Let us, therefore, live together in mutual harmony, trying to figure out for each new situation the best mutual accommodation of interests, unencumbered by the myth that there is some higher road to salvation. Let us walk together along a path towards a better world, but let us keep an eye out for solid ground, not stumble along looking into the sky for guidance.

Comment by V. M. Tarkunde on Hocutt Article

I agree with many, and disagree with some, of Prof. Max Hocutt's observa- tions. In a brief commentary like this, the points of difference are bound to be highlighted. Given below are the points on which I am not in full agreement with Prof. Hocutt.

1. Prof. Hocutt has rightly stated that ethical rules are made by man and not by God. Man-made ethical rules, however, do not constitute the primary source of morality. Moral conduct is usually spontaneous and even impulsive, and its primary source is found, not in the prevailing

ethical rules, but in what Darwin called the "social instincts" of human beings. Biological evolution, which endowed us with altruistic (in addition to egoistic) impulses, is the main source of morality. These altruistic impulse or "social instincts" of an individual are usually assisted, and sometimes hindered, by the prevailing ethical rules which reflect themselves in social approval and disapproval. At a later stage of an individual's development, self-approval and disapproval may take the place of social approval and disapproval. While ethical rules may contribute to moral conduct, biological evolution remains the main source of morality.

2. I cannot fully share Prof. Hocutt's statement that the yardstick for evaluating ethical rules is the "satisfaction of our needs" and that "the value of moral practice... is its utility." This approach has led Prof. Hocutt to conclude that there is no absolute right or wrong, and that "a practice right for one society in one situation might be wrong for another society or under different circumstances."

It is true that, in a very indirect way, the utility principle may explain the origin of the moral conscience. Human beings have developed altruistic impulses because cooperative social relations were essential for their individual survival. But once these altruistic impulses have become a part of our mental makeup, they influence our conduct, without being directly influenced by the utility principle. If a person helps in relieving human suffering, he does so because of his impulse of sympathy, aided by the moral code which he has accepted, and not because such conduct has any utility for himself. And if he is engaged in helping a minority of the people, such as the blind or the deaf and dumb, even the principle of the greatest good of the greatest number has no relevance to his conduct.

Moral values, since they have been derived from the biologically inherited altruistic impulses, contribute to cooperative social existence. They are therefore as absolute and permanent as human society itself. What is right for one society is also right for another society, since the objective of cooperation in living is common to both. It does not happen that honesty, consideration for others, kindness, fellow-feeling, and other moral values are right for one society and wrong for another.

While considering this subject, a distinction must be made between moral values and the conduct resulting therefrom. Situations may arise when there is a conflict between two moral values, one of which is required to be adhered to in preference to the other. A situation may also arise on rare occasions when a moral value may have to be sacrificed for one's survival. Even on such occasions a morally sensitive person continues to cherish the moral values which he is, for the time being, unable to practice. The absoluteness and permanence of moral values are not negated by their occasional impracticability.

3. While the history given by Prof. Hocutt of the concept of Free Will is of absorbing interest and makes delightful reading, I do wish to say that a humanist has every reason to believe in freedom of the will. This is because in the course of his life an individual is able to develop his character so as to bring about substantial modifications in the strength and direction of his will. Each one of us has a different will today than what we had years ago and we have done a lot to make it better or worse than what it was. Our will is free because to a large extent it is our creation.

4. If the question "Does the end justify the means?" is properly formulated, it is in my view not capable of being answered in an emphatic affirmative as Prof. Hocutt has done. The question really is, Is it right to try to achieve a morally good end by recourse to morally bad means? The answer as a general rule must be in the negative, because the quality of the means normally affects the quality of the end. In other words, it is usually not possible to attain a good end except by good means.

5. I find it very difficult to appreciate Prof. Hocutt's conclusion that the conflicting ends of individuals cannot be reconciled on any generally acceptable principles of justice, that there is no reason why a superior person should treat his inferiors as if they were his equals, and that in order to reconcile our conflicting ends, we must "either negotiate or compete."

If principles of justice must differ from individual to individual, how is morality possible? If 'A' and 'B' are morally sensitive persons, their ends will be so conceived as not to cause injustice to each other. Morality implies self-imposed discipline which renders externally imposed discipline redundant. A "superior" person, if his moral development measures up to his superiority, will respect the dignity of each individual and will insist that every person, however "inferior" he may appear to be, will have the same chance of achieving success in life as anybody else. To say that in case of conflicting ends we must negotiate or compete, implies that might is right.

6. Indeed, while dealing with the basis of rights and duties, Prof. Hocutt accepts in terms the view that "might makes right." This, it appears to me, means that morality has no place in human affairs, except to the extent to which it takes the form of legal or social coercion and ceases to be itself. Morality must be voluntary; morality ends where coercion begins.

Reply by Max Hocutt to Tarkunde

Professor Tarkunde's criticism of my remarks helps me to understand and appreciate his own views better. If I still do not entirely agree with him, it is because I am less convinced than he is of the existence of what Darwin called "social instincts" and what Hume called "natural sympathy." I know of no arguments good enough (those by E. L. Wilson and other sociobiologists do not seem to me to be good enough), to prove that we are all "endowed with altruistic impulses." I have much the same skeptical attitude towards the contrary belief that we are all innately selfish.

Besides, I can't attach much moral significance to the question whether our impulses are innate or learned. The form of inference "X is innate; therefore X is good" is invalid. Ignorance is innate, but that does not make it good. If selfishness were innate, that would not make it good. So if altruism turns out to be innate, that won't make it good. It matters, of course, whether people are selfish or unselfish, but it does not matter how they got that way. If unselfishness is good, it is good whether it was learned or is innate. As I understand ethics, it must start with people as they are, not with people as they were born. So what matters morally is whether people are selfish or unselfish as we find them, not whether they were born selfish or unselfish.

Now if we speak of people as we find them, the plain fact is that some are extremely selfish and some are extremely unselfish but most are somewhere in between. A few people love nobody but themselves and a few people love everybody but themselves, but most of us love a few people besides ourselves. Since we don't all love each other, we have conflicting interests. As I see it, the question of morality is "What to do about that?"

Of course, the answer to the question is obvious: do what is right. But what is "right" to me is what advances my interests, while what is "right" to you is what advances your conflicting interests. To each person "X is right" means "doing X will advance my interests." Therefore, the obvious answer is not obviously an answer.

There would be no problem of ethics if, as Tarkunde assumes, our interests coincided. Then, by advancing your interests, I would simultaneously advance mine, and vice versa. Sometimes, of course, our interests do coincide. For example, if we both love the same person, we can both advance our common interest by doing whatever benefits that person, our common interest being that person. Furthermore, even when interests don't thus coincide, one can sometimes advance one's own interests by doing, and being rewarded for doing, what advances the interests of others. For example, by scratching your back, I can induce you to scratch mine in return. When they exist, both of these sorts of situations provide a basis for the sort of cooperative and mutually beneficial society that Tarkunde desires. I agree that such a society is the ideal, but, unlike Tarkunde, I am not so sanguine as to believe that the basis for it exists.

Just as common, I think, as coincidence of interests is divergence and conflict of interests. When such conflicts are unresolvable, there is no right or wrong. What serves your interests but defeats mine is right for you, wrong for me, and vice versa. The issue then becomes a question, not of morality, but of power: which of us will have the power to advance his own interests at the expense of the other? Where one of us enjoys the balance of power, questions of right and wrong become idle. In such a case, might makes the only right there is any point in acknowledging.

Comment by Alastair Hannay on Hocutt Article

Professor Hocutt says that our concern for others is a matter of the "best mutual accommodation of interests." The interests he talks about are the individual's own, his or her interest in happiness or the avoidance of pain, misery, and discontent. He says we help others because we need them (to help us), though the accommodation presumably means that we also "help" them *indirectly* by trimming our own interests in order to avoid trespassing unduly upon theirs. The former help seems to be no more than an extension of the individual's own personal goals, while the latter is achieved by the individual's submission to a set of man-made rules which put moral and legal constraints on those goals and on the individual's conduct. The *in*humanist alternative sketched by Hocutt is one in their opposition to which I suppose all humanists are united. It says that the coordination of interests is to be achieved by imposing an absolute, God-made morality, which denies the inherent value of natural human needs and desires, and makes their suppression a requirement of human freedom and fulfillment.

My own view differs by saying we help others not because we need them but because they need us. This is not just looking at the same facts from another point of view. Hocutt seems to me to leave something essential out, namely *mutual* human concern or care. He mentions care only once, to say, and I quite agree, that "whatever a person cares for, whether himself or something else, must constitute the basis of all moral argument." But the basis must, on my view, include a person's care for some*one* else. There are, I believe, two alternative positions for one who accepts, as I do and perhaps Hocutt also, that mutual concern is a human value. One is the view that natural sympathy is too restricted in scope to be the foundation of social morality. Rather, social morality, as a system of constraints designed to protect individual interests and rights, has *first* to be founded in order to protect, among other rights, that of exercising natural sympathy within the immediate circle to which it "naturally" belongs. The other view, expressed in my own paper, is that this sympathy is the root of social morality, that it provides the proper insights for locating the constraints (for constraining *them*), and that the general intention behind these should be that of widening the scope of this natural capacity, thus blurring the rather sharp distinctions we tend initially to make between our own others and others in general. Although I appear to disagree fundamentally with Hocutt on this, the disagreement strikes me as being one that can be discussed and even resolved within a humanistic framework. On the other hand, or rather because of that, agreement here does not seem to me to be a matter of great urgency. What is more pressing is the need to develop or enrich the conceptual content of the humanistic framework itself.

In this respect I find Hocutt's paper a little disappointing. The humanism he offers as an alternative to theism is based on distinctions which many people would now reject as failing to do justice to human reality. Indeed their inadequacy is closely linked with their having been developed within the kind of metaphysics which humanists oppose. I see no reason why a humanist must accept determinism just because free will has so long been associated with theism. It is not impossible that we may arrive at humanistic conceptions of free will and responsibility which do better justice to human reality than traditional determinism, though of course determinism too might be developed in ways which make it fit, or throw light on, the human case.

Finally, although my own paper says too little about the connection between rights and rules, I think Hocutt stresses unduly the function of rules in ethics. True, humanists do indeed differ from others by the answer they give to the question, "Who makes the rules, God or men?"; but having given it, the main question facing them is not, "Who says I should do *X*?" or "How do I establish my right to do *X*?", but, "What is the value in doing *X*?" or "Why should an ability to do *X* be protected or encouraged?" What is unhumanistic, not to say inhuman, about a theistic answer (and not all theistic answers are unhumanistic in this respect) is not that the rules are not man-made, but that nothing that is man-made, including what man makes of himself, is said to have inherent value. Once that prohibition is lifted we are left with the task of agreeing upon what *is* value-able, not only in the man-made world, but in the natural world as a whole. If I understand Hocutt's remarks on rights correctly, he would not assign rights to animals since they cannot claim them. This for me is symptomatic of an unfortunate anthropocentrism to which humanists are too easily prone, and which is reinforced by making the question of who makes the rules the fundamental one. Values are not pieces of legislation; legislation is, or should be, a rational response to our experience of values.

Reply by Max Hocutt to Hannay

Professor Hannay locates the difference between us in our metaphysics. If by "metaphysics" he means beliefs as to what is real, he is right; we have different metaphysics. If by "metaphysics" he means belief in such trans-empirical entities as God and the soul, the difference between us is that he bases his morality on metaphysics and I don't. Thus, where Hannay postulates an autonomous will, human equality, and natural rights as bases for his morality, I reject such postulates for their lack of empirical justification.

Since the issue between us does turn on differences in metaphysics, Professor Hannay begs the question when he accuses me of "failing to do justice to human reality." That means merely "Hocutt does not accept Hannay's concept of human reality." But why should I? Why should I believe in that for which there is not a shred of empirical evidence? So far as I can see, the only reason that Hannay has is that, without his metaphysics, he would have no rational basis for his morality; but the right conclusion to draw from these premises is that Hannay's morality has no rational basis.

The issue can be focused on two points. First, Hannay objects that I must reject talk of "animal rights" as nonsensical. Apparently he thinks that this result constitutes a *reductio ad absurdum* of my views, but one man's *reductio ad absurdum* is another man's *modus ponens*. For the reasons I have stated, talk of "animal rights" is nonsensical. Second, Hannay says that "natural sympathy" is a sufficient basis for his kind of morality. That may be so, but Hannay nowhere gives us any reason to believe that everybody has a "natural sympathy" for others, and the behavioral evidence suggests that some do, but others don't. Revealingly, Hannay confuses my recognition of the existence of egoism with advocacy of egoism. Blurring this distinction is characteristic of those who, like Hannay, base their metaphysics on their morality, for, as they reason, if people ought to be unselfish, then people must already have a disposition to be unselfish. Therefore, Hannay postulates "natural sympathy" as the basis of a humanistic morality. Well, if "humanistic morality" requires such fictions, we are better off without it.

Towards a Fuller Consensus in Humanistic Ethics

V. M. Tarkunde

THE MEANING AND SOURCE OF MORALITY

What is morality?

According to criminal jurisprudence, an offense consists of two components—criminal intention and criminal act. Intention without any act in pursuance thereof, or an act not accompanied by the necessary intention, do not constitute an offense. No offense is committed if one intends to steal somebody's umbrella without actually proceeding to take it; no offense is also committed if one takes away somebody's umbrella thinking is to be one's own.

Morality also has two corresponding components — intention and conduct. It is the latter component, consisting of do's and don'ts, which is emphasized in the moral codes of different societies. But conduct, unaccompanied by the necessary mental component, is not moral conduct. "Thou shalt not steal" is an injunction common to all moral codes, but a person who desists from stealing, even when he is tempted do do so, is not necessarily moral. He may desist from stealing because he is afraid of the law, in which case his conduct is lawful but not moral. He may also desist from stealing because he is afraid of punishment in hell, in which case his conduct is wise or foolish (depending upon whether his fear is or is not well founded) but not moral. His conduct is moral when he desists from stealing because he feels that it is not right to do so.

Moral conduct is often instinctive. Sometimes it is deliberate, involving a choice between two or more alternatives. In either case the mental component of moral behavior can be identified as consisting of certain values such as kindness, honesty, truthfulness, and so forth. Morality consists of conduct impelled by such values.

Since the concept of value is often needlessly mystified, it is desirable that we should be clear about what a value means. Anything which is 'good' has a value. Value consists of the goodness of what is good. It is the quality of being valuable. The question to ask, however, is, Valuable to whom? A climate which is not congenial to disease-carrying germs is 'good' for human beings; it is clearly not 'good' for the germs. Malarial fever is obviously bad for human beings but probably 'good' for the germs which multiply in the human body and cause the fever. Value consists of whatever is valuable to human beings.

Obviously, values are of different kinds. Some of them, such as the cleanliness or climate or wholesomeness of food, are related to a person's physical well-being. Other values like courage, discretion, and perseverance are mental qualities which are useful to an individual's success in life. Moral values fall into a third category. They have a social purpose. They contribute to the maintenance of a mutually beneficial, cooperative society. Kindness, honesty, truthfulness, and on a higher level of sophistication, justice and equality—all these and other moral values have this common characteristic. They are "valuable" because cooperative social existence is essential to the well-being of the human individual.

Morality then consists of conduct impelled by moral values, and moral values are values which contribute to cooperative social existence.

Source of morality

Modern science is reared on the basic postulate that no supernatural factor interferes in the affairs of the world. Increasing knowledge of the physical world has been made possible on the basis of this postulate of monistic naturalism. Since man is part of nature, the same postulate must be adhered to for understanding the complexities of the human mind and behavior. We must therefore look into the history of biological evolution to discover the sources of the various attributes and impulses of human beings, including the moral impulses.

Struggle for existence is the basic characteristic of the entire biological world. In the course of that struggle, different biological species have developed marvelous adaptations which serve the primary purpose of survival. It is not surprising that in the animal world such adaptations are mental as well as physical. In the long history of biological evolution, the ancestors of *homo sapiens* and *homo sapiens* himself must have developed appropriate adaptive mental attributes. Man's will as well as man's reason are thus the products of biological evolution.

Homo sapiens is a gregarious species. The biological ancestors of *homo sapiens* had probably the same characteristic. Living together in cooperative communities was obviously necessary for the survival of individual human beings. Society gave protection to the human individual and passed on to him such knowledge as was accumulated in the past. Cooperative social relations being essential for the survival of the human individual, it was but natural that during the aeons of biological evolution, the human mind should have developed complimentary attributes. That is the source of what Darwin called the "social instincts" of man—the instincts or impulses which go into the formation of moral values.

Moral behavior of a rudimentary type is found in the higher animals and can be traced even to lower forms of life. This fact is enough to establish that the source of morality is biological and not theological. Religion cannot be the source of morality, because the process of moral development started before the emergence of religion.

As Spinoza emphasized, human beings are not only conscious but also self-conscious. They not only feel, but know what they feel. When they experience an impulse of kindness and say to themselves that this is a good impulse, a value is born. Moral values arise from the appreciation of moral impulses.

In the course of biological evolution, human beings have developed competitive or egoistic, as well as cooperative or altruistic, impulses. The former were just as necessary for the individual's survival as the latter. Moral development requires that the competitive or egoistic impulses of the individual should be subordinated to the cooperative or altruistic impulses.

Moral development of the individual

In early life the moral development of the individual is brought about almost entirely by his elders in the family and by the rest of society. The individual therefore absorbs the current social norms, including those which are socially inequitable or individually restrictive. His conduct is guided by the necessity of social approval. He internalizes social norms and is afraid to transgress them. In later life, some individuals develop sufficient intellectual independence to examine the authenticity of the prevailing social norms and to develop their own scale of values. Their morality becomes progressively voluntary. It consists, not of external authority internalized, but of internal authority externalized. They are free as well as moral. Their conduct is guided by self-approval, more than by social approval.

Inadequate understanding of human nature leads to the traditional belief that man is basically selfish and that he can act morally only under the compulsion of the spiritual sanction of religion or the physical sanction of the penal code. Once it is realized that man is endowed with altruistic as well as egoistic impulses, it becomes obvious that morality need not be imposed on him by spiritual or physical coercion. By giving vent to his natural altruistic impulses, he can act morally of his own accord.

Generally speaking, the fulfillment of a natural impulse leads to the satisfaction of the individual. This applies to altruistic as well as egoistic impulses. If you behave kindly towards another person, or perform a well-deserved act of charity, you experience a tangible sense of satisfaction. On the other hand an act of unkindness, done by yielding to an egoistic impulse, gives you tangible pain, and if you are morally sensitive, wipes out whatever pleasure you might have derived from the fulfillment of the egoistic impulse. That is how moral life is essentially a life of enlightened selfishness. It is a life of happiness derived from the satisfaction of the natural moral impulses. From the point of view of an external observer, you are leading a selfless, altruistic life; from your own experience, you are living in a delightfully selfish way. The moral life was never better described than by Epicurus. He is reported to have said; "I want to be moral, not to please the gods, but to please myself."

The moral development of a free individual is essentially a function of the individual's rational faculty. The choice between rival impulses in a given situation is a rational process. If the individual decides to give vent to his moral impulse and to curb his antimoral impulses on a particular occasion, the reason is that he regards a morally enlightened life as the happier life. It is often said that reason has only an instrumental value; that it enables you to adopt appropriate means to achieve a particular end, but not to make a choice between two ends. Like most other fallacies in the sphere of ethics, this fallacy also results from the naive assumption that moral life is a life of suffering and that it cannot be freely chosen by a rational individual. Once it is realized that morality is an essential part of an enlightened life and that an enlightened life is far more satisfactory to an individual than a life of mere physical enjoyment, reason becomes the main instrument of an individual's moral development.

Some explanation is perhaps necessary of the above statement that an enlightened life is far more satisfactory to an individual than a life of mere physical enjoyment. Human life is enriched in quality when those natural impulses which are individually and socially beneficial become independent and additional sources of satisfaction. This process can be illustrated with the aid of a simple instance. The food impulse is obviously associated with the primary urge for survival. The impulse, however, becomes an independent and additional source of satisfaction when food is eaten, not merely for physical sustenance, but also for the enjoyment of its taste. One may partake of food only for its taste, even when one is not hungry. In a comparable way, the natural human impulse to search for the necessities of life develops into a search for truth, and the fulfillment of this impulse becomes an independent and additional source of satisfaction to the individual. Every one can recall the deep satisfaction he experienced when, as a student, he was able to solve a problem in geometry or an equation in algebra. The search impulse can thus become the source of tremendous additional satisfaction derived from the search for truth and acquisition of knowledge. Human life is enriched in another direction by the satisfaction derived from art and beauty, and in yet another direction by the satisfaction derived from the fulfillment of our moral impulses. The Greek ideals of truth, beauty, and goodness (corresponding to the ancient Indian ideals of Satyam, Sundaram, and Shivam) represent the enrichment of human life by the manifold satisfactions derived from intellectual, aesthetic, and moral pursuits. These satisfactions are consistent with, and additional to, the satisfaction derived from a balanced fulfillment of our physical ("animal") appetites. Such an enlightened life, of which morality is an integral part, can be rationally preferred by an individual to a life of mere physical enjoyment. Reason can enable us, not only to choose the means to attain a particular end, but also to choose one end in preference to another.

We have seen earlier that the moral impulses in man are rationally connected with the primary urge for survival, because cooperative social existence was essential for the survival of the individual. We have also seen that, on the conscious plane, reason enables an individual to prefer a morally enlightened life as the better (because happier) life. Reason, objective as well as subjective, is thus the basis of the emergence and development of morality. To the extent to which man is moral, he is so because he is rational.

Moral development of society

Morality prevailing in a community is not merely the sum total of the morality of the individuals who constitute the community. Reason plays a more decisive role in the moral development of society than the role it plays in the moral development of an individual. Spread of rationalism enables the disadvantaged sections of society to rid themselves of spiritual and material exploitation and to establish a more just and more equitable social order.

It is possible that in the earlier stages of human civilization, religion had played a positive function in curbing the turbulent egocentric tendencies of unruly individuals. In more recent times, its role has been largely negative. Religious orthodoxy buttressed the exploitation of the people by priests, princes, and landlords. It also helped the old to dominate the young and the male to dominate the female. It set up false (because biologically untenable) ideals of austerity, self-denial, and even self-torture, and led to self-deception and social deception on a vast scale. Moral standards improved when, with the spread of rationalism, religious orthodoxy began to decline and the underprivileged majority could gradually rise in human dignity and become self-reliant and assertive of its social rights. Except perhaps at the early period of civilization, the equation between religion and moral standards in society has been negative, not positive. If there is again an apparent fall in moral standards today, the reason is not that religion has declined, but that society is becoming increasingly more complex and requires an increasingly higher level of morality.

Fact vs. Value

Philosophers often amuse themselves with self-created conundrums. One such conundrum consists of the question whether values can be derived from facts, and if not, whether one value-system can be said to be better than another. A fact, it is pointed out, consists of what "is," whereas a value indicates what "should be." From what is, you cannot infer what should be. It is claimed therefore that there cannot be a science of values, and that one value-system cannot be held to be superior to another.

The question ceases to be intriguing as soon as it is realized that the values we are discussing are human values, not values in the abstract, nor the values of some other biological species. There is, therefore, a standard for judging the goodness of the values we cherish. A value is 'good' if it is good for human beings. There are, and will be, differences on whether a particular value-system is good for human beings. But once there is a commonly acceptable standard of judgment (namely, the good of human beings), the differences can be discussed on a rational plane. Moral philosophy, since it is concerned with one class of values, can therefore be legitimately looked upon as a social science.

A little thinking will show that moral philosophy is basic to other social sciences like politics and economics. Controversies in political and economic theories are often the result of different value-systems consciously or unconsciously cherished by the adversaries. Increasing consensus on the underlying system of values would widen the noncontroversial areas in the political and economic sciences.

It is generally recognized that one value can be rationally derived from another. If good health of human beings is a value, temperance in the enjoyment of physical pleasures can also be deduced as a value. It follows that if any one value can be rationally established as the basic human value, a coherent value system can be deduced from that basic value.

Since survival is the primary urge of the whole biological world, the basic human value must have a direct connection with the human urge to live. But a human being would rather die than live permanently on a subhuman level. The basic human urge is to live a "human" life.

Freedom the basic value

While many values are widely cherished, freedom is the value which has the most universal appeal. The reason probably is that freedom means the freedom to live on the human plane. It implies not only freedeom from externally imposed restrictions, but also freedom from want and insecurity. The struggle for freedom is the struggle for existence on the human plane. So understood, freedom is the basic value from which a hierarchy of values can be derived.

Society is not a biological entity. Values can be conceived and cherished only by individuals and not by any collectivity. It follows that society is for the individuals who compose it, and not vice versa. The function of society is to promote the freedom (success in life) of its constituents. Society is the means; the individual, the end. It is, however, inherent in the logic of social existence that society is for all the individuals who compose it, and not for only some of them. Since all the individuals in a society aspire to live as human beings, and since all of them are capable of achieving that objective in different degrees, society must ensure equal opportunity to all its constituents to achieve success in life. It must respect the dignity of each individual and eliminate discrimination arising from race, religion, age, sex, class, or inherited wealth. Equality means equal freedom for all.

A society cannot promote the freedom and equality of its constituents unless mutual relations therein are governed by honesty, justice, kindness, and the other moral values which make a society truly fraternal. Freedom and equality are not capable of being realized except in a moral society—a society of moral men and women. Freedom, equality, and fraternity are thus the essential elements of a good culture.

Is one culture better than another?

A culture has many facets. One of its important facets is the value-system it represents. In practice we do prefer one culture to another on the basis of our preferred values.

What is stated earlier shows that there can be a rational standard for judging the "goodness" of the value-system represented by any culture. A society's culture can be judged on the extent to which freedom, equality, and fraternity are available to the individuals who compose it.

These values—freedom, equality, and fraternity—are known to be the basic values of democracy. Although democracy has not been realized to a material extent in any part of the world so far, it is remarkable that even those countries which have departed widely from the democratic ideal prefer to attach some democratic appellation to themselves. This is perhaps an indication that there is a great deal of "truth" in these values.

HUMANKIND AND NATURE—FREE WILL AND RESPONSIBILITY

Inherent rationality of human beings

The word 'rational' is used in two different senses. Human beings are both rational and irrational, depending on the sense in which the word 'rational' is used.

The thinking faculty, the faculty of associating two events or things as cause and effect, is inherent in human nature. In the absence of such a faculty, a human being could not have survived even for a day. If a child extends his hand towards a fire, and if he does not apprehend that the heat he feels is caused by the fire, he would be burnt to death. He realizes instinctively that fire burns and withdraws his hand. Even the instinct of food requires for its fulfillment an appreciation of the connection between hunger and the means by which it can be assuaged.

In a rudimentary form, instinctive reasoning faculty is found in the higher animals and is probably present in the entire animal world. Its origin can be traced to determinism in nature. It is indisputable that the whole biological world tends to adapt itself to physical nature. Since physical nature is law-governed, only those forms of life survive whose consciousness possesses the rudimentary faculty of reason. Reason is thus a biological adaptation to physical determinism. Because man is an animal, he is rational.

Indeed the obvious superiority of human beings to the rest of the animal world is derived solely from the fact that the instinctive thinking faculty is more developed in humans than in any other biological species. Knowledge is the source of man's power, and knowledge is acquired by synthesizing experience with the aid of reason. The distinction of human beings lies, not in the power of their limbs or the force of their emotions, but in their greater ability to think and to know.

While man is thus 'rational' in the sense that the reasoning faculty is an inherent part of his mental makeup, he is often not 'rational' if by that term we mean a person whose reason is free from the domination of emotions and preconceived notions. In other words, reason is an inherent part of human nature but not necessarily the dominant part.

Ignorance and fear are the main factors which induce a person to adhere to beliefs which had a 'rational' origin in the past but which, in view of modern knowledge, no longer have a 'rational' justification. Many instances can be given, but one would suffice. The biblical story of creation was a 'rational' hypothesis of how man and the world could have come into existence. It was 'rational' because the belief that the world must have had a cause had its origin in man's inherent rationality. While being 'rational' in this sense, the belief in the biblical story is not 'rational' in the other sense, as it is contrary to the overwhelming evidence about physical and biological evolution.

Free will and determinism

The problem of free will arises in two different types of questions. One question is, How far is human will free (i.e., potent) in shaping history? Are events determined by factors other than the human will, the latter being merely an "epiphenomenon" which has no effective role to play? The other question is, In a given situation, is not the strength and direction of the human will already predetermined by other factors? Just as, in the case of an interplay of several physical forces, you are able to anticipate the energy and direction of the resultant force, can you not, supposing you had the requisite knowledge, anticipate how a particular person will act in a particular situation? If the theory of determinism requires you to answer this question in the affirmative, is it not a fact that when a person makes a choice between two alternatives and feels that his choice was freely made, he does not really act as a free agent and that his will is not really free in making the choice?

In deciding whether a human being is a free moral agent, it is the latter type of question that we have to deal with. If a person, faced with a moral choice, yields to temptation and acts contrary to his moral judgment, a determinist will have to concede that the person was not a free agent in making the choice. Was he then not responsible for the moral lapse?

The answer is that the person in the above instance *was* responsible for the moral lapse, despite the fact that in the given situation all the factors which resulted in the lapse, including the force of his will, were what they were and the result was therefore inevitable. What was not inevitable was the weakness of his will in relation to the temptation which it had to face at the given moment. A human being is responsible for his actions because he has the capacity to mold his character. His failure to do so may render his lapses inevitable but he is responsible for the lapses nevertheless. It is true of course that social environment influences the character of an individual, but the individual also plays a decisive part in shaping or failing to shape his own character. Determinism does not exclude freedom of the will, because to some extent the human will is self-determined. Man is the maker of his future because he is the maker of himself.

The process of character formation goes on throughout the individual's lifetime. In early age, the process is guided by parents and other elders in society. In later life, the process is guided by oneself. A person gradually learns to control his impulses and to avoid mistakes committed in the past. The unpleasant consequences of the earlier mistake teach him to avoid a similar mistake on a second occasion. Although his will was "determined" on both the occasions, it was stronger and therefore more "free" on the second occasion. Free will is not inconsistent with determinism.

MORALITY AS WORKABILITY VS. MORALITY AS JUSTICE

Ends and means

When it is claimed that a good end justifies bad means employed to achieve it, the question to ask is whether a good end remains good if it is achieved by bad means.

It is easy to see that bad means compromise the goodness of a good end and what is achieved is an inferior version of the initial objective. In most cases, therefore, the employment of bad means is not justified.

Take the ordinary case of an employee who has a modest salary and a large family to support. Would he be justified in committing a fraud on his employer in order to maintain himself and his family in greater comfort? The answer will, of course, be in the negative. Even if the fraud succeeds, he would have in the result made himself a morally coarser and inferior person, a result not justified by the greater physical comfort achieved by himself and his family members.

The employee in the above instance had the choice of continuing to work on a modest salary without recourse to fraud, and that is why the means chosen by him were morally responsible. An end which cannot be attained except by immoral means is usually not worth attaining. This, however, cannot be an invariable rule. There are occasions when the only choice before a person is between two evils. The choice in such cases is by no means easy to make.

164   V. M. Tarkunde

It is not necessary to multiply instances of situations of this type. Books on morality are full of such true or imaginary situations. A typical case is that of a country craft on the open sea which contains four survivors, one of whom must die if the other three are to be saved. Since it is obviously preferable that one should die rather than all the four, the unavoidable conclusion is that the death of one of them, preferably the oldest of the lot, would be morally justified.

In all such cases, the choice is not between one of two possible means to achieve an end, but between two moral ends, one of which is to be sacrificed for achieving the other.

A choice between two moral principles, sacrificing one for the other, has often to be made in life. This topic, however, falls logically under the heading Principles in Situational Morality.

Greatest good of the greatest number

Since a good end does not justify bad means, the principle of the greatest good of the greatest number cannot be an absolute principle of State policy. Interests of the few should not be sacrificed for the good of the many, unless the latter cannot be achieved without the former. Sacrifice of the interests of the few would be justified only when the alternative is to sacrifice the interests of the many.

An instance in point is the recent abolition of the Zamindari system (absentee landlordism) in India. Abolition of landlordism was essential in the interests of the vast number of small cultivators. It was, on the other hand, not possible to pay full compensation to the landlords for the extinguishment of their rights. These rights were therefore extinguished by paying a very moderate compensation. The measure was morally justified.

The hub of morality

It has been submitted earlier that morality consists of those values which contribute to cooperative social existence, values which in other words make a 'good' society. Honesty, kindness, love, equality, and justice are instances of these values. Each moral value is vital in some situations and not in others.

The basic human value is freedom, which means the right of a human being to live a human life. Since cooperative social existence is essential for individual freedom, all moral values are contributory to the basic value of freedom. Among the moral values, none can be said to be the hub of morality.

BASIS OF RIGHTS AND DUTIES

Rights, duties, obligations

While law is essentially coercive, morality is essentially voluntary. Rights and duties (obligations) are legal concepts. Rights and duties can be enforced by law. To bring these concepts into the voluntary sphere of morality is to cause confusion.

If one person is kind to another, it is because he has the natural impulse of fellow-feeling which he might have encouraged in himself as a cherished value. It is misleading to say that it is his "duty" to be kind or that it is the "right" of his counterpart to receive kindness. The same is true of other moral values like honesty, truthfulness, and the like.

Law begins where morality ends. If you give false evidence, you fail in your duty and are punished by law. Even if you give true evidence but you do so for fear of legal consequences, you are acting lawfully but not morally. You are moral when you give true evidence because you do not like telling lies.

We do of course speak of moral duties, moral obligations, and moral rights. That appears to be a legacy of the time when human nature was believed to be wholly selfish and morality was consequently regarded as something imposed on the individual by society. If we appreciate that human beings have social impulses and that a moral life is a life of enlightened happiness, we would cease to think of morality in terms of rights and duties.

Human equality

All humans are not born with the same physical or mental attributes. They differ in their physical and mental abilities. Yet they are entitled to be treated equally and without discrimination.

The reasons are, firstly, that all humans have the basic biological urge to live, to live as humans. They have, in other words, the same basic urge for freedom. They are consequently ends in themselves, and not the means to the end of any other person or body of persons.

Secondly, all humans have the basic biological faculty of rationality, the ability to think. They may differ in the extent of that faculty, but the existence of the faculty in all humans cannot be denied. Consequently, all humans have the ability to learn, to know, and to progress in life, in the attainment of freedom. They must, therefore, have an equal opportunity to make a success of their lives, although they may not succeed in life to the same extent by making use of the equal opportunity made available to them.

Thirdly, a society is not a biological being. It is not by itself capable of feeling pleasure or pain, or experiencing progress. An individual cannot therefore be asked to sacrifice for society or for any other collectivity. Society is a means and not an end. The purpose of social existence is to promote the success in life of the individuals who constitute the society. Now, in the absence of any justifying principle, society must promote equally the interests of all its constituents, and not of some of them at the cost of others. There is no principle on which society would be justified in giving better opportunities to some to succeed in life than to others. Society is therefore for all the individuals who compose it and not for only some of them.

The principle of equality has different implications in the economic, the social, and the political spheres.

In the economic sphere, the principle of equality implies that all the constituents of society should have an equal opportunity of receiving education and securing employment (including self-employment) in gainful activity. It also implies equal pay for equal work to men and women, and a limitation on disparities of income and wealth of different individuals and families.

In the social sphere, the principle of equality implies nondiscrimination on the ground of race, religion, sex, age, place of birth, or any of them. One person may attain higher social status than another, but the difference must be attributable to his individual attainment or contribution to society.

In the political sphere, the principle of equality implies the widest diffusion of political power. Adult franchise and decentralization of both power and responsibility, are some of the possible means of political equality.

PRINCIPLES IN SITUATIONAL MORALITY

When is deviation from principle justified?

Since moral principles are derived from moral values, the above question may be formulated thus: When is departure from a moral value justified?

It appears that as a general rule, departure from one moral value is justified only when adherence to another moral value is preferable in a given situation. The only exception to this rule is the rare instance when saving oneself is clearly preferable to compliance with a moral value.

Situations of moral conflict, when one moral value is required to be sacrificed in preference to another, occur frequently in life. Take the case of a doctor who is treating a cancer patient and is asked by the patient about the time when he is likely to get better. Suppose further that the patient does not know the nature of his ailment and that the doctor knows that the patient would die within a few days. The doctor has to decide between telling the truth and being kind to the patient. Unless the patient is known to be a strong-minded person, the doctor will prefer to tell a lie in order to save the patient from avoidable mental agony.

Does the doctor act immorally in telling a lie? No, if he is conscious of the moral conflict and feels sorry for being required to tell a lie. Yes, if he tells a lie without feeling any discomfort, with no qualm of conscience.

It is important to notice that when the doctor acted morally in the above instance, he had not really departed from either of the two moral values. He continued to cherish the values of truthfulness as well as kindness, although the situation compelled him to act in accordance with one in preference to the other.

The same principle applies in more complex and morally tormenting situations, like the instance of a country craft on the open sea when one person has to die in order that the other three may survive. In such a situation, if killing becomes quite unavoidable "killing with kindness" may become a moral necessity.

It is more difficult to say when one is justified in saving oneself by sacrificing a moral value. There would be some occasions when sacrificing one's life may be morally necessary, others when saving oneself would be the right course. No generalization appears to be possible. It would certainly not be proper to say that one should never save oneself by acting contrary to a moral value. If you are ambushed and caught by an enemy and you can escape by telling a lie, why not do so?

Are moral values permanent?

Since the biological origin and rational purpose of moral values is to enable individual human beings to have a cooperative social existence, moral values are as permanent as human society itself. Kindness, honesty, truthfulness, fellow feeling, and other moral values will exist as long as human beings exist and live in social groups.

Situational morality, as explained above, does not imply that any moral value is required to be abandoned in a given situation. A morally sensitive person, even when he is required to act contrary to a moral value, continues to cherish that value and remains a moral being. Moral conflict does not affect the permanence of moral values.

Comment by Alastair Hannay on Tarkunde Article

I agree with most of what Tarkunde says about free will and determinism, about ends and means, and about which values (kindness, love, honesty, truthfulness, equality, and justice) are to be counted among the moral ones. And I think he is right in saying that no one of these values should be singled out as pivotal, since which of them is (are) central will, as Tarkunde says, depend on the situation. I also agree that "morality consists of conduct impelled by such values," and furthermore, that if these values *are* to impel that conduct they must be seen to contribute to some more basic value, since moral values themselves are not inherently appealing. Where we seem to disagree is in our understanding of this more basic value.

In line with his evolutionary approach to the justification of moral conduct, Tarkunde links it with the urge to survival, a goal for which the immediate product of moral behavior, a "cooperative social existence," is an essential requirement. In its developed form the urge to survival becomes the urge to live a "human" life, or more generally the individual's desire for his or her "well-being," and the ability to live this life or to achieve this state is what Tarkunde calls "human freedom." Thus moral conduct commends itself to the individual because it contributes via social cohesion to the individual's own betterment or fulfillment. One leads a moral life, a life of "enlightened selfishness," because it secures one the satisfaction of "natural moral impulses."

If, as Tarkunde accepts, acting morally is to do, or refrain from doing, something because one *feels* that the alternative (not doing it or doing it, as the case may be) would not be right, what one satisfies, surely, is not first and foremost an impulse to improve one's own lot, but an impulse to obviate or alleviate the suffering of another sentient being. What must be *felt* is not the rightness of one's own enrichment through the exercise of compassion, but the wrongness of the other's disenrichment, a feeling which prompts the compassion and is not evoked by it. A person who lacks compassion may be led to exercise benevolence, or to act in kindly ways, by being told that it pays, as no doubt it does, in the ways Tarkunde says. Perhaps, as Kant suggests, the habit of kindliness is one way of acquiring the capacity for compassion. But for a person who genuinely has that capacity, whose feeling for the rightness of his or her acts is aroused by the needs of others, the thought that the moral life pays in these ways will be irrelevant. And were such a person to turn devil's advocate, he or she could probably find as many reasons for warning the moral novice off the moral life as for recommending it.

The evolutionary perspective forces the facts of human society into too narrow a mold. Once it is allowed that rudimentary moral behavior exists in higher (nonhuman) animals, and can even be traced to "lower forms of life," it is difficult to admit that evolved morality contains anything essentially new. I think it obviously does, not least in virtue of what is specific to *human* powers of cognition and reason, and compassion. A humanist should have no difficulty in accepting that. Moreover, the assumption that the justification for morality must be that it pays off, together with the evolutionary argument that it always has (otherwise we wouldn't be here!), as if the justification of moral behavior was built into the species by virtue of its very existence, blinds us to the real problems—the need for the enlargement and dissemination of moral insight. That is why I argue in my own paper that the justification for moral behavior is basically cognitive, that the appeal of the moral life to us humans must be to a sense of the irrationality and injustice of confining our natural "moral" responses to the immediate circle, which is where evolution has left them. On the whole, I would say that the moral life, or one might force the point by saying the moral life we need in our time—though I would hesitate to recommend the moral life because it is needed, since that too seems to me to direct attention away from the source of the genuine moral impulse—is a more strenuous life than the one Tarkunde portrays. I think I would like to offer the Stoic as a counterbalance to Tarkunde's Epicurean. Neither of them wants to be moral because it pleases the gods, but Epicurus' idea that one should want to be moral to please oneself seems complacent and superficial when contrasted with the Stoic's sense of the need to serve the interests of others, and his awareness of the obstacles in the way of the cultivation of this sense and of its practical expression.

Reply by V. M. Tarkunde to Hannay

The editor of this Symposium prescribed, very rightly, a certain limitation of space within which every contributor had to attempt a presentation of his views on different aspects of humanistic ethics. This limitation, coupled with the inherent complexity of the subject, led to a considerable terseness of expression and consequent lack of clarity, which can be a fruitful source of misunderstanding. It appears to me that Professor Hannay's comment is to a large extent the result of such lack of clarity on my part. I am glad that he has given me an opportunity of clarifying some parts of my original contribution which have apparently remained vague and misleading.

Hannay has understood me to say that when an individual acts on his impulse of compassion and tries to alleviate the suffering of another, he does so "because it contributes via social cohesion to the individual's own betterment in life." That is not my view. In fact, I agree with Hannay that the individual in such a case is actuated by the impulse to alleviate the suffering of another and not by the impulse to improve his own lot. I would, however, emphasize in this connection a psychological fact of vital importance which appears to have escaped Hannay's notice. A compassionate person suffers with the suffering of others, and when he tries to alleviate the misery of another person, he is incidentally trying to alleviate his own misery as well. He would suffer even more if he were to do nothing to help a suffering individual. On the other hand, if his help achieves the desired result, he is positively happy. That is why his compassionate act is also an act of enlightened self-interest.

I have referred to social cohesion, or rather to "co-operative social existence," in an entirely different context. If the impulse of compassion is one of the main moral impulses, as it undoubtedly is, where does it come from? Why is a compassionate individual compassionate? Is compassion a God-given gift or a product of biological evolution? In his own paper Hannay has not dealt with this question. I have expressed the view that since the urge for survival is the primary urge of all biological species, and since cooperative social living was essential for the very survival of *homo sapiens*, the moral impulses of human beings which facilitate such cooperative association are a natural product of biological evolution. Correspondingly, the social purpose of moral values, the reason why they are "valuable," is that they contribute to a cooperative social life.

To say this is not to say that when an individual acts on a moral impulse such as the impulse of compassion, he does so with the conscious object of securing his own betterment via social cohesion. I have already in my paper given instances to show how an impulse, arising from the basic urge for survival, becomes an independent source of satisfaction. Let me, however, take a more telling instance. The sex impulse is undoubtedly connected with the survival of the species. In the fierce biological struggle for existence, the species *homo sapiens* could not have survived unless its members had a well-developed sex instinct. To say this, however, is not to say that when a human individual acts on his sex impulse, his object is to augment the species. Very often he takes steps to prevent that result, because the sex impulse has become an independent source of satisfaction. Similarly, a person who acts on the impulse of compassion does so in order to fulfill that impulse and not to secure a cooperative society for the betterment of his own lot.

Hannay has also assumed that, according to me, "moral values themselves are not inherently appealing" and that "they must be seen to contribute to some more basic value" if they are to impel moral conduct. Hannay agrees with this view, but it is not my view at all. My view is that every moral impulse, when fulfilled, is an independent source of satisfaction and that, therefore, it *is* inherently appealing. While dealing with a very different subject, namely the distinction between facts and values and the question whether there can be a science of morality, I pointed out that all values are human values, that existence on the human level (freedom) is therefore the basic value, and that other values (including moral values) can be rationally derived therefrom. The question in that context was whether values can have a scientific justification, and not whether they are inherently appealing.

I have some difference with Hannay in regard to his statement that the moral life of our time is a "strenuous life" and his preference to the Stoic as against the Epicurean. At an early stage of an individual's moral development, when he tries to see that his egoistic impulses are subordinated to his altruistic impulses, some strain is necessarily involved. When that stage is over, moral behavior is voluntary and without strain. Morality then is a matter of self-expression and not of self-denial. Surely it is much better to be an Epicurean than a Stoic, to be a cheerful person who is voluntarily and spontaneously moral than a cheerless person who is under the constant tyranny of his puritanic self.

The evolutionary approach adopted by me does not imply that the moral development of man and society is confined to what is achieved by biological (i.e., genetic) evolution. I have explained in my paper how the inherited moral impulses of man are molded by social approval and disapproval and later by self-approval and self-disapproval, and how the spread of rationalism in society helps its moral development. The "psycho-social" (Julian Huxley) or "socio-genetic" (C.H. Waddington) mechanism of evolution, which has taken the place of biological evolution, serves to develop morality beyond the stage where biological evolution has left it. I fully share Hannay's view that our moral response must no longer be confined to a circle smaller than humanity as a whole.

Comment by Max Hocutt on Tarkunde Article

I cannot decide whether I agree or disagree with V. M. Tarkunde. I think I agree that morality has to do with maintaining a mutually beneficial society, but I do not agree that commitment to abstract "values" is either necessary or sufficient to morality. I prefer a man honest out of habit but not out of principle to one honest in principle but not in practice.

I agree that God has nothing to do with morality, but that seems to me to be a demonstrable fact, not a postulate. I agree, too, that human biology is relevant to morality, but I have not yet seen convincing proof that either egoism or altruism is "instinctive," and seeing purposes in biological evolution sounds suspiciously like claiming that God does have something to do with morality after all. Indeed, Tarkunde's belief that we are biologically "endowed" with a faculty of practical reason (and with associated moral instincts) sounds to me like Kantian transcendentalism in biological dress. Tarkunde's remarks about free will and responsibility are also reminiscent of Kant. I fear, therefore, that Tarkunde's humanism is a form of theistic transcendentalism posing as a biologically based naturalism.

I think, therefore, that I agree with Tarkunde's morality, but not with his moral theory. He seems to me to be reading abstract moral principles into human nature while purporting to read them out of human nature. I prefer construing social virtues like honesty as devices for satisfying biologically determined human needs for such concrete values as food, water, and sex.

On Suffering*

Marvin Kohl

It is generally admitted that the presence of suffering in the world poses a problem for theistic religion insofar as it seems to contradict the notion of an all-powerful benevolent God. It would seem that if God were good, He would not want His creatures to suffer, and if all-powerful, He would be able to prevent their suffering. In this note I will suggest that the presence of enduring pain also poses a problem for the humanist, a problem that cannot be met simply by rejecting theism or by embracing egoism. Then I shall proceed to present an outline of a Promethean humanist's position, an outline that I hope will encourage further inquiry into the nature and limits of remedial suffering.

We can roughly distinguish two radically different and extreme ideological positions, one which holds that all suffering is good and a second which holds that all suffering is bad. Fortunately, few hold, and even fewer would be prepared to defend, these positions. Let us therefore confine our attention to two parallel claims, namely, the belief that almost all suffering is extrinsically good and the belief that, since almost all suffering is bad and happiness good, a person should place his own happiness or interests above the happiness or interests of all other persons. For the sake of convenience, I shall call the former "mortifying asceticism" or "asceticism"; I shall call the latter "extreme egoistic hedonism" or "egoism" for short.

Asceticism may be seen at its best in the writings of St. John of the Cross. In his *Precautions* he takes care to point out that, although suffering in itself is an evil for the one enduring it, it is most often the cause of great benefits. According to St. John, suffering expiates and sanctifies, it frees the soul from debasement and selfishness, and it renders us most like our Lord Jesus Christ. In other words, suffering has a clearly defined instrumental value. It is valuable because it purifies and greatly strengthens our spiritual and moral character. Moreover, suffering is of the greatest value, and is sacred, because it confers upon those whom it rends the most intimate resemblance to the sorrowful Son and does so in a perfectly egalitarian way. While all men can find God, those in the most pain, the greatest distress, are in an especially fortunate position to do so.

There are several reasons why this view should be rejected: first of all, why would a benevolent and all-powerful God insist that we must come to Him through suffering and mortification? Why would a truly loving father want his children to suffer?

Second, if suffering is to be viewed as a blessing, as almost the greatest gift of God's love, then why do anything to reduce it? If we are enjoined to view our own suffering as being blessed, then what logically prevents us from drawing the conclusion that all human suffering is good? Why not follow the example of Paneloux, the priest, who, in Camus's book *The Plague*, concludes that it is illogical for a true religious believer to call in a doctor or struggle against affliction?

Finally, let us recognize the palliative value of this outlook. Let us admit that it often cloaks, softens, and at its height seems to transubstantiate suffering. But even the use of a relatively good palliative has its limits. Suppose we compare the ascetic attitude towards suffering with the use of a drug like alcohol. The modest drinking of alcoholic beverages often enables an individual to escape temporarily from the woes of this world. But this is not in itself an argument for excessive drinking. Nor is it an argument for facing every problematic situation with bottle in hand. Similarly, wisdom seems to command that we endure suffering when it is irremediable. But it does not demand that we endure suffering that can be intelligently diminished or eliminated. Nor does it suggest that we overdose with ideological palliatives, or that we begin to worship our natural enemy.

One of the most persuasive advocates of extreme egoism is Ayn Rand. In a series of intellectually absorbing novels (including *The Fountainhead* and *Altas Shrugged*), and in *The Virtue of Selfishness*, Rand states that man is (and therefore should be) objectively egoistic, that is, rationally and completely selfish. She maintains that an individual's achievement of his own happiness is his highest moral purpose. What makes this position different, and open to acclaim or scorn, is that Rand rejects all forms and acts of altruism, believing that they are unnecessary and dangerous to the human good. She repeatedly suggests that she knows of no worse injustice than the giving of what is undeserved. From this perspective, an altruistic person is, at best, misguided or weak and, at worst, immoral. Similarly, a charitable or welfare society is morally degenerate, and one that is in danger of destroying itself.

Before examining some of the difficulties of this position, it may be well to try to understand why many humanists, after leaving the abode of asceticism, readily move to this extreme. After all, why not shift from a philosophy of self-sacrifice to a modest egoism? Why not say that, since almost all suffering is bad and happiness good, a person should place his own happiness or interests above that of any other individual? Or why not be content to say that since the rational end of conduct for each individual is the maximum of his own happiness or interests, most (but not all) forms of altruism are undesirable? The most obvious answer is that these positions do not go far enough. And I suspect that we would once again be reminded by the advocate of egoism that all forms of altruism are to be rejected; that, to the extent a person is rational, he must place his own happiness, not merely above that of any other person, but above the happiness of all other persons, taken collectively.

Let us, therefore, ask a different question. Let us ask the egoist, what is the task of morality? He probably would reply that morality has to do with how we are to treat ourselves and how we are to maximize our own happiness. In more candid moments he may even suggest that, while asceticism stultified his own pursuit of happiness, egoism allows for its most natural and fullest expression. This is an important clue. For the radical shift from asceticism to egoism often seems to be grounded in a combination of the desire to be happy and the belief that the best way of doing so is by adopting an ethical theory that views this end to be the highest good.

Knowing this takes much of the sting out of the first criticism of egoism. For we are often told: via the linguistic mode, that while the value judgments of the egoist may be maxims of prudence or self-love, they are not, literally speaking, moral judgments; or, via the material mode, that it is eminently clear that morality primarily has to do with how we should treat one another, and not primarily with how we are to treat ourselves. The difficulty with both arguments is that they appear to beg the question: the first by assuming that we must accept the apparent nonegoistic bias of ordinary language, one of the very points at issue; the second, by assuming that it is somehow self-evident that morality is primarily concerned with the good of others. An objection that does not beg the question and has more force is as follows: Ethics is necessary because men's desires conflict, and since the egoistic belief—the belief that it must always be an agent's positive duty to do what is best for himself—is the primary cause of this conflict, egoism must be rejected.

A second objection is that egoism is inaccurate in its assessment of the worth and viability of the welfare state. The historical evidence does not substantiate Rand's claim that a welfare state cannot ultimately protect its best and brightest and therefore must fail. Experiences in Great Britain, Sweden, and the United States indicates that, while grave difficulties may result in a social welfare state which emphasizes almost complete social and economic equality, a social security state which aims at a guaranteed minimum-type protection is more than viable.

There is yet another reason why this view should be rejected. It may be held that even if it is reasonable for a man always to act in the manner most conducive to his own happiness, it is not reasonable for society (and most groups) to accept this as its own credo. For example, it may be reasonable for a man to open a nuclear power plant before it has been properly checked out in order to obtain tax benefits, and thereby maximize his own profits or interests, as seems to be the case in the Three Mile Island situation. But it is certainly not reasonable for the fifty people who will die prematurely of cancer because of the radiation leak, to acquiesce. Nor is it reasonable for the hundred thousand or so individuals who were threatened to support this purported ethic. In fact, most disinterested parties would be inclined to say that the support of egoistic belief in this and similar situations is more than unreasonable—it is irrational. It is irrational because one of the primary functions of a society is to provide for protection against general suffering. And when we say this we imply that so long as man requires a rational social life, selfishness cannot be the supreme principle of ethics.

And finally even if this analysis were mistaken, egoism is not an alternative open to humanists who claim Prometheus as their patron saint. Promethean humanism must be universalistic and altruistic. Prometheus stole fire from the gods and gave it as a gift, knowing that he might be blamed or punished, because he took pity on the helplessness of men. As Bryon suggests, his only God-like crime was to be kind, to render less the sum of human wretchedness. To the extent that we emulate this great and loving Titan, we should be caring *and* giving to our fellow creatures, even though this, at times, may entail considerable risk or sacrifice.

But a Promethean approach also has its difficulties. The greatest danger is that it excites in many minds, among them the most compassionate in feeling and benevolent in purpose, the belief that all suffering can be eliminated. But can this really be accomplished? Even if we could eliminate war, poverty, and disease, can we eliminate the possibility of failure, accident, and the pain that normally accompanies the loss of loved ones? In other words, if one of our major goals is to eliminate suffering, and if it is true that this cannot be done (at least not in the foreseeable future), then the goal is a futile one. And if the pursuit of futile goals is often (though not always) a cause of misery, it follows that the attempt to eliminate all suffering is often a cause of misery, and thereby self-defeating.

The encouragement of unrealistic expectation also tends to promote disillusionment and noncritical retreat. Because men aim too high, they often cry out as to the impossibility of any welfare program or, in moments of despair, urge that human suffering is intractable. Again: how often do we find men who, after noble battle to conquer the unconquerable, turn in their failure to the Epimethean idol, an idol which insists that we have blind faith in nature and accept life, more or less, as we find it?

In order that we may be able to avoid these and the pitfalls mentioned earlier, the following seems preferable as a preliminary stance: Man is not challenged to eliminate all suffering. Man is challenged only to know the difference between remediable and irremediable suffering, to remedy suffering wherever it can be remedied, to endure it without chronic complaint when it is irremediable, and to understand that the enemy is great and that the battle may be endless.

Comment by Paul Kurtz on Kohl Article

I agree with Marvin Kohl's indictment of religious asceticism, and also with his criticisms of egoism, but only of an exacerbated self-centered one, since some measure of reflective self-interest is essential, in my judgment, to humanist ethics. Professor Kohl raises many important issues in his short paper, but I will only focus on his concluding remarks on the Promethean saint. It is not clear to me that Promethean humanism must be universalistic and altruistic. Although Prometheus gave the gift of fire and the arts of civilization to humanity, it is not apparent that this was done solely or primarily out of a motive of sympathy and compassion. Kohl seems to be drawing the model of Christ rather than that of Prometheus. In a fundamental sense, Prometheus expresses the quality of audacity to do battle with the gods. Granted that Prometheus had a philanthropic concern for humanity; yet, he expresses independence as a chief virtue in so far as he was willing to challenge the gods. The value he represents is moral courage, a virtue especially appreciated by freethinkers and humanists. That is why he stands as their patron saint, for they wish to cultivate the arts of intelligence in order to cope with the problems of human life. Accordingly, I don't know that the Prometheus myth implies the belief that all suffering can be eliminated. This surely would be a naive optimism. On the contrary, the Promethean myth suggests an awareness of suffering and an appreciation for the need for continuing heroic efforts to overcome it.

Kohl's last paragraph seems to me to be eminently sensible: we cannot eliminate all suffering, but we should do our best to eradicate whatever we can. To this I would add a further positive moral obligation, which is incumbent upon us: to distribute goods, wherever possible, first to oneself (a modified egoism), and second, where possible and with their voluntary consent, to our fellow humans who are within the range of our activities.

Reply by Marvin Kohl

Professor Kurtz suggests, with his usual subtlety and clarity, the Prometheus' actions fundamentally express the quality of audacity to do battle with the gods and that his form of humanism has successfully avoided a major pitfall of egoism. I have my doubts about both of these points.

In order for Prometheus to actually do great good to and for others, it was necessary for him to violate the prevailing rules of sovereignty and be prepared to do battle with Zeus. According to this interpretation, his end was that of doing good in a universalistic and altruistic sense and his means, or at least one of his means, was that of having an unusual amount of courage and even greater fortitude. If this interpretation is mistaken, and if Prometheus' definance is not a means but the primary end (as Kurtz seems to suggest), then Prometheus is something of a megalomaniac, and I fail to see the moral worth of loving power for its own sake or of emulating those who do.

I have urged that ethics is necessary because men's desires conflict, and since the egoistic belief that it must always be an agent's positive duty to do what is best for himself is the primary cause of this conflict, egoism must be rejected. To attempt to modify this position by saying that, where possible, we have a positive moral obligation to distribute goods first to ourselves and then to others does not, in itself, meet this objection. It may be notoriously difficult to get nonaltruistic men to teach their children altruistic desires. But it is even greater folly to pretend to have successfully avoided the pitfalls of eogism when the evidence indicates that unless a theory offers a proposal that would enable us to avoid the conflicting serious interests and activities of different men it leaves the door open to unnecessary suffering and, in a significant way, welcomes the tyranny of the powerful and selfish against the majority of mankind.

Propositions Toward a Humanist Consensus in Ethics

Alastair Hannay

THE MEANING AND SOURCE OF MORALITY

Perhaps the first thing humanists should come to agreement about in ethics is what it is they should agree upon. Enlightened but troubled by the latest Humanist Manifesto, I have the suspicion that agreement is being sought about the wrong things and for the wrong reasons. Am I right in suspecting, for example, that we are being encouraged to provide materials for the establishment of a new, humanist code of moral conduct? To propose, in the words of the Manifesto, "radically new human purposes and goals" to replace "traditional moral codes and newer irrational cults"? If so, the enterprise is misguided. Whatever faults the codes and cults may have, I cannot believe that moral codes can be generated by debate, or that having them endorsed by persons of academic standing or good will, or both, is the way to give moral directives effect. Or even that moral codes are good things. The Manifesto also talks of the failure of the traditional codes and newer cults to "meet the pressing needs of today and tomorrow." Are we being asked, therefore, to modernize morality so that it can "speak to the problems of the times"? Admittedly there are new and expanding areas of choice where moral guidance is needed, but the generally instrumental view of morality which such a request expresses represents, for me, a grave distortion of morality's "source" and "meaning." The idea that morality is a functional institution which, like any other human device, needs updating in order to cope with the contingencies of the age wrongly suggests that the question, What is morality basically about?, can be

179

answered satisfactorily by specifying an institutional goal, for example, social cohesion or, a matter which much concerns us these days, human survival. I do not believe that it is a moral task to pronounce on human goals at all, not even (I should rather say, least of all) the goal of human survival. Morality is concerned not with human purposes and interests, but with the concern humans show one another in their devotion to their own purposes and interests.

This gives morality at least one purpose, namely influencing people to adopt courses of action which take other people's interests into consideration. This of course implies that there is something about other people or their interests which can attract a person's consideration. A humanist ethics must therefore, like any other, be able to say what that is. Having deprived itself of the functionally effective expedient of conceiving all persons as God's children, it must identify whatever it is that is worthy of this consideration with some universal human characteristic, something capable of evoking the appropriate positive response. The requirement of universality means that it must do better, for example, than Hobbes, whose economics of human value ("the value, or worth, of a man is as of all other things his price, so much as would be given for the use of his power") satisfies the requirements of humanist metaphysics but not yet of humanist ethics. Hobbes's account makes the individual replaceable and human worth a matter of the state of the human market. The characteristic we need must be a human constant and must secure the indispensability of the individual. An obvious candidate is *suffering*, understood as broadly as possible. The appropriate response to suffering is compassion or concern, and it is directed uniquely at the suffering individual. Humanist morality is, or should be, the "institution" of concern for the suffering of all beings that suffer, which of course includes other than human beings. This does not mean that suffering in itself is a moral concept or the absence of suffering a moral value. Strictly the alleviation and prevention of suffering are not moral goals but goals which moral people set themselves when the occasion has arisen and the means are available. The primary notion of moral value is of a value to be attributed *to* those who demonstrate concern and *by* those who themselves view such concern with approval.

Approval and reproach are of course the traditional means by which people are encouraged to act morally. But how do they work? If someone knowingly and unnecessarily causes suffering, but *never* feels concern or contrition, what will his response to reproach be? Not guilt in any *moral* sense, and if guilt at all, then only out of some ingrained respect for the source from which the reproach stems, for example, a stern father, God, or the voices of common moral opinion. Reproach in such a case is a crude instrument of conformity in the hands of those with authority to wield it and the response, depending on the respect in which that authority is held, will vary from humiliation through indifference to contempt, all counter-productive responses in terms of the moral end sought, as indeed would be conformity with moral opinion if brought about simply by a desire for rehabilitation in the eyes of the public. But few people are totally without compassion. If we can suppose that our person is capable of concern in *some* cases, that there are *certain* persons who are to him "near and dear," then reproach—and approval—can take the form of a moral communication, an observation, if you like, directed at something which both parties have the formal competence to judge. The moralizer can point out and the moral offender in principle acknowledge that the partiality of his concern is "inconsistent," "unfair," the concern itself "limited," even "egoistic." Given certain conditions to do with the reproached person's willingness to subject his behavior to a scrutiny suggested by another (for example, respect for the latter or ability to swallow one's pride), the reproach can then function as a positive provocation or incentive to do better.

Since "doing better" has in part the sense of "acting more appropriately to the truth," the moral "ought" has an epistemological aspect with strict parallels in the scientific norms that truth is better than falsity and greater knowledge better than less. This gives charity its link with rationality. The charity which both begins and ends at home is incompletely rational; it corresponds to the assumption that the only true statements are those which strike you as true. The problem of morality, in this light, is to confront moral consciousness with its true object and elicit in it a sense of the parochiality of its initial concerns. There is certainly more to it than that, but I suggest that it is seriously misleading to suppose that the more includes a quite separate problem of setting up and developing the moral consciousness, distinct from that of locating its object. I suggest that it is nearer the truth to say that moral consciousness grows with recognition of its object, that moral consciousness is to be conceived not as the juxtaposition of two separate "faculties," in this case (as against other views which see morality as willed rationality in defiance of feeling) perceiving and feeling, but as that blending of perceptiveness and responsiveness we sometimes call "sensibility." I won't argue for this conception here, but merely assume that if there are indeed two problems, then perception is the principal if not the prior one. I propose that this problem be assigned to the following areas of inquiry.

First, a matter of philosophy rather than science, though really it would be a matter of common sense were it not for the corruption of common sense by scientific and philosophical theories which therefore need countertheoretical remedies. The relevant fact here is that "the" world really breaks down into a multiplicity of centers of consciousness or sentience. Of course, no one really supposes that his or her own experiences are the only ones. Yet the fact that they are not is a peculiarly elusive one, not only in terms of rational epistemological reconstruction, but also in respect of the plain human ability to grasp it. We know in a formal sense what we mean by such a multiplicity and manage without difficulty to use an expression like "center of consciousness" in the plural. But we have no perceptual or any other concrete access to the fact that corresponds to the multiplicity or the plural form. The moral problem here is to give the elusive fact substance enough to appeal to our natural powers of compassion.

Secondly, two areas of psychological facts. First, facts of human and other suffering, of its kinds and causes. The difficulty with these is not their elusiveness, for they are facts to which as sufferers we can all in principle have direct access, but their variety, complexity, and uneven distribution. In practice, our own experiences of suffering differ widely, both in kind and depth. Nor are our sufferings equally apparent to each of us; we do not always see that the brave face we put on things is a mask. Since we learn suffering from our own case, however much that learning may be amplified by what we read and imagine, our capacities for compassion have very variable limits. The problem here is to enlarge our knowledge, to cultivate our moral imaginations, so as to produce a greater likelihood of the coincidence and mutual correspondence of suffering and concern.

Thirdly, an area of facts, not only psychological, but also bound up with the contingent nature of our political and social institutions and with the motivations and prevailing ideologies behind them. Here we find a wide variety of obstacles to the free unfolding of a general concern: for example, the requirements of ego-identity which conflict with the moral requirement that concern be directed also beyond the circles, membership in which helps to establish that identity; the social setting which on the one hand creates the requirement that identity and self-respect be established in this way, and on the other provides the institutional means of satisfying the requirement; the pressures in public opinion which can stigmatize the very investigation of these factors as "cynical" or "corrupting," and so on. Since the difficulties here include those of personal and social acceptance, there is, apart from the complexity of the facts themselves, the additional practical problem of their unpalatability—its existence not an insignificant fact of the kind in question.

FREE WILL AND RESPONSIBILITY

We said that it is only under certain conditions that approval and reproach can be forms of moral communication, the suggestion being that that is what they should be. We have so far postulated two conditions, first, that the moral approver or disapprover has had access to suffering, and secondly, that the recipient of approval or reproach be able to make moral judgments. But there is of course another condition. The moral approver or disapprover must believe that the person of whose action he approves or disapproves acted freely. Otherwise there can be no default and so no blame.

The problem of free will is usually construed as the quite general question of whether a human being is capable in principle of intervening in a causal chain of (let us, in order to avoid complications, say psychophysical) events without the intervention being itself explainable as a *fully* determined event in such a chain. I do not see that there is a specifically humanist solution to this quite general question. On the other hand I think that anyone interested in how ethics does or could change the world for the better will, in the absence of conclusive arguments to the contrary, continue to accept the prima facie plausibility of the proposition that all of us could have done better in the past and that it is open to everyone to choose the (contextually) optimal moral course in the future. But it should be possible to do that without denying the possibility of explaining, by appeal to determinable regularities or to rational strategies, why particular moral performances are good or bad; without denying the appropriateness of citing such explanations when judging a person's moral record; and without denying that what is optimal in one situation may not be so in another. The belief that causal explanations exclude moral assessments is based on the assumption that morality must be a defiance of nature, the battle of the better against the bad self, a contest in which moral failure is put down to weakness of will. I am suggesting that moral failure is very largely a failure of knowledge, perception, or imagination. In saying that it is (largely) failure of this kind, however, I am not suggesting that this is an ignorance which excuses, and thus offers an escape from reproach, any more than I am suggesting that the *state* of a person's knowledge is determined by factors which do not include personal initiative. As noted in the first section, The Meaning and Source of Morality, there are pressures which hinder a free unfolding of an appropriate moral response to the facts of suffering, pressures which also encourage reluctance to face or become acquainted with these latter facts. Some of these pressures are beyond the singleperson's powers of control (they are "givens" of this social time and place and restrict the moral range we can expect of him), but others are not, or not altogether, for they have to do with the attitude or role he adopts in his given circumstances. Does he choose the role of "victim" of those circumstances and let this further narrow the range of his concern for the suffering of others, or does he try to widen and deepen his grasp of the suffering of others within that range, perhaps even try to extend the range himself? Whatever psychological or sociological explanations can be given of the selection of the passive rather than the active role, or vice versa, it still seems meaningful to talk here of a fundamental choice. Some claim that the morally passive, other-denying option is really an active defense, and recognized "deep down" as such by the "chooser," so that even here there is some minimal intervention in a psychophysical causal sequence. But where a particularly oppressive environment makes the passivity of the moral reprobate seem natural, it may be better to concentrate on future positive initiatives rather than moralize about past negative ones. The important thing is that the positive, other-affirming option represents the promise of a moral development while the negative, other-denying one does not. Anyone who favors such a development will try to create the conditions in which it is more "natural" for the other-denying option to be rejected and in which the "chooser" is himself able and willing to make and respond to moral judgments. From then on the development can be a mutual process involving a willingness to treat adverse moral judgments as cues to further relevant discoveries about oneself and others.

Traditional wisdom conceives the will as pure energy, the spiritual muscle needed to subdue human nature to rational moral dictates. But on the whole it seems unlikely that a boosting of moral capacity in the form of sheer willpower, even if it exists, is a useful tool in the shaping of moral development, more likely that this end will be served by the provision of an environment which, on the one hand, gives less justification for the role of victim, and, on the other, presents fewer obstacles to a cognitive development which, by expanding the range of natural sympathy, can reduce that unfortunate tension between nature and morality which tradition valued as setting the necessary stage for moral performance. From a humanist point of view, moral engineering is preferable to moral gymnastics.

Still, it would betray a serious lack of insight into certain relevant facts to suppose that expanding the range of natural sympathy didn't also create problems for the will. Initially self-centered and combining its concern with a strong measure of self-regard, the will has to accommodate itself to the thought of being but one center of interests among all others. Full and genuine accommodation to this thought represents an ideal of humanistic saintliness which it would be unrealistic to pose as a universal moral goal. But some progress in that direction is called for, and therefore some effort of self-improvement on the part of the will. The path itself can be briefly outlined as a generation of the moral self out of the nonmoral beginnings of self-interest and a merely instinctive sympathy. Self-interest proceeds, via the notion of what is the prudent thing to do, to the realization that immediate personal goals can be subordinated with benefit to more distant ones. Combining this realization with the idea, already resident in natural sympathy, that some others are to be benefited, this generates the thought of sometimes subordinating one's own interests to those of others. The idea that these specified others have interests and therefore rights of indepen- dence and dependence (including, respectively, of and on oneself), implies that they are genuinely others, and in this respect not to be discriminated from the unspecified remainder. The ability to conceive oneself as just one, in many respects in principle replaceable, center of interests among others within the immediate circle proceeds, via this universalization of the other, to the ability to conceive oneself as one equally among all others. For the less than saintly it is no doubt enough, but it is also a lot, that one acquire a sense of the merely relative importance of one's own interests in the light of the interests of those principally affected by one's actions.

MORALITY: WORKABILITY OR JUSTICE

The view so far sketched is Kantian rather than utilitarian. The exercise or, where that is prevented, just the existence of compassion is the end-all of morality. There is no ulterior goal, for example, human survival or, more luxuriously, human fulfillment, not even the greatest possible happiness. There will be objections and I will mention three, the first of which can be partly upheld but I think with credit to the view being advocated. To uphold the other two would be to the view's discredit, but they are not to be upheld.

First, those who insist that the goal of morality is at least in part a harmonious state of society will object that compassion, even if effective within a certain range, is not sufficient. Now if the objector will agree that the state in question is one in which compassion reigns as far as it can, I will agree; there must also be institutional guarantees of the respect due to individuals where that respect cannot be sustained by mere compassion. If, however, the objector assumes that social harmony can be measured by external indicators compatible with a merely mechanical application of principles of justice, a situation in which compassion, if it exists, is no more than an epiphenomenon, then that state of affairs, on the present view, is not a moral one, nor therefore can it constitute a moral goal. Since compassion, if it is not sufficient, is at least a necessary component of any moral state of affairs, there is no moral goal other than one in which compassion is an essential ingredient to which it is a means.

Secondly, that compassion is not enough is an objection we have already accommodated. Although one individual's concern for the suffer- ing of another, not necessarily near or dear, individual is the basic moral interest, we have noted the secondary interest in producing a better match between individual concern and actual suffering, an interest furthered by moral communication but also, where possible and necessary, by "moral engineering." The goal of such engineering is in the first instance to discourage the sense of victimization which prevents the unfolding of a moral attitude. The means of discouraging the sense of victimization include, naturally enough, altering those external arrangements which make victimization both a possibility and a likely fact. The kind of arrangement which excludes the possibility, or at least decreases the likelihood of the fact, is what one calls a "just" arrangement; it provides protection from unfair treatment or restitution for it. It is true that just practices and institutions are often the result of collective aggression and assertiveness on the part of those who have been treated unjustly, rather than of the compassion of those in a position to make improvements constitutionally. But to assert one's rights militantly on behalf of one's fellows as well as one's self can also be to act with compassion. The goal of moral engineering is justice. Concretely, the aim of institutionalized justice is to reduce the possibility of the harmful consequences of the failure of people to show concern, and to take up the slack of the inevitable limits and oversights of our natural sympathies. Abstractly, justice is a *moral* ideal because it is a requirement of the respect for persons as such. To respect persons as such requires, in political terms, a guarantee of a certain basic inviolability which unconditionally protects *any* individual from victimization or "use" in the cause of some further end. It goes without saying that this unconditional protection cannot be guaranteed when morality itself is conceived as serving other ends than the interests of the individual. Thus no social ethics which allows the welfare of society as a whole to override the individual's right of acknowledgment can provide the guarantee of justice; nor can utilitarianism, which countenances the victimization of the innocent as the cost of a correspondingly greater gain of general happiness.

Thirdly, it can be objected that the identification of morality with a concern for suffering, rather than, say, for happiness or fulfillment, is implicitly to postulate at least one general goal in which compassion is not an ingredient, namely, the elimination of suffering. So if suffering could be eliminated by painlessly eliminating the sufferer, then, on the present account's own assumption of the universality of suffering, this would mean that the annihilation of the human race could in principle be a moral act. That would be as perverse a conclusion for a humanist to have to draw as would be, for his Kant-inspired colleague, the conclusion that the race should be preserved simply to provide objects of concern. But the view does not deny the *right* to happiness or fulfillment, nor does it imply that suffering in general is an evil and should be eliminated (it could conceivably be a condition of the richest forms of human fulfillment, as well as of compassion, and perhaps even of happiness). It is in fact compatible with the belief—surely a paradigmatic humanist belief—that it is better that there should be human beings—even suffering ones—than that there should not. We should stress again that the rationale for moral concern is a respect for persons and, therefore, for persons as, amongst other things, capable of choosing their own forms of happiness and fulfillment, though always within the limits of morality. Some may conceive of fulfillment as a kind of comprehensive contentment in the performance of specifically human activities. But although that sounds like the characteristically humanist way, such eudaemonism will not satisfy everyone. Indeed I believe that those whom it does satisfy betray a serious lack of insight into the kinds and causes of human suffering. They wrongly assume that suffering is a contingent, that is to say an uncharacteristic, feature of the truly human life, and in their misplaced glorification of the species (a vainly Promethean attempt to retroject eternal values onto a temporal domain that cannot support them) they turn their back on the primary source of moral competence, knowledge of human (and other) suffering. Eudaemonism is therefore a suspect choice for individual fulfillment. All the more reason that it should not be erected into official humanist moral policy. On the other hand, a religious conception of personal fulfillment should not be excluded on humanist principles. Even if the principles prohibit the founding of morality upon religious dogma, they should not prohibit a conception of morality in which morality acquires a transcendent religious value.

THE BASIS OF RIGHTS AND DUTIES

Humanists naturally want to believe that we have moral obligations, duties in some virtually legalistic sense but not the product of arbitrary legislation, to one another. But on what can the belief be based? The divine legislator and guarantor of human value has gone by the board, but the human legislator doesn't seem to have the credentials. Take the contractualist account of obligation. The individual facing a "solitary, poor, nasty, brutish, and short" life tries to improve his prospects by binding himself to others in ties of mutual obligation. But it is the restrictions he ties himself to, not the others, and his sociality is merely an extension of his selfishness. In other words, the obligations are not moral. Kant construes the individual as a potentially *un*selfish self-legislator whose directives automatically accord respect to persons (as free and rational beings). But Kantian obligations have to be carried out for their own sake, and to let the Moral Law impose them upon him, the individual must project himself above the full-blooded psychophysical network of desire and aversion in which humanists would (or should) prefer to ground their moral concepts.

As an attempt to satisfy this preference, and in line with the view here proffered, I suggest that the origin of moral obligation may be found in the experience (not just the fact) of disappointing what one admits is another's justified expectation. The experience of regret and shame (loss of self) is one which discloses an obligation, a personal, perhaps even unique, obligation. The assumption here is that a primitive and natural tie of mutual dependence and trust can exist prior to any contract or submission to laws, moral or otherwise. The precise expectations will vary with culture and context, but common to all cases will be a sense of regret and shame at betraying a trust, a trust so simple and basic that it would be pointless to ask oneself, Why do I have this sense? It would be pointless because there is no further authority or explanation to appeal to in justification. On a very limited scale one is doing the divine legislator's job. Although the important thing here is not the content of the expectation but the interest in fulfilling it, this interest will nevertheless always presuppose the expectations that are, by law or custom, justified in a given situation. Morality as an institution is concerned with enforcing, encouraging, and cultivating recognition of the expectations people actually have. It is also concerned with inducing in people a more balanced, rightful, conception of what is due to them, the notion of "balance" or "rightfulness" here being based on insights of the kinds mentioned earlier. Just as importantly it is concerned with enforcing the recognition of rightful expectations in cases where they are not consciously entertained, because those whose rightful expectations they are do not suspect that they might be being disappointed (e.g., by those who deposit dangerous chemicals on land liable to be developed for housing or cultivation). By extension, morality is also concerned with the expectations of those (e.g., nonhuman animals and mentally enfeebled humans) not in a position to entertain them because entertaining expectations is not something they can do, though here the absence of this ability nust surely limit the nature and extent of the expectations in question.

Right and *duty* or *obligation* are terms often affixed to very general deals or safeguards. In actual moral practice it is perhaps better to think in terms of specific expectations. Few courses of action are in themselves, independently of context, morally prescribed or prohibited. Thus in most cultures children learn to expect favors (as well as disfavors) of their parents which they do not expect of other adults. Parents and other adults thus acquire correspondingly different obligations to those children. But as the children grow into adulthood, their expectations of preference should wane. The only general moral obligation is that one have an interest in meeting justified expectations. And the only general moral right is the expectation that one's justified expectations be fulfilled, including the primary expectation that one be an object of concern. I have no moral obligation to alleviate suffering *wherever* I acknowledge its existence; broadening my insight into the extent of suffering, however much it extends the range of my concern, does not extend automatically the range of my moral obligations. The reason is that much of the suffering I acknowledge will not be suffering which the sufferer can justifiably expect *me* to alleviate, therefore not suffering which the sufferer will (or can rightfully) feel is due to any infringement of basic trust and dependence. But having acquired a greater insight into suffering and its extent I might deliberately put myself into a position where I would *become* the object of such expectations of trust and dependence on the part of these new-found sufferers. My philanthropism is not morally obligatory (it may even be partly selfish), but the position into which it puts me is one which imposes new moral obligations upon me.

The notion of equality goes properly with that of rights, particularly rights of opportunity and reward, though also of punishment. Its negations are undeserved privilege or deprivation. The idea of equality (in a moral as opposed to a taxonomic sense) is that there is a status which all humans enjoy whatever inequities they actually suffer at the hands of nature or their fellows. The point of according humans this status is not, however, to allow them to ignore these inequities (as the religious conception of equality in the eyes of God is sometimes claimed to do), but on the contrary to contribute somehow to their elimination. This, however, must be seen as a moral goal, not just a political one. Certainly there must be political and legal guarantees of human rights and the principle of the inviolability of the individual must be proclaimed loudly and repeatedly not only by, but also to, those in authority. In the end, however, it is the close moral encounter which gives the ideal of equality its content. Not, therefore, in the form of predetermined directives derived from general moral principles, or uniform expectations tailored to some agreed specification of the optimally fulfilled social individual, but as the single moral rule that each person is entitled to the compassion of any other, regardless of intraspecific distinctions of race, sex, nationality, creed, or "class."

PRINCIPLES IN SITUATIONAL MORALITY

Our primary moral obligations are to those whose needs we are best placed to understand and satisfy. More particularly they are to those who have a right to expect that we are the persons to satisfy them. This implies, however, that morality is *inherently* situational, that the moral course is determined by insight into particular people's needs and expectations at particular times. But then where do general moral principles come in? There are of course such principles, and we can formulate them. Thus we can set about specifying the main kinds of needs and expectations, or the various categories of suffering we should be concerned to avoid in others, and also the main qualities of mind required by one who genuinely seeks to avoid them, for example, principles enjoining respect for life, limb, and property on the one hand, and honesty, trust, and fellowship on the other. For the concerned individual in his close moral encounters, however, these principles will be of no use at all. What he needs are his moral sensibility and insight.

But that is too simple an account. If we note a significant asymmetry in the two sets of principles just illustrated, we can see how they each separately, and in combination, perform important moral functions. The first set does not comprise absolutes while the latter does. That is to say, in certain (progressively less critical) circumstances life, limb, and property can be offered in a moral cause, but honesty, trust, and fellowship cannot. The reason is that these define the moral attitude which determines whether or not the cause in which something is offered is in fact a moral one. But since it is easier to identify and prevent breaches of the first set of principles than of the second, it is reasonable for society to give the former a certain precedence and to put the onus of justifying deviations upon the deviator. We want to be sure that his attitude is moral and his insight sound. Moreover since, in virtue of our wider social functions and engagements, we have moral obligations to people into whose particular circumstances we lack insight, it is fitting that in respect of those long-distance moral encounters, we guide ourselves, or are effectively influenced, by general principles which minimize undue discrimination in favor of those with whose situations we are familiar. Though it is important to remember that, since close or direct personal interactions generate *special* bonds of trust and dependence, there are cases where such discrimination is not undue.

But the general principles must not be too specific. The more detailed the specifications of general rights, the greater the likelihood that they merely reflect and thereby help to perpetuate habits of thought and action no longer appropriate to current advances in moral insight. Worse, a detailed moral code tends to eliminate the part played by moral insight, conscience, and compassion altogether. A society whose morality consists in a body of codes and practices has lost its moral core. Without it, without faith in the reliableness of individual moral insight, it acquires the neurotic belief that deviation from principle is a threat to society and therefore to human survival. It begins to conceive of morality as a means to nonmoral ends, or, from its own point of view, to treat nonmoral ends as moral ones. Moreover without an acknowledged part to play in social morality, moral insight and the close moral encounter easily degenerate into obscurantist dogma on the one hand and dropout cults and sects on the other—sects which thrive on a sense of moral superiority and on opposition to one another and to society at large, and base their doctrines on primitive categorizations which positively hinder the spread of insight and concern. In resisting this development humanists should dedicate themselves to the centrality of compassion and of its locus, the close moral encounter, as the core of morality.

Comment by Max Hocutt on Hannay Article

Reading Alistair Hannay makes me suspect that the "humanist consensus" will reduce in the end to agreement that God does not exist. The nonexistence of God makes more difference to some of us than to others. To me, it means that there is no absolute morality, that moralities are sets of social conventions devised by humans to satisfy their needs. To Hannay, it means that we must postulate an alternative basis for moral absolutism.

Hannay's postulates are essentially the same as Kant's: equality, the right to be respected as a person, the obligation to regard others as ends in themselves, et cetera. That these are metaphysical postulates, not demonstrable truths, is revealed by the fact that there is no empirical basis for them. No fact is plainer than the fact that people are extremely unequal, or that some people, being worth more, deserve more respect, compassion, affection, et cetera. Nobody who has examined the facts can maintain that we ought to love James Earl Ray as much as we loved Martin Luther King, or that a shapeless blob of protoplasm with an IQ too low to measure is worth as much as a creative genius like Leonardo da Vinci. For my part, I would show Ray no compassion or affection whatsoever, and I see no reason why I should treat idiots with the same respect I would pay Leornardo.

To put the point in another way, we humanists all agree that God is a myth, but some of us are glad to be rid of both the myth and the morality that was founded in it, while others, like Hannay, are so anxious to preserve the morality as to create another myth to replace the first one.

Reply by Alastair Hannay to Hocutt

I think Max Hocutt's neat account of how he and I differ makes the difference more a matter of principle than it really is. He says I am trying to base moral absolutism on something other than God, while he wants to get rid of moral absolutism along with God. And he says the basis I offer is not an empirical one, so I am simply replacing one myth by another.

I do not mean to defend moral absolutism, and I *do* mean to offer an empirical basis for morality. Our real disagreement seems to be about what this empirical basis should be. Hocutt says it is human need, I say it is the experience of others' needs. I choose the latter because compassion exists and because it seems a promising foundation for humanistic ethics. If all there is to our practical cognizance of others is self-interest, then morality boils down to watching your step (not because if you tread on another person's toes it hurts *them*, but because the result of you hurting them is that they might hurt *you*) or helping others to provide you with otherwise unobtainable goods (automobiles, for example). But there *is* this special concern for the well-being of others, so why not build on it?

As for Ray and King, I certainly don't wish to argue that everyone should be loved by anyone, or if so, equally, only that the need or call for concern and love be properly recognized in particular instances. Assassins fail abysmally to recognize it, at least in their victims, while others such as King succeed gloriously. I personally feel no compassion for Ray, but that might be due to lack of knowledge or imagination on my part. It would be relevant from the point of view of my paper to suggest that Ray's failure may even be due in some measure to the same lack of knowledge and imagination on the part of those who have less excuse for it than I have. Morally, however, I share Hocutt's evaluation of the two, except I would say that I held King in great respect rather than that I loved him. I admired him for the quality and quantity of *his* love.

This agreement diminishes the importance of the allegedly crucial question of God's existence. King believed in God, so he was not a humanist. But it would have been a complete waste of time to try to convert him. Not because it would have been difficult, as no doubt it would, but because for all *practical* purposes he was already a humanist, according to my view. The crucial question is how to make practicing humanists out of moral primitives. It doesn't seem obvious to me that it can best be done by getting them to take note of their own needs. But I may be wrong.

PANEL IV

LESTER A. KIRKENDALL
ARCHIE J. BAHM
HOWARD B. RADEST
LEE NISBET

An Ethical System For Now And The Future

Lester A. Kirkendall

In 1949 an experience which forever altered my thinking about ethical-moral[1] issues engulfed me; I began teaching courses in marriage and family relations at Oregon State University. My students were unflaggingly concerned about optimum ways of relating to others. Even then the enrollment in my classes was quite cosmopolitan. Through the years I had students from all parts of the world bringing with them a wide range of experiences and inquiring minds. Very shortly they made me aware of how diverse and how alike were their patterns of cultural behavior.

My overseas students, along with my American students, did not ask ethical questions in a philosophical sense, or moral questions in a theological framework. A common concern for basic values permeated their questions as they explored marriage and family behavior. "Is it right to spank a child?" "Should there be arranged marriages?" "Is divorce wrong?" "Is sexual intercourse outside marriage ever right?" "Should adults appear publicly in the nude?" "Are homosexual relations wrong?" Their questions might have been answered by reciting the concepts of a particular religion, the mores of a specific culture, or the customs of some racial or ethnic group. But I, the instructor, did not want to divide them into cultural groups. I wanted an umbrella covering them all as human beings.

American students would discuss a situation they had experienced, then an overseas student might relate a similar circumstance in his/her own culture. One Arabian girl raised vexing questions about the American process of mate selection. When she returned home she expected to marry a male to whom her parents had betrothed her when she was two and the male was five or six. Their parents had betrothed them hoping to unite the two families. They felt the personalities of the two would mesh, and so did she. Was this not better than the romantic love-pairing she had observed in America?

An African male whose father was a tribal chieftain told how young couples of a particular tribe avoided unwanted pregnancy. They merely walked into the bushes where they engaged in erotic play ending in mutual masturbation. There was no penile-vaginal penetration. Was this not better than unwanted pregnancies where everyone, including the child-to-be, was disadvantaged?

An American male, a former exchange student in Sweden, described a winter visit with a Lapland family. One day the parents and their adolescent male and female children were planning for a sauna bath. He was invited to go and accepted. Then he realized that everyone would be nude and all would occupy the sauna at the same time. "Would this have been right?"

The overseas students were basically uncertain, too. They talked with great assurance, but they faced perplexing situations in both our culture and theirs. They often felt walled-off and separated. They appreciated my concern for including all persons simultaneously, regardless of background, in the discussion of value questions. Thus I embarked upon a search for an ethical/moral framework which has intrigued me ever since.

Perplexing issues faced me at once. Why need there be concern for an ethical/moral system? Is it to please a Deity; to support cultural patterns and mores; to insure obedience? Can one be delineated? Upon what authoritative foundation can it rest? Should it be concerned only with face-to-face associations and daily life experiences, or can it apply to business, national, and international affairs? Can it apply to all persons or must some differentiations be made? If so, on what basis? Do changing local and world situations and new knowledge alter our ethical/moral concepts, or are they foreordained, never-changing?

In considering these issues I arrived at some assumptions, which in turn raised baffling, perhaps insoluble questions. Not everyone will agree with my assumptions, but they gave direction to my thinking.

I assumed there should be an ethical/moral system and that it:

1. *Should serve to insure the survival of humankind.* Survival, however, should be interpreted as more than mere existence. It should be survival with joy and satisfaction; both physical and mental. It should encompass all aspects of living. Survival starts with the individual, for one cannot be permanently separated from others and survive.

2. *Must rest upon a logical, rational, openly-acknowledged framework.* Ethical decision making must have an authoritative basis. Otherwise it is

likely to be capricious and inconsistent, often contradictory. This means more, however, than simply balancing one research fact against another. It requires a respect for the intuitive wisdom acquired through the ages. A suggested framework will emerge in the following discussion.

3. *Should be applicable universally.* Increasingly we are living in a world where cross-cultural contacts are more readily experienced and communication between people and groups is becoming easier, even almost instantaneous. Global consciousness is increasing; compare our current awareness of the Middle East, Iran, Egypt, Rhodesia, and Uganda with what we knew even a few years ago. This intermingling increases the number of choices with ethical implications. Widely differing customs, practices, and ways of thinking now often exist side by side. Differences in race, religion, family, marriage and sexual patterns, social concerns, and ethnic customs which have been either subjects of curiosity or anxiety, now become issues of choice, matters of moral concern. Paul Kurtz[2] had the need for universality in mind when he asked, "How far shall we extend our moral concern: to our nation, state, race, ethnic group, religion—to the whole of humanity?" His reply: "The ultimate source of moral choice should be human experience; and its test, the consequences of the choice in action."

4. *Should rest upon the basic need for enhancing altruistic experience, both in giving and receiving.* The desire for edifying associations, both immediately and in the long run, is highly important and a deeply ingrained human need. Kurtz[3] comments here: "Human beings cannot live caring only for themselves, their own families, and close friends. At some point there should be a broader outreach and concern.... we should not neglect the greater moral universe."

The concern for this outreach is not optional I feel; it is a necessity if humankind is to survive and is an essential quality of human nature itself. But to what degree are we certain about the nature of human nature? And to what extent does it include outreach, compassion, and altruism? Are human beings essentially egocentric and unsocially aggressive? Can these qualities be modified, or are they genetically determined?

This debate has gone on continuously for eons.[4] Scientists in divergent fields of learning are amassing evidence indicating that while human beings experience conflicting impulses, the cooperative, outreaching, altruistic impulses are there and can be addressed.

Several scientists have written to this point.[5] For example, W. C. Allee, a social-biologist says: that after much consideration he has concluded that

...the balance between the cooperative and altruistic tendencies and those which are disoperative and egoistic is relatively close. Under many conditions the cooperative forces lose. In the long run, however, the group centered, more altruistic drives are slightly stronger.

> Despite many known appearances to the contrary, human altruistic drives are as firmly based on an animal ancestry as is man himself.[6]

Niko Tinbergen, an English animal biologist, leans a bit more in the direction of genetic determinism than does Allee. But quite apart from any disagreement he hopes we may diminish the aggressive impulse, perhaps through educational measures.

> Whatever the causation of our aggression, the simple fact is that for the time being we are saddled with it. This means that there is a crying need for a crash program, for finding ways and means for keeping our intergroup aggression in check. . . .in our short-term cure we are not aiming at the elimination of aggression, but at 'taking the sting out of it'.[7]

How do you take the sting out of unsocial aggression? By recognizing that human beings do experience conflicting impulses and drives which carry them in contradictory directions, but recognizing also that these can be ameliorated in direct, personal contact. We need to return to an ancient concept of human relating, clarifying and observing it in terms of everyday living, and acknowledging it as an ethical/moral system which, sincerely implemented, will vastly alter our existing civilization.

This sounds like advertising puffery, yet my convictions have grown out of the university teaching situation outlined earlier and what I have experienced since. The students' questions and concerns were not satisfied with philosophical abstractions. They hoped for a concrete crystallization and examples. Ultimately this statement was developed.

> Whenever a decision or a choice is to be made concerning behavior, the moral decision will be the one which works toward the creation of trust, confidence, and integrity in relationships. It should increase the capacity of individuals to cooperate, and enhance the sense of self-respect in the individual. Acts which create distrust, suspicion, and misunderstanding, which build barriers and destroy integrity, are immoral. They decrease the individual's sense of self-respect, and rather than producing a capacity to work together they separate people and break down the capacity for communication.

When stated in chart form this is the way it appears.

THE BASIS FOR MAKING MORAL/ETHICAL DECISIONS

These Actions, Decisions and Attitudes are

Ethical/Moral	Unethical/Immoral

which produce

Ethical/Moral	Unethical/Immoral
1. increased capacity to trust people	1. increased distrust of people
2. greater integrity in relationships	2. deceit and duplicity in relationships
3. dissolution of barriers separating people	3. barriers between persons and groups
4. cooperative attitudes	4. resistant, uncooperative attitudes
5. faith and confidence in people	5. exploitive behavior toward others
6. enhanced self-respect	6. diminished self-respect
7. fulfillment of individual potentialities and a zest for living	7. thwarted and dwarfed individual capacities and disillusionment

Three consequences flow from this approach. First, we have moved away from the act-centered focus of the traditional ethical/moral approach, toward a process-centered approach. In the former the concentration is on acts, forbidden or accepted. The process-centered approach does not mean a complete lack of interest in overt acts but the major concern is now the processes they generate. What are their character and their consequences? It means also that interest is now in developing and establishing a moral climate, not in enforcing an act-centered moral code.

Second, in the process-centered approach no behavior can be regarded as beyond moral concern. Even isolated experiences which produce elation and an enhanced feeling of self-worth (or conversely, one of guilt, shame, and self-depreciation) affect one's capacity for outreach, for relating, and responding to others.[8]

The third consequence is this. Everyone is somehow responsibly involved in any process-centered moral/ethical situation. Under the act-centered approach, persons conceiving themselves as not directly involved can stand back and scorn the person being faulted. Certain phrases express this view—"It's his own fault," "She asked for it." "He made his own bed, let him lie in it." "They have none of my sympathy."

At one time I was involved in helping teachers concerned with improving classroom morale and creating a better atmosphere for learning. Most of the teachers seemed to feel that the problems of low morale lay entirely with the pupils—if only they would somehow change, everything would be fine. There was much discussion of classroom dishonesty, cheating, and ways for dealing with this. To emphasize the point that teachers were involved as well I gave this assignment: "Plan situations in your classroom which will insure cheating and dishonesty. The objective is to have all pupils cheating. How would you proceed?" It became clear very shortly that classroom methods, teachers' attitudes, the worth or lack of worth of the subject matter itself, parental pressures—all of these and more could affect pupil cheating. Some common procedures seemed ingeniously devised to produce cheating.

The next assignment: "Set up classroom situations which will encourage honesty." It became clear that strict rules, separate seating arrangements, forbidding textbooks in the classroom, or stern injunctions to be honest were not the answers. Rather it was important for pupils to feel that what they were to learn was valuable, worthwhile for them, that the teacher trusted them and was there to help. Under these circumstances teachers were also learners. They had to know both their pupils and the subject matter and its significance to them; they could no longer stand apart, focus on the act of cheating, and fault the pupils for being dishonest. They needed, too, to understand what forces were playing upon the pupils. To eliminate dishonesty they needed now to create a moral climate and build morale.

Early in my career as a professional educator I was principal of an eighth-grade elementary school. At the opening of school we moved into a brand-new building. The school grounds had been leveled by tractors and were completely bare; nothing was growing. The building itself, however, was new and exciting and everyone hoped to keep it that way for as long as possible. But how was this to be accomplished? Should guards be posted to prevent vandalism? Should pupils check in knives to prevent carving on desks? Should someone be stationed in the toilets to prevent the appearance of toilet graffiti?

The faculty decided that the pupils must be genuine and effective partners in maintaining the school. Numerous procedures followed for establishing a moral climate. They included:

1. The arithmetic teachers had class members go to the courthouse to get the tax levy on property and the proportion of tax money allocated to education. With approximate costs of construction and outfitting classrooms, and information on the amount of taxes paid by a family it was possible for a pupil to say "My family paid for this chalkboard," or "We purchased four desks."

2. The school board was contemplating putting out a lawn. The English teachers in the upper three grades asked each pupil to write a paper on "Ways to Improve the Appearance of Our School." The overwhelming concern was the need for a lawn. This was no surprise—it could hardly have been anything else! In any event a pupil delegation went to a school board meeting, presented the results, and explained their interest. The

presentation went so well that the board increased the lawn appropriation. From then on the pupils were truly partners. At the request of the pupils and faculty the added appropriation was used to purchase trees. At tree-planting time the pupils sponsored an Arbor Day program for parents and the public. Afterward everyone adjourned to the lawn-to-be. Each room had an assigned spot for setting out a tree and every pupil assisted in some manner.

Now it was the pupils' lawn! One day in a hurry to get to my office I cut corners and walked across the grass. I, the principal, was greeted by the voice of a child in the first or second grade: "Mr. Kirkendall, you're not supposed to walk on the lawn."

3. One day three or four pupils appeared at my office door to say that someone had walked from the first grade room to the boy's toilet dragging a green crayon along the wall. I went with them to see what had happened. Already several other pupils had obtained soap and hot water, and were erasing the crayon mark. Who had done this? No one ever asked. Seemingly everyone assumed it was a mistake. Rather than seeking to punish the child, they were concerned with getting rid of the mark.

4. Once graffiti depicting male and female genitals were etched on the walls of the boy's toilet. The toilet, adjacent to the gym, was used by high school basketball players, and visitors at the time of games. I called together six or seven upper-grade boys and asked them to go with me to the toilet. Here we examined the graffiti. I asked if the toilet as it stood presented an image they wanted the community to hold? No, it did not! "What should be done?" "Why don't we ask the custodian what to do?" And so this was done. The custodian, with the boys' help, soon had the walls in shape again. Once again we never knew who inscribed the graffiti—someone within or someone outside the school. Knowing who did it was never a consuming issue; restoring the appearance was.

5. Twice in two years, with the aid of the faculty, the Student Council arranged for a traveling art exhibit to come to the school. The pupils were so successful in selling tickets to parents and the public that at the end of the second year each classroom had two framed pictures chosen by vote of the pupils.

6. One noon the Student Council officers, the upper grade teachers and I, the principal, attended a downtown luncheon to discuss the part that pupils played in the school. The program was delayed so we returned some twenty minutes after the automatic bell system had called school into session. No plans had been made for this. With the absence of all student leaders and the faculty, would we find the school in rank disorder? To everyone's delight in each classroom the pupils were going ahead with their assigned work, with no teacher present.

Some will call this procedure indoctrination, perhaps manipulation. However, I would say that making the pupils partners created an environment in which they behaved as responsible citizens. The school was theirs in a very real sense, so they protected and improved it; their altruistic impulses were aroused. A moral climate had been created.

The illustrations show how the process-centered moral/ethical system is pervasive and all-inclusive. We have behaved toward the act-centered system as though it were all-pervasive, but it has not been. Chasms have existed because of variations in cultural patterns, racial and sex memberships; there have been religious rifts, for clear divisions have existed between religious leaders.

The real question is, how can the process-centered approach be made effective? Obviously it works most satisfyingly at the personal and community levels. Here people can meet each other straightforwardly and directly. Our society has become increasingly depersonalized. Face-to-face interchanges, whether altruistic in nature or aggressive confrontations, occur less and less frequently. Whatever their nature they enable individuals to assess deep-seated personality attributes in others. In a complicated society it is hard to know people as persons. We see them rather as related to some specialized function—this one a clerk, another as a librarian, still another as a teacher, that one a medical person, but few are seen as individual personalities, as people with hopes and aspirations, passions and apathies, experiencing defeats and successes, feeling emotions often much like our own. Yet when conditions permit, people respond to one another, and as Allee says (and I agree) that in the long run, " group-centered, more altruistic drives are slightly stronger."

The Christian Science Monitor in September-December, 1978 ran twelve articles, "A Nation of Neighborhoods" describing the rejuvenation of city living areas by the residents themselves. People who had formerly lived a disjointed existence, isolated in adjacent apartments but strangers for all intents and purposes, had joined in the revitalization of their neighborhoods. At the same time they became human beings to one another, and in a number of cases became allies in other projects.

Hope exists, too, in a growing flexibility in social arrangements and formalized structures. Marriage, for example, was at one time a social structure which, once entered, bound the spouses to numerous rigid patterns of behavior. Gender roles were crisply divided. In the patriarchal family the male was the financial supporter. He also ruled the family, otherwise his masculinity was in question. The female cared for the family, did not take part in decision-making processes, and accepted those restrictions as a part of her lot. It was expected that all emotional needs of the spouses would be satisfied in marriage. If not, then they would have to remain unsatisfied. For a married person to express strong affection for an opposite-sex person of similar age was scandalous and smacked of infidelity. Many difficulties seemed solved, undesired situations avoided, merely by entering the marriage structure. Too, a lifetime commitment was involved, for getting out of marriage was extremely difficult.[9]

Such rigidity was at times ridiculous. Thus, the Bulloughs[10] make a reference to a British writer of the Victorian period who urged "the perfect hostess to assure herself that the works of male and female authors be properly separated on her bookshelves. Their proximity unless they happen to be married should not be tolerated."

Variations in family forms have been looked at askance.[11] Single parenthood has been strongly disapproved, as have been couples who deliberately and forthrightly chose not to have children. A sexually open marriage, a commune organized to permit sexual accessibility of all members to each other, or couples living together without marriage—all were condemned. The ready acceptance of an alternative family form, unmarried couples living together (cohabitation), represents the discarding of one long-standing pattern. Nor is this abandonment confined to youth; many older persons as well have regarded it favorably.

To name these changing forms implies neither approval nor disapproval; it does say, however, that as rigidities are relaxed ethical assessments are more likely to be made rationally and within the process-centered framework.

Now to turn to more complicated situations, as when arbitrary authority still controls behavior, or some other human attribute such as the urge for power has triumphed over any sense of altruism. These are most often situations in which practically all face-to-face exchanges have disappeared. Any remaining interchange often involves only persons in control, who seldom see those subservient to their authority. And those face-to-face situations which do occur are often confrontations, rather than situations in which people are attempting to be open and expose themselves as persons.

To me the courageous decision of President Sadat to move directly into the Egyptian-Israeli maelstrom was valiant in the extreme. His hope was to apply the process-centered ethical approach to a threatening international affair. The ensuing involvement of Prime Minister Begin and President Jimmy Carter is likewise gratifying. Their efforts inspire a hope that even complex and dangerous situations can be approached in a positive moral manner.

I would like now to note three establishments wielding tremendous significance in matters of moral relating, worldwide. There are others, but my intent is not to evaluate, only to bring them to your attention. One is the government itself. Particularly in the more industrialized, technologized countries leaders are remote from the people themselves. With the complexity, the intricacies of today's societies, often over-populated, some of them highly industrialized and fragmented, unethical/immoral conditions are certain to exist. Is to take "the sting out of it" the best we can hope for? How can we cut down on immorality? How can we make the moral climate operative and satisfying.

Some rail against "big government," but this misses the point. The problem is not bigness, but depersonalization and a general remoteness which encourages exploitation by those persons in the controlling group who are so inclined. Globally, however, a highly interdependent "big society" has been created; this being the case, "big government" is inevitable. Added complications result from the pressures of special interest groups pushing a single issue but disregarding the whole political scene.

The extent to which the sting can be removed must rely on citizens' everlasting vigilance of governmental operations. Citizen support is needed for organizations like Common Cause, Committee for an Effective Congress, the American Civil Liberties Union, and others working for a more direct and personal approach in government.

The support of a democratic form of government is highly important. Note what happens when dictatorial and autocratic forms of government come to power. But maintaining democracy becomes more and more difficult in an increasingly complex society. This saddles even the best of governmental leaders with insurmountable demands.[12]

Another established force is "big business." It, too, produces depersonalization while concentrating on maximum production and increased consumership. Government policies at all levels may suffer from "big business" manipulation. The power of multinational corporations is increasing. I do not intend this to be indictment of all persons in the business world, only of manipulative, divisive, dishonest practices, which are certain to increase as the chasm between producer and customer widens.

The established third force, the most immoral of all as I see it, is rampant nationalism, that is, the existence of arbitrarily drawn boundaries walling in people who are then taught to defend and support their nation in any encroachment on or from others.[13] The leaders of each nation strive to make their nation powerful and more powerful. The success of their efforts commonly depends on settling all disputes by force, by military power. Suspicion, distrust, a sense of being manipulated permeates the thinking of people throughout the world. We have governments of the superpowers selling arms to smaller nations, ostensibly to maintain peace; actually to deplete resources, to bleed citizens financially as they pay for the military establishments. Another devastating global war is clearly a possibility. Perhaps the ultimate in weaponry was noted in a recent Department of Defense annual report.

> One of the responses that must surely be available to the President is what has been called 'assured destruction.' It is essential that we retain the capacity at all times to inflict an unacceptable level of damage on the Soviet Union, including the destruction of 200 major Soviet cities.

> .....no potential enemy should be permitted to think that he could, at some point, attack the U.S. or allied population and industry, or subject it to collateral damage, without prompt retaliation in kind.[14]

Robert Cahn adds still another area of ethical concern, namely a concern for the natural environment. This is certainly sound since human behavior is so strongly conditioned by environmental influences. If we are thus concerned we come closer to the "one-world" concept. As Cahn puts it "we all dwell in a house of one room—the world with the firmament for a roof and are sailing the celestial spaces without leaving any track."[15]

It is far easier, of course, to point out deficiencies and shortcomings in government, business and at the nationalistic level than to say what should be done. I plead guilty to this charge. But can we agree that these powerful forces should be evaluated, just as are individuals, by the criteria basic to an altruistic, process-centered morality? It will be a great step forward if we can.

Apropos of the preceding discussion are comments made by the late André Malraux in an interview which was excerpted in *Atlas*.[16] Malraux was asked "Can ethical factors influence history?" He replied,

> It depends on your definition of ethics. There are two different concepts in the word: One is guilt, and the other quality. We discussed quality; civilizations come into being only when they strive for the kind of man who believes he has more duties than rights. Then there's guilt. It comes from Christianity. Marxism is filled with it.... I believe that dignity changes history in the long run. That's the reason I have often spoken of brotherhood.... [In brotherhood one sees others] as more important than oneself. It's a very old idea. You ask if it could change history. I wonder if it hasn't already changed it profoundly. We are evolving from the farthest reaches of time, and I don't know if what impresses me most is the enormity of what is behind us or the enormity of what lies ahead.

This being a book on humanistic ethics some attention should be paid to organized religion. When dogma—for that is what is usually being talked about, not religion—becomes hardened into an autocracy with no adjustment to changing conditions, it is just as unethical in its processes as is authoritarian, depersonalized "big government" or "big business." Of course some religions are relaxing aspects of their rigid structure. The Catholic hierarchy, for example, is embattled. Some opt for the unchanging God-given commandment; others, particularly those who are close to the people, opt for a more flexible structure.

In the past the Judeo-Christian dogma has been a dour one. Once embraced, there was no longer much joy to be found in surviving. It has been act-centered and essentially negative toward earthly pleasures. The miseries and dissatisfactions of the here-and-now could be endured by thinking of the pleasure to be found in the afterlife. As a matter of fact one was taught not to think, but to accept concepts which created guilt and heightened one's sense of inadequacy and subservience. The sad part is that this concept has become deeply embedded and ritualized. As May Sarton writes

> ..the American ethos is still fundamentally puritanical and its values based not on a flowering of life... but on restrictions, disciplines, mores that have to be questioned before any human being can become fully human. And it is just this questioning that is now cracking this society in a healthy way, as the young batter their way through to a new ethos. The process seems often chaotic and even violent, but eventually we have to find an ethos that includes stability and harmony, for growth is not possible without them.[17]

My hope is that this battering will not be confined solely to the young.

Many of the ethical concepts espoused by religious leaders, however, have been significant and enduring—"Peace on earth," "Love thy neighbor as thyself"—and are process-centered in nature. Whether these concepts are realized will be determined by the extent to which this ethical/moral system can be made effective.

The process-centered approach will make heavy demands upon everyone. At the same time it promises much in the way of a more joyous, exciting society.

Some will argue that it is too complicated; a specific code will be much more easily understood and enforced. True, but the process-centered approach is no more, nor any less, complicated than life itself. Nor does the bottom line read "enforcement." Some enforcement may be necessary, but the ultimate objective is to create a climate in which all persons feel respected and included. And this can be a joyful experience.

Another argument against this approach is that it never settles anything, and is again all too often true. Nor is this anything new. As Zeik [18] says,

From Plato on, however, more philosophers have observed that ethical judgments become increasingly difficult as they descend from the purity of abstract principle to the murkiness of concrete application. None of us is excused from the anguish of application; we all necessarily bear on our shoulders the twin burdens of ambiguity and ambivalence.

In everyday life, numerous factors, both internal and external, are constantly changing one's living arrangements, and these in turn affect the way in which we relate to others and they to us. Aging, moving from one developmental level to another, one's mental and physical condition are illustrations of internal factors; industrialization and militaristic arming are examples of external forces.

In the process-centered approach one is always a learner. This ethical/moral system becomes more and more effective as one's knowledge of humankind increases, and of course there is no limit to this knowledge. The same must be said about knowledge of the environment, a crucial element in the process-centered approach. So while one will never have the final and complete answer, there is always growth and a furthering of one's outreach.

In closing I return to the final sentence from the Malraux quote:

> We are evolving from the farthest reaches of time, and I don't know if what impresses me most is the enormity of what is behind us or the enormity of what lies ahead.

NOTES

1. I use these terms synonymously to reflect a concern for human conduct considered within a right/wrong framework.

2. Kurtz, Paul. *Exuberance: A Philosophy of Happiness* (Buffalo: Prometheus Books, 1977).

3. Ibid, chapter 8, "The Beloved Cause."

4. Caplin, Arthur L. (ed.). *The Sociobiology Debate: Readings on Ethical and Scientific Issues* (New York: Harper and Row, 1978). This book, 514 pages, is composed of 42 chapters, treating of such matters as genetic determinism, the nature of human nature, the relation of biology, sociobiology, evolution, and philosophy to ethical concepts. Thomas Huxley, Allee, Lorenz, Darwin, E. O. Wilson, Lionel Tiger, Caplan, Tinbergen, and Eisenberg are featured, among others.
Also see Wilson, Edward O. *Sociobiology: The New Synthesis* (Cambridge: Harvard University Press, 1975).

5. Op. cit. *The Sociobiology Debate.*

6. W. C. Allee, "Where Angels Fear to Tread: A Contribution from General Sociology to Human Ethics," *Science*, 97:517-525, 1943. p. 521. Also in *The Sociobiology Debate* by *Arthur* Caplin, (ed.), pages 41-56.

7. Tinbergen, Niko. "On War and Peace in Animals and Men." *Science*, 160:1411-1418, June 28, 1968. Also in *The Sociobiology Debate* by Arthur L. Caplin, (ed.), pages 76-99.

8. Storer, Morris B. "Foundation Stones of Humanistic Ethics." *The Humanist,* 39:41-44, March/April, 1979. Storer concludes that morality "is always concerned with what is honorable and commendable *from the point of view of the overall community, never with what is merely desirable from the individual's perspective."* (Italics not in original.)

9. The title used in a treatise dealing with marriage carries a contemporary ring, "*Until Death Do Us Part, Or Something Else Comes Along.*"

10. Bullough, Vern and Bullough, Bonnie. *Sin, Sickness and Sanity* (New York: New American Library, 1978), p. 3.

11. Riemer, John J. "An Interview with Lester A. Kirkendall." *Alternative Lifestyles.* 2:101-119, Feb., 1979.

12. See, for example, the March 3, 1979, *Saturday Review* article, "Is Congress Obsolete?" by Tad Szulc.

13. Huxley, Julian. "A New World Vision." *The Humanist,* 39:34-40, March/April, 1979. In this article many points made in this chapter are discussed by Huxley, first Director General of UNESCO. He was concerned with achieving world unity, and was concerned with ways of transcending "nationality and nationalism."

14. Brown, Harold, Defense Secretary, "Department of Defense Annual Report, Fiscal Year 1979." Quoted in *Parade,* Feb. 25, 1979. p. 14. Also for realistic, gripping, and harrowing portrayal of the immoral effects of warfare on soldiers directly involved, see the article, "The Spell of War," by Liane Ellison Norman, March/April, 1979 issue of *The Center Magazine,* published by the Center for the Study of Democratic Institution, Santa Barbara, California. This fully coincides with my experience in counseling American service men in Italy in 1945.

15. Cahn, Robert. *Footprints on the Planet: A Search for an Environmental Ethic* (New York: Universe Books, 1978).

16. Malraux, André, "Ethics for a New Era." *Atlas: World Press Review.* 26: 25-27, March, 1979.

17. Sarton, May. *Journal of Solitude* (New York: Norton, 1973).

18. Zeik, Michael. Commentary in "A Condemned Man's Last Wish: Organ Donation & a 'Meaningful' Death." *The Hastings Center Report,* 9:16-17. Feb., 1979.

Comment by Archie Bahm on Kirkendall Article

As a former teacher of sociology, including Marriage, I find myself at home in Kirkendall's thinking, and I agree with most of his statements. Decline in acceptance of traditional explanations of the ultimate bases for moral appeals calls for some new ways of thinking about ethics.

Yet I find his concluding statement, perhaps justified by required brevity of treatment, incomplete. He says that "Our assessment of ethical decision will always be in the process of changing as we learn more...." But is it not also true that, as we learn more about human nature and its environment, we discover and test more universal principles operating in them? He claims that his system "should be applicable universally." We discover new samenesses as well as new differences. Is not Kirkendall's "always" itself intended as a universal principle? Is he inconsistent when he says "We need to return to an ancient concept," or does he imply recognition of some enduring universals?

He advocates moving "from an act-centered to a process-centered approach" and "from a concern for. a moral code to concern for...a moral climate." These are excellent moves. They can be effective in local situations when a competent counsellor is in charge. How they can be extended to big government, big business, rampant nationalism, and traditional religions has not been made clear.

A favorable moral climate is indeed necessary for confident moral living. But also, as he says, an "ethical system must rest on a rational, logical foundation." Although he promises a suggested "framework" for such a foundation, an actual foundation seems missing. An ethical system should be axiological as well as logical, based in intrinsic values as well as in reasoning based upon them. "Ethical decision making must have an authoritative basis." "The ultimate source of moral choice should be human experience." Agreed. But, except for appealing to human nature, biologically evolved and genetically determined, as having a "basic need for enhancing altruistic experience," explanation of the "authoritative basis" and "ultimate source" seems missing. Each person is also naturally self-interested (which interests also have biological and genetic sources) and his own primary intuitions of what is good. Showing how the need for altruism grows naturally (genetically, historically, psychologically, and in examples of his process approach) out of enlightened self-interest would provide an authoritative, rational, ultimate source for his system.

Reply by Lester Kirkendall to Bahm

Archie Bahm's critique of my chapter is appreciated. It is straightforward and direct. I will comment on certain points beginning with the second paragraph.

I did intend to imply an "enduring universal," namely, the human need for altrustic experiencing which I myself believe is inherent in the nature of human nature. But since we are forever learning more about the qualities of human beings, we are forever being challenged to be more

208   Lester A. Kirkendall

insightful and understanding in ethical decision making. The "ancient concept" I had in mind was the philanthropic, compassionate concern which renowned humanitarian leaders have expressed over the ages.

I did not outline in detail how to extend the process-centered approach to "big government, big business, rampant nationalism, and traditional religions." I had too little space to be detailed (and lack the knowledge as well), but I did cite illustrations in face-to-face situations which bear upon this concern. Traditional religion has relied upon a supernaturalistic deity, a concept which has played into the hands of demagogues. It favors exclusivism ("ours is the true faith"). At the business levels we need less materialistic striving and greater emphasis on caring and humane life goals. The governments of advanced nations must withdraw from the armament race and cease being "merchants of death." Competitive striving to be number one in military power must be dropped in favor of some kind of world control or government. A redirection of an economy away from militarism and toward cultural exchanges and a sharing of health care, natural resources, and intellectual know-how among the world's people is necessary. And certainly I wonder much of the time whether we can ever achieve it.

This caring concern for one another is the authoritative base for ethical decision-making since it is rooted in human nature, and our very existence depends upon whether it can be realized.

Comment by Howard Radest on Kirkendall Article

I am grateful for the air of reality that Professor Kirkendall introduces. Too often discussions of ethics (including my own) suffer from an abstractness that makes an already elusive subject even more elusive. The use of notions of cultural variety is also apropos—particularly since we humanists are easily tempted by a facile universalism despite our pretentions to pluralism.

Nevertheless, certain problems arise. For example: does the fact of cultural variety necessarily imply a type of indifferentism? Professor Kirkendall avoids this by identifying trends toward universality, for example, evidence of growing moral concurrence as exhibited in the chart he shares with us. Yet, as with any empirical approach to ethics, the possibility always remains that some group or groups with cultural bonafides may depart from that concurrence in some significant (moral) way. At that point, unless we introduce criteria that are transcultural, we are left with merely accepting—even if regretting—the direction such a group takes.

Since Professor Kirkendall does not intend this, there must be some implicit universal premises in his argument. For example, is he relying on some species-wide biopsychological base or is he working out a moral evolution theory (e.g., following Huxley)? I suspect this is so and it could be crucial to our common task. But I need more about this than I get in the essay. I am reassured about Professor Kirkendall's reliance on some universality that underlies (transcends) plurality when he identifies common ends under the general heading of "joyous survival." Unfortunately, this raises yet a further question since I am not convinced that "joy" can carry the weight that Professor Kirkendall assigns to it. Again, unless we can be confident that joy has some universal objective content (psychologically, socially), we can run into serious trouble. For instance, is it or is it not possible for my experience of joy to arise out of your suffering? Nor need this be a vicious experience at all since a case can be made that there is a rightful joy among the virtuous at the pain—guilt, remorse, punishment— of the wicked. But if that is so, then in what sense are we using "joyous" in the phrase, "joyous survival"?

I am naturally drawn to Professor Kirkendall's defense of the interpersonal as against the nonpersonal villains—governments, corporations, nations. Yet, I am puzzled by the problem of how interpersonal processes can transform transpersonal entities that rely on transpersonality for their usefulness. Is Professor Kirkendall, in other words, importing anarchist suppositions into his ethical theory—and if so, wouldn't we all be benefited if he dealt with these explicitly? I have no objection to such an approach and, intuitively, I share it. I am concerned, however, to have it brought forth for discussion and not left in the background. In education, for example, such moral anarchism characterizes views of schooling developed by the late Paul Goodman. What do these views contribute to our common moral task?

A striking hypothesis that piques my curiosity is Professor Kirkendall's statement that as "rigidity is relaxed, ethical assessments are more likely to be rational..." Since this view—again one I share—is in radical contrast to normal ethical usage (rules, duties, disciplines, etc.) I would hope that it might be the base of further inquiry. Of course, it has its moral neighborhood in notions of moral autonomy and moral democracy—but I think that Professor Kirkendall is adding something to these. I simply want to hear more.

Humanist Ethics as the Science of Oughtness

Archie J. Bahm

Humanists agree that persons are or have intrinsic value. Persons are ends-in-themselves. There is something ultimate about human nature and human values that cannot be reduced to anything else. Although persons depend upon many causes and conditions instrumental to their coming into being and continuing in existence, they do not exist fully as persons until they become aware of the worthwhileness of living and of themselves as embodiments of intrinsic value. The enjoyment of life as an end-in-itself and prospects for, because of potentialities for, more future enjoyment is the ultimate basis for morality.

If complete and perpetual enjoyment of life were assured, as is dreamed by those believing in a heaven after life, there would be no need for ethics. But since life perpetually presents us with problems, we have to decide and choose which course of action will best solve these problems. If one course of action, or kind of behavior, promises a better solution than another, then one ought to choose and act in that way. Oughtness consists in the power that an apparently greater good has over an apparently lesser good (or an apparently lesser evil has over an apparently greater evil) in compelling our choices. Why ought one choose the apparently greater good? Just because it appears to be the greater good. Such greater goodness may appear as a better means or a better end; but the apparent greater end-in-itself which the better means serves is the ultimate basis for morality.

The problems persons face are of many kinds, and so the kinds of choices persons must make are of many kinds. Some of these kinds are common to all persons, such as needing food, drink, protection from enemies, warmth, companionship, and adaptive skills. Other kinds are peculiar to differing environments and cultural conditions. To the extent that people and their circumstances are alike, we have bases for generalizations about them. To the extent that they differ, we do not. To the extent that we have generalizations, we have bases for an inductive science of ethics. Observed likenesses provide data for hypotheses about how people do behave, about what kinds of behavior beget better results than others, and about how people ought to choose in order to obtain the better results. Such hypotheses, stated as principles, can be tested repeatedly when the same problems recur.

ACTUAL AND CONDITIONAL OUGHTS

A fundamental distinction, too often neglected, between actual and conditional oughts helps to clarify many confusions commonly occuring in ethical theory and practice. Oughts are actual when a person is confronted with a situation in which he must choose between two alternatives, one of which seems better. But when persons learn from experience that certain kinds of choices and behavior generally, or always, achieve better results, he can remember his generalizations and discuss them with others even when he is not confronting such choices actually. For example, whenever a person has eaten too much of a favored food he experiences a stomachache, he can conclude that "I ought not to eat too much of this food so that I will not suffer a stomachache." He is stating an ought as a general principle regarding his own behavior. It is both conditional and universal. It is conditional in the sense that, if and when he is confronted with a choice of eating or not eating too much, he ought not to eat too much. But such conditional ought is not an actual ought because he is not now confronted with such a choice. It is universal in the sense that it is believed to apply to all occasions in which he is confronted with a choice about overeating his favorite food.

Actual oughts are situational. Conditional oughts are universal. Confusion occurs when conditional oughts, which are universal, are mistaken as actual oughts, and as equally compelling in all actual situations. When a son returns home for a visit with his mother who is pleased to cook his favorite food, he may believe that he actually ought to overeat to please his mother. Another conditional ought, when faced with a choice between pleasing and not pleasing one's mother, one ought always choose to please, other things being equal. Finding himself in a situation where two conditional oughts conflict, one's actual ought will depend on whether pleasing-mother-plus-stomachache ᴏɪ not-pleasing-mother-minus-stomachache appears to be the greater good.

Conditional oughts, stated as principles, normally involve "other things being equal." Most scientific principles or laws also normally involve "other things being equal." Curiously, we commonly neglect to observe that almost every scientific principle can serve as a basis for a conditional ought. For example, presumably scientists have demonstrated that unleaded gasoline pollutes air less than leaded gasoline under certain conditions (e.g., by using an electronic ignition). This demonstrated principle often serves a basis for a conditional ought: Whenever choosing between leaded and unleaded gasoline, one ought always choose the latter, other things being equal. But when other things are not equal, such as higher prices and insufficient money, insufficient supply of unleaded gasoline, or the rented car does not burn unleaded gasoline, then other conditional oughts enter consideration in actual oughts involving choices between leaded and unleaded gasoline.

The more complicated problems become, the more different kinds of principles need consideration in reaching decisions about them. The more science we study, for example, the more knowledge we can call on for help. Each scientist, and each specialist, by learning what is best in the field becomes an ethical authority relative to those principles in his field that can serve as a basis for conditional oughts. A specialist does not automatically achieve understanding of how a person ought to choose actually when and because he is not acquainted with the other conditional oughts entering into a person's actual oughts. But humanists do well to heed the advice of experts in all fields to the extent that they speak conditionally about what is the best in the way of decision and action.

ENLIGHTENED SELF-INTEREST

Each person has interests. Each person is naturally self-interested or interested in what is best for himself. In fact, rightness consists in intending to choose and act to produce the best results for one's self in the long run. Such intending is natural. In this sense, persons naturally intend to act rightly. But difficulties with knowing how to produce the best results, how to understand the nature of self, and how long is the long run often result in claims about acting wrongly.

The nature of self, seemingly most obvious to each person, involves multiplicities of complexities all somehow so organically unified and persisting that each person remains the same person throughout his life and its changes. Each self has a body, with organs, cells, molecules, and atoms; and we have developed physical, chemical, biological, and physiological sciences to help us understand it. Each self has a mind, with awareness, perception, memory, conception, imagination, feelings, emotions, desires, frustrations, hopes, fears, and so forth; and we have developed psychological, epistemological, and axiological sciences to explain its nature. Each self is social, being born of a mother, dependent on others for infant care, humanized through intimate association, provided with language, culture, adaptive skills, social roles, and productive ideals; and we have developed the social, economic, and political sciences to investigate and reveal its social nature. Growing numbers of subsciences constantly reveal more intricate complexities in the nature of things, including selves, that make the problems of self-realization more and more richly complex and difficult and challenging.

An important clue to the nature of each self is the number and kinds of things with which it feels indentified and to which it feels opposed. Some Christians, Jains, and Yogins, believing that a self is a soul detachable from its body, often feel opposed to their bodies. But most humanists identify themselves with their bodies, including its organs and cells. Some include their molecules, atoms, and subatomic particles. Some persons feel identified with their own past experiences, their mother, grandparents, ancestors, race, mankind, and even prehuman antecedents. Some selves feel identified with their groups, family, neighborhood, village, city, state, nation, and world, both general and more specialized such as educational, occupational, recreational, commercial, political, and scientific groups. Relative to each thing, digestive system, parent, village, or profession, with which a person feels identified, he naturally acquires interests in its welfare. Each becomes a part of him. His interest in it is his interest, and as naturally self-interested he is interested in what is best for it.

The question of how to obtain the best results for one's self in the long run becomes more complicated as one's self expands to include interests in more groups, more social roles, more cultures, and in the potentialities for still further development inherent in all of them. Enlightened self-interest involves feelings of obligation to learn more about the natures of all of the things with which a self feels identified. A self is naturally interested also in things with which it does not feel identified, both as possible additional enriching identifications and as dangers to its own welfare, including the welfare of all of the things with which it feels identified. Although increasing numbers and kinds of enjoyment resulting from expanding identifications ought always be sought, other things being equal, there are limits to growth for each self, both because limited amounts of time and energy prevent appropriate attention to all and because conflicts of interests, both within each person when his interests compete with each other and between groups with which he feels identified, often function as evils to be avoided if possible. Persons ought not join some groups, for example, those they do not understand, those demanding too great a percentage of their time and energy, and those producing more conflicts of interests, and especially those endangering their existence and other desirable potentialities. Aging and enfeebled persons should withdraw from groups and functions making demands they cannot fulfill. Some selves develop rigid personalities; others acquire flexibility in the ease with which they identify with and withdraw from interests bringing enjoyable satisfactions.

SELF AS SOCIAL

Each self is social, not only in the several ways already suggested above, but also in the sense that principles of association, including social interaction, are observable as inherent in its nature. One of the most obvious principles is that of reciprocity. Persons tend to treat others as they are treated by others. When a mother feels identified with her child, the child naturally feels indentified with its mother. Slap me and I will want to slap you. Esteem me, and I will esteem you, at least for esteeming me. The principle operates both negatively and positively. Help me and I will want to help you if I can.

Persons associating in more intimate groups, where feelings of identity make shared interests seem more obvious, tend to be more sensitive about reciprocating benefits. Persons associating in less intimate groups tend to limit feelings of responsibility for appropriate reciprocation to the specialized interests shared in common. Persons meeting at a bank window expect monetary exchanges to involve exact reciprocation, but they do not normally exchange sympathies regarding bereavement or other misfortune. The principle of reciprocity operates differentially in different groups. It seldom works with mathematical exactness. People with differing abilities, for example, in mother-child, teacher-pupil, wealthy-poor, strong-weak, timid-aggressive, and skilled-unskilled relationships, cannot always reciprocate in kind. Delays often occur before reciprocation. And others may forget to reciprocate even as we forget.

To the extent that the principle does operate, a person who desires benefits from associating can initiate benefits to others. Anyone who doubts its workability can experimentally initiate helping others satisfy their interests. Those who do so usually report coming out with increased benefits. The principle also tends to reflect sincerity. For if it becomes obvious that I am helping you merely so that you will help me, the genuineness of my interest in you tends to be depreciated. If my gift is genuine, I do not expect a return. Then when a return comes unexpectedly, it comes as a surprise with added enjoyment. We naturally believe that selfish persons do not deserve our help. In spite of its variability, the principle operates with sufficient beneficence that wisely self-interested persons will avoid developing attitudes and habits of selfishness and will try to be generous in at least those groups in which considerable beneficial reciprocation can be expected.

SOCIAL ETHICS

The views that ethics is merely social or merely individual are both mistaken. Ethics involves both individual and social problems, principles and solutions. The foregoing discussion has been limited primarily to individual ethics, for even "self as social," both when a self identifies itself with groups and recognizes the principle of reciprocity operating in human association, is intended as explaining something essential to the nature of selves. Although individual and social ethics interdepend intricately, each being in its own way foundational to the other, social ethics, strictly speaking, depends on the existences of groups as groups.

Groups consist of persons and continue to exist only by depending on persons. Groups come into existence to serve the needs of persons, and different kinds of such needs are the cause of different kinds of groups. But groups do exist, and have structures, functions, and casual influence over and above those of individual members. Some groups are momentary and some endure for centuries, lasting longer than any particular member. Institutions exist in persons and nowhere else. Yet institutions as established behavior patterns of persons in groups sometimes achieve a stability, endurance, and causal influence in addition to their functioning in particular persons. Once in existence, groups too, in the minds of their responsible officers or voting populace, confront problems requiring adaptation and decision. Groups too have interests and are naturally self-interested. When persons self-interestedly accept membership in a group and then think as members concerned about that group's purposes, nature, and problems, they naturally think in terms of how that group may best self-interestedly serve its purposes and solve its problems.

Central problems in social ethics pertain to group—person relations and to group-group relations. Since groups tend to be made up of many persons, each one somewhat different from the others, the values that each group has for its members tends to differ from member to member. Also, the demands that a group sometimes must make on its members will differ from member to member. So problems of justice, distributive and retributive, occur naturally in groups. If a person seeks more from his group than the group can give, or more than his share relative to other members, the principle of reciprocity may result in his getting less. But also groups may demand more from some members than from others, and more from all of them than its services to them are worth. Then problems occur regarding rights and duties, both those of persons as members in relation to the group and to other members, and those of the group relative to its members.

Group-group relations proliferate many complications regarding interests and conflicts and value accommodations. I cannot here go into all of the kinds of group-group relations (group-subgroup, group-peer group, group as member of a larger group, hierarchy of groups), all of the kinds of functions of groups, general or specialized (economic, political, military, educational, scientific, recreational, etc.), and all of the variations in kinds of groups and group functions. Humanists must accept the fact that social ethics is very complicated and is becoming more so.

Culture, including ethical conceptions and ideals, and institutions, including mores, laws, and incorporations structuring our social behavior, condition social ethics by providing conceptions about values and obligations and explanations about good and bad, right and wrong, rights and duties, and ways of behaving appropriately. Persons born into a particular society find its mores and institutions as something given, already existing as something to accept and adjust to. But social scientists studying the history of societies have been able to generalize about how societies and cultures are formed, mature, age, and decay. Cultural lag occurs whenever institutions designed to serve particular purposes no longer do so sufficiently and when needs arise for which no suitable institution exists. When persons in groups believe they can achieve a surplus benefit from establishing an institution, they ought to do so, other things being equal. When such an institution does serve member's needs, then personality values and institutional forms go hand in hand and persons naturally conform willingly to its conditions. When needs change but the institution does not, it tends to require conformity without sufficient benefit. When institutions persist in exacting dues from members without reciprocating benefits, they become formalistic (even antihumanistic) and persons ought to terminate them if possible. When some members do and some do not conform, an institution becomes disorganized. When none conform, it distintegrates.[1] If the needs it served persist, it tends to be reorganized. Social intelligence characterizes groups that keep their institutions in the stage of efficiency, and thus avoid or minimize cultural lag, according to humanist John Dewey.

RIGHTS AND DUTIES

Rights and duties are of many kinds and more complicated kinds emerge as society becomes increasingly complex and globally more interdependent. Some result from contractual agreement between two persons. Some result from contract between a person and a corporation, such as an insurance company, a bank, a labor union, or a manufacturing company. Some result from the voluntary formation of a group whose members commit themselves to rights and duties decided upon for fulfilling its purposes. Some are inherited through political institutions in groups into which we are born. Some are embedded mores, more rigidly in simpler, more rural, and more conservative societies, and less so in more complex, more megalopolitan, and more rapidly changing societies. Despite diversities in kind and origin, the ultimate bases of morality are the intrinsic values of persons. Humanists, at least, can trace the values of all rights and duties back to the intrinsic values of human beings. A right is always a right to some good, and a duty always involves a good owed.

Each person's first duty is to himself, that is, to his own intrinsic values, their creation, preservation, increase, and consumption. Whenever a person faces a choice between alternatives, one of which appears better than the other, he ought to choose the better. That is, he owes it to himself to choose the better. The fact that he is essentially social and that more of his interests tend to be extended to and achieved through groups extends his duties to himself through his duties to his groups. By doing his duties to others, others realize their rights. Actualizing one's own rights depends on others doing their duties. Rights and duties are correlative at least somewhat. At least they interdepend. For if others do not do their duties, our rights do not exist actually.

Rights and duties are not completely correlative, for when a person owing me some favors dies, when a bank goes bankrupt, or when a government guaranteeing bank deposits ceases to exist, I cannot collect. Individual differences, group difference, and differing circumstances all influence variations in the correlativity of rights and duties. Yet without sufficient correlativity to assure members that a normal minimum of justice is possible and probable, withdrawal or rebellion tend to occur. Justice, both distributive and retributive, has its existence in the correlativity of rights and duties. Justice is seldom exact, for even in a simple act of changing a five dollar bill for five ones, the person requesting the exchange tends to benefit in his own way more than the other. Yet without faith that sufficient justice can be expected from cooperative association, persons and groups will refuse to cooperate, other things being equal.

Recent emphasis on rights without duties testifies to growing moral degeneration, in the United States at least, and, even if variably, throughout the world. Increasing education, publication, communication, and political agitation all tend to emphasize human rights and to motivate each person to seek their attainment. But popular, professional, media and political neglect of equal emphasis on correlative duties contributes to unrealistic expectations. One reason why a science of ethics is needed is to

demonstrate how mistaken are such expectations and how fuller understanding of the nature of intrinsic values inherent in human beings and the
principles of benefits from mutual cooperation will motivate enlightened
self-interested persons and groups to emphasize duties as necessary foundations for rights.

ETHICS AS A SCIENCE

All of the foregoing problems are intended as problems open to scientific
investigation and all of the assertions are intended as hypotheses available
for testing, if not already sufficiently tested. All of them can be seen as
involving principles functioning as conditional oughts.

Not all humanists agree about whether a science of ethics is possible or
desirable. Editor Storer recently asserted that "We will never have a
science of ethics."[2] But Corliss Lamont says, "The Humanist contends that
a true science of ethics is possible and will yet be established."[3] The
Humanist Manifestos do not explicitly advocate developing ethics as a
science. But they do so implicitly. Manifesto I: "Religion must formulate
its hopes and plans in the light of the scientific spirit and method."
Presumably ethics must do the same. Manifesto II, in its section on
"Ethics," asserts: "The controlled use of scientific methods ... must be
extended further in the solution of human problems."

The first formulator of the Humanist Manifesto, Roy Wood Sellars,
not only regarded "Ethics as an empirical science" but also stated that
"Ethics is a very old science and has had a varied and distinctly controversial career very much as have epistemology and metaphysics."[4] John
Dewey, American Humanism's most influential philosopher, early asserted
that "Ethics is the science that deals with conduct, in so far as it is
considered right or wrong, good or bad."[5] As a founding member of the
American Humanist Association, I held, as I still do, that ethics is a
philosophical science.[6] I expect that, as more humanists become aware of
how ethics exists as an inductive science, its acceptance, use, and promotion will help to shape a humanist consensus in ethics.

POPULAR MISCONCEPTIONS

Turning to editor Storer's five packages of questions, I comment on three
issues not treated in the foregoing.

1. The freedom-determinism controversy persists because so many
mistakenly believe that freedom and determinism are incompatible. One is
free whenever he is able to do what he wants to do. But, since nothing
happens without being caused to happen in the way that it does happen,

one's wants are caused and his abilities are caused. One is caused to be free whenever his wants correspond with his abilities and is caused to be unfree whenever he wants what he cannot have. There are two ways to increase one's freedom: by acquiring additional abilities (both capacities and opportunities) to satisfy one's desires,[7] and by acquiring additional willingness to want what one actually gets.[8] Persisting misunderstanding results partly from misconceiving causation as merely mechanical. Such misunderstanding can be reduced by recognizing that the emergence of novelty is essential to the nature of causation[9] and that the evolutionary causes of human beings have caused each to exist and function as a new originating source of causation feeling its own agency in intending, choosing, and acting.

2. The question, "Does the end justify the means?" persists as troublesome when some ends are ignored or disregarded. The ends do justify the means because nothing else can. But all of the ends together do or do not justify all of the means involved in a particular situation. The common "Was the robber justified in killing the bank teller?" example either ignores the intrinsic values inherent in the life of the teller or asks whether the robber was justified in disregarding them when seeking his own ends selfishly. When the teller's ends are included, the killing is usually regarded as unjustified. When the killer selfishly ignores the teller's ends, we judge him blameworthy, we fear him as socially dangerous, and we seek to arrest, convict, and incarcerate him and to make him repay as much as possible for the damages (ultimately the deprived intrinsic goods and suffered intrinsic evils) he has caused. The answer to the question, "Does the end justify the means?" is "No" whenever any important ends are omitted because the ends, that is, only the ends and all of the ends, can and do justify the means.

3. Serious students of ethics discover many claims about what is the ultimate basis, the central foundation, or "the hub" of ethics. Editor Storer suggests three alternatives for consideration: "Greatest happiness of the greatest number versus justice versus love?" There are many more: custom, conscience, group approval, self-realization, et cetera. But why "versus"? Granted that some proponents of each claim argue for exclusive priority. But all of the theories grow out of human experience and each expresses something fundamental about it. A fully adequate theory will include all of these claims within its purview and show how, and in how far, each does express something fundamental. I claim that a humanistic ethics, one that locates the ends of human beings within it, both provides a more ultimate basis for all other claims and shows how love and justice, self-realization and the greatest good for the greatest number, conscience and authority, and so forth, not only have their roots in, but are richly extensive develop-

ments resulting from and continuing to depend on them, is best. Each supplements the other in rounding out the good life that ethical decisions ought to seek.

HUMANIST CONSENSUS

I am confident that greater consensus among humanists is possible. Expected proliferation of still newer ideas among humanists does not eliminate a shared basis, unless some mistakenly become exclusivistic in their claims. P. T. Raju, expert in comparing even more diverse philosophical traditions, recognizes that all philosophies are human, expressions of human nature, and, despite their diversity, actually supplement each other as manifestations of a common source, "man, who is already an integrality given in reality." He predicts that a study of even more diverse philosophies "will lead to a new kind of humanism."[10] Fuller understanding of human nature should promote greater consensus among humanists. I believe that a scientific study of the nature of human values and obligations to optimize those values is the best way of achieving such fuller understanding.

NOTES

1. For a most enlightened account of the problem of cultural lag, see "The Cycle of Institutional Development" described in Charles Horton Cooley, et al., *Introductory Sociology*, Charles Scribner's Sons, N.Y., 1933, pp. 406-415.
2. *Religious Humanism*, Vol. XII, No. 3, Summer, 1978, p. 117.
3. *The Philosophy of Humanism*, fifth edition, revised and enlarged, Frederick Ungar Publishing Co., N.Y., 1949, 1977, p. 232.
4. *The Principles and Problems of Philosophy*, Macmillan Company, N.Y., 1926, pp. 399, 395.
5. *Ethics*, Henry Holt, N.Y., 1908, revised edition, 1932, p.3.
6. See: "What is Philosophy?" *The Scientific Monthly*, June, 1941, Vol. LII, pp. 556-557; *Philosophy, An Introduction*, John Wiley and Sons, N.Y., 1953, pp. 4-6, 303; *Ethics as a Behavioral Science*, Charles C. Thomas, Springfield, Illinois, 1974; *The Philosopher's World Model*, Greenwood Press, Westport, Conn., 1979, pp. 156-166; *Why Be Moral? An Introduction to Ethics*, Munshiram Manoharlal Publishers, New Delhi, in press; *Axiology: The Science of Values*; and *Ethics: The Science of Oughtness*, submitted to publisher.
7. See my "Freedom as Fitness," *The Scientific Monthly*, Vol. LXIII, August, 1946, pp. 135-136.
8. See my *Philosophy of the Buddha*, Harper and Brothers, N.Y., 1958, pp. 15-15.
9. See my *Metaphysics: An Introduction*, Harper and Row's Barnes and Noble Books, N.Y., 1974, pp. 127-200.
10. *The Concept of Man. A Study in Comparative Philosophy*, Johnsen Publishing Co., Lincoln, Nebraska, 1960, 1966, p. 378. See also Raju's *Introduction to Comparative Philosophy*, University of Nebraska Press, Lincoln, 1962.

Comment by Lester Kirkendall on Bahm Article

Professor Bahm's chapter, "Humanistic Ethics as the Science of Oughtness" is concerned with ways people "ought to choose" in order to obtain satisfying results in moral decision making. He notes two kinds of oughtness: actual, used in particular situations, and conditional, which has universality. Decisions based on conditional oughts can be guided by principles which go beyond a specific situation. Professor Bahm mentioned two principles, reciprocity and self-identification. The concept of underlying principles is good but needs expansion. The recognition that there are such principles and that a number exist in any moral situation has important implication for the moral decision maker. In the first place, the principles Professor Bahm cites when further analyzed demonstrate that in every behavioral situation (and each situation poses its own moral dilemmas) there is an interaction in which other persons are involved, and are or have been moral decision makers themselves. In each specific situation, if one is aware of it one is not isolated as a chooser. Others face or have faced moral choices also.

When Professor Bahm discussed the principles of reciprocity he balanced the likelihood of a stomachache from overeating for the son, against the pleasure he would experience through pleasing his mother. But where does the mother stand in all this? Does reciprocity not involve her also? Has communication been so poor that she is unaware that overeating may cause her son digestive trouble? Has she based her self-esteem upon such a narrow base that the only way the son can please her is to overeat? Are there not other things he could do that would delight her, while he excused himself from overeating? Or perhaps he has walled himself off from his mother to the extent that the pleasure he finds in their relationship is confined mainly or entirely to the food he consumes. Or has he failed in some way to identify himself with his mother? And, of course, in terms of reciprocity other questions still could be asked.

The same is true of the self-identification principle. To begin with Professor Bahm lists a number of things that a person may identify with, then adds that relative to each one, "he naturally acquires interest in its welfare." True, but the principle of reciprocity is a part of this situation just as the principle of identification was involved in the overeating versus pleasing-mother illustration. Reciprocity is involved in the identification issue in this way. One does not "naturally" acquire interest in the welfare of the thing or person(s) with whom one identifies, except as there is at least something of a reciprocating response.

Reliance upon these principles, plus others which may be a part of the picture as well, makes moral oughtnesses and moral choosing very complex. But choosing in terms of these principles is complex only because life itself is complex. And it certainly means that moral decision making calls for rational and logical thinking, combined with intuitive awareness, and a knowledge of human behavior that goes much beyond esoteric philosophizing. This is the essence of the humanistic challenge.

Reply by Archie Bahm to Kirkendall

By raising the question "But where does the mother stand in all this?" Kirkendall reveals that he does not fully understand the nature of conditional oughts, which normally involve "other things being equal." He proceeds to list a series of other things which are not equal. When other alternatives enter a choosing perspective, then one particular conditional ought is not intended as alone compelling. Each of the alternatives can itself be stated in terms of one or more conditional oughts. Kirkendall does not cite an example of an actual ought with one or more of his additional conditions, each with its own conditional ought. The mother has her own actual oughts in terms of how the alternatives appear to her at a particular time. Asking how one ought to choose if the alternatives were different does not change the fact that one actually chooses in terms of how the alternatives appear at the time of choosing.

Although a principle of reciprocity appears to operate naturally in human association, variations in its operation can also be noted, including many good intentions and efforts that are not reciprocated. Since I can identify with my deceased mother or child, with a fellow human being in Tibet with whom I can never communicate, and with my totally wrecked car, I regard as false Kirkendall's statement that "One does not 'naturally' acquire interest in the welfare of a thing or person(s) with whom one identifies, except as there is at least something of a reciprocating response."

Moral choosing may be simple (as it must be with infants) or complex. Since moral choosing becomes increasingly more complex as we live more interdependently in megalopolitan and global society, our understanding of the complexities inherent in some choices can be aided by greater awareness of more relevant conditional oughts.

Comment by Howard Radest on Bahm Article

I found Archie Bahm's essay helpful, although, unlike him, I began my essay by denying the value of "ultimates," even the ultimacy of human beings. By way of corroborating my own sense of the problem, I noticed that while Professor Bahm's essay nodded to ultimacy at the beginning, he quickly moved to "process" questions, for example, focusing on choices and their requirements. So one question I have is: what purpose is served by an announcement of ultimates at the outset and do those ultimates help or confuse the ideas of "rightness" and "science" which are central to the essay?

Secondly, I am concerned by Professor Bahm's description of "rightness" in terms of long-run self-interest. As an opportunity to help the reader reflect on "self," on "interest," and on "long-run" the statement has a certain heuristic value. But, as a definition of rightness I find it problematic. For example, unless we are prepared to accept some "objective" or third-party definition of "my" interest, I am left with an invitation to ethical subjectivism which I know is contrary to Professor Bahm's purposes. He does try to guard against this subjectivist possibility by defining self as "social self" and by attaching instructions to what shall count as "long-run." But interest is simply too open a term of moral psychology for my taste and "long-run" varies with the respective position of the person judging his or her own time scale, for example, what is "long-run" for a child is not the same as "long-run" for a "senior citizen." I wonder then if we might not be better served by direct attention to such matters as biological responsiveness (e.g., problem-solving as in Dewey) and history (e.g., time is not a private matter although it is experienced personally). I think that's where Professor Bahm winds up, but I think he takes us in a needlessly subjectivist direction.

I am also puzzled by the use of the term "science." Scientific activity begins with assumptions and includes some kind of "world picture" to be sure. But these are functional and not metaphysical ultimates. In other words, as working assumptions, replacement assumptions and radical modifications are possible without prejudice. On the other hand, I do not think that Professor Bahm would be prepared to accept assumptions other than the ones he announces at the outset, for example, about the ultimacy of human beings, et cetera. Hence, I don't think we have assumptions at all here but rather something much stronger. That is why I referred considerations like this to "faith" in my own essay (e.g., as in a "religious" humanism, perhaps). But, if our root assumptions aren't assumptions, then in what sense do we have a "science"? I notice that Professor Bahm is uneasy about his claim for a scientific ethics when he adds the adjective "philosophic" as in his phrase, "ethics as a philosophic science." But, if that is necessary, then what would count as an *un*philosophic science, an *a*philosophic science, and an *anti*philosophic science? I'm not sure we gain much by entering that kind of debate so the use of the term "science" is to me only confusing. It seems to make a promise that the adjective quickly takes back.

Despite these comments, it should be obvious that the naturalistic commitments which inform Professor Bahm's views are clearly shared by me. My comments then are not intended to suggest some ultimate disagreements at all but some search for clarifications and usages that can help achieve the "common ground" which I suspect (believe, trust) is really present.

Reply by Archie Bahm to Radest

Radest's misconception of ultimates leads him to fail to understand that I regard processes as ultimates and to be confused further about "rightness" and "science."

My enlightened self-interest theory of ethics is intended, not as heuristic, but as self-evident, that is, one which Radest practices even when he is not aware of doing so. My explanation does not intend to invite subjectivism but enlightenment which is understood to include aid from all of the sciences, with all of the objective evidence available about the nature of self as well as its world. I do interpret persons as biological beings surviving by solving problems (as in Dewey) and I see those problems as the source of ethics (choosing between alternative hypotheses), rightness (survival, etc., presently and in the long run, by solving them), and science (as theory and practice of solving problems).

One of the assumptions of pragmatic science is the need for retaining an attitude of tentativity about conclusions. Such tentativity is one of the ultimates in the nature of science. Scientific conclusions continue to function as working hypotheses, and thus as assumptions for further practice until disproved or modified. Faith in the worthwhileness of solving problems, and in retaining an attitude of tentativity regarding solutions, is required as part of the faith needed in the worthwhileness of life itself. I regard scientific activity as religious whenever it aims to serve the value of a life as a whole (including its long run). Thus promotion of science is a natural ingredient in humanistic religion.

Those who distinguish between "the sciences and the humanities" and classify philosophy with the humanities often infer, mistakenly, that philosophy is necessarily unscientific. My view is that scientific attitudes and methods can and should be used in inquiring into philosophic problems. So I regard metaphysics, epistemology, logic, axiology, aesthetics, ethics and philosophy of religion, language, science, history, government, education, and so forth, as sciences. Since these sciences are not usually included among the physical, biological, and social sciences, it is natural to call them all philosophical sciences. Including ethics as a science causes no uneasiness.

Comment by Morris Storer On Bahm Article

Professor Bahm quotes Editor Storer as saying that "We will never have a Science of Ethics" and forthwith refutes him by quoting from many distinguished authorities. There is nothing that Editor Storer would rather be refuted on than this prediction, and speaking for him, I applaud every effort to bring such a science into being. I can think of no single thing that might be more salutary for the future of mankind than for ethicists and the whole world to be united around a comprehensive body of verified truth in ethics (and to be so guided) as physicists and biologists (except for psychologists), and the whole informed world with them, are united around the findings of those sciences (and are so guided, mostly). My prediction concerned "science" in this sense.

There are formidable obstacles in the way of achieving and communicating such a science, but I have every confidence that we can make progress toward that end by way of this symposium if we are united and single-minded in its pursuit.

One considerable obstacle that we need to clear concerns some differences about the meaning and central concern of ethics itself. "Rightness," states Prof. Bahm early in his article, "consists in intending to choose and act to produce the best results for oneself in the long run." Read out of context of the entire article, this might seem to signal a fairly sharp difference of viewpoint as compared with my interpretation of "oughtness" as a kind of "owing"—every individual's debt to the community. But I do entirely agree that the excellent person, the morally worthy person, does accept responsiblity for his own life and is concerned for "best results" in that life. And it is clear, at the same time that Bahm has those debts to others very much in mind and that "best results" are tied up in some way with performance of our duties to others. One of the strongest paragraphs in his article, in my opinion, is one about the overemphasis on rights in our time to the neglect of duties, those "goods owed" to others, as he defines them.

Could this devaluation of duties conceivably be related to the idea that the *ultimately* important principle of morality is "best results for self?" Perhaps people get the idea that a duty is null and void unless it is clear that something is to be gained by performing it. Do we have duties to members of groups with which we have not identified? Perhaps this is part of the problem. And can people always count on best results for self by performance of duties?

I would be glad too to have Bahm's comment on some particulars of those duties. What should be included: Honesty? Good faith? Respect of life, person, and property? A fair trial for anyone accused? An equal chance for all? An end of discrimination? I miss specifics. Are these categorical obligations?

One point of difference that might take several exchanges to resolve is Dr. Bahm's proposal that " 'oughtness' consists in the power that an apparently greater good has over an apparently lesser good . . . in compelling our choices." This might involve that people can afford to relax and let appearances make their choices for them since they are going to be compelled anyway.

Relativism and Responsibility

(A Discussion of Ethics From a Naturalistic Point of View.)

Howard B. Radest

THE MORAL AGENT

Careless sentimentalism and, at times, vicious mindlessness often pose as liberation. Without deserting personal freedom for order, we do need to find alternatives to this destructive individualism of our time. It is this need that I want to explore in this essay.[1]

Moral judgments and moral acts arise in the middle of things. Fortunately, the inherited store of moral habits that we find there often serves us well. However, we meet with puzzles in which the choice between moral goods or between moral evils is unclear. This is particularly true when changes accelerate and when multicultural environments are the rule. We turn in vain then to our habits but are uninstructed by them; we seek dependable replies but find the gods are silent too.[2]

At such times of serious doubting, we become aware in a visceral way of what we learned in history: that moral judgments occur differently in different times and places, and vary for people who are situated differently within their own societies. This confusing variability is successfully masked by effective moral conventions but now becomes visible, for example, as when women insist rightly that unadmitted masculine values have shaped culture, practice, language itself. This actual variability in moral judgments violates our expectations and our desires. We tend to react in one of two ways. We may deny variability itself by becoming more and more morally rigid—as in the reawakened fundamentalism and political fanaticism characteristic of crisis. Or, we may deny the valuableness of moral judgments entirely as in our so-called realism and evident moral cynicism. Since neither moral rigidity nor cynicism make much sense, we need other alternatives.

We do much better when we 'shift attention away from moral ulti-mates and toward moral activity. Like doing politics or art or business, so doing morality benefits from rubbing against all the other things we do. Once we humanize, as it were, moral activity, we cease to have perfectionist expectations of ethics. We come to understand that moral judgments like other human judgments are going to be partial, temporary, changeable, et cetera. In short, we desacralize and demystify morals. Ironically, this is both more necessary and more difficult in transitional times which increase our anxiety and tempt us to greater rigidities.

We may begin to understand doing morals by attending to the moral agent and not the moral rule. How might such an agent be described? Clearly, we are talking about someone who can have experience, learn from it, and do things with that learning. If we reflect on these require-ments, we can also understand something of the moral world in which such an agent must live, that is, a world which provides experience, which permits knowing, and which can change. Moreover, by describing both agent and world this way we recognize affinities between doing morals and doing other human things.

Experiencing, learning, and acting imply development or moral growth. Ordinarily, we think of this in individualistic terms alone and clearly moral agency is located in the notion of personal moral maturity. But, moral development includes much more. If we want an effective moral agent, then we ought to look to the community in which we find him/her in order to assess whether moral change has occurred in that community, that is, community as well as person may be said to develop morally. Other relevant questions come to mind once we situate a moral agent in a moral community. For example, we know that "good" people (e.g., moral heroes) do appear in "bad" societies, and that "good" societies exist even where their members are not so good. There appears to be no way of deciding in advance about the relationships between moral persons and moral communities. Variety, then, is not just personal and cultural but relational as well.

By now, I am sure we are convinced that dealing with moral judg-ments empirically, naturally, and historically is a trap and we can appre-ciate the reasons people have for turning to absolute extranatural moral authorities. We need to be able to say of others and of ourselves that what we are up to is or is not morally good. Yet, our evidence of moral variability seems to make it impossible to make such judgments. This is, however, the result of describing doing morals too abstractly and of seeking moral permanence. In context—that is, when genuine moral judg-ments are required—the situation is not hopeless at all.

Let us take two opposing moral judgments of slavery. In fifth century Greece a moral man could defend slavery on moral grounds. In twentieth century America, a moral man could not defend slavery on moral grounds. It would be nice if we could say finally that we are right and that the Greek was wrong—and I suppose we could say it if we wanted to. That, however, would ignore the moral realities of fifth century Greece and more generally ignore the way in which moral history happens. So while we might get a certain pleasure from being morally superior we would also be misled and not just about the past.

Are we then simply agreeing to whatever cultural norms exist at a given time and place? And if we are, then can we ever say that any culture is immoral? Clearly, for example, we judge Athens and Sparta differently just as we describe Hitler's Germany as immoral. How is this possible?

On analysis, we find that a moral defense of slavery—as against an opportunistic exploitation of slaves with attendant post-facto rationalizations, relies on a distinction between the moral status of the owner and the slave. So, for example, Aristotle argued that "some men were slaves by nature"; Plato distinguished between "bronze, silver, and golden" souls; pre-Civil War moralists relied on Old Testament distinctions between the various "tribes of Israel"; and so forth. The moral discussion of slavery resolves itself then into a discussion of whether or not some such distinctions are defensible; and if defensible, relevant; and if both defensible and relevant then do they justify domination? Since the record of these distinctions is that they turn out not to meet these tests, slavery may continue but its moral status disappears.

The latter point calls attention to the fact that doing morals is one activity among many. It should not be freighted, therefore, with more than it can bear. So, having drawn defensible moral conclusions, we yet have no guarantees about moral motivation or about moral commitment, et cetera. Doing morals has a necessary but limited role to play in human experience, that is, to identify moral judgments for the moral agent and so undergird the moral actions which may follow from such judgments. It is important, precisely because of our traditions, to distinguish doing morals from doing religion and other good and useful things. These bring to our experience the richness of commitment and the glories of faith; doing morals has the task of providing reasonable substance and critical apparatus so that our commitments do not run riot and our society does not become an arena of holy warfare.

Surely by now, however, we should be able to assert, "slavery is wrong." Of course we can, but we have not thereby achieved moral security. A moral rule—which this would become—works well precisely where moral options no longer exist. Rules represent our tacit moral agreements and are useful reminders. If I am correct, however, in thinking that the problem of "slavery" is found in determining what qualifies a being for status as a "free person," then the issue remains with us still. Let me illustrate.

Custom, as we know, continues slavery in some parts of the world. But a defensible moral case of slavery (e.g., of women in some Middle Eastern countries) is no longer possible. This, in fact, is the genuine achievement recognized by a moral codification like the "Universal Declaration of Human Rights." It leaves the slave owner with two options: to be a slave owner in secret which is in itself a confession; or to deny that the slaves are persons which is factual nonsense. However, before we congratulate ourselves on our moral enlightenment, we need to notice that the question of slavery appears for us in new shape. For example, we treat certain species of "animals"—for example, dolphins and higher apes—as property although we have evidence that tells us that we can reasonably attribute moral agency to them, that is, they would not seem to be morally inferior to us. We have here a genuine puzzle since a moral case can be made both for treating "animals" as "animals" and for treating some "animals" at least as moral agents. We notice that the rule, "Slavery is wrong," does not help us in any important way in developing a definitive moral case since the rule may be used with equal cogency by opposing sides in the moral argument. We notice finally that resolving the case is simply not in our power at this time. In a sense, that is paradigmatic of "doing morals" in genuinely interesting moral situations. By the way, discussion of this matter has obvious implications for developing morally sensible answers to problems of relations with nonterrestrial life when and if we meet with it and it meets with us.

My concern in these last remarks is not with science fiction but to illustrate the necessity of doing morals as against relying on moral codifications. Doing morals—which admittedly gives us only "second bests"— permits us to be open to the developing moral situation. It calls our attention to the need to educate moral agents, which is a different matter from mere moral training. In other words, insecure and tentative moral empiricism—which I describe under the name of doing morals—is not only defensible on the record but indeed sensible in a world like ours. Rather than apologizing, then, for our lack of certainty, we might well proclaim our moral way as preferable to those ways that, unfortunately, are misleading at best and disastrous at worst.

CHOOSING

Moral empiricism and moral development entail a world in which moral agency is possible. Yet, we continue to be fascinated by the idea of determinism. It attracts us both because it relieves us of moral responsibility and because it allows us to paint an absolutely coherent world picture. Determinism, moreover, is all the more appealing when madness rules. Unfortunately, a deterministic strategy makes the notion of strategy itself meaningless. If everything happens as it must, then we behave but we do not act. At that point moral agency vanishes. A bit of reflection shows why this must be so. Let us take as an example the idea of a "discovery." The implications of the idea are that we might not have made the discovery; that we made it and others did not; et cetera. Hence, we enjoy finding what we were looking for; we are surprised at it; we deserve the praise of others; we have a right to a sense of achievement. However, in a deterministic universe, discovery can have no meaning for what had to happen to our knowledge as to everything else just had to happen. Our ordinary responses to discovery then are unjustified. For example, why be praised or blamed for what we could not help but do. Of course, our responses also were inevitable since even our feelings had to happen.

One escape is to put the responder—or some part of him like "mind"—outside the world of experience. This two-world hypothesis, however, makes moral doing itself problematic. Where would we be about moral action and with whom would we be engaged? On reflection then, determinism despite its comforts achieves its ends by trivializing experience.

Now it may well be that the world is determined. However, we cannot decide the question, for such a decision would require a standpoint outside the world from which to perceive it entire. Since we remain inside the world, the question of determinism itself is indeterminate.[3] And since, moreover, the implications of determinism are such as to make human activity in the world pointless from a human point of view, it would seem the part of wisdom to resist its appeal.

This becomes crucial if we want to do morals for as we have seen morality rests in a relationship between an active agent and a responsive world. If agency is to be nontrivial, then any situation must permit more than one choice, that is, choice itself must be possible. At the same time, unless we reduce choice to a subjective event, more than one actual future has to be possible too. The very notion of moral outcomes necessitates a nondeterministic view of the world. That seems to be the logic of the question.

More is at stake, however. For example, we want to be able to take a position on this or that moral act; we want to be able to assign responsibility; we want to praise or blame; we want to learn and improve. Now all of this needs a world with possibilities in it rather than with certainties only. Hence doing morals sets limits on ontology—on the characteristics of the world—and on anthropology—on the characteristics of the agent.

We should notice, by contrast, that traditional moral views which derive ethics from some ultimate reality turn out to be morally problematic. For example, if the moral law is a natural law of the universe, then moral agency is reduced to obedience or disobedience and then only if the moral agent is in part nonnatural. Indeed, from a certain point of view, disobedience is idiotic since it must be followed by inevitable punishment. Often, the choice of obedience is reduced to psychological posing, that is, I will assert myself against the law although I know that this is really impossible. We then arrive at a morality of "fallen angels" who have defied legitimate authority or we agree that moral failure is the result of our inadequacy as moral knowers. Human beings are thus perceived as moral villains or as moral children. The historic debate over the "free will" of God's creatures is a painful rehearsal of this problem.

We must also distinguish moral agency, as we view it, from mere spontaneity. To deny determinism is not to deny causality and predictability. Our habit of polarizing points of view often leads us into such absurdities—so that denying determinism is taken to mean affirming chaos. But, doing morality requires that there be some intelligible relationships between the doing and the done. So, for example, the very idea of a lie requires that language be dependable enough so that reference to the events being misreported can be made in the future about the past. If this is impossible, then we cannot tell what a lie is either linguistically or ontologically.

Choice is not equivalent then to random movement but can only happen within some kinds of structures and in accordance with some kinds of reasonable rules of order. In fact, our actual moral judgments reflect precisely this point of view. For example, when we can show that there is no assignable connection between someone's act and a later event, then we admit that we do not have a morally judicable situation and that we cannot assign responsibility, for example, as in deciding a case of negligence. Similarly, unintentional harm doing is not punishable. Further, in chaotic situations—interestingly enough called "acts of God"—responsibility is voided.

Agency then implies choice and choice in turn implies a world in which choices are possible and agents for whom choices are intelligible. By contrast, both determinism and chaos make agency impossible. Thus doing morality happens in the middle of things both historically and metaphysically; we require a universe in which connections may be said to be loose, but still exist.

Morality cannot appear in a world that is entirely ordered or entirely nonordered. We may notice too that orderliness is not always given. In fact the morally interesting orderliness is that which is achieved. This achievement is the meaning of workability in morals, that is, moral realism and practicality are identified with the achievement of moral orderliness. So, for example, a world in which "a man's word is his bond" is to that extent a morally ordered world. It is obviously achieved and not given at birth. It is also incomplete since the achievement is never final.

WORKABILITY

Moral order is the evidence that moral judgments are at work. Unfortunately, nothing has been more misunderstood than the relationship between morality and practice. Popularly, for example, we talk as if realism and morality had to be enemies. Of course, what we mean by realism in such instances is some form of mere egoism and to that extent the enmity between morals and realism is rightly drawn. However, neither prudence nor opportunism exhaust realism. For example, it is realistic for a parent to provide for the future of his/her child although parental love does not require prudential justification. Similarly, some people are simply "truth-tellers" although on occasion this may be inopportune and even painful. So we can find instances of life-serving conduct that "works"—say by contributing to joyful survival—but that has no egoistic "pay-off" in the ordinary sense of the term, "What's in it for me?"

On the other side of the question, it is seldom noticed but ought to be that the view that the moral is that which ought not work (i.e., do the good for its own sake and only for its own sake) turns out to be a strange morality indeed. It begins with the austere appeal like those of a "duty-based" morality; it is sensible only if we accept distinctions Kant made, that is, between an autonomous human character in the "noumenal" world and a determinate causal human existence in the "phenomenal" world. If we take this view, however, then clearly even on deontological grounds, a duty-based morality may be said to "work" in the deep sense that it is the most complete expression of the nature of human nature.

The popular view that morality is "unrealistic" is only a pale echo of such a dutiful morality. We might better ask for the kinds of realism that are consistent with and that help us do morality. What should the moral agent be looking for by way of effectiveness. For example, if lying is immoral, then we should expect to find out about the moral (and other effects) of lying on the liar and the misled; for example, in addition to psychological and other practical consequences, we should expect to find consequences to character, to maturity, and to freedom. As it happens, we can and do find these things, that is, we do discover morally poor results following from morally poor judgments.[4]

We can, in other words, develop criteria for moral workability by examining moral experience. For example, a moral agent who could not discover the effects of moral actions could not be a moral agent. This implies that moral agency requires the possibility of moral knowledge.

Since an agent chooses, an agent must be free in order to do morality. There are, in other words, some clear and general things we can say about moral workability. By implication, then, policies and practices which restrict freedom and knowledge would be judged to be morally undesirable. Inevitably, however, the unforeseen and the unforeseeable occur. The moral agent, therefore, runs into the limits of knowledge. It follows that global moral judgments are suspect precisely because they are global, or, to put this traditionally, humility remains a virtue for us. Logically, this casts doubt on unconditional moral judgments beginning, "all...", and forces us to examine and reexamine the variable scope of judgments beginning, "some..." (e.g., as we saw in our discussion of slavery).

Other criteria appear when we take moral agency seriously. For example, benefits sought by an agent for himself alone are suspect. So, if I authorize myself to steal but am not prepared to authorize others like myself to do the same thing, I generate morally contradictory or chaotic behavior. Our reasons for the defensibility of moral exceptionalism follow from living in a world in which the consequences of acts reverberate. Hence, when I make myself an exception I still have to take account of effects I would like to ignore. So, even if I try to authorize myself alone to steal, it turns out that I have authorized others, each of whom can now perceive himself to be in "my" case too, that is, makes himself an exception.[5] Since stealing is intended to benefit me above others, my act turns out to be self defeating. I am not saved by the argument that most people, after all, will not know about or act on my authorization. Since I cannot find out whether or not this is the case (i.e., stealing to be effective must be undetected), I am left not only with doubt about my own benefits but doubts about the acts of other moral agents. The process of making myself into an exception turns out to be untenable. Moreover, it subverts all moral agency since the freedom to act relies upon dependability in experience. Exceptionalism by destroying dependability increases randomness in that experience. In a deep sense—morally and ontologically—trust vanishes. Behaviorally, truth claims come to be greeted with cynicism.

Workability thus turns out to be a nexus for the necessary interactions of facts and values. A note on why the ill repute of workability then is in order. To be sure, our secularized Puritanism takes a certain pleasure in making moral demands that are moral just because they are painful. More significantly, doubts about workability arise from the limits of knowledge. Since consequences can never be fully known, it is difficult to assign responsibility for events. So, we try to find ways of judging ourselves and others apart from events.[6] Unfortunately, this leads us literally out of this world in a search for eternity or for stasis. More sensible, it would seem, is to attribute responsibility carefully, minimally, and humbly.

Finally, moral consequences compete with other kinds of consequences, for example, with political power, economic wealth, and so forth,
and sometimes we prefer these other results. The moral agent cannot
simply impose his preferences over all others. He can, however, exhibit the
moral consequences of our choices.

At times, we can claim that other outcomes must take precedence over
morally desirable outcomes and we can give good (but not moral) reasons
for this judgment. However, it is not possible simply to convert such a
nonmoral claim—say for the "national interest"—into a moral claim
without meeting moral criteria. Since we human beings seldom are con-
tented with a merely political or economic argument, we find that despite a
rhetorical "realism" we do usually seek moral justifications. So survival is
not merely desired but desirable because we not only want to survive but
ought to survive. We are, in other words, "ethical animals".[7]

We cannot, in doing morals, then, insist that everyone always be doing
morals too. We can insist, however, that if we shift ground from doing
something else to doing morals—as is the habit of politicians, business-
men, labor leaders, scientists, et cetera—that we be required to meet moral
criteria. So, for example, we may claim economic justification for a
"bottom line" but we cannot claim it to be moral without moral analysis
and defense. That, really, is as far as doing morals can or ought to take us.
Since our aim is neither moral authoritarianism nor moral hierarchy, other
values have a legitimate claim on us too.

RIGHTS AND DUTIES

The search for morally effective agents leads naturally to questions of the
moral limits on an agent and the moral obligations of an agent. What, in
other words, must be predicated of a moral agent in order for him/her to
qualify? Ordinarily we answer this question with moral rights and moral
duties. Here, again, our developmental view would imply that new or
revised rights and duties may be expected to emerge as human capacities
change and as the nature of experience undergoes transformation.

The derivation of rights from moral agency frees us of the need to fix
rights for all time or to base rights in "Nature," "God," or "Truth." We
need not suspend natural and historic processes or perform an act of faith
in order to speak intelligibly of rights. One practical outcome of this view is
that we need not demand agreement to some global creed as a prerequisite
to developing meaningful worldwide rights.

If rights can be said to develop along with moral agency, it follows
that rights cannot be eternal. To take an example, the right to determine
the shape of our personal lives, as in family size, may be legitimately

curtailed by developments which justify limiting rights of association. Similar limits on the personal life are taken for granted by now, for example, limits on the rights of property, but we are less troubled by these limits because we are accustomed to them and because such limits are reasonable. More generally, we depart from both natural law and enlightenment traditions. Rights come into being and pass away just like the rest of our experience.

This approach to rights may also be stated as a description of the capacities of a moral agent. Capacities, however, do not necessarily require any given act. So a moral agent may choose to exercise a right but need not do so. On the other hand, since a right that could not be exercised would not be a right, it follows that the world of moral agents must be so constructed as to permit exercise but not demand it. On this ground, we may describe the minimal acceptable legal structure of a society, that is, agency leads through rights to society.

A right, finally, may be understood as that which is had by a moral agent. That enables us to distinguish having a right from performing a duty. So, I cannot be required to exercise a right since other legitimate considerations may suggest that I not exercise it, for example, the right of free speech need not be exercised in the interest of courtesy. By contrast, I am morally required to perform a duty. For example, if I have a right to know and exercise it by asking you a question, then you have a duty to see to it that information is available or else give good reasons for not doing so. It is in this way that we may describe moral relationships.

It would seem that rights and duties are correlative; that is, if we find someone exercising a right we should find someone else performing a reciprocal duty. However, it isn't as clear as that in all cases. For example, a child has a right to know in order to develop as a moral agent. Someone then may be said to have a duty to teach. Yet, we cannot expect the child to be a teacher and so we cannot say of the child that he has a duty to teach. Duties, in other words, flow from qualifications. Where qualification is present then someone may be morally coerced to act. Does a right to know, however, necessarily imply a duty to learn? I would suggest that we here confuse a rational judgment with a moral obligation, that is, if I exercise a right to know then it is senseless for me to refuse to do the things attendant on learning. But a choice of options initiates the process. That is not the case with duty.

Unfortunately, we further confuse the issue these days by using phrases like a "right to be loved," et cetera. Yet, it is clear enough that I cannot exercise a "right to be loved" in the same way that I can exercise a right to know. Because rights have a certain popular appeal in democratic cultures, we tend to use rights language to describe legitimate moral and other needs. We would be better off, however, to limit such usage to possibilities of exercise, and duty language to required moral performance. Other features of the moral biography of an agent are better dealt with differently, for example, in a moral psychology.

Another way of understanding rights and duties is to associate duties with moral development and rights with moral existence. We may then have a duty to help someone because we are capable while not having a correlative right to expect assistance from that someone in return. He or she may simply be incapable of assisting us. The interactions of rights and duties are not then to be modeled after a marketplace.

We can judge someone to be immoral if he or she fails to perform a duty where the qualifications exist. However, we cannot make that judgment if he or she fails to exercise a right. Our judgment with respect to free exercise differs. So, we may regret our differences about exercise but we could not legitimately make a judgment of immorality. On the other hand, there is a strong case for a negative moral judgment and for moral sanctions when someone fails in his or her duty. An examination of our experience shows that we do take a different stance toward the moral agent when confronted by failure to exercise as against failure to perform.

Of course, we have feelings in such situations. We associate with rights those feelings that have to do generally with exercised abilities—satisfaction, pride, achievement. Feelings associated with duties derive from notions of obligation and vindication. Thus, we are not justified in feeling proud for having done our duty since that is just what we had to do. Pride then is correctly viewed as casting a shadow on moral performance. On the other hand, we might even feel good about failing to exercise a right; for example, I may feel good in choosing courtesy over free speech.

Among the more complex feelings associated with the nonperformance of duties is the feeling of guilt. Guilt, however, is not appropriate with respect to nonexercise. So, if I have a right to vote and fail to do so, I may feel quite justified. Perhaps, nonexercise may be understood as evoking feelings of regret and sadness rather than guilt and self condemnation. Appropriately, we may expect to atone for nonperformance while we may simply be sorry for nonexercise.

THE MORAL SITUATION

I have been sketching the picture of a moral agent and his world. Clearly, the view is relativistic and situational. But, as I trust is clear, this does not lead us to an incoherent and utterly undependable morality. Since, however, relativism and situationism are alleged to have such a result, it is useful to examine the question a bit more thoroughly.

After all, it may be claimed, if moral judgments arise and end within the situation, then it would seem to follow that each event could in principle call for its own unique judgment. Any collection of judgments, then, might well produce morally contradictory recommendations. One way out of this dilemma is to deny that moral judgments can be compared at all since they would literally disappear with the situation that evoked them. Of course, if this approach were taken, then guidance from moral experience would be impossible and moral recommendations would be pointless.

Relativism it would seem reaches its extreme condition in such a pure situation ethics. However, doing morals in the middle of things does not require us to opt for this most radical formulation of the meaning of situations. Indeed, it is literally impossible to understand situations in this utterly atomistic way. We must, for example, carry some language over from situation to situation unless we make the strange claim that we also invent a new language for each situation and that we dispense with that language when the situation ends.

Situation ethics, then, is not at all the same as relativistic ethics. So, by denying that the moral agent is found in some noumenal or other permanent nonnatural order, we do not have to surrender ethics to chaos. Nor need we surrender doing morals to mere subjectivity in order to be naturalistic. Indeed, both radical situation ethics and radical subjectivity turn out to be satires of relativism. After all, doing morals requires an assessment of contexts and consequences—both of which need objective transsituational inquiry in order to have a content.

The empirical ethics I have been talking about occupies its own distinctive ground. It is not subjectivist, situationist, or absolutist. My view presumes continuities in nature and history. If this were not the case both the subjectivists and the absolutists would be correct—but the former could not know it and the latter wouldn't be interested.

I really think, however, that I have been describing our actual moral conduct. Why is it then that subjectivism, absolutism, and situationism seem to have such appeal? All three, despite their manifest differences, promise a certain security. Subjectivism promises liberation and sanctions reliance on inner certainties. Absolutism, in complementary fashion, promises coherence and sanctions reliance on ontological certainties. And situationism promises relevance and sanctions-reliance on completed experience. By contrast, in doing morals we expect uncertainty to continue and inquiry as a permanent diet. So, each of the popular alternatives may well meet some deeply rooted psychological and practical need.

Even when we boast of our "realism," doing morals is quite serious for all of us. Yet, we are seldom if ever in position to know enough to make our moral judgments certain. Nor can we temporize, since to delay, as moralists have noticed over and over again, is also to decide. This makes it quite understandable for us to search for ways of dispensing with the limits of experience and of seeking security. Yet, just as we accept limits in other weighty areas of judgment, so we need to learn to accept limits on moral judgment too. This becomes possible once we accept the notion that moral error—no matter how serious or painful—does not jeopardize our eternal souls. The historic connection between the ways of the Gods and the ways of the good made it impossible to live with moral doubts which we find entirely reasonable in politics, economics, the arts, the sciences.

Finally, I do not want to exaggerate our problems. We are not morally helpless or morally unintelligible. In the middle of things, the choices are always finite and resources for making choices do not have to be created from the beginning.[8] Moreover, when we examine what our neighbors do morally—not what they say they are doing—we find that they, like us, do morals very much as I have been describing it. On that point, relativists can make the claim that they more closely describe what doing morals is all about—and not just for relativists. At the very least, this makes doing morals a more credible and responsible human activity than when it is performed under the claim of untenable moral certainties.

NOTES

1. In this essay I focus on agency and do not do very much with relations. I trust, however, that I will not be understood as ignoring the moral significance of society, community, state, etc. Since the presenting problem for me is the claim of radical moral individualism as the danger into which humanist liberation easily falls, it seems crucial to take a look at what might count legitimately as the moral individual.

2. As should be obvious, I think that John Dewey's naturalism makes good sense. I do not believe that it entails a so-called "naturalistic" fallacy, i.e., that moral inquiry is forced to confuse the desired and the desirable. On the other hand, moral inquiry which ignored actual desires, etc. would simply not reach to the moral questions worth asking and would turn moral activity into an arid exercise.

3. For a cogent development of this view, see William James, "The Dilemma of Determinism."

4. See, Sisella Bok, *Lying* (New York: Random House, 1979) for a discussion of moral effects.

5. This view is in line with Kant's recommendation that we act as if we were willing a universal law. However, I also think we have to examine the outcomes of universalization in experience so, unlike Kant, my suggestion is not categorical.

6. We do fix responsibility in situations—e.g., in law, in relationships. However, actual fixing of responsibility is revisable and so as with other serious activities is attended by risk.

7 C. H. Waddington, in *The Ethical Animal* (Chicago: The University of Chicago Press, 1967) provides a sound and useful discussion of this theme.

8 Dewey's term, "funded experience," is appropos here.

Comment by Archie Bahm on Radest Article

I believe that I agree with most of the views Radest holds. But the language he uses causes me to disagree with how he states them.

1. He locates morality as always an activity in the middle of things and not a matter of ultimates, first principles, or final ends. His statement appears to me to be self-contradictory. "Activity in the middle of things" *is his ultimate*. His stating that morality is always in the middle of things *is his principle*. Because he looks no further than "the middle of things" for his explanation, it *is his final end*. I believe that the constructive statement of his views does not depend upon his negative, limited, and to me mistaken, use of "ultimates."

2. The freedom-determinism controversy is fraught with perpetual misunderstandings, and Radest allows himself to get trapped in them. He accepts causation of consequences by choices, of conditions requiring choices, and of evidences influencing persons when choosing. But he rejects determinism completely, thus implying that causation, which he accepts, does not determine. He mistakenly rejects "permanence" as a condition of existing, history, and morality because he identifies it with "absolutes" and interprets it as "eternal." Then, still needing permanence, he "requires a universe with structures and connections" to serve as bases for "dependable knowledge."

3. Rights and duties, I agree, are somewhat correlative but not completely so. Both, he says, "appear with the character of the moral agent." But how and why remain unexplained. If ethics were merely social, then the "rights are owed me, duties are debts to others" view might seem more reasonable. But, as I see it, each person's duty is first of all to himself and second (or still first) to others because he himself is essentially social in nature and fulfillment. A person owns, or "has," his duties as much as he owns, or "has," his rights. I disagree with the statement that "duties of moral agents are not matters of 'free exercise' but of obligation" because I believe that actual obligations do not exist apart from awareness, intention, and choice. Conditional oughts, duties one would choose to accept actually under certain conditions, are often mistaken as rules having no exceptions. One is not, except potentially, a moral agent until he is actually choosing. Duties become actualized only in and through choosing.

Thus, although I regard Radest's views as obviously humanistic, absence of distinctions between intrinsic and instrumental values and between actual and conditional obligations, which appear to me to be essential to understanding the nature of values and ethics, makes me regard his development as still inadequate.

Kulturkampf

Lee Nisbet

Cultures that nourish are outcomes of deliberate effort. They do not just happen. A rich harvest demands cultivation. Admittedly one cannot produce a good crop like one produces a good car, for life is more subtle, stronger, more demanding than dead material. The conditions, however, that encourage bounty can be studied and created. Morality and ethics are concerned about the cultivation of individual and wise character.

Unfortunately, in most cultures human beings, both historically and in contemporary times, have thought it their duty to produce sturdy reproductions of themselves or fantasized selves. They suffered and suffer the misfortune of misidentifying themselves and the rigid ideals, dreams, and purposes of their times with a rich harvest. The result of this misidentification has been the confusion of dog training with the moral process of cultivating fine character. With the best of intentions and the worst of motivations they imposed and impose sweeping directives of "ought" and "should" willy nilly on everyone. One should always *act* in these ways and certainly ought to *be* just like this. It was and is thought relevant to provide rationales for these directives. Appeals to the supernatural, fear, pity, duty, society, humanity, the greatest good for the greatest number, reason, intuition, family, manhood, womanhood, shame, niceness, and so on were and are thought to suffice.

These rationales and the rewards and punishments intimately attached to them in fact are not very desirable. The very connection of these sweeping directives, with multitudes of rationales, widespread bribery of innumerable rewards, and threats of awful punishments provides evidence that casts doubt on the desirability of dog training for human beings. Obviously, if people have to be directed, shamed, coerced, seduced, and otherwise manipulated into behaving in certain ways, they either don't *want* to behave in those ways or don't know what *they* want. In the former case, life will always be a struggle between submission and defiance, and, in the latter, life is a vacuum which will be filled by authority. Either situation is undesirable since the opportunity for intelligent choice among known alternatives is rendered difficult, if not impossible, as is the opportunity to take responsibility for those choices.

Morality, if it is to be desirable, must therefore be something more than dog training. Morality, worthwhile morality, is inquiry. This distinction between dog-training morality and moral inquiry redefines the function, method, and ends of the art of judgment and has profound implications for the development of character in modern industrial culture.

Behaviors defined as virtues by traditional moralities *may* be worthwhile. Virtues, however, such as dedication, courage, altruism, self-reliance, and assertiveness *are* virtuous only in reference to integrated and worthwhile ends. A Nazi may very well be dedicated, courageous, self-reliant, and assertive in his search for the final solution but hardly a person we would consider virtuous. Inquiry substitutes inquiry into particular situations for generalizations, knowledge for opinion. A primary task of moral inquiry, therefore, is the study of how to determine what ends of conduct are worthwhile pursuing under what circumstances.

The second central task of inquiry is to determine what cultural conditions are most likely to produce the sort of character capable of and likely to select better ends of conduct. We should understand by now that men of worse character have a distinctly different conception of what is good than men of better character. The good of the sadist can be painful for the good man to behold.

The difference between moral inquiry and dog training or moralizing is quite apparent. Telling persons what they should be like goes nowhere simply because one is telling them to behave differently than they know how to. The result, of course, is that they can't do what they are told even if they wanted to. They simply don't know how. But what if individuals *want* to know how to behave differently? We might be able to teach them how to teach themselves how to do so. What sort of persons are most likely to want to do so? What sort of character would they have? Such persons would be those who experience life as the scene of manifold opportunities to become more than they are. They understand that the secret of becoming, of happiness, of achieving a unified self is to *know how to* and to *want to.* Such beings understand that *should* now means "should you *want* to

244 Howard B. Radest

achieve this end you *must* do this." Such persons experience in all its glory and pain the iron necessity in freedom. They submit and they are free. They select the ends that chart the course of their conduct. They impose upon themselves the duties designed to secure those ends. They act to test their wisdom and thus even in failure they master their own destiny. Irony sides with the strong.

The question remains, What sort of culture would nourish such strength of character? Ironically, a hypothesis might be developed through an investigation of slavishness and the conditions that nourish it.

The slavish are those who cannot establish their own direction. They are lost in the worst sense of being lost. They do not know where to go because they do not know where they want to go. Since they lack courage as well as wisdom, they fear to find out even where they now are.

The first instinct of the lost soul is to cry out for rescue. The cry for help in the wilderness turns to rage. "Why does no one hear me? Why does no one take care of me? The world is alien, hostile; it is purposeless." The Christian and the anguished atheist share the same wretched conclusion. Since free existence requires effort, discipline, courage, and intelligence, life is absurd.

The character of the slave comes to be dominated by resentment. Nietzsche wrote that resentment is the substitution of imaginary revenge for the deed. The slave wishes to revenge himself on the creative, powerful, all those who are able to establish purpose and direction in their lives, all that is growing beyond itself. Their fantasies of revenge, their hostility to all who are better than they are, drives the slavish to execute their first hostile act. They demand that something or somebody exist such that they can justify their servileness. The slavish demand a master to impose upon them purposes and duties which they believe themselves incapable of doing for themselves. No master, however, worthy enough to rationalize servileness would immediately accept such a demand. The master, like the haughty King of Prussia, would, out of necessity, turn down a crown offered by trembling hands. The slaves can demand nothing, for demands imply obligations and slaves do not merit obligations. The slavish can offer only servileness. The slavish, therefore, cannot demand a master. They must *seduce* a master.

The slavish, though not wise, are cunning. They know that any person wishing to be a master is also slavish. A master is also one who can establish no direction, nor purpose of his own. He therefore desires to be used, to be useful. Feigning contempt for the sweet pleadings of the slavish, the master is secretly attracted. He wants parasites to dominate and to dominate him. Domination establishes a direction, a goal, a purpose, apparent power, and prerogatives. Frederick William IV did, after all, finally submit to the seductions of the frightened burghers of Prussia.

Every master is but a master-slave. Cleverly concealed in the cloak of power is his own slavishness, his substitution of the responsibilities of others for his own. The master is literally created by the slavish to serve, maintain, and, most importantly, to rationalize their bad habits. "We cannot be free; our master does not permit it. We cannot impose our *own* purposes on life, formulate our own duties; our master must impose ends and duties upon us."

What ways of living nourish slavishness? Why, our ways of course. How do *we* encourage, seduce our children and ourselves to become entangled in a web of purposes and obligations that discourage seeking our own ends and duties? The answer lies all around us—and in us?

We utilize a variety of sources actively to develop, promote, and reward the view that life consists of the obligation to achieve a set of fixed purposes of fixed value. Consider the prevailing view that we *should* all aspire to be handsome, beautiful, wealthy, admired, smart, nice, occupationally successful, useful—Winners in the Great Game of Life. Mass entertainment, mass media, mass education, mass advertising, families, and peers all support this view. If these ends appear to be *the end* of life, then behaviors which are virtues are those which are effective in achieving these fixed ends. We learn quickly, therefore, the "virtue" of manipulating, seducing, bullying, posing as master or slave or both in our quest for success. We learn quickly and well that the supreme virtue in modern living is to master the well-timed pose.

The systems of rewards and punishments, of monotony of thought, work and entertainment are so effective that many believe they have an "obligation" to be slavish. Obligations and duties which *are* obligatory are so only because they promote conditions which support the possibility of achieving good for all. When good is thought of as a fixed set of goods of fixed rank then the person may well believe he has an obligation to be slavish, to disown the search for *his* priorities.

Stronger natures, those who sense, who feel the trap of fixed systems of purposes and oughts, rebel. Rebellion however, too often, becomes merely another form of slavish reaction. The rebel says "no" but his "no" may merely be the substitution of one set of fixed values for the other. "Whatever you tell me is good; I will do the opposite," becomes the slogan of the bad boy, the small rebel of our age, the rebel without a cause.

To repeat, traditional moralities have been supplanted by contemporary slave moralities because they lack support of existing conditions. What ends of conduct do contemporary economies, sciences, technologies, political systems, media systems, family systems, educational systems, and so on support and fix?

Ascetic, contemplative ends are certainly not supported as they were in earlier times for they hardly exist in the behavior of the industrialized masses. A primary end that "modern" culture does worship is usefulness. Being "useful" is held to be the essence of true being. Usefulness is synonymous with being good. A person is regarded as a tool, an instrument in the hands of employers, parents, teachers, priests, and all other users who want to produce some desired (not necessarily desirable) outcome. A good person is good in so far as he or she produces what *others* want. Initiative, discipline, intelligence, and kindliness are qualities of conduct regarded as virtues only so far as they support achievement of what *others* want. The good boy or girl is one who is quickly trained for slavery. The incentive for the victim is, of course, the approval of others *and* the understanding that with enough effort and servility, one day he can be in the position to demand the same sort of performances from others on the "way up."

We live in a sophisticated culture. Slaves need to revolt from time to time. We provide sensuous "revolt" through drugs and sex, escape into the thrill of sport and entertainment, into wild play. Every good boy and girl is angry at what they have done to themselves and hence the very existence of phony "forbidden" areas provides temporary expressions of revolt against "the system," the "rat race." Temporary transgressions against usefulness are expected and forgiven and hence the slaves can return.

This picture can easily be overdrawn. The fetish of usefulness and phony revolt are tendencies experienced more or less and sometimes not at all in individual members of industrialized cultures. We find, however, that an age which worships all the goods which mass organizations of "busy bees" can produce decidedly does not support reflective and discriminating thinking regarding the course of our own lives. The advertisers are the philosophers of our age. We give them billions of dollars to convert the quality of life into an effective slogan designed to sell another product.

Those who wish to be free, genuinely free, do then have a great cause and task. If we believe in freedom, the task of reform becomes the central task, the duty of moral inquiry and action. Art, work, play, family life, and communications, even more than formal education, *should* be studied and reformed so as to support individuals in establishing and realizing their own distinguishing goals. All moral concern centers on how to reform value-creating institutions to encourage people to reflect intelligently on what they want to do with their lives and accept responsibility for the choices they make. Curiously, what we lack today is not so much knowledge of how to do this, but rather the faith that this course *ought* to be followed. We live in a culture in which people view self as an indwelling, somewhat corrupt "soul" which cannot be trusted to act well without external restraint. Saying that someone is self-serving is immediately interpreted to mean that the person in question is nastily selfish. The fascination of today's arts and media with the bizarre and the brutal is further evidence of our paltry conception of ourselves. Strong and reverent beings focus on the potentialities for struggle and growth in human nature and encourage each other to achieve more for *themselves*. Difficulties are viewed, not as occasions for wailing and resentment, but as occasions for thought and action. Such *persons*, useless as they are to those who wish to use them, know the secret of being: When want sustains should, when faith nourishes action, life forms itself anew! They have the radical faith that all that we now are constitutes the seeds of an ever richer becoming. Do we, you and I, have such faith?

With this question raised we are now able to formulate the hypothesis to which this essay is dedicated. Earlier, it was asked: What sort of culture would be required to support, to cultivate, the strength of character necessary to seek freedom? A testable hypothesis now is forwarded: A culture willing to make the attempt.

Comment by Lester Kirkendall on Nisbet Article

Lee Nisbet's essay, *Kulturkampf*, is one we can all generally agree with, particularly the negative assessment he makes of our materialistic, master-slave society. His concern for the development of character based upon inquiry will surely be supported by this collection of essays.

He does not go far enough in his analysis, however. He is undoubtedly right when he says that Nazis are persons we would not consider "virtuous." That is, most of us, for we have certainly had some evidence that Nazism is supported by at least a few persons in the United States; doubtless some of them are American citizens.

Nisbet also says, "We should understand by now that men of worse character have a distinctly different conception of what is good than men of better character." But who is doing the defining and by what criteria are the definitions arrived at? I doubt not that some, maybe most of the Nazis thought their objectives and character as virtuous, or more virtuous, than those opposing them. Finally, Nisbet says that "A primary task of moral inquiry, therefore, is the study of how to determine what ends of conduct are worthwhile pursuing under what circumstances." At this point I wish Nisbet had gone further! What ends of conduct should we pursue and what circumstances make them worth pursuing?

At another point he wrote that many of our social structures and ways of communicating should "support individuals in establishing and realizıng their own distinguishing goals." What if their goal is to be a Nazi? In the last paragraph Nisbet does hypothesize that our culture should be supporting freedom. But again freedom for what purpose—all humankind, or particular groups? Will this freedom be in harmony with the essential nature of human nature—or do humans have an essential nature that requires freedom? If they do, what characteristics must we look for?

Of course Lee Nisbet was outlining social deficiencies and raising questions; now we must go beyond these questions to probe deeper concepts of fundamental human needs.

Reply by Lee Nisbet to Kirkendall

Lester Kirkendall has raised some questions about whether my essay goes far enough in exploring certain important issues regarding moral character, human nature, and freedom. I thank him for doing so for it gives me the opportunity to further clarify my position, method, and presuppositions.

He believes that my essay doesn't adequately deal with the "deeper concepts of fundamental human needs." He is correct. I deal with surfaces. The depths are over my head. The world I deal with is the world we all experience; it has its "realities" and yet unknown potentialities. I do not divide the world into realms of mere appearance versus fixed "true" realities. I leave that move to the deep thinkers.

I also do not prescribe how people should act. It doesn't work for the reasons made clear in the essay. I also do not prescribe what ends people should strive to achieve. As I indicated, such prescription is the essence of master-slave dog-training mentality. Nazis were superb at telling their followers what they should be like and what ends they should strive to achieve.

Herein possibly lies the problem for Mr. Kirkendall. He seems to ask, "Here is what you are against, but what are you for?" I had hoped that this question was answered both explicitly and implicitly in the essay, but maybe not.

What I am for is, of course, the wholeness of character that is both the outcome and the facilitator of growth. Wholeness requires reflective intelligence and support for becoming more than you are. I used the example of the Nazi who was assertive, courageous, innovative, and so on in search of the "final solution" to make the following point: People who are not virtuous are not without virtues. They may be brave, smart, and determined; but what they lack is the ability to intelligently decide what ends they should put their virtues in the service of. Good men, men who are not prejudiced, men who have learned to inquire into what a situation is and what needs to be done to remedy its ills, develop ends with discrimination and wisdom. They know that life situations are not fixed but are more or less unique and that answers, if there are any, must be made in reference to this uniqueness. Nazis or fanatics lack wholeness of character precisely because they refuse or don't know how to inquire into the means and ends of developing situations. They substitute prejudgments for judgments and they don't know the difference. They do not grow. They remain deficient. Their goods are not the developed goods of good men. They love the uniform and hate the unique.

When Mr. Kirkendall asks then of me, "What ends of conduct should we pursue and what circumstances make them worth pursuing," I can say only what I said in *Kulturkampf.* We should aim to study and establish the conditions which support the development of habits of intelligent reflection. We certainly can't tell people what ends to choose in their conduct for if they did so, *we* would be doing the choosing, not they. You don't develop intelligence and discrimination in choosing by having someone else do the thinking and choosing for you. You also don't tend to produce many Nazis or other fanatics if you learn how to encourage and develop habits of intelligent reflection. Simply, the role of morality is to teach, when people are ready, *how* to think and choose, not *what* to think and choose. The latter course could hardly be called freedom.

Mr. Kirkendall also believes that I did not define whom freedom is for and whether we have an essential nature that *requires* freedom. These are interesting questions but remember my clarifications will be those of a surface rather than a deep thinker. I will address the latter question first.

Freedom of choice is not essential to human nature if by "essential" you mean necessary for survival, happiness, and other important things. Nazis, Stalinists, Maoists, and fascists, for example, not only did not require freedom, but totally despised it and stamped out free choice at every opportunity. Freedom of choice and its encouragement is a rather new and tenuous development on the human scene.

Is there an "essential nature" to human nature? Skipping over the mountains of anthropological, philosophical, psychological, and religious literature on the subject let me suggest this answer I don't know and nobody else does either. What if we found, through a monumental anthropological, sociobiological study, after all the variances of culture had been taken into account, some invariant behavior or structure to behavior. If by essence one means some fixed, uniform behavior or structure one could still not say for sure that an essential or fixed human nature had been found. Why not? Processes change. Who could guarantee in an evolving world that such an essential nature would not change?

Here we come to a key point. If all things have the potential to become other than what they are, then we can never know what a thing or process ultimately is. If human nature is such an evolving process, then the concept of freedom developed here is in accord with human nature. By refusing to prescribe in an arbitrary way what ends are to be achieved, we facilitate, given the necessary cultural support, the development of a *unique person*. Humanism above all is an ethic of freedom. Brave voyagers are required in its uncharted seas, for their ends, their destinations, arise out of their own explorations.

Comment by John Anton on Nisbet Article

It is far from clear why a cultural humanism of the type Nisbet intimates must rest its case mainly on the thesis that the conception of "fixed ends," whether of the secular or the supernatural sort, should be discarded as impossible or restrictive. The only alternative to "fixed ends" has been stated in the fashionable idiom of "open-textured" and "open-ended" approaches to the conceptualization of values and objectives. Supporting this trend is the widespread conviction that an existentially conceived freedom is incompatible with closed systems of value. The arguments in support of these positions constitute a separate issue. Be that as it may, I think the issue of alternatives must be raised again. What has not been given a chance at all in this controversy is the possibility of arguing in favor of a third alternative, which, if defensible, may emerge as a viable solution. Let us assume that the meaning of "fixed ends" has not been exhausted by the negativism of recent discussions. If so, we may want to entertain a suggestion to explore the possibility of there being *bona fide* fixed ends. Unless there is a chance of assigning meaning to this third alternative, I am afraid that the cultural humanism Nisbet advocates may never overcome the inherent vagueness that plagues all solutions of the "our ends" type as the only viable alternative to suspect theories of "fixed ends." Furthermore, if we agree with Nisbet and others who have taken a similar stance that the virtues belong to the means, then we must conclude that "false" fixed ends, once admitted as "true," not only advocate the employment of virtues of questionable serviceability, but, what is worse, they distort in the long run our native capacities to think and act with functional rectitude. The point I have been trying to make in the preceding paragraph is that by rejecting all instances of fixed ends as manipulative devices peculiar to supernaturalisms or secular mass cultures, Nisbet has to opt for the open-ended approach to values. The choice, if it is one, not only leaves the problem of vagueness about ends unresolved, it also, and comparably so, forces him to employ an approach to virtue which is destined to leave this ethical concept obscure.

Professor Nisbet registers strong disapproval of the slave morality contemporary culture has induced us to accept in certain sectors as well as in areas of conduct as yet to be detected. In order to prevent further deterioration of the prevailing cultural conditions where the worship of usefulness almost invariably necessitates the treatment of persons as tools, Nisbet urges upon us the task of reform and the acceptance of the duty of moral inquiry. The purpose behind both assignments is "to support individuals in establishing and realizing their own distinguishing goals."

It is precisely at this point where the desirablity of such a program is transformed into a hornet's nest. I suspect that at the heart of this noble recommendation lies a nasty paradox: if distinguishing goals belong to individuals and since support for realizing them must come from certain peculiar entities called "institutions" for some mysterious reason, which threatens to cancel all of a sudden the initial meaning of inquiry, the roots of possible disagreement about ends, possible discord and conflict are somehow kept in a secret vault. If such is the case, I fear that Nisbet's optimism depends too heavily on the appealing abstractions he selects to state the cause. That this version of humanism is not tough enough to carry out the tasks it recommends is further evidenced by the following admission: "... what we lack today is not so much knowledge of how to do this, but rather the faith that this course *ought* to be followed."

On the whole my comments were directed to this basic issue: knowledge. I happened to believe that at this very moment we are still more deficient in relevant knowledge than most of us are willing to admit. We are still wanting in moral wisdom. Regardles of how assertive humanists and nonhumanists appear, the facts indicate otherwise. Faith in the sense of confidence in a plan is certainly needed to initiate reforms, but as such it is a poor substitute for the requisite science of the good life. Without possession of the latter, mankind profits accidentally and a culture that lacks it can never stay on a steady course of self-correction.

Reply by Lee Nisbet to Anton

Professor Anton argues that unless one can find "bona fide" fixed or "constant" ends in situations where choices between competing values or goods are required, no culture "could stay on a steady course of self correction." He is of course right to say that with no ends in view action is aimless. Navigation does require reference points. The crux of the disagreement, however, is whether in each and all situations demanding choice there is a fixed hierarchy of goods or ends to be realized. Professor Anton would perform a great service if he were to give us a list of such universal goods so we might better understand his hypothesis. Until such a scheme is forthcoming and especially in light of the failure of all such preexisting schemes, I remain skeptical. Whether we face choices in education, politics, statecraft, economics, sex, love, and so on, it seems to me that persons who exhibit both the willingness and ability to render informed, fair judgments on what needs to be done constitute the necessary condition for moral progress. Certainly such persons do not constitute a sufficient condition for progress, as human affairs often defy even the most heroic, sustained and informed efforts of their participants. Those who want guarantees, however, need gods, not fellow humans.

In sum, the call for the reform of character-forming institutions so as to better cultivate courageous, intelligent conduct is neither "moral atomism" nor romantic anarchy. It is simply a project, an end to be achieved; and how to achieve it in our culture demands inquiry and action. Inquiry, courage and their other attendant virtues when embodied in character constitute the dynamic substance most capable of keeping a culture "on a steady course of self-correction."

PANEL V

JOSEPH FLETCHER
MARVIN ZIMMERMAN
JOHN P. ANTON
MORRIS B. STORER

Humanist Ethics: The Groundwork

Joseph Fletcher

To describe any kind of ethics as humanist tells us too little. Nobody admits to being inhumane. After all, there is even the Renaissance model of "the Christian humanist." Some inquiry is in order, then, into what is or ought to be entailed by the term. Consensus is desirable, if possible, but after all consensus is not a closed circle of theory or practice. Our present condition is not so much a danger of hard and fast definition but of discourse and language too loose to represent an authentic philosophical affinity. We need to take a second hard look at both ethics (how to decide what is right) and metaethics (what our presuppositions are about such matters as values, obligation, moral cognition, freedom, and the like).

A POST-THEOLOGICAL PREFACE

Once upon a time I looked for the basis of morality and found it, I thought, in religion. There had to be some source and sanction for a standard of right and wrong, it seemed, and I concluded that it lay in the will of God. That is to say, we ought to be moral because God commanded it. Without the divine will to back up the human will, to act morally, Nietzsche's cry was correct—that if God is dead, everything goes ethically. (It took me a while to see that this was not a logical inference from atheism, this Dostoevskian grief and despair; it was only Nietzsche's way of sneaking the "superman" into the ethical forum.)

In short, I thought morality depended on a *commandment* ethic. Some believers might obey the divine will because they wanted to, of course, but in any case, willingly or unwillingly, they were commanded to obey—their obedience being backed up by various eschatological sanctions, as promises of salvation. This was the ethical position, for example, of the Five Big Bs: Buber, Barth, Brunner, Bultmann, Bonhoeffer, plus the Americanized Niebuhrs (Richard and Reinhold).

Then I began to wonder. Did I accept the commandments because of the commander, or the commander because of the commandments? I decided that the commandments are decisive. I would have to repudiate the commander if the commandments, however revealed or discovered, called for pain or indifference instead of happiness and loving concern. This meant, to use an old saw, that theology stands at the bar of ethics, that doctrine has to measure up to moral values, that religion depends on morality *and not vice versa*. This upset the theological claim that ethics needs a religious basis. Kai Nielsen's *Ethics Without God* was correct; morality had escaped the *odium theologicum*.

We have to validate happiness and moral concern humanly, not theistically. There are good gods and bad gods and we have to choose among them according to whether they pass our moral tests. We approve or disapprove of any particular divine command by a prereligious criterion. The ancient maxim was true, *conscientia semper sequenda est*, but it is *our* conscience, not God's.

The perennial problem of evil in theology arises precisely because of the inconsistencies between God's putative will and the facts of experience under his putative dominion; as even Saint Augustine saw it, God either is all-powerful but not all-good or is all-good but not all-powerful. Medieval "realists" such as Aquinas took the right road when they decided that God wills a thing because it is right, not that it is right because God wills it. They were unable, of course, to accept fully what was implied, but at least they said it plainly: morality has an antecedent status, so that even God would be subject to it.

By definition religious beliefs are nonrational and subjective (intuitive). So, indeed, for that matter, are moral values. If, as they say, theology is a rational reflection on the nonrational, ethics too is a rational reflection on the nonrational. In both cases the reflection is in the interest of tidiness and coherence. But the main point here is that the primary datum is moral, not religious; right and wrong are humanly perceived, not religiously revealed. In a word, ethics is humanist.

Teleological ethics (in which rightness comes from aiming at good consequences, as opposed to "deontological" ethics which finds rightness in obedience to normative principles) is typical of humanists. The mainstreams of Christianity, however, have never managed to pull loose from legalism and the absurd contradictions arising between universalized moral rules. Such rules or "moral laws" as "theft is always wrong" or "abortion is always wrong" are attributed by religionists to the divine will—a will which is universal, eternal, final, whether known directly, as in Protestant biblical ethics, or indirectly, as in Catholic natural-law ethics. And since this authority is sacred and absolute, it is easy to absolutize moral rules, twisting what may often be wise generalizations into rigid and unrealistic "laws" of morality.

Situation ethics offered them a way out of rule ethics and its dilemmas, both theoretical and practical. It posited that the divine will is indeed that humans act out of loving concern, but it then contended that this is God's *only* moral imperative—leaving it up to human beings as moral agents (individually and corporately) to determine what the most loving thing would be in every situation, unencumbered by prejudicial rules. This they could not and would not do.

THE MEANING OF MORALITY

Deciding what it means to be moral is really deciding "for the sake of whom?" Is it my own sake that has the first-order interest (egoistic ethics, like Ayn Rand's), or God's sake (as in religious ethics), or humanity's (a social ethic, such as utilitarianism)? Who comes first, not what, in this question.

In every kind of ethics the good is the survival, and more broadly the benefit, of some specified individual, phylum, species, or genus; that is, the good is always what benefits animal life. (*Benefit*, literally, is "doing good.") A moral agent is necessarily a subject (conscious), not an object (nonconscious), and the moral agent's "loyalty" (as William James' colleague, Josiah Royce, liked to say) goes to subjects, not to objects. In ethics, by a play on words, subjects only are the objects of moral concern.

This means that inanimate objects are, at most, nonmoral values. It means also that in the hierarchy or evolutionary series of animal life, the more conscious a creature is the higher it stands in the scale of relative values and the greater its claim on moral agents. Humans are more precious than nonhumans, and rational than nonrational; for example, the absence or loss of cerebral function, irreparably, is arguably the absence or loss of moral status.

Just as good and evil are value judgments (the interests of human beings taking first place in the priority or preference scale) so rights and wrongs are determined by objective facts or circumstances, that is, by the situations in which moral agents have to decide for the most beneficial course open to choice.

Ethics deals with values and their realization. The purpose of a moral agent is to optimize human benefits (a more realistic goal than "maximizing"). Whatever course of action seems to conduce most to human well-being is right, what does not is wrong. To act morally, in any case, is in part a matter of knowledge (of the facts involved) and in part a matter of how one *feels* about the values at stake.

A full and rich humanness, the *bene esse* of being human, calls for a creative balance of the Apollonian and Dionysian principles, a sensitive commixture of reason and feeling. When the cerebral and the visceral fail to work together we are crippled morally. Mind without emotion is dessicate; emotion without mind is squalid. But mind, not emotion, is the essence. Feeling fuels thought, but only if brains are boss. In William James's language, both "tender" and "tough" mindedness are needed.

Moral conduct is, in part, a matter of verification as to the factual or situational considerations, and in part a matter of justification, of pleading for one value rather than another or for one bundle of values rather than another. The cognitive or "truth" status of moral judgments never simply hangs on either verification or justification. It is a combination of both. Sooner or later, when we try to make sense of what we choose to do, we find we cannot explain it solely by rational means—there is no way to "prove" that beauty is "better" than ugliness nor that goodness is better than badness. Although a strong case might be made pragmatically, there is no way, for example, that the Supreme Court could *prove* that privacy is a "human right"—at least in the sense that we can prove one part carbon and two parts oxygen is toxic, or that a syllogism in Barbara is correct.

Kant came to the conclusion that human intention has two rational ends or goals; one, he said, is virtue, and the other is happiness. It is the great merit of the English utilitarians that they were able to show Kant's redundancy: virtue *is* happiness; happiness, virtue. Goodness (virtue) consists in human beings being happy rather than miserable, they contended; in having pleasure rather than pain. They called it "utility." It might be any human pleasure—intellectual, physical, emotional—although, as Mill put it, a hungry Socrates' happiness is better than a well-fed pig's. Utilitarianism was really the first ethical system deliberately to socialize or politicalize virtue, with its standard of the greatest happiness of the greatest number of human beings possible. It is a humanist ethic, rather than theist, and a societal ethic rather than egotistical. It was made to order for humanists.

FREE WILL AND RESPONSIBILITY

Every vigorous study of ethical questions comes sooner or later to the question whether freedom is (1) necessary to moral conduct, and (2) humanly possible. The answer on the first score seems fairly obvious: Yes. If we are not free to choose between whatever alternative courses of action happen to be open to us; if, that is to say, we are either helpless to choose or our choices have already been determined, then nothing we do lies in the forum of conscience; not being free we are neither responsible nor culpable for what we do. (This condition might be the case effectively in some situations, but the question is whether it obtains in *all* situations.) What we cannot help doing is amoral.

Freedom is not absolute, any more than life or other human values are. The whole question of moral freedom, therefore, is only to be understood in terms of the tension between freedom and necessity. As Friedrich Engels said in his *Dialectics of Nature*, freedom is founded "on the knowledge of necessity." To imagine we are utterly free, able to do whatever we might want, is to be imprisoned in a fantasy. To know what the limits are on our powers frees us to make optimum use of them. Philosophers have always respected the distinction between "hard" determinism—really a mechanistic theory that everything is due to ineluctable cause and effect, with no real choice possible—and "soft" determinism, of the sort that Engels typified.

Freedom without order is license; order without freedom is tyranny. Actually, there are three positions, not two, we may choose among on the spectrum of responsibility. At one extreme is mechanism, which eliminates freedom (and therefore ethics); at the other extreme is randomness or a radical voluntarism according to which we are always free to choose what we do; and in between lies determinism—of the soft kind. *Real* determinism, not mechanism. This is the stance of truly humanistic ethics. It acknowledges that human freedom is limited or finite but recognizes at the same time that there must always be at least whatever cause-and-effect is required to provide the connection between means and ends—to establish a meaningful basis for judging moral acts in terms of their foreseeable consequences.

MORALITY AND THE PRAGMATIC TEST

Pilate's question "What is truth?" is close in nature to "What is good?" The pragmatic test for the *verum* and the *bonum* is the same, and no other test makes as much obvious sense. As the Cambridge ethicist G. E. Moore said, moral propositions "are merely statements that certain kinds of actions will have good effects." What makes anything we do right is that it aims at desirable *consequences*; if it succeeds, if it works out in fact, twice blessed is the moral agent. Any ethical system in which what is "right" and what is "useful" can come into conflict is absurd. To be good, to be right, is to help human beings. Anything else is in principle, and may well be in practice, inhumane.

Moral judgments or decisions to be right must "work." William James used "expeditious" as his test term, John Dewey used "satisfaction," the utilitarians set happy (i.e., humanly beneficial) consequences as the test.

The good, in short, is whatever works. Moral conduct is aimed at *doing* good; it acts out a value commitment.

This pragmatic test of moral actions, however, is not in itself sufficient. Pragmatism, which validates thoughts and actions by whether they work or not, is really only a method—vitally important though it may be. Correct ideas and right actions must work, yes; *but work to what end*, for the sake of whom? This is the crucial question, and pragmatism as such has no answer. A rapist can be as pragmatic as a philanthropist. What values are served in a moral action is the final criterion, over and beyond the requirements of "practical reason." Humanist ethics, as we have seen, has a cleancut answer to the values question—human beings are values, and whatever they value is value.

RIGHTS AND DUTIES

Given what we have already explained, it is plain enough that there is much merit in what the conventional wisdom has to offer about rights and duties. Perhaps the most succinct statement of it is the familiar saying, "Every right carries a duty, and vice versa." They are coinherent. Rights are morally valid claims to acts or things (such as privacy, personal liberty, possessions, health, travel, and so on). They are *owed*. Conversely, to speak of duties is to presuppose that there are morally valid claims which others make upon us.

There are no "absolute" rights, just as there are no absolute duties (obligations). Always it depends on the situation. To be valid, in any case, it must be evident that the exercise of rights and duties would not injure others. "Doing justice" is unjust if it victimizes innocent third parties Obligation, in a humanist ethic, is to do whatever we can (including respecting human rights) to make as many people as possible happy.

SITUATION ETHICS

When we make moral judgments or value choices—decisions as to right and wrong, good and bad, desirable and undesirable—we are consciously or not following one or the other of two alternative ethical modes. One is rule ethics and the other is situation ethics. Humanists are situationists. No genuine humanist would ever act out of what Kant called a "sense of duty" to follow any general principle of conduct, if and when foreseeably one or more persons would be hurt by doing so (unless by hurting a few many would be helped). Principles of conduct are normative generalizations, to be followed ordinarily—that is, except where to do so hurts or hinders people instead of helping them. Humanist ethics, in a word, is goal oriented, not rule bound.

In rule ethics what we ought to do is decided *a priori*, by some predetermined precept or categorical imperative. It is decided abstractly, not on the facts. Variables are ignored or downgraded. Such rules might be "No abortion," or "No lying," or "No violence." This ethical modality means that some things may or may not be done regardless of the consequences. "Right is right," they say, acknowledging the circularity of their ethical reasoning. This also means that effectually "conscience" is eliminated; responsible decision making is set aside. If you follow a rule that dictates your deeds, conscience is preempted and irrelevant. The moral agent is a null whenever a rule is relevant; he is passive and amoral.

Situation ethics (philosophers commonly call it "act ethics") functions, in contrast, with responsible moral agents—agents who judge what is best in the circumstances and in view of the foreseeable consequences. Like science, it is *a posteriori*, after or according to the facts, not *a priori*. You choose the course of action offering the greatest benefit, if need be even violating a generally sound normative principle ("rule") if in the particular case more good can be done. It is not that situationists have no normative principles; they have them, but they are used as guidelines, not as prefabricated decisions.

"The end does not justify the means" is a common but nonsensical saying. It is precisely the end sought (the consequences) which justifies the means employed. (It should be obvious, of course, that some ends cannot justify some means, because of the ethical principle of proportionate good.) What requires justification is the *end*, not the means. Humanism keeps this order intact; it puts human interest or benefit before moral rules. A humanist is morally bound to say, for example, "It is better to end this pregnancy than to bear a baby with Tay-Sachs disease." The humanist cannot say, "That's too bad, but abortion is wrong."

THEOLOGICAL POSTSCRIPT

Coming back to God again, there is, we should note, no theologically-necessary conflict between humanist ethics and religion. The drift to rule ethics in religious groups is due to the psychology of religion, not theology. Belief in God and opinions about God do not, except in some brands, exclude the view that we first have to consult our own human perceptions of morality, before we can accept any alleged command of a divine will. One such position could be that God as creator implanted our moral perceptions in us *ab initio* (natural law theory). Another is the doctrine that deity is impassive, as in the ancient Greek outlook and in Buddhist metaphysics. Still another (finite theism) is that both God and man are as yet only in "process" of moral development. However—these and other philo-theological questions having ethical significance should be left to another time and place.

Comment by Morris Storer on Fletcher Article

Joseph Fletcher's article is full of things that I want to applaud, including: (1) his advocacy of utilitarianism as "made to order for humanists" (this with some reservations), (2) his emphasis on "generally sound normative principles" as guidelines for ordinary circumstances, (3) the relevance of situation in moral judgment, (4) the reality of human freedom, and (5) his interpretation of "rights" as what others "owe" to you. But we seem to read *Utilitarianism* with focus on different passages in Mill's text. All in all I think our positions are not so far apart in practical intent as might seem to be involved in apparent collisions in statement. I'm sure that mine can gain from Fletcher certain balancing emphases, and conceivably vice versa.

Fletcher slights J. S. Mill's early emphasis in *Utilitarianism* on "*the rules and precepts* which would lead to the greatest happiness altogether" as definitive of utility. Mill leaves this important phrase relatively undeveloped, but it signals his sharp divergence from Bentham and his calculus of "total pleasures less total pains," as key to the "right course." Bentham's formula would inevitably work serious injustice since it offers no protection for the luckless innocents who suffer the pains of the equation. Mill in the crucial passage cited is saying (I think), "Let's aim at the greatest happiness, but we don't want any injustice to anyone." We must not "use" anyone for the sake of others. The way to avoid this is to think always in terms of general principles—always *inquiring* for the course that we would approve as reasonable and just if our positions were reversed—you in my corner and I in yours—but none the less keeping greatest happiness (the "ends of love," as Fletcher phrases it) in view as a major goal; as much happiness as possible without injustice.

Fletcher imports the consideration of justice into the picture behind his own back by his statement that "doing justice is unjust if it victimizes innocent third parties." The crucial question here is: What is victimization? Is a person "victimized" only when he literally gets a knife in the back, only when he suffers physical harm? I believe we would agree that he is victimized if he is deceived or if truth is witheld that he/she has a right to know or if what was promised is undelivered. Ultimate human goods are involved here: peace and good feeling between people and in a person's life with himself/herself—harmony and health in the minds of people and in their community.

Fletcher is trapped in Bentham's mistaken logic when he writes (in the section on *Situation Ethics*) that "No humanist would ever act from sense of duty to principle if foreseeably one or more persons would be hurt by doing so (*unless by hurting a few, many would be helped.*)" This is the logic that prompts some people to say "A good big lie about X will cook his goose. We can get him out of the way by that lie, and go ahead to accomplish all the great and good things that we have it in mind to accomplish—and we will be justified." This is the way to division and conflict in the community, to bitter and violent feelings, and to curtains for good enterprises. Fletcher is perfectly right in emphasizing the great importance of "the end," the human good, in ethics, but would lead us into no green pastures and beside no still waters by his "end justifies means" emphasis. This is the way to no human good, to put it mildly, because to most people it means what it meant to Cesar Borgia.

Only principle justifies—constitutes an act as right and just. *Not* preordained principles. Fletcher is right: situations do arise where our customary normative generalizations require adjustment, sometimes minor, sometimes radical. But in such situations we do not find the right course (the course of the human good) by fixing on the end and forgetting principle, but rather by reaching for an adjustment of the principle—sometimes for a new principle—appropriate to situations like the one in hand, which would serve the greatest good if observed by everyone in such situations. In sum, ends and only ends ultimately justify principles, and only principles justify means—justify actions.

A final question for our common reflection: are we so sure that our pleasure-bent civilization is on the right track? Is the "human good" adequately understood in terms of "happiness," interpreted as most pleasure and least pain? The priceless ingredient in Fletcher is his beneficence: concern for the happiness of all. I would join in fixing as humanist goal happiness, researched as profoundly as possible, coupled with justice interpreted as fairness.

How "Humanistic" are Humanists?

Marvin Zimmerman

Are humanists scientific? Do humanists practice what they preach? Humanists have claimed their superiority to supernaturalists in their belief in scientific method and empirical truth. The humanist commitment to Reason and Science meant that scientific method could be used as a means to achieve ends even if these ends turned out to be egoistic or emotional. Furthermore, ends could be treated scientifically as means to, and in relation to, other ends. Thus, whether we supported our personal good or the public good as ends, we could explore scientifically the effect of one on the other. Unfortunately, in practice, humanists often misuse science or do not even pretend to use it at all, in taking positions on a variety of issues.

Human values are frequently egoistic or emotional, but this is not the most significant point. Judgments based on knowledge and science are most important in satisfying emotions. David Hume maintained that Reason is the servant of passions.

Many of our social problems involve individual liberty, equality, the relationship between individual freedom and society, and the extent to which authority should restrict individual freedom. Even the libertarian acknowledges that restrictions are needed for stability and order. The egalitarian acknowledges that men are not equally qualified to perform surgery. The principle of inequality is justifiable, but not the principle of equality. The principle of individuality, fulfillment of individual need, individual potential and individual differences, sounds better. Though humanists acknowledge the Deweyan principle of individuality, they seem to succumb to the myth of equality.

The role of government restriction of the individual transcends the question of equality. The role of the Supreme Court is the significant factor in the expansion of the power of authority, particularly in constitutional questions. If restrictions go far enough, even with equality, we may end up with the equality of slaves.

In fairness to the humanists, a lack of sophistication and historical insight into the judicial tyranny developing in our country characterizes a much larger segment of our people. But it does seem more prevalent in liberal, secular, and humanist quarters, probably because of the recent thrust of the Supreme Court decisions in their direction. Compounding the error of accepting decisions on a basis of emotion rather than evidence, humanists have been indifferent to this abuse and growth of judicial power by the Supreme Court, a usurpation of the legislative and executive functions.

Almost anyone can claim to be scientific in ethics, but whether one actually looks to experience and scientific evidence is an entirely different matter. Thus, whether humans are equal, races are equal, men and women are equal, different cultures are equal, and in what ways, are difficult questions to analyze scientifically. Yet, they seem to be easily answered by humanists (and others) and in anything but a scientific fashion. Thus, though there is evidence against belief in equality in all these areas, such suggestions are met by cries of racism, sexism, chauvinism, prejudice, and so on. New absolutes are proclaimed, even as old absolutes are rejected.

There is overwhelming evidence that humans are different in more ways than they are the same, whether physically, mentally, culturally, or educationally. Most are not qualified to practice medicine, law, engineering, police work, firefighting, teaching, et cetera. Yet the reality of ability and achievement or merit is being ignored in order to promote the illusion of equality by use of quotas, reverse discrimination, goals, executive and judicial decrees, charges of discrimination or what have you. In general, many humanists have condoned, if not advocated such measures.

In the name of equality, innocent individuals are being penalized because of their race or sex, and others rewarded because of their race or sex, all this under some form of quota system. Humanists who should be in the forefront of the battle against this new form of original sin, have barely voiced their opposition. Though humanists oppose discrimination against atheists, blacks, and females, they condone, if not accept, discrimination against theists, whites, and males.

Conflicts between individual and community interests can sometimes be reconciled by looking for shared, coinciding, or overlapping interests. But disagreements concerning what are, and what will promote, individual or community interests clearly guarantee the impossibility of overwhelming, let alone complete, reconciliation. Given the fact that factual elements in the judgments are usually inadequately supported, fallible, and subject to change in the light of new evidence, it is amazing that any agreement can be reached. Thus, all may agree that police and fire departments are needed but hardly anything else in implementing this.

Even where there is apparent shared interest between the individual and society, for example, crime (police), fire, health, and sanitation protections, disagreement about means, ends, and alternatives prevent strong agreement. Indeed, the question of individual liberty and government coercion, in these and other areas, raise the usual confrontations and dilemmas.

For example, in the field of crime, there is strong feeling that the community interest in reducing crime has suffered in favor of protecting the individual rights and interests of criminals, both in jail and in the abandonment of capital punishment. Factual knowledge of how to deal effectively with crime and criminals is not very conclusive, which makes it difficult to arrive at means and ends and to project consequences. However, that punishment, particularly capital punishment, does frighten and deter some people can hardly be denied.

Most humanists oppose capital punishment, not on the basis of scientific evidence that it does not deter crime, but on grounds indistinguishable from religious faith or dogma, namely emotions. They accept blindly the claim that capital punishment does not deter killing because people who kill are too emotional to even consider the consequences of their actions. What about the calm premeditative killer and even the emotionally disturbed? What is the effect of capital punishment on recidivists? They accept the argument that innocent people might be executed and that minority groups make up a disproportionate number on death row. They ignore the fact that most of the victims of crime are also innocent people and also minority members. The issue is not whether the data supports capital punishment, but whether the humanists have taken a stand against capital punishment without regard to the data or scientific method.

Even apart from capital punishment, the humanists' attitude toward crime appears to be based on sentimental emotions rather than reason. They express sympathy for rehabilitation, parole, and prisoners' rights, whether or not supported by evidence, and a virtual disregard for victims of crime. In spite of the increasing evidence that the use of parole, rehabilitation, and prisoners' rights have been ineffective for the most part and, as a matter of fact, tend to increase crime, the humanists continue to support them.

To the extent that satisfaction is good, the defense of human freedom, that is, making free choices to meet one's desires, contributes to the good. In this sense human liberty is vital and needs protection against encroachment by government and other institutions. Thus, interference by government is to be permitted only in the most extreme cases, the burden being on anyone defending interference to make a conclusive case. Most extreme cases would include "clear and present danger" situations, a threat to life or limb, and so on. Anything short of life and limb, such as economic benefits or educational advances, would have to be shown to be of greater value than loss of freedom and the danger of further interference with liberty.

One of the basic problems of scientific method is that agreement to follow it is not necessarily an indication that it will be carried out. Thus, a whole series of alleged justifications for expanding power of government over individuals has been based on claims that these policies are effective in promoting the common good, in spite of little empirical evidence. Claims about crime, welfare, inflation, education, cyclamates, saccharin, estrogen, tobacco, pornography, et cetera, have frequently turned out to be mistaken. Wishful thinking seems to prevail over scientific thinking.

A fundamental error of the Supreme Court in abolishing compulsory segregation in the South, was extending this to the imposition of compulsory integration. Compulsion is no less compulsion whether for segregation or integration; it is a restriction of individual freedom without any significant compensatory evidence to justify it. It is a mistake to believe that in order to terminate one kind of compulsion one is required to force an opposite compulsion. One might just as well argue that to remove a ban on intermarriage between races or religions or smoking or drinking, one must compel people to intermarry, smoke, or drink.

The quest for integration growing out of the principle of equality illustrates quite graphically the dangers of governmental interference in individual freedom. Thus, the assumption that integration is desirable because it promotes social interaction and harmony and educational uplifting has generally been proven to be mistaken, and yet it is still being imposed by the government on all levels. Masses of children have been moved around by compulsory bussing and other means in order to achieve racial balance, even though the mass exodus of the middle class has brought about even greater segregation then before. Yet compulsory integration continues. The principle is apparently maintained regardless of consequences, and humanists have accepted it without reservation.

It is interesting to note the two extreme principles of compulsory exclusion (i.e., separation of whites and blacks; separation of religious and secular courses), and compulsory inclusion (i.e., integration of whites and blacks; and integration of religious and secular courses). Though most humanists oppose compulsory racial segregation and compulsory prayer in schools, they also tend to support compulsory racial integration and compulsory exclusion of prayers in the schools, though there is no significant empirical support.

Compulsory racial segregation in the South had no significant evidence in consequences to support it. Nevertheless, recent compulsory racial integration has similarly not been sustained as justifiable. Just as compulsory prayer in public schools had little to support it, recent compulsory exclusion of religious activities from public schools is equally unjustifiable. The basic assumption underlying these different compulsions, that they would have desirable consequences, is a claim for which there is no scientific or conclusive evidence.

We learn from experience that there are no eternal (absolute) ethical principles. We realize that killing is justified in self-defense, sometimes in war, and perhaps in capital punishment, if an effective deterrent. Even incest or rape could be justified by the last two people on earth, and adultery or torture might be necessary during war. Circumstances and situations need to be evaluated, using our best knowledge, before action on them is advocated. But this does not suggest that these actions are not usually wrong, immoral, or unethical, or that killing, incest, or torture are evil most of the time. That there are exceptions, does not imply that these exceptions do not require strong, indeed conclusive, justification. Thus the call for mercy killing by many humanists and other liberal enthusiasts, requires so many precautions against abuse and error by relatives, doctors, and government, that it raises serious doubt whether the danger of euthanasia does not outweigh any advantages.

As an exception to our moral prohibition against killing, mercy killing lends itself more easily to abuse and corruption by doctors and relatives than killing in self-defense, capital punishment, and, perhaps, war. Ironically, humanists are more sympathetic to mercy killing than to other kinds of killing.

Despite witnessing Fundamentalists' mistaken support of compulsory integration of religion and education in Tennessee during the famous Scopes (monkey) trial, by banning teaching of evolution in biology classes, many contemporary humanists are similarly supporting compulsory separation of church and state by banning theistic views in biology classes. It is odd that they grant that theism may be taught in history of biology though not in biology, because allegedly theism is not part of science. But they fail to recognize that any biology course worth anything incorporates the history of biology into the course. Humanists are indistinguishable from the Fundamentalists in their support of a ban of distasteful ideas. The same

consideration applies to the humanist attempt to replace the foolish imposition of compulsory prayer in the schools with a compulsory ban on
prayer. All that is needed is to allow it to be voluntary.

Even on abortion, the humanists and others are apparently influenced
by their anti-Roman Catholic attitude instead of dealing with the fundamental question, When does human life begin? in a purely scientific
fashion. There are no scientific grounds for accepting the views that human
life begins at conception, birth, or (as per the Supreme Court) at six
months of pregnancy. Scientific grounds for consideration are: at what
point does the fetus seem to possess the characteristics associated with
human life, for example, heartbeat, brain activity, bodily shape and form,
and biological responses?

The secular worship of what is "natural" is a replacement of what is
supernatural and raises the same kinds of confused, emotional, and
unscientific reactions. There is no more reason to worship what we can see
(natural), than what we cannot see (supernatural), or to believe that nature
is moral or good and should therefore be preserved. Should we welcome
poisoned mushrooms, bacteria, viruses, (all of which are natural), and
reject antibiotics, aspirin, or buildings (all of which are artificial)? To
welcome the balance of nature and reject the interference with nature, is to
substitute new myths for old: nature for God, natural purpose for God's
purpose.

Some equate ecological or natural balance with the good of society
because this is sometimes the case; for example, cleaning polluted streams
or air presumably restores the "balance" in nature. But there is the vague
notion of balance since anything that happens can be looked at as a kind of
balance as long as it refers to what exists independently of what is man-
made. If pollution is man-made, the viruses and bacteria responsible for
millions of deaths are not, and indeed have been virtually eliminated by
man-made (artificial) means, for example, smallpox, diphtheria, yellow
fever, et cetera. The jungles and swamps of "virgin" areas may reflect a
natural balance, but are hardly fit for man's survival.

If man interferes in nature, it is referred to as creating an imbalance in
nature. If elements in nature interfere with or destroy each other then it is
called "restoring" the balance in nature. But these activites in the abstract
are neither good nor bad, right nor wrong, moral nor immoral.

It is somehow assumed that balance is "good" and imbalance is "bad,"
which may be true in walking a tightrope or managing a budget, but surely
not in all things.

The whole evolutionary process of survival of the fittest and adjustment and adaptation involves continuous conflict and destruction of
different elements, continuous upset and restoration of balance. If we take

human betterment and survival as being the highest priority, then whatever in nature, including all lower animal, plant, and other life, can contribute to it by preservation or destruction or manipulation, can be ethically justified. Calling these things balance or imbalance, natural or unnatural (artificial), is irrelevant.

Humanists seem to buy the antinuclear energy hysteria, an area in which science would seem to be most relevant and yet has been mostly ignored. Though so many other activities are far more dangerous to life and limb (e.g., coal mining, automobile driving, flying in airplanes, or merely crossing a city street), the humanists succumb to the emotions rather than to reason. Again Dewey's call for more scientific method is ignored.

Again and again, on issue after issue, it seems clear that the humanists have failed to practice what they preach, and can hardly be distinguished from the supernaturalists whom they ridicule for being unscientific.

Comment by Lee Nisbet on Zimmerman Article

How humanistic is Marvin Zimmerman? Is Marvin Zimmerman's conduct scientific? Does Marvin Zimmerman practice what he preaches?

He certainly is outrageous. In his wicked little essay he attacks (and surely offends) integrationists, segregationists, theists, atheists, ecologists, pollutionists, liberals, conservatives, proabortionists, antiabortionists, and worst of all, "humanists."

Marvin Zimmerman has apparently forgotten that one must strive to form convictions and find the proper label to sanctify these strong and fixed beliefs. Once properly formed, once finally a part of our habits, these convictions are happily impervious to almost any form of persuasion, especially that of contrary evidence presented in the form of sound argumentation. A person of strong conviction is considered admirable in conduct even by humanists if, of course, the person is a humanist. If the person is not a humanist he or she is considered a dogmatic ignoramus or, worse yet, irrational.

This writer clearly shares Professor Zimmerman's displeasure with some of the hypocrisy found in institutionalized humanism. The point that his essay effectively constructs is that many humanists don't understand what humanism means. Humanism cannot be identified with any one position concerning any particular issue save one. There is not and cannot be, for example, any one humanist view on abortion. Humanists might and do have a variety of views on abortion, euthanasia, gun control, crime, punishment, and so on. The belief, however, that does distinguish humanism from other approaches to moral and social issues concerns the principle of fallibilism. Central to the development of modern humanism is the belief that no belief can be confirmed absolutely for further evidence could always falsify it. The principle of fallibilism, not coincidently, is the foundation of modern scientific method. When followed, whether in science or moral affairs, the principle eliminates dogmatism, requires tolerance of (but not agreement with) conflicting viewpoints, encourages debate and inquiry, and supports free choice. The principle also supports the right to be wrong, the right to blunder, to make mistakes for if you can never know for sure if you are right, you certainly can know when you are wrong. What you think is the right position on an issue might be supported by coincidence, ignorance, and so on; but when events prove you wrong, you know you are wrong. Here lies the great strength of the principle and, therefore, of humanism when it is practiced: We can learn from our mistakes. It is our mistakes that teach us and promote growth—if we let them. Dogmatism is the refusal to recognize error and this refusal destroys the opportunity for choice, learning, and going beyond ourselves. Humanism, therefore, is a distinctive way, a mode, a means of conducting ourselves; and it is our characteristic conduct that identifies us as humanistic or nonhumanistic.

Humanists who are dogmatic are hardly humanistic. Persons who are characteristically dogmatic cannot be considered humanists no matter what they call themselves or what organizations they belong to. Conversely, people who do not think of themselves as humanists may well be. So, how humanistic is Marvin Zimmerman? Knowing that his essay is an outcome of his characteristic behavior, it may very well be that he is one of the few humanists around.

Comment by Morris Storer on Zimmerman Article

Marvin Zimmerman's article is bound to stir up a pervasive reexamination of humanist ideals on many fronts: compulsory integration of schools, quotas and reverse discrimination, human equality in general, compulsory exclusion of prayer in schools, capital punishment, euthanasia and mercy killing, abortion, nature worship, and nuclear energy. And it's bound to be healthy.

We might generalize his main point in these terms: We ought to be very sure of the good and bad consequences in each particular case of (1) unfettered individual freedom, and of (2) government intervention in the interest of ideal purposes. In this he emphasizes sins against science as responsible for what he considers to be questionable crusades, although I think he might agree that failures of philosophical severity—superficiality in analysis and articulation of meanings—may be as often responsible.

Possibly he has sinned a little himself in this last regard in pressing the importance of the principle of individuality as against the principle of equality to the point of referring to equality as a myth. Actually he is insisting here on the equal right of individuals to freedom in fulfillment of individual needs and potentials. This commitment to "equal rights" is not without foundation in a certain underlying equality of persons in themselves. Human beings are roughly equal in their ability to play one responsible part or another in the human enterprise—speak truth, understand simple language, grow in understanding, and perform according to commitment. A person's a person for a' that, qualifying for equal freedom (where animals without understanding do not) unless and until that freedom is abused by violence to principles of reason.

Zimmerman's point on the need for scientific study of consequences has special point in relation to forced integration of schools. But if he is right that the consequences have not justified the means, humanists should not lose sight of the goal of a society free from discrimination, mindful of the values of free and easy association and full communication, without walls. This will certainly take time, but possibly voluntary integration of schools, public and private, supported by a program of incentives and the support of humanist and civic and religious organizations can do better than forced integration toward these ends. And I believe that it is toward such unconstrained programs that Marvin Zimmerman looks for solid accomplishment.

On the issue of capital punishment, it seems clear with Zimmerman that people have been more moved to opposition by selectively merciful hearts and a short span of recall for the tragic end of victims than by sober concern for security of life in the large. But studies of the effects of death penalty versus life imprisonment on the murder rate seem inconclusive, and there is not much reason to hope for more revealing research. Meantime the principle is worth considering that a right to life is a *qualified* right, subject to an individual's stable determination to respect life and conserve it except in the extremity where self-defense calls for the ultimate defense against attack.

Reply by Marvin Zimmerman to Storer

Morris Storer has touched upon some of my basic points.

I agree that errors in philosophy and analysis, as well as scientific method, contribute to faulty conclusions drawn by many humanists. I merely tend to lump philosophy with science.

I do not accept the equal right of all to fulfill their needs or potential. I would tend to give those more gifted or with greater need *more* rather than equal opportunity to fulfill and develop their abilities. Shall we spend equal time, money, and energy on the retarded and the geniuses, or the sick and the healthy? I would challenge the claim that "people are even roughly equal in their ability to play one responsible part or another in the human enterprise." Do young and old have equal ability as athletes and firemen or as soldiers? What about the mentally and physically ill and disabled?

Though I oppose compulsory segregation or integration and prefer a voluntary approach, I am not convinced that voluntary integration is more desirable than voluntary segregation. It depends. I can see where people may wish to separate on a basis of sex, age, religion, ethnic background, race cultural interest, and so many other reasons. To suggest that integration, even if voluntary, is preferable to separate associations, is to substitute myth for reality. For example, having separate schools, churches, prisons, clubs, hospitals, social organizations, toilets, gyms, and so on, seems quite reasonable.

Incidentally, the effects of the death penalty versus life imprisonment is not entirely inconclusive. Capital punishment is quite effective as a deterrent on repeaters, whereas life imprisonment is not. I am, of course, ignoring the fact that life imprisonment has usually not meant life imprisonment. I agree with Morris Storer however, that far more research is needed here. I agree with Lee Nisbet that fallibility is a basic characteristic of scientific method. It may not be clear however, that only supporters of fallibility and scientific method are true humanists. Of course many humanists have claimed to be scientific and this is the burden of my criticism, with which Lee Nisbet is in agreement. Though we cannot legislate language, we can point out an important and traditional use of the word *humanist* to which so many self-described humanists do not adhere.

A Note Toward a Theory
of Political Humanism

John P. Anton

This brief note is an attempt to tie together a philosophy of humanism and a view which is not so much about "politics" as it is about the political aspect of human conduct. I hope to communicate the concern to restore the meaning of what the ancient philosophers meant by the expression *politikē technē*, the art and science of the political life. As a concept it may serve to intimate the broadest and most appropriate context for the identification of our problems as well as the direction to search for practical solutions.

The possibility of arriving at a theory of political humanism is hardly news to the students of government and public affairs throughout the centuries. Hence while I am fully aware of how ancient and venerable the quest is, I believe that a renewed effort to resurrect an old usage under a new expression may not be without some value to those at least who have been looking for integrative approaches to the domain of human affairs. Those of us who look at the past and the present with the eyes of the humanist consider the abuses of the original meaning of the term *political* a source of disturbance. They interfere with our thinking when we try to come to grips with the terminology employed by such recent manipulative enterprises as geo-politics. To what extent the so-called principles of geo-politics are ultimately compatible with the objectives of a theory of political humanism is a real issue and deserves to be carefully analyzed. But there is also another reason why I believe there is need to restate the political dimension of humanism. By recognizing it as one which provides the broadest context for the scrutiny of the human condition, we stand a good chance of reducing disagreement among the diverse sectors within the humanist camp. I shall try to explain how both objectives can be served by starting with the latter.

Generally speaking, humanists of different persuasions tend to agree on the need to develop a comprehensive theory that would offer a satisfactory interpretation of moral responsibility in line with a naturalistic approach to the problem of value so that the ensuing lessons may be held together with logical bonds. On the practical side, it is expected that a philosophy of humanism will give full credit to all the basic traits of human conduct, either in their initial stage or at any later phase, as they develop and take on the structure of habits.

The basic considerations that guide the building of a humanistic outlook are usually two: (a) confidence in the native capacity of human intelligence to find answers to all the mysteries and wonders of nature, and (b) a deep conviction that as members of the human species we are all subject to the same hazards and promises of life regardless of sex, color, or geographical location. By taking the general features and natural conditions of life more seriously than the particular circumstances of groups and individuals due to religion, ethnicity, local traditions, social status and the like, humanism as a philosophical outlook attains the same empirical directness we associate with the objective and impersonal procedures of the social sciences. Yet all types of humanism share an explicit concern: they all display a manifest interest in the qualitative aspects of human conduct and all communicate a sense of urgency for personal development and social cooperation. However, despite their common objectives and procedures, it is not unusual to discern disagreements which often tend to divide the humanist movement at some deeper level of commitment. The purpose of my advocacy for a theory of political humanism is in no small measure conciliatory. It is hoped that by removing certain conceptual blocks among humanists, the theory can be of some assistance to those who are fighting to neutralize the debilitating effects of divisiveness, the provincialisms of all kinds, the overt and covert forms of alienation, and the other negative forces that continue to cause suffering to large numbers of people in the human community.

The fact that our cultural and intellectual history has given rise to different types of humanistic philosophies should not be held as a strike against the common ground they share. Nor is it reason to discount the contribution each variety of humanism is capable of making. However, the fact that certain differences continue to persevere is not without negative significance insofar as they tend to block the integration of perspectives so sorely needed for the furthering of the humanistic cause on a global scale. Thus it is not unusual for humanists to have special commitments and

institutional affiliations which in turn force upon them a sense of obligation to promote particular objectives. It is a simple fact of ordinary life that
as individuals we are all products of our personal involvement with the
forces of acculturation. Given this fact, each person manages to work out
in varying degrees a pattern of responses to the values of the society in
which one grows, and does so by effecting different intensities and arrang-
ing within certain limits his or her own priorities. As a matter of course, the
grade of response qualifies the degree of dependence one feels as cultural
loyalty. On the other hand, the pattern of priorities one calls one's own
determines limits of the critical attitude one can exhibit toward the established values. No matter what the reservations one may have toward the
soundness of the ideals a society sustains through its institutions, it is next
to the impossible for anyone to escape their effects while forming his or her
personality. Societies are free or restrictive depending on the measure in
which they allow for deviations from approved norms and acceptable
patterns of value priorities.

There is no humanist vision that has proved able to ignore the limits
which distinct cultural structures set up as legitimate parameters for the
formation of character. Even the most flexible of societies have found it
impossible to discard certain explicit limits beyond which an individual
may reach without risk to loyalty or loss of identity. Given these considerations it is understandable that a plurality of humanistic outlooks may
flourish in the course of history. Of greater interest is the fact that choice of
commitment in the activity of constructing an intellectual outlook is
anything but monolithic. The freer the society the richer the variety of
commitments and thus the greater the diversity of personal styles. The
issue that pertains to the present discussion is not whether all types of
commitment and all life styles are legitimate or not, but whether they may
be coordinated to function as a cooperative set to promote the common
concerns of humanity. What needs to be decided here is which types of
commitment are agreeable to a genuine humanistic philosophy, and if
more than one, what is the relative worth of each.

The fact that there are a number of humanistic interpretations of
human experience is itself a problem that calls for cooperation and adjust-
ments. A commitment to a pattern of value priorities and a preference for a
certain hierarchical arrangement of institutions reflect strong convictions
for humanist and nonhumanist alike. As such, these convictions find their
way into the set of beliefs that determine one's evaluative attitude, one's
philosophical criteria of significance. It is here that disagreements often
turn into polemics and differences of approach degenerate into counter-
productive splinterings of the humanistic movement. Consider, for
instance, the variety of humanistic responses to the institution of religion.

With the separation of church and state, legal devices were introduced to allow for the protection of a number of commitments and interpretations of the use and value of religious institutions. Thus it was permissible, at least in principle, to hold any one of a variety of approaches to matters of worship, ranging from unquestioned loyalty to a supernatural type of deity to an uninhibited condemnation of all objects of worship and all observances of religious ceremony. The last two centuries especially have seen a large number of humanist frameworks constructed as part of a critical movement that brought in its wake many interpretations of religion ranging from theories spun with the aid of the sociology of religion to the variety of our liberalized philosophical theologies. In this regard alone, it is not surprising to see that humanists have run the gamut from naturalistic theism to the religion of humanity.

The case of the humanist response to the institution of religion can also be used to discuss comparable evaluations of other institutions and the related programs of reforms either for their improvement or, in certain extreme cases, elimination. The issue which relates directly to the present discussion is not the particular action a humanist response may or may not generate under certain conditions but the fact that the diversity of responses gives rise to counterproductive disagreements within the humanist ranks. Judging from the splintering in the case of the debate on the problem of religion and its detrimental effects, one can see how they multiply rapidly by bringing into the picture the intellectual responses to other institutions. Therefore, it is not difficult to see why the humanist outlook has yet to reach the stage of a unified movement. The difficulties that result from sharp disagreements are mainly due to partial commitments and related intellectual projections of preferred value stratifications.

As attempts to illumine human conduct, the humanistic philosophies are no different than any other *bona fide* intellectual activity which starts out with a candid analysis of problems and states openly its particular commitment to a set of values, religious, artistic, ethical, social, or any combination thereof. The important thing to note here is that, more often than not, *commitment* is turned into a decisive factor in the construction of a more comprehensive viewpoint. Thus what was initially a distinctive feature, an adjective, is elevated to the status of a conceptual determinant for all other types of evaluation. Hence the tacit ultimacy claimed for this or that life style, artistic, religious, ethical, social, legal, existential, and so on, should be of no surprise; and the humanist life style is no exception.

It would be desirable from a practical and theoretical point of view to seek a course of action that would permit some degree of doctrinal unification without falling into the errors of reductionism. Though a full defense in favor of such a proposal cannot be presented here, this may be as good a time to suggest the theory of political humanism as the one which affords the most comprehensive context for the integration of a vital yet diversified movement. The main problem in this case is not the terminological one, how to bring under the same banner the diversity of adjectives that stand for this or that brand of humanism. It is hoped that by introducing the needed political component to broaden the theoretical basis of the humanist outlook, not only can fresh analyses of traditional ethical and cultural problems be undertaken, but also more efficient ways to meet the persistent need for international cooperation will hopefully emerge. On the contrary, by continuing along the lines of the established partisan views within the humanistic movement, it is rather unlikely that an integrative theory can be arrived at and consistently illuminate the problems of free will and responsibility, the source of morality, the general concept of justice, the basis of rights and duties, and also what seems to be the toughest problem of all applied ethics: how to assign meaning to the practical excellences in a period when this area of concern is being steadily taken over by private taste and personal caprice.

It is worth repeating here that one of the first tasks of a theory of political humanism would be to restore the meaning of the term *political*. It is a task that has to be defined in light of a comprehensive view of objectives that transcend vested interests and ideological loyalties. Once the political conduct is seen as the matrix for all other types of institutional concerns and habits, there would be nothing to prevent the inquiry into this domain from reaching the level of service it had with Aristotle and thus becoming again the supreme practical science, with a normative as well as a descriptive side to it. Should this shift in the direction of political inquiry prove possible, not only will practical humanism acquire a much needed theoretical scope, it may equally signal the termination of the provincial offshoots of humanism which continue to draw their effectiveness from suggestive yet abstract characterizations of the human condition.

A theory of the type we are proposing here would aim at doing justice to all human activities and institutions and also provide the requisite criteria for the diagnosis and prognosis of deviations from productive and cooperative conduct. Of course, there is always the danger of moving in the direction of axiological dogmatism once we allow normative considerations to define the principal tasks of political theorizing. However, no matter what the cost of intellectual labor in pursuing the tasks as stated, the losses we incur through neglect to investigate the conditions of institutional degeneracy and political aberrations are far too serious to ignore. As in the case of biological ecosystems, once the balance of the factors responsible for the state of health is disturbed, the prospects for the removal of disease decrease as the process of corruption remains unchecked. But whereas the biological world requires no subjective references for the identification of the normative patterns which constitute the specific states of health, the cultural and political works of human beings demand the active engagement of intelligence to produce and maintain healthy institutions and balanced personalities. It is precisely this broadened concept of health with respect to civilized life that should be recognized as the fundamental task of the science of politics. By extension, the art of politics has as its primary obligation the active control of the conditions that ensure the preservation of social and individual health. Anything else, insofar as it tends to threaten or disturb and distort the normal conditions for fulfillment of the human potential, falls within the purview of curing: removing the deviant.

All this may sound as portending advocacy of conservatism or inflexible moralizing for the sake of promoting a fixed pattern of absolute ends. However, the point of the thesis is not one of preaching against having a variety of value systems or cultivating cultural diversity in order to control human beings through standardized behavior. As was said earlier in this paper, the proposal to construct a theory of political humanism was tied to the concern to guide our efforts in the direction of securing a more complete grasp of the means and ends of group life and personal fulfillment. Since varieties of institutional structures, values and life styles arise no matter what we wish or think in abstract, the issue is not whether such facts are allowed to come to be but what sort of refinement they deserve to attain. Starting out with the facts of life is a sign of intellectual sanity; giving these facts the direction they deserve through a reasoned vision of perfectibility is a gift of wisdom. In fact, it is the sort of collective wisdom any group may aspire to attain provided it succeeds in reinstating the political aspect to its rightful position. With this process under way there would be little resistance on the part of theory to recognize what the term *political* can mean when it occupies the place of the most significant *differentia* in any definition of the human animal.

The issue therefore is not one of resurrecting some wornout terminology to enrich the value connotations of our theoretical formulations of the human condition. Rather, the cardinal point is how to come to grips with the substantive pursuits in personal and public conduct. I will discuss briefly two such areas where substantive matters call for intense attention: (a) the problem of the practical excellences, and (b) the problem of social cooperation. It is hoped that in both these areas a theory of political humanism can open new vistas by offering fresh approaches and making valuable recommendations.

The problem of the practical excellences is perhaps one of the most difficult of all cultural and educational issues we face at every turn of our lives. For one thing, it is a most demanding task to formulate the basic premises upon which to rest a theory of perfectible habits and in line with an unbiased inquiry into the nature of human desires. For another, it is even more difficult to produce the requisite leadership and persuasive means in order to induce the acceptance of a set of practical excellences. If changing the prevailing customs and habits of a given social group is in itself an educational undertaking of extraordinary magnitude, it should be evident that introducing principles which demand the perfection of already structured responses borders on revolutionary reforms. Experience has shown that it is easier to induce people to accept refinements in the area of intellectual habits and logical procedures, that is, processes which are essential to securing theoretical excellences, than it is to reorient the entrenched values to which desires attach themselves. Insofar as the problem of practical excellences, what they are and how to inculcate them under given historical and cultural circumstances, is inseparable from that of forming character, it belongs to a cluster of disciplines, and chiefly among them the philosophy of education. Therefore to explore it in all its complexity requires the assistance of psychology, biology, the medical sciences, and the social disciplines. Unless we are prepared to enlarge the field of ethical inquiry and recast its objectives so as to allow them to overlap with those of a theory of political humanism, the chances that we may bridge the already wide gap between ethics and politics remain rather slim.

It is equally important to consider the service which a theory of political humanism can offer to the educational process both as a critique of cultural practices and as an inquiry which studies the public ends and means as they relate to individual fulfillment and social cooperation. As such it provides the broadest context for: (a) an inquiry into the human condition, whereby political humanism can function as a continuous exploration of the problematic relationship between the pedagogic demands for the transmission of "approved" practical excellences and the justification of authority; and (b) an inquiry into the special cultural factors which as such hinder or advance the recognition of the pervasive values on which intercommunity understanding depends.

Every organized society preserves its identity by means of certain agencies which are responsible for the education and acculturation of its members. That there are processes which effect certain cultural types or characters is not an issue up for debate. What is of special interest in this connection is the set of commitments and values that determine the qualitative controls each society exercises in the production of character. Hence the function of a critique of institutions is to identify the special features each society allows to enter into the formation of character and also to evaluate the claims to producing what is believed in each case to be good character. Whether the issues involved can be brushed aside by appealing to the verities of cultural relativism and situational ethics will always be open to debate. However, what a theory of political humanism may manage to establish in this connection is a set of minimal criteria which claims to "good character" would have to satisfy. Only thus will it be able to defend the meaningfulness of the concept of practical excellences while also satisfying the demands for the preservation of freedom and individuality.

At the other end of the spectrum of the forces involved in character formation are those that point to the dangers of serving fixed ends and stereotype moralities. The protests that have been registered against the forces which promote stability through contrived ideals and policed ends are too familiar to be recounted here. What is more pertinent to our theme is the fact that such practices continue to persist under the cloak of the mystique of law and order despite the spreading adoption of democratic ideas. Thus one of the most disturbing paradoxes of contemporary culture is that whereas freedom remains a primary cultural condition for the formation of character it is also being used for the production of stereotypes obedient to the values of mass culture. The abuse of freedom in the case of the manipulation of desires through the mass media is itself a major political development; it is one that affects directly the qualitative conditions for conceptualizing the relationship between desires, needs, and habits. Once the political issue is made clear it is easier to see why a theory of political humanism has to include among its concerns both the criticism of fixed ends of traditional moralities, including the attendant supernaturalisms, and the more subtle systems of secular values, especially the ones we readily associate with mass culture and technics.

It is routine practice among liberal intellectuals to oppose fixed ends and to state the alternative in the fashionable idiom of "open-ended" or "open-textured" values. Supporting their approach is the conviction that authentic freedom is incompatible with closed systems of value. Perhaps the time has come to reexamine the validity of the disjunction and raise anew the possibility of a third alternative. What has not been considered as creditable in this controversy is that a third alternative may well prove to contain the promise of a viable solution. Let us assume that the meaning of "fixed ends" has not been exhausted by what the opposing parties have propounded. Should this prove to be the case, the third alternative may lie in the direction of discovering *bona fide* fixed ends. Now since the practical excellences belong to the means, we may proceed to argue that "false" fixed ends, when admitted under the guise of "true" fixed ends, not only have to introduce some set of practical virtues, but, what is damaging to the concept of fixed ends, their eventual downfall as pseudovirtues brings discredit to the ends they serve. Such "virtues" flatter us at the start, as Plato would say, but as their employment continues they distort our native capacities to attain genuine happiness and prevent us from acting with deliberative rectitude.

If the problem of clarifying the meaning of practical excellences lies at the top of the pressing needs which ethical theory must face, the task of redefining the common ends of mankind is no less urgent. Perhaps the need for a theory of political humanism is destined to be felt most acutely in the field of international cooperation. It has often been said by skeptics of all types that in view of the fluid nature of economic systems and the plurality of social styles, the quest for a worldwide humanism with binding political authority, one which is capable of generating broad agreements in matters of peace, production, health, and education, is but a fool's dream. That may well be the case but the truth of the claim must always assume the mysterious existence of some ultimate arbitrator of human affairs, a force that resists all efforts toward universal cooperation. At best, this is a conviction, not a fact. I think we are on better grounds when planning for the future or assessing the present to keep reminding ourselves that human intelligence is both a means and an end. As end, it constitutes a substantial component in the thinking of the ideal of self-fulfillment. As means, human rationality, while it can be used to defend and promote any set of vested interests, it also serves as the most reliable instrument for the critical evaluation of all hitherto proposed models of political life. We have at least this much to go by: the ubiquitous features of human intelligence.

The time has come to act and initiate debate on the pressing problems of our generation, from that of increasing international cooperation between the superstates to that of ensuring the independence of the smaller nations. If we take into consideration that of all types of organization it is the "united states" model that has become the most workable, then the chances that it may succeed in the case of the continents of Europe, Africa, and South America are indeed very good. This trend alone justifies the careful examination of the theoretical basis that would help sharpen the tools to further the constructive interaction among the four or five massive "united states" of the future. The task is bound to assume the dimensions of a formidable practical and theoretical operation. At least we can anticipate this much: that it will call for the successive crystallization of the pertinent practical excellences which the emerging political organizations need to employ in order that human beings may function as citizens. It is in this regard that I consider the theoretical program of political humanism to be most timely and most appropriate to the study of the future of mankind.

A Factual Investigation of the Foundations of Morality

Morris B. Storer

"Morality thou deadly bane," wrote Robert Burns,
"Thy tens o' thousands hast thou slain!
Vain is his hope, whose stay and trust is
In moral mercy, truth and justice."[1]

In such terms humanist Burns condemned the tyranny of the Kirk of Scotland of his day, and the moral standpoint that was at that very time, by way of the Kirk-Session, prosecuting his friend and benefactor, Gavin Hamilton, for "causing his servants to dig new potatoes in his garden on the 'last Lord's Day' of the month" (July 1789); also the same morality that, under the Spanish Inquisition, had burned at the stake somewhere between 4,000 and 341,042 (by various estimates)[2] Spanish and Portuguese unbelievers, a "deadly bane" indeed.

We may say that this "morality," this set of fiats from the paramoral, was just a counterfeit of the real thing, an ecclesiastical ploy and substitute for the veritable "mercy, truth and justice" which Burns knew full well to be the foundation of human society and which are bound to be major objects of our study here.

In probing for the real thing, my procedure will be to start by trying, through some examples, to get clear on what morality is about, what sources it flows from, what our stake in it is, and then to see if there are some things that can be truthfully said about how a person "ought" to live in terms of what he/she "owes" to society in moral terms. This will precipitate an investigation of the facts that can be said to define and inhere in and verify these "moral debts."

Let us consider two perennial truth problems that are as urgent today as ever:

Behind the post-World War II iron curtain, Alexander Solzhenitsyn spends eight years in jail, then three at forced labor, for writing a letter criticizing Stalin. The issue: the *right* to speak the truth.

On this side of the curtain, a post-Vietnam president is forced to resign as the price of suppressions and distortions of the truth. The issue: the *obligation* to speak the truth.

Where does humanism stand? Erich Fromm expressed a dominant emphasis of contemporary humanism when he wrote in *Man for Himself* (twenty-five years before E. R. A.): "The aim of man's life is to be understood as the unfolding of his powers, according to the laws of his nature....Good in humanistic ethics is this unfolding, the affirmation of his life....Virtue is responsibility toward his own existence. Vice is irresponsibility toward himself."[3] Is it so? Is this all? Is this emphasis equal to the strain and demands of those problems and of today's problems overall. In its essence, is this enough?

Ethics is properly a study of human excellence in total perspective, neglecting nothing that has a bearing. Right action is action worthy of approval, wrong action deserving disapproval. Solzhenitsyn's action was right—perhaps heroic—not because it was calculated to bring great good to himself or because it *did* so. It *didn't* in any material sense. It doubtless enhanced his self-respect. But it was right because it challenged abominable violations of human rights. It was a necessary step on the way to a cure of the society. The President's actions were wrong not because they brought pain to himself. They *did*, but in the moral standpoint this was incidental. They were wrong because they undermined the confidence of a nation in their government.

For total perspective in ethics, a combined emphasis would seem to be called for on (1) fulfillment of the potentialities of the person who acts (society does have an interest in this), and on (2) justice or whatever constitutes virtue in relations with the community. Everyone has observed that without this second factor, it is not uncommon for people intent on the "unfolding of their own powers" to become caught up in a *struggle* for power which leads to injuries and slanders and alienation quite shattering to the environment of trust and good will, and obstructive to that unfolding of the individual's powers. So we must expect to find that the "affirmation of life" of the excellent person must be continually qualified by a regard for other persons as ends in themselves. And we may find profound truth in Cicero's observation that "nothing opposed to right can be advantageous."[4]

THE SOURCES OF MORALITY

We might learn something of the essence by examining the sources of morality.

Feeling as Source. Some humanists are persuaded with David Hume that right and wrong are simply proclamations of the heart, of emotion, of sentiment—and a follow-up command. So "Murder is wrong" means "I don't like murder," and "Don't you murder." Only this and nothing more. If this is true, consensus would seem totally out of reach, since hearts quicken in response to quite different drummers. But in the view of this essay the skepticism of the emotivists is quite unnecessarily desperate, and a solid foundation for accord does exist in facts which are before everyone and whose surface we will try to scratch in this essay: judgments of right and wrong in the moral sense are factual judgments, and we get clear on facts by sense and reason, not by emoting over anything.

Custom as Source. Another highly respected group among humanists who seem to be hopeless of accord on any essentials are the cultural relativists. These take the position that morality is defined in every culture or tribe by the particular "mores" or settled customs of that group, and that there is no basis for moral judgment beyond custom. The mores reflect the circumstances and the tribal wisdom of the community in meeting local problems, and no one can reasonably say that a free culture here is superior to a slave culture there, or that an aboriginal tribe has made progress in turning its back on the lively "head hunting" days in opting for civilization. There's nothing intrinsically wrong in the traditions of the headhunters, and there's no sense in trying to convert them to a respect for heads. Their customs are just right for them. So say the relativists.

Back of this skepticism about discoverable roots of morality in universal human nature, I believe, lie two notable factors: (1) the necessities under which anthropological researchers work. If you are to live with a primitive tribe on a reasonably pleasant and fruitful basis for a few years, it is needful that you shall discretely leave "judgment" behind, show respect for what you encounter, and set "understanding" as goal. (2) A meticulous scientific objectivity has traditionally discouraged value judgments. "A scientist's role is to examine and report, not to judge."

What seems to be needed in this drive for overview and consensus is a united effort to stand above the limiting aspects of our callings as social scientists or philosophers in reaching for an unlimited perspective. As in the case of the emotivists, we may find an escape from skepticism for all if we can identify facts, open to the examination of all, which eventually define and provide foundations for our judgments of "good" and "bad" and "right" and "wrong." It is the objective of this article to marshall crucial ones.

Law as Source. A considerable part of the world business community conceives that there is absolutely no obligation to moral principles beyond the requirements of law, and that laws obligate only when it is impossible to circumvent them. The drive for profits justifies bribery, conspiracy, collusion, strong-arm robberies, crimes at all levels.

There is a growing self-consciousness in the business community about the degradation of business morality and the depression of credibility which results from this, and an entire half of the world has expressed it's aversion to the consequent iniquities by turning to Communism.

No humanist can be blind to the inequities and injuries suffered by millions of people at the bottom of the pile under our economic system— the indecent concentration of wealth and income, the spectacle of outrageous profits fueling a menace of inflation that can only be slowed by a period of recession and attendant unemployment, the inescapable interpretation by many of a sky-high profit system as exploitation and highway robbery and a justification for everything from shoplifting to organized crime operating on national and world levels.

But the centralized concentration of power over the lives of the people in the hands of the State, which is of the essence under Communism and which is always a strong trend under a socialized economy, leads in the words of Soviet mathematician Shafarevich in his forthcoming book *Socialism* to a "total destruction of the human spirit and to a leveling of mankind unto death."[5]

Humanism must lead the way in finding the middle course which will provide at the same time the environment of an open society, and a corrected and responsible and justified economy "with liberty and justice and opportunity for all." But no correction of the economy and the laws under which it operates can give us a good and healthy society unless human individuals are committed to high standards of personal morality beyond the requirement of law. Law simply fixes the *minimum* of absolutely essential morality which shall be enforced on all persons. That minimum itself is open to constant reexamination, and for good human life much more is required than conformity to law.

ALTERNATIVE STANDARDS OF MORALITY

Our differences about the substance of a humanist ethic result in part from our differences concerning what ethics is "about." Three options are prominent: One will say, "Clearly the measure of right and wrong for you is the impact of your actions in personal gains and losses for yourself." People, like the less rational animals, have but one life to live, and survival is the first order of business, and "getting ahead" or happiness or fulfillment is next—the greatest "value" for self, however interpreted. The private end justifies the means, and actually dictates the course for humans in the view of many. Others in this category simply view self-interest as the inescapably *rational* choice. A certain consideration for others and their own distinguishing standards may be seen as important, *instrumental* to personal advantage, but it has no moral worth in itself, and the morally "right" course always involves a hard-nosed calculation of long-range advantage. You think of examples as various as Raskolnikov or Lady Macbeth or Napoleon or Ayn Rand or a wealthy benefactor of public causes and needy people. Call this "egoism."

Or a second will say, "Clearly survival is a sine qua non, and personal security and fulfillment are important to individual and community alike, but the 'excellence' of a person involves much more than this." "Excellent" is the *community's* judgment of the individual, and the excellent person is the one who, in all his getting, keeps other people in mind, not instrumentally toward a payoff in later relations, but taking thought for the greatest happiness—the greatest preponderance of pleasure over pain, or the least preponderance of pain over pleasure, if pain there must be—for all who are affected. The composite end justifies the means. You think of examples as various as Karl Marx or Castro or Mao invoking violent revolutions in the interest of oppressed peoples, or Harry Truman deciding for the atomic bomb at Hiroshima. Call this "arithmetic utilitarianism."

Or a third may say, "No, neither formula will do. Yes, of course, rich value and balanced fulfillment for self is to be taken for granted as a major goal, and the happiness of other people as well, but beyond this the essential and unexceptional principle is 'justice', 'fairness', concern for the move that you would approve in everyone else's doing, conformity to the law of your own legislation, regard for every individual as an end in himself. The human end justifies the principle, and only principle justifies the means." Some in this class would say "In the end there is no entire fulfillment apart from this justice." One thinks of Socrates or Epictetus or Cicero or Abraham Lincoln or Jane Adams or Mahatma Gandhi. Call this "universalism."

Who is the realist, who the idealist, and who the visionary in this apparent collision of minds? Is the basic concern of ethics self-interest or greatest happiness or justice? And is a person really free to choose between ultimate self-interest and total human interest when the conflict arises? Are we all grooved and committed by inborn animal nature to the pursuit of our own happiness?

Our decision between the claims of these alternative emphases depends ultimately on our conclusions on matters of fact which we will survey in our next section. But the question about the central concern of ethics should be easy, depending only on the history of the use of words. Since humans began to talk, to communicate through the use of word-symbols, and to think on the same basis, they have recognized that some talk and some actions have had good effects on persons concerned and on the community generally, and other talk and action have had bad effects on the same. ("Good," in this elementary use means helpful, pleasing, gratifying because serving "toward the creation of trust, confidence, and integrity in relationships," "cooperative attitudes," "enhanced self-respect," "fulfillment of individual potentialities" as summarized in Lester Kirkendall's valuable proposals on Page 196 of this book. "Bad" means displeasing, disturbing, injurious because serving to undermine these goods.) Good and bad effects on single individuals are apt to be observed by others or communicated quickly by word of mouth to communities at large with resultant reassurance, pleasure, and comfort, on the one hand, or distress, anxiety, and fear on the other. The words "right" and "wrong" are used then by the community to commend and encourage the former kind of talk and action, and to condemn and disparage the latter kind. Such have been the definitive concerns of morality as reflected in our notes on Solzhenitsyn and President Nixon and their careers on the "truth" front early in this article.

The word "right" is also used with just as clear precedent to express "prudent," "wise," "commendable" from the angle of a particular individual or group, and the objective in view. So if I am trying to cut down a dead tree, I call my strategy "right" if my guy-line brings the tree down clear of the threatened fence, if it "works" to the end in view. But no one would call my strategy a "moral" one. Similarly we might call a person "shrewd," "sagacious," or "astute" who is very discerning in planning his moves—his statements and actions—to the end of private advantage, independent of any concern for the impact of his actions in other lives. But if to this end he makes lying statements and acts injuriously or irresponsibly or "unjustly" in relation to others, his actions are correctly called morally "wrong" or "corrupt" and he is condemned for them. His or her actions *are* the community's business if they undermine the environment of trust and security.

Of course people are free to use words in any sense they choose, so long as they make their meanings clear. But there are always difficulties in understanding when there is departure from the meanings sanctioned by usage. Thus if "morally right" is privately conceived and defined as "shrewdness," independent of principle, shrewd actions will not thus be rendered more honorable, and other words will have to be coined to identify the humanly praiseworthy—what is praiseworthy from the point of view of humanity because beneficent in the life of people immediately or distantly affected.

There is an understandable impulse among humanists and among thinking people broadly to disassociate themselves from all vestiges of Calvinist or other authoritarian Judao-Christian morality, but we must not let that impulse disassociate us from *morality*—from the morality which is dictated by the facts of life. Because life approaches the intolerable in proportion as the level of public morality declines and the community is poisoned by injuriousness, suspicion, ill will, vengefulness, and hatred.

The spokespersons for ethical egoism have performed an immense service in rejecting the hair shirt, the irrational guilt consciousness, the sense of original sin, and the disparagement of human nature which played so large a part in Calvinist morality. This has led to a great clearing of the air and a freeing of human potentialities, but with this accomplished, there is a need to face the facts of human interrelatedness.

Our proposal in answer to the original question about the rock-bottom concern of ethics, then, would be, "the commendable from the standpoint of the community—what works good, what accomplishes good in the community." This includes the good of the individual in the middle—whose actions are in question—as a significant consideration, but not when in conflict with the greater good of the whole.

What is the underlying concern of ethics? An end of conflict in the community and in the world; an end of suspicion and rancor and mistrust, an end of hatred and use and abuse of persons; the establishment of a humane environment—an environment of clean water and clean air and clean land and clean human relations where people can enjoy life together and bring their powers to fullest realization. What excellence in persons are required to bring about such a world? What excellences in persons would be made possible by such a world? That's what ethics is about.

These goals would have slight chance of realization under the "greatest happiness" option that we barely described, because at the center of such a calculated program, balancing pleasures here against pains there, is a factor of exploitation which is unimaginable under humanist idealism. It would tend inevitably to the abuse of persons who happen to stand at the losing end of the equation. If we are to have that clean air and make progress toward a world of trust and security and good feeling between people, our ethic must commit us to equity in human relations, to justice and fairness and equal acknowledgment of all people.

What is the meaning of justice? Justice takes on meaning first in relation to law, commending one and the same law to govern all, with equal penalties for violation. We take this ideal for granted in this country for the most part, although we are just four generations from slavery, and the battle over discrimination is not yet won everywhere in America. But justice, translated as fairness, has meaning entirely apart from law: what we assert to be right for ourselves we assert to be right for others under the same conditions, what wrong for others, then wrong for ourselves similarly. This translates into a morality of principles, but unrelated to rules from supernature, rules from any source to be written down and conveyed identically to all mankind. In this justice, responsibility for definition of principle falls on the one who is doing the choosing. This is the fate of the humanist: to have to choose without ordained guidelines. But we are not really as forlorn and bereft of standards by our liberation from the paramoral as Sartre has represented. We do not have to "invent" principles out of whole cloth. Everyone knows what he would not want others to do to him/her in a particular situation. This lead is available to every human being from the most primitive, and has been articulated again and again since humanist Confucius offered his negative golden rule 500 years before Christ and Hillel of Babylon formulated it for the western world in the first century B. C.—"Do not do to others what you would not want them to do to you." Since there are few situations where I want others to lie to me or steal from me or cheat me or knife me, those principles come without a struggle. But since I am writing the guidelines for myself, the door is always open to "license." Shall I cheat a little myself if I see that I can gain by it and think that I can get by with it—offer a makeshift justification if I get caught? But others see through it, and all the time I am looking on, myself. I know that what I have done is destructive to those ends of a humanist society which we have examined.

Do we have obligations beyond avoiding injustice? The traditional golden rule seems to fall short in its unrealistic response to the injuries and injustices of others. Should humanism add its own affirmative rule: Stand for yourself against injustice, and deal justly in all relations with others?

THE "OUGHT" AS A KIND OF OWING

Under what "obligations" do people live to govern themselves by such a principle of justice? What basis in fact, or otherwise, confronts us for saying that everyone ought to so live? We fly in the face of highly accredited and fairly massive judgment to the contrary in looking for facts: "You can't get an 'ought' form an 'is'; beware the 'naturalistic fallacy'." But all the evidence of language indicates that people everywhere have sensed the "ought" as a kind of "owing," a kind of debt, and since every other kind of debt is a kind of "is," a very sensible factual confirmable reality, we are encouraged to explore "moral debt" for factual content.

About that evidence of language, the Anglo-Saxon "agan" at the source of the "ought" served both meanings, the "ought" of morality and the debt at the market. Both meanings were packed in the Latin "debeo" and its Romance language derivatives. The same in the Greek "chreos" and the Russian "doljen" and the Hebrew "chovah" and the Chinese "ying kai."

The same in our English "duty"—what our forefathers refused to pay in Boston when they dumped the tea in the harbor, and what people tend to shun today in their thinking because in a free country they like to think they are doing everything of their own free will or on free impulse, as if there were something offensive about meeting a debt.

But there is something incongruous here. In our everyday debts we owe for what we have received. But if we do have moral debts, it would appear that we owe in advance of receiving and independent of it. If we are going to build a community of justice, we will have to deal justly in first relations and from that point on.

There is no mystery in this. We have many other debts of this kind. The school tax is a case in point. Many who have no children in school, and who have never had any, pay the tax without a thought. There is a common sense that it is important from everyone's point of view that all the children have a certain level of education. We have a common cause in this. All should pay a share of the cost. Call this a "debt of shared responsibility." Membership dues are commonly debts of the same kind. Members pay without too much thought of a balanced return of goods or services for what is invested: A share in the costs.

If we have moral debts, they are clearly of the same kind. We have a common cause: it is of vital importance to all people that they should be able to believe what is told them, rely on what is promised, count on the honest intentions of people—no purpose to deceive or cheat or betray or burglarize or assault. It is as important to other persons as to self. We have an urgent common cause in maintaining such a community of honesty and mutual respect and responsibility and justice and good will. My share in the cost, my debt to the community, is to govern my own life accordingly, putting at least such limits on my liberty in pursuit of my own ends as I ask others to put on theirs.

FACTS UNDERNEATH MORAL OBLIGATION

The interpretation and recognition of moral obligation, as a particular kind of debt puts us just a step on the road to a factual interpretation. All in all, what facts are needed to confirm this debt and that obligation?

(1) As very first step, we have to recognize elementary value judgments as factual. "Good" in the elementary sense means "responding to need or desire; what gives pleasure." "Bad: Whatever blocks the satisfaction of these; what causes pain." "Right" and "wrong" are different from these (as has been developed) and much more complicated.

(2) The human community is conspicuously interdependent. (So the "common cause.") The prehominoid community much less so. The development of verbal communication vastly increased this interdependence in

ways that do not need elaboration. With this came true and false, good faith and bad faith, and of course understanding and misunderstanding. And out of these emerged:

(3) "Elementary freedom," the capability and necessity of choosing and deciding, of assimilating the reality we meet in experience into "ideas" attached to words, meaningful symbols, and through these instruments making personal judgments of true and false and personal determinations for action, independent of instinctual pressures and genetic inspiration. Without this capacity for understanding, this freedom to choose, no plausible debt or obligation. There are premonitions of this human power of judgment in advanced lower animals (for instance the black labrador retriever and its miscellaneous progeny), but essentially humans are alone under the sun (and almost certainly in our solar system) in this emancipation from irrational determination.

We should not be lightly persuaded that, because we are part of nature, we are like the rest of nature in being objects of natural determinism, without autonomous force. We know ourselves better than that. We know ourselves (and only ourselves) from within, and ourselves as knowers, capable of acting on knowledge, no matter what pressure from genes or operant conditioning, and capable of acting in complete *violation* of knowledge if we choose—capable of choosing—responsible for choosing—responsible for the act. We take this freedom and this capability for granted in every conversation with a friend. In particular we take it for granted when we require people to swear that they will speak the truth in court. If we are mistaken, our system is grievously at fault in its penalties for perjury. We must not send people to jail for crimes that they cannot save themselves from committing, unless to discourage others from crime, and there would be no justice in that.

It is hard to contradict the reality of human freedom and independence from conditioning forces, operant or otherwise, since the person who contradicts asserts the truth of what he contradicts—asserts that *he* is capable of knowing the truth and speaking it, asserts that he knows "the most useful way of talking," the best evidenced way of talking about human behavior, asserts that his beliefs or his way to talking have *not* been determined or swayed by the conditioning factors that have operated in his own life.

Consensus or no consensus—by way of this symposium or otherwise—would appear to hang in the balance on this issue. If there is a truth about human behavior and what moves it and about our moral debts—about how people ought to behave—if there are facts to be assimilated into and reported by those judgments—and if people are free to perceive those facts and recognize that *truth* and embrace it, that *truth* would seem to offer the only promising basis for consensus. Consensus *is* convergence on truth, agreement based on a common conviction of truth.

(4) The freedom and the ability to choose to act—to determine to act—on a perception and judgment of truth about right and wrong as about any other truth.

What is there that's different about a human being that dictates the right to life for all humans (unarguably in most circumstances) where most people acknowledge no such right in other animals? That justifies equal right to liberty where we fence the others in, equal justice under law where the other animals are not granted any trial at all. Yes, people are ends in themselves, but what does that mean, and what facts support it? How are people equal?

Of course, people are equal in having an equal stake in life. Everyone has only one chance at life and what it offers. They are born into unequal circumstances, but the potentialities of life are boundless for everyone. But then the other animals have only one chance at life too. There must be another explanation.

There *are* other aspects of equality that we are apt to overlook that, I believe, stand at the root of the matter: equal understanding of right and wrong, of just and unjust; equal ability to speak the truth and keep a promise and *do* justice; equal awareness of injustice when it is suffered and equal suffering in the face of it; equal ability (more or less) to play a part in a responsible enterprise.

To say that human beings have intrinsic worth and must be recognized as ends in themselves, means simply that others must not use them as means to their own ends without recognizing that they have ends of their own, that they must be seen as factors in every moral equation where they play a part, not victimized, not forgotten as centers of human rights.

The debt is as factual as the debt at the bank, but obviously different in character. In one case I owe in return for what has been received. In the other case, I owe continually a portion of my freedom, equal to what I ask continually of others in the common cause (always relative to situations as they arise). I owe this discipline of myself, if it takes discipline. The respect of the community and my self-respect depend in one case as much as in the other on my meeting obligations as they come due. I am conscious, if I live in continuous delinquency in paying my moral debts, that I am a living parasite on the community, a "free-loader," a "sponge." I am not paying the share that is due.

The obligation to the principle of justice or "fairness" is as real, as concrete, as actual, as factual as this debt. It is independent of the *debtor's* feelings about it and of the *creditor's* feelings about it. It *dictates* to feeling. It is independent of all speculations about what might be gained by forgetting it. Perhaps the very wealthy grandparent might give the school its new library if his granddaughter is passed in spite of scandalous cheating on the examination. But if she is, other students will sense the sellout and cynicism will take over. The debt of fairness and the obligation to pay are indistinguishable. The obligation *is* the debt and the debt the obligation. It is utterly independent of sermons and appeals and claims of supernatural sanctions. It is simply and unconditionally there.

This analysis has had its disproportions. In focus on our debts to others, it has underemphasized the debts to self. They are important and need emphasis because slighted in many lives. But the crying need of the world is for a clarified and reverberant consciousness and recognition of our debts to each other, toward establishing peace and an environment of mutual trust and respect among nations and people. Egocentricity, intent on maneuvering increase in power and advantage for self as primary objective without acknowledgment of inherent obligations to others and without respect for the worth of other persons as ends in themselves, is apt to be the ultimately shattering blow to associated effort toward that world of peace and good will.

The analysis has been disproportionate in slighting the factor of "situation" in moral choice. But it has been there all the time underneath. If the chooser himself thinks through the principle of action in place (Would I be willing to have others do this?), he has the situation before him in every decision. There are commonly binding principles that admit of exceptions only in very extraordinary circumstances (the escaping prisoner of war lying his way through the countryside, or the father of hungry family without recourse, stealing what is needed), but the principle of principled behavior asserts its imperative categorically ("Would I believe others to be justified in such a situation in doing what I contemplate?) There is no magic that converts injustice to justice.

The analysis has been lopsided in slighting Robert Burns's concern for veritable "mercy" to go with his veritable "truth and justice" which *have* been emphasized, and undoubtedly it has slighted mercy's first cousin "love." But I count on correction by fellow-contributors. I am confident that a solid entirety will be the issue of our shared effort.

NOTES

1. *The Complete Poetical Works of Robert Burns*, Cambridge Edition Houghton, Miffin & Co., page 42.
2. The New International Encyclopedia on "Inquisition."
3. Erich Fromm, Man for Himself. Fawcett Publications, Inc., page 29.

4. Cicero, *Selected Works*, a Penguin Classic, translation by Michael Grant, page 162.
5. *Harvard Magazine*, July-August, 1978. Alexander Solzhenitsyn on *The Exhausted West*, page 24.

Comment by Archie Bahm on Storer Article

"Ethics is properly a study of human excellence in total perspective, neglecting nothing that has a bearing." I agree with this definition, except for a question about its key word, "excellence." Ethics, presupposing axiology, is concerned with goods and bads, better and worse, and best and worst. Acts are right because they are intended to produce the best results. If by "excellence" you mean "best results," my question is answered satisfactorily. But since "excel" also connotes excess, and since moderation, even humility, are often what is best, the term "excellence" in a definition needlessly entraps the definer in problems that must be dealt with later. Although I do idealize excellence when appropriate and advocate such an ideal for others, a more realistic (you aim to "probe for the real thing") statement will use the term "best" (or "optimum" as against "maximum").

But in the next sentence you restrict the "total perspective" to only some parts and, in doing so, omit, it seems to me, some essential parts of the total. Although you speak truly when you say that "right action is action...," you mislocate the actual existence of rightness, which is in the *intention* of the person acting (to be intending is already to be acting mentally, and unintended action is ethically neutral), by locating it in "approval" or "worthy of approval." Unintended actions producing good results may be "worthy of approval," but they are neither right nor wrong. Although many, perhaps most, right acts are also worthy of approval, being approved, or being "worthy of approval," are neither necessary nor sufficient to constitute the rightness of an act.

Granted that plenty of examples can be found in literature of people locating rightness in acts (vs. intentions) and in approval. Granted that people, tending to be naive realists epistemologically, tend thereby to locate rightness in overt actions. But I trust that, in your probe for "the real thing," you will not be satisfied with the naive realistic habit so obviously prevalent. Granted that actions having bad results should be condemned as bad (and "be judged worthy of disapproval"), but badness of unintended results does not constitute wrongness of intention. [In fact, when a condemner intends to condemn an act producing unintended bad results as wrongly intended, he himself is acting, because intending, wrongly.] [I suspect that one of the reasons why ethics suffers ill repute is that people not only resent others mistakenly condemning their own rightly intended actions but also feel uncomfortable when discovering that they themselves have been mistaken in ignoring the intentions of others when condemning bad results.]

In summarizing your "total perspective in ethics," you rightly include both the individual and the social in "a combined emphasis" on "fulfillment of the potentialities of the person who acts" and "on justice or whatever constitutes virtue in relations with the community." You later expand your "in relations with the community" to "commendable from the standpoint of the community" where you then "include the good of the individual in the middle . . . but not when in conflict with the greater good of the whole or the equal rights of others."

I am disturbed by an apparent ambiguity in your treatment which seems at times to involve a contradiction. At times you speak as if the good results of acts, whether the good of the individual or the good of the whole, are the ultimate foundation of rightness and morality. But at times, even at the same time, you speak as if the approval of action or the standpoint of the community were the ultimate location of rightness and morality. Since persons can be misled to approve false views, and persons and communities apparently can and do hold views actually harmful to themselves, commendation and condemnation can hardly be regarded as ultimate. You sometimes add "worthy of approval" and "deserving condemnation," but the basis of worthiness and of deservingness needs to be made clear. If you intended to define what you mean by these words in terms of good results, then introducing them as if part of your definition of rightness seems to postpone leading your reader to a clear conception of such good results. When you assert, in conclusion, regarding "the obligation to the principle of justice" that "it is simply and unconditionally there," approval seems not to be required. It not only does not require approval but "is independent of the debtor's feelings about it. It dictates to feeling."

Your ideal of good results includes both clean air and justice. Justice is needed so that conflict in the community and world will end. Justice involves equality, "the actual equality of persons underneath equal rights." Granted that equality is a central concept inherent in the principle of reciprocity functioning variably in human association. But people are both alike in many respects and differ in many respects. Surely people who *differ* have an *equal* right to have their differences (*inequalities*) respected. Is it not as wrong to treat unequals as equals as it is to treat equals as unequals? You mention several likenesses, but only one difference (born into unequal circumstances). You cite Confucius' "negative rule" but omit the essential phrase "if you were that person," intended to make clear that discriminating carefully regarding differences is essential to justice. I agree that "moral debts are factual." But the facts about moral debts are complex and conditional, not "simply and unconditionally there."

Reply by Morris Storer to Bahm

We try to improve our communication by way of these exchanges. They are needed. A few responsive thoughts here on results, intentions, and principles as factors in morality.

In the view which I have outlined, if a person achieves to outstanding results in his own life—goes to the top in business or profession, and is able to surround himself and family with the best things—if this "success" has been achieved at the cost of violence to moral principle and related violations of other people—treacheries, betrayals, duplicity, conspiracy, et cetera, then there is nothing "commend-able" or "honor-able," nothing worthy, in those successes, though they may be honored by some. We condemn the injuries and the injustices whether we believe they were done intentionally or carelessly in the conviction that people have a responsibility to intend justice.

Similarly if a person aspires to public service and works purposefully for the "greatest good of the greatest number" but is indifferent to neglect or violations of minority groups, we see this as a serious fault in the program and demand something closer to justice in purpose and program.

I want to join you in your emphasis on the importance of intention. No one deserves any particular respect for the good result or the semblance of justice that is accomplished accidentally, but people have to answer for their irresponsibilities as well as their bad intentions. The drunk who carelessly drives his car across the sidewalk and kills two or three people is not guiltless because he/she "did not mean to do it." And the measure of intentions from a moral point of view is not the results in view but the principles to which one is committed. And since humanists disavow the authority of commandments from on high and from here below except for such as are embodied in the laws of a free people, we are left with the principle of principles: Deal justly as you would be dealt by, and judge others a little mercifully in view of the built-in neuroses and psychoses and traumata under which all rational animals function to a greater or lesser degree. This makes each of us sovereign and subject, legislator and bounden citizen, under heavy double obligation in the moral sphere, but this is the best that good free-thinking animals can do in and toward a good free society.

In this view, the good principle which is the measure of the good intention or good purpose is the principle that you would desire everyone to be guided by in circumstances where some self-restraint or self-discipline is called for (in the public interest) in the entirely appropriate normal pursuit of private ends. This is what I meant in saying that the standpoint of morality is that of the community. I did not at all mean that the current standards of the community are the proper measure of morality for every individual. The ultimate consideration in such self-restraints is the good order of the community, in which all have a stake.

Comment by Joseph Fletcher on Storer Article

The language of Morris Storer's title is, we may be sure, carefully chosen. It is precisely with respect to his belief that ethical investigation is fundamentally factual, that "judgments of right and wrong in the moral sense are factual judgments," that he poses a significant issue around which many moralists ("of equally good kidney," as Sidney Smith liked to say) disagree and dispute.

First, however, it seems right and proper, and a privilege, to rejoice in Storer's moral vision. Appeals to legality and rights are rife in the world today, but justice and duty seem to be almost completely eclipsed. To speak of justice as straightforwardly as Morris Storer does, and to put it—the social dimension of the cardinal virtues—in the driver's seat, over the sister virtues of temperance, fortitude, and prudence, is to stand in the grand tradition of Western philosophy and jurisprudence. In the same way, his emphasis on obligation as primary in ethics has the ring of a sturdy humanistic challenge to the narcissism of so much of the contemporary insistence on individual rights—a moral malady which has even infected the American Civil Liberties Union.

I must say that I feel great sympathy with these two foci in Storer's essay: the imperative importance ethically of the concepts of justice and obligation. They fuse or join together in the ideal of social interest. As one who has a lot in common with the ideal of classical utilitarianism, I see in this social interest a close parallel to the "utility" of humanistic ethics worked out by John Stuart Mill and others—Sidgwick, for example. My commentary, therefore, is not on what Morris Storer proposes, but on how he supports it. (I need hardly remark, surely, that humanists are to be found in many different schools of ethical theory.)

Perhaps my chief complaint is that he may be guilty (note that I do not say he *is*) of what G. E. Moore called the "naturalistic fallacy," that is, of at least suggesting that, in Hume's figure of speech, "ought" can be derived from "is"—that we can cross over by logical inference from facts to moral obligations. Philosophically regarded, this was the fatal error beneath the "natural law" ethic of Catholicism.

Storer's unelaborated reference to this trap (he mentions it twice) shows that he is aware of it, but he chooses to ignore it; how else are we to understand such language as "...judgments of right and wrong in the moral sense are factual judgments..." and "...if we can identify facts, open to the examination of all, which eventually define and provide foundations for our judgments of 'good' and 'bad'..."? He also makes it plain in the second of his two Bergsonian "two sources of morality"—custom.

The tone of Storer's paper as a whole, however, suggests that he means not "brute" facts but "institutional" facts, as they have been distinguished by John Searle and G. E. M. Anscombe. To say that a child is a biological organism is a plain or a brute fact but to say the child is a person is not; it is a statement about a moral or social phenomenon, a complex or syndrome of brute fact with attitudes and values. Exponents of naturalistic ethics have sometimes tried to argue, as Storer seems to, that "ought" or obligation is derived from facts (is-ness), that is, facts of the second or institutional kind.

Storer may want to make this claim, too. In a startling but plain-spoken use of the notion of "moral fact," he says "...we have to recognize elementary value judgments as factual." I have to admit that with him I feel inclined to regard attitudinal phenomena as genuinely empirical.

The trouble with this, though, is that it does not escape the logical fallacy in any attempt to make inferences from "ought" (value judgments) to "is" (facts). Granted that our personal and cultural sentiments are facts just as much as physical things are, this only means that their existence is not evidence that they are correct. To say, as Storer and I would both say, that most people disapprove incest means nothing more than that most people disapprove incest. In short, I want to say that ethics, including humanist ethics, is normative, not descriptive. Precisely because it is factual, what is sometimes called "descriptive ethics," is really psychology and anthropology, not ethics.

As I have pointed out elsewhere, there is no way in the world to "prove" that the Supreme Court's decision against racial discrimination in the schools (*Brown v. Board of Education*) was "true." Like religious beliefs, moral beliefs are matters for justification, but not for verification. Moral judgments may be justified but neither verified nor falsified. In our thirst for the good (bonum) and the true (verum) we must not forget that from ancient to modern times we have kept them distinct.

(Nothing I say here should be taken to mean that facts are unimportant or irrelevant or ethically insignificant. On the contrary, as a consequentialist—one who determines that actions are right or wrong according to whether they result in more human well-being or less—it is obvious that I must take both kinds of facts into full account. I am not clear whether Storer would accept this as sufficient or not.)

At one juncture in his paper Morris Storer plainly links his focus on moral obligation to the naturalistic fallacy. The focus is certainly a proper one; nevertheless, many of us could not accept his claim that since the sense of obligation (Kant's "oughtness"?) is an observable fact (as he puts it, "a kind of 'is' ") it therefore has factual content. Not so. The sense of oughtness is a fact but it has no factual content, anymore than Ludwig Feuerbach's nearly universal "sense of dependency" had any data or evidence to support any religious belief of any kind whatsoever.

There are other elements in Storer's discussion which could provide us with a rich profit if we could meet to discuss humanist ethics vis-á-vis. For example, I resist his way of looking at what he calls "arithmetic utilitarianism." It happens to be a conviction with me that "mathematical morality" or "ethical arithmetic" is essential to distributive justice in huge societies and massive populations. Indeed, we might go so far as to contend that equalitarian morality is incompatible with distributive justice—a contention which would be of special interest to Storer because of his heartwarming concern for justice. Our discussion could be illumined, for example, by picking his brains on the age-old distinction between justice distributively, commutatively, and retributively interpreted. But this is for another time and place.

I might add one more word of thanks. I agree that freedom to choose (not necessarily to act, but at least to favor) is essential to a humanist ethics. We may go farther; we may say that any and all ethics, not only humanist but nonhumanist and antihumanist ethics, must presuppose the moral agent's freedom to select a course of action. If he/she is physically or psychologically totally determined, helpless or "invincibly ignorant" of the alternatives open, nothing takes place in the forum of conscience. This is why even authoritarian morality, such as the churches teach, allows, no matter how low in key, that *conscientia semper sequenda est*—conscience is always to be followed—not church nor state nor party nor friend. "To thine own self be true..."

Reply by Morris Storer to Fletcher

It is very gratifying to have Joseph Fletcher's accord with my conclusions (or at least with their *emphasis* on justice and on obligation) in spite of his misgivings about my supporting logic. I would like to strengthen our accord on these conclusions by clarifying my logic, which clearly has failed to communicate fully.

I will be plain: I do plead guilty to deviation from the gospel according to G. E. Moore. I not only admit this apostasy, I proclaim it. In my view the "naturalistic fallacy" is a bugaboo which we should put behind us. If we contemplate the "ought" as a kind of "owing," I think it will be clear that moral obligation, moral debt, is every bit as factual as market debt, although the factors are more complex. My debt at the bank is what I owe to square the account—loan amount less amount paid off plus interest as agreed on. My moral debt is my equal share in the cost of a good community in which with others I have an equal stake. I owe it to others to exercise just such a discipline over my words and actions as I expect and ask others to exercise over theirs—to govern my speech and actions by such "rules and precepts" (Cf. John Stuart Mill) as I ask others to govern theirs by, with an eye to the happiest community for all. Moral debt is what is required of me and of everyone in order to maintain a relation of equal worth in sustenance of the good community and so qualify for self-respect and the respect of others. The facts which I have accented in my article are the unique aspects or elements of human nature and human situation that are involved in establishing this fact of moral obligation.

As a footnote, in my vocabulary "elementary values" are contrasted, not identified with moral values. Food is an elementary (and universal) value or good, valued and good because it satisfies a very factual human need. Oysters are conspicuously relative particular goods. Some like them, some do not. Shelter is a universal good, exposure to the storm bad. None of these are moral values, all of them very simply and directly factual as satisfying need or desire or as gratifying taste. These are *factors* in moral values, but are without moral aspect in themselves. Moral obligation—moral debt—is "a complex or syndrome" of *human* facts—solid, but not "brute" or "institutional." (I incorporate in part, with appreciation, the Searle-Anscombe phrase which you quote.) And I would insist on obligation's independence of attitude. Obligations stand whether I like them or not and whether I regard them as relevant or irrelevant.

A debt is a debt. And I acknowledge one to Joseph Fletcher.

NOTES ON CONTRIBUTORS

JOHN ANTON—Professor of Philosophy, Emory University. He is author of *Aristotle's Theory of Contrariety, Naturalism and Historical Understanding, Essays in Greek Philosophy*, and others. Editor of Greek Authors series.

ARCHIE J. BAHM—Professor Emeritus of Philosophy, University of New Mexico. Editor, *Directory of American Philosophy*. Author of *What Makes Acts Right?; Ethics as a Behavioural Science; Why Be Moral?* and *An Introduction to Ethics.*

KURT ERICH BAIER—Professor of Philosophy, University of Pittsburgh. Past President, American Philosophical Association. Author of *The Moral Point of View.*

WILL DURANT—Author of *The Story of Philosophy* and *Transition* (autobiographical novel) 1927; and with Ariel Durant, *The Story of Civilization* in eleven volumes, and *A Dual Autobiography*, 1977.

JOSEPH FLETCHER—Professor of Pastoral Theology and Christian Ethics, Episcopal Theological School, Cambridge 1944-70; and Visiting Scholar, Medical Ethics, University of Virginia 1970-75. Author of *Situation Ethics; Moral Responsibility; The Ethics of Genetic Control; Humanhood, Essays in Biomedical Ethics;* and other books.

ALASTAIR HANNAY—Professor of Philosophy at the University of Trondheim, Norway, and Editor of *Inquiry*. Author of *Mental Images—A Defense*. Co-editor with Avne Noess of *Invitation to Chinese Philosophy.*

MAX HOCUTT—Professor of Philosophy and Chairman of Department, University of Alabama. Author with others of *Human Behavior*.

LESTER A. KIRKENDALL—Professor Emeritus of Family Life, Oregon State University. Co-founder of SIECUS. Author of *Premarital Intercourse and Interpersonal Relationships; The New Sexual Revolution; The New Bill of Sexual Rights and Responsibilities;* and other books.

KONSTANTIN KOLENDA—McManis Professor of Philosophy, Rice University. Author of *The Freedom of Reason; In Defense of Practical Reason; Philosophy's Journey; Religion Without God;* and other books.

MARVIN KOHL—Professor of Philosophy, State University of New York at Fredonia. Author of *The Morality of Killing*. Editor of *Beneficent Euthanasia;* and *Infanticide and the Value of Life.*

PAUL KURTZ—Professor of Philosophy, State University of New York at Buffalo. Chairman, Committee for the Scientific Investigation of Claims of the Paranormal. Author of *Decision and the Condition of Man; The Fullness of Life; Exuberance; Moral Problems in Contemporary Society;* and other books.

MIHAILO MARKOVIC —Serbian Institute of Arts and Sciences. Formerly, Professor of Philosophy, University of Belgrade, Yugoslavia. Visiting Professor, U. of Penn., Fall '78, '79. Author of *From Affluence to Praxis: Philosophy and Social Criticism.*

KAI NIELSEN—Professor of Philosophy, University of Calgary, Canada. Author of *Ethics Without God, Reason and Practice,* and other books.

LEE NISBET—Assistant Professor of Philosophy, Medaille College. Executive Director, Committee for the Scientific Investigation of Claims of the Paranormal.

HOWARD RADEST—Director of Ethical Culture Schools in New York City. Professor of Philosophy, Ramapo College of New Jersey. Co-Chairman, International Humanist and Ethical Union. Editor, *International Humanism.* Author of *Toward Common Ground, To Seek a Human World.*

HERBERT W. SCHNEIDER—Lecturer in Philosophy, Carleton College, California. Professor Emeritus of Philosophy and Religion, Columbia University. Former Editor, *Journal of Philosophy*. Former President, American Philosophical Association. Author of *History of American Philosophy; Morals for Mankind;* and other books.

JAMES R. SIMPSON—Associate Professor, Food and Resource Economics, University of Florida. Past President, Inter-American Research Associates.

MORRIS B. STORER—Professor Emeritus, Humanities, University of Florida. Author of three-part monograph "Theory of Moral Debt" in *Inquiry* (Parts I and II) and *Religious Humanism* (Part III).

V. M. TARKUNDE—Senior Advocate of the Supreme Court of India. Former Judge of the Bombay High Court. Chairman of the Indian Radical Humanist Association. Editor, *The Radical Humanist*. General Secretary, Citizens for Democracy. International Humanist Award 1978.

MARVIN ZIMMERMAN—Professor of Philosophy, State University of New York at Buffalo. Author of *Contemporary Problems of Democracy*.

CRITIQUES OF THE PARANORMAL

____ESP & PARAPSYCHOLOGY: A CRITICAL RE-EVALUATION C.E.M. Hansel $7.95

____EXTRA-TERRESTRIAL INTELLIGENCE James L. Christian, editor   6.95

____OBJECTIONS TO ASTROLOGY L. Jerome & B. Bok   3.95

____THE PSYCHOLOGY OF THE PSYCHIC David Marks & Richard Kammann   7.95

____PHILOSOPHY & PARAPSYCHOLOGY J. Ludwig, editor   8.95

HUMANISM

____ETHICS WITHOUT GOD K. Nielsen   4.95

____HUMANIST ALTERNATIVE Paul Kurtz, editor   4.95

____HUMANIST ETHICS Morris Storer, editor   8.95

____HUMANIST FUNERAL SERVICE Corliss Lamont   2.95

____HUMANIST MANIFESTOS I & II   1.95

____HUMANIST WEDDING SERVICE Corliss Lamont   1.95

____HUMANISTIC PSYCHOLOGY I. David Welch, George Tate,
Fred Richards, editors   8.95

____MORAL PROBLEMS IN CONTEMPORARY SOCIETY Paul Kurtz, editor   5.95

____VOICE IN THE WILDERNESS Corliss Lamont   4.95

____RABBI AND MINISTER: THE FRIENDSHIP OF STEPHEN S. WISE AND
JOHN HAYNES HOLMES Carl Hermann Voss   6.95

PHILOSOPHY & ETHICS

____ART OF DECEPTION Nicholas Capaldi   5.95

____BENEFICENT EUTHANASIA M. Kohl, editor   7.95

____ESTHETICS CONTEMPORARY Richard Kostelanetz, editor   9.95

____EXUBERANCE: A PHILOSOPHY OF HAPPINESS Paul Kurtz   3.00

____FULLNESS OF LIFE Paul Kurtz   5.95

____FREEDOM OF CHOICE AFFIRMED Corliss Lamont   4.95

____HUMANHOOD: ESSAYS IN BIOMEDICAL ETHICS Joseph Fletcher   6.95

____JOURNEYS THROUGH PHILOSOPHY N. Capaldi & L. Navia, editors   10.95

____MORAL EDUCATION IN THEORY & PRACTICE Robert Hall & John Davis   7.95

____TEACH YOURSELF PHILOSOPHY Antony Flew   5.95

____THINKING STRAIGHT Antony Flew   4.95

____WORLDS OF PLATO & ARISTOTLE J.B. Wilbur & H.J. Allen, editors   5.95

____WORLDS OF THE EARLY GREEK PHILOSOPHERS J.B. Wilbur &
H.J. Allen, editors   5.95

____PHILOSOPHY: AN INTRODUCTION Antony Flew   6.95

____INTRODUCTORY READINGS IN THE PHILOSOPHY OF SCIENCE E.D. Klemke,
Robert Hollinger, A. David Kline, editors   10.95

SEXOLOGY

____THE FRONTIERS OF SEX RESEARCH *Vern Bullough, editor*   6.95

____NEW BILL OF SEXUAL RIGHTS & RESPONSIBILITIES *Lester Kirkendall*   1.95

____NEW SEXUAL REVOLUTION *Lester Kirkendall, editor*   4.95

____PHILOSOPHY & SEX *Robert Baker & Fred Elliston, editors*   6.95

____SEX WITHOUT LOVE: A PHILOSOPHICAL EXPLORATION *Russell Vannoy*   8.95

SKEPTICS BOOKSHELF

____ATHEISM: THE CASE AGAINST GOD *George H. Smith*   6.95

____CLASSICS OF FREE THOUGHT *Paul Blanshard, editor*   5.95

____CRITIQUES OF GOD *Peter Angeles, editor*   6.95

____WHAT ABOUT GODS? (for children) *Chris Brockman*   3.95

SOCIAL ISSUES

____AGE OF AGING: A READER IN SOCIAL GERONTOLOGY
  Abraham Monk, editor   8.95

____REVERSE DISCRIMINATION *Barry Gross, editor*   7.95

The books listed above can be obtained from your book dealer
or directly from Prometheus Books.
Please check off the appropriate books.
Remittance must accompany all orders from individuals.
Please include $1.00 postage and handling for each book.
(N.Y. State Residents add 7% sales tax)

Send to _____
(Please type or print clearly)

Address _____

City _____ State_____Zip_____

Amount Enclosed_____

℞ *Prometheus Books*

1203 Kensington Avenue
Buffalo, New York 14215